# HAUNTED SKIES

*PRESERVING THE SOCIAL HISTORY OF UFO RESEARCH*

## VOLUME FOUR  1976-1977

*REPLACING EARLIER VOLUME REMOVED FROM SALE*
*NOW IN COLOUR: REVISED AND EXPANDED*

**JOHN HANSON**
**VICTORIA JANE HYDE**

HAUNTED SKIES VOLUME 4 Revised 1976-1977

Copyright © 2018 John Hanson & Victoria Jane Hyde. All rights reserved.

First paperback edition printed 2018 in the United Kingdom.

A catalogue record for this book is available from the British Library.

ISBN 978-09956428-4-3

Published by
*Haunted Skies Publishing*

*For more copies of this book, please email:* johndawn1@sky.com

Telephone: 01527 279199

Designed and typeset by Bob Tibbitts

Printed in Great Britain

# *Silver Jubilee Edition*

## 1952-1977

### Celebrating the reign of our
### Queen Elizabeth II

Authors: During our recent research (2017) into this revised *Haunted Skies* Volume 4, which covers the period of 1976 to 1977, when a 'wave' of UFO activity took place around the Broad Haven area of Wales, we discovered that Scottish citizen, Malcolm Robinson – a veteran of the UFO/Paranormal subject, going back many years – had visited the location in 1980 and carried out a thorough interview with Rosa Granville, of the Haven Fort Hotel, whom we ourselves met some years ago.

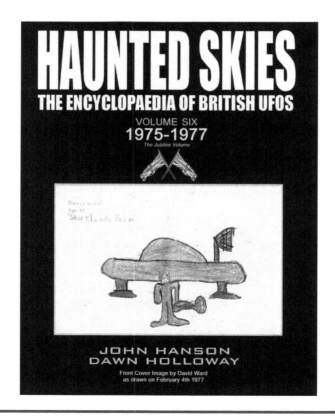

# FOREWORD

## By MALCOLM ROBINSON

FOLLOWING on from a period of UFO activity recorded for the UK 1976 period, which increased dramatically during 1977, Wales featured a higher concentration of UFO sightings as compared to the rest of the country. Why this should be so, we at present don't know. Most of the Welsh sightings were localised in the West Wales area, particularly the St. Brides Bay region. It was inevitable then, that books would be written about these fascinating UFO sightings over Wales. Author Randall Jones Pugh, with F.W. Holiday, wrote the book – *The Dyfed Enigma* (Faber & Faber, 1979). Peter Paget wrote the book – *The Welsh Triangle*, whilst Clive Harold wrote and documented the strange incidents which happened to the Coombs family in his book – *The Uninvited* (Star Books, 1979).

At this time I was avidly reading all those reports concerning these UFO sightings in the National newspapers, and eventually I picked up and read a copy of Peter Paget's book – *The Welsh Triangle*. This book really did stir up my interest, and reading the accounts of the Welsh people confronted by these amazing aerial displays, gave me such an inkling into visiting Wales and talking to these people, that I just had to make my next annual works holiday in the Welsh direction . . . and that's exactly what I did. The year was 1980; fully three years had elapsed since the Welsh people had witnessed these strange objects. Were these sightings still going on? Well I now had the opportunity to find out.

So with my wife Rosemary to accompany me, we set off for Wales in the summer of 1980. We boarded a *Dan Air* aircraft at Glasgow Airport and were soon taxiing down the runway. This was not one of the usual aircraft that one boards today; this was a propeller-driven plane, and the noise of it just had to be heard to be believed; it was like having a swarm of bees inside both ears! I thought to myself, would it last the journey to Wales? Well needless to say it did, and by the time my wife and I departed the aircraft, we could hardly hear . . . still, it was an experience that we both won't forget in a hurry, and I almost felt that I should do what the Pope does and kiss the ground!

*Carole Peck*

At the time of receiving the above text on the 12th of November 2017 we learned that it was his current partner, Carole Peck's, birthday so – Happy Birthday Carole. (John and Dawn)

**David Young** – *"I first actually met Malcolm at Warminster when he gave a great presentation. Since then he's been following me about! I can't seem to avoid him, Hastings, Glasgow, Nottingham, (where we had a strange occurrence of an apparently 'apported' stone), Hull, Essex . . . What's going on?' Only joking. He's a great guy and always gives an interesting presentation, and I have all his books."*

**Philip Mantle,** *FLYING DISK PRESS* – *"Malcolm has been actively involved in all forms of 'paranormal' research for longer than most researchers and as a result he has certainly earned our respect. His passion and dedication to his research remains undiminished to this very day. If you have ever attended one of his lectures you will know exactly what I mean. There are those researchers who claim that they've "done it all" when in reality all they are doing is massaging their own ego. However, when it comes to Malcolm Robinson he really has done it all. You may not, of course, always agree with Malcolm's conclusions and I know only too well that he does not have a problem with that. There are many active researchers of all things paranormal out there but Malcolm is one of a kind and long may he last."*

**'Alien Bill Rooke' 2017** – *"Where do I start on my great buddy Malcolm Robinson. What I have found so interesting is he set out with such disbelief and tried to prove many paranormal & Ufo sighting as explainable in the "normal scheme of things". Then finds so much evidence to the contary that he is a convert in the belief now on both subjects. A true cosmic trooper of a researcher. When we first met in London nearly 5 years ago for the first time I knew I had met the right fellow within minutes to open up my Ufo & paranormal files to and sure pushed him even more into the belief side of all things truly strange going on in this and other Universes, His dedicaction is of the highest order and proud to have him as a friend and fellow researcher. Hence I am delighted he has written the foreword for this book and it is spot on. Just to add his sense of humour is ace and I would have an alien ale with him any day of the week"*

**Alyson Dunlop, 1st Jan 2018** – *"I first met our esteemed colleague, Malcolm Robinson, in the mid-90s when I travelled through to Stirling from Glasgow to join Strange Phenomena Investigations. From the start, he was a motivational person who clearly had a great enthusiasm for the paranormal and UFOs. We collaborated on a couple of cases, but, unfortunately, he moved to England shortly after this and life got in the way of keeping in touch. SPI, to all intents and purposes, folded in Scotland. However, a few years ago, we were reunited and Malcolm gave me his blessing to resurrect SPI in Scotland. We then discussed the possibility of running conferences with another respected colleague, Ron Halliday, and that also has been a very successful venture. Malcolm's positivity and dynamic exuberance plays no small part in that. He spurs us on with that remarkable driving spirit he is so well-known for. He is definitely a motivating force behind both the group and the conferences.*

*Since I've known him, Malcolm Robinson has always encouraged and believed in me, no matter what. Over the years he has supported and had unconditional faith in me through some very rough times. He's more than just a colleague. I consider him to be the epitome of the word friend. I'm very honoured to have been entrusted with the safe-keeping of SPI in Scotland, and I'm truly grateful to know someone as loyal as Malcolm. I think all who know him would agree that, in the paranormal and UFO community, there is no one as dedicated to the subject as this man. Unfailing commitment to the truth and passion for his beloved subject is the hallmark of Malcolm Robinson."*

# INTRODUCTION

WE will now examine the UFO events that occurred between 1976 and 1977 when, once again, the skies and occasionally the ground played host to all manner of strange phenomena in a period of UFO history now often referred to as the 'Welsh Wave of 1977', which is somewhat misleading, as our research was to show the events which took place along the Welsh coast only formed part of an enormous number of UFO sightings

We felt ourselves fortunate to visit such people as BUFORA representative Randall Jones Pugh, a vet by trade and a leading authority on the activity that took place in and around the Haverfordwest area of Wales, and Pauline and Billy Combes – central characters to some of the strange events that occurred there – not forgetting some of the children at the Broad Haven County Primary School, who witnessed something very peculiar on the slope of the hill next to the school, in early February 1977, which was to attract a huge 'wave' of worldwide media publicity.

Many people whom we came across over the intervening years felt frustrated with the attitude adopted by the MOD, who have always declined to be drawn into any discussion over sightings of UFOs brought to their attention, and seek to convince us that the majority of UFO sightings can be explained and, as they are of no Defence significance, are of no interest. People just want answers!

At the time of preparation of this revised volume, in late 2017, it is difficult to believe that now (18 years ago, in December 2009) of the closure of the MOD Air Desk 2a, which was the first port of call for many members of the public wishing to report a UFO sighting. The reason given was part of a cost-cutting exercise, which may form the impression that UFOs are no longer of any importance to the authorities. This is puzzling, to say the least, knowing the many occasions involving what appear to have been attempts to intercept UFOs by the RAF. The simple truth is, of course, they don't want the public to know about the reality of the existence of something, or someone, whose daily incursions into our space and time continues unabated to this present day.

Most people on the street are aware of the existence of UFOs. The MOD (and some UFO organisations) has always tried to convince us that 99% of sightings can be explained away rationally. Statistics like this cannot be true if one accepts the evidence painstakingly accumulated by us (with now over 15 Volumes) showing the reality rather than the opposite of something which is often disposed of as being of no interest by the authorities. However, surely something or someone who has the propensity to move at incredible speeds, change shape, and occasionally land (leaving traces), is of very much of interest to the military. Our *apparent* inability to determine the nature of what UFOs represent, and where they come from, should not prevent us asking questions about something we deserve an answer to.

One of our greatest problems is ever having been able to obtain publicity about the books in the media, which appears not so much to be part of any conspiracy or 'D' Notice issued, but the way in which the National newspapers now compete with the social media with the ever constant stream of crazy and ridiculous stories, many of them regurgitated, bizarre, accounts of alien hordes invading Planet Earth – pure entertainment rather than anything based on serious investigations into subject that should be of concern to us all.

### *Dedicated to*

Chief Petty Officer Edward 'Ted' West formerly of *HMS Kelly*, seen below, piping the King aboard in 2nd Word War – later awarded a medal by the Queen at Buckingham Palace – proud to have known him. RIP

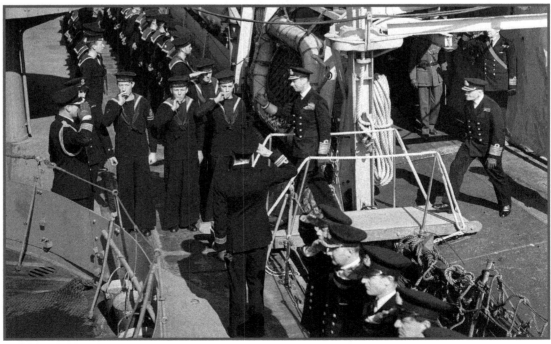

# 1976

## BEGINNING OF THE 'WAVE'

### CHAPTER 1 – JANUARY 1976

6th January 1976 – USA: Close encounter at Stanford
10th January 1976 – UK: Winged UFO over Essex
15th January 1976 – UK: UFO over Isle of Wight
19th January 1976 – UK: Strange phenomena over Kent
20th January 1976 – USA: USO seen, Ventnor, New Jersey
21st January 1976 – USA: FOI re Cannon Air Force Base
23rd January 1976 – UK: Rotating object over Wembley, Middlesex
23rd January 1976 – UK: Close encounter with UFO causes medical ailments
25th January 1976 – UK: 'Flying Saucer' over Lancashire
25th January 1976 – UK: Police Officer chased by UFO, Wyoming
27th January 1976 – UK: Two UFOs sighted over Essex
29th January 1976 – UFO over Basildon, Essex
29th January 1976 – USA: Singer reports close encounter, Nevada

### CHAPTER 2 – FEBRUARY 1976

February 1976 – UFO display over the Peak District
5th February 1976 – Fort Shaw, Montana – UFO landing
7th February 1976 – Rectangular-shaped UFO over Farmersville, Indiana
10th February 1976 – 'Flying Saucer' sighted over High Springs, Florida
10th February 1976 – UFO display over Peterborough
17th February 1976 – UFO paces truck drivers
18th February 1976 – Alabama women followed by five UFOs
19th February 1976 – Three red-orange glowing objects seen in triangular formation
19th February 1976 – Two 'balls of light' seen from aboard ship
20th February 1976 – Motorist encounters three triangular lights
22nd February 1976 – Giant humanoid seen
24th February 1976 – Domed 'disc' seen, with legs
25th February 1976 – Strange 'beings' seen by motorist
26th February 1976 – Domed UFO sighted, Long Island, New York
26th February 1976 – Alabama Police Officers sight UFOs

### CHAPTER 3 – MARCH 1976

2nd March 1976 – Strange object over Essex
5th March 1976 – Disc-shaped UFO over Oregon

8th March 1976 – Saucer-shaped UFOs seen
16th March 1976 – UFO sighted by Gatwick Airport worker
19th March 1976 – Letter sent to the newspaper
21st March 1976 – Film on UFOs
22nd March 1976 – UFO over Essex
23rd March 1976 – *The Evening News*, Bolton – UFO photographed!
25th March 1976 – same account different newspaper
27th/28th March 1976 – NUFORA Investigation at Highdown Hill

### CHAPTER 4 – APRIL 1976

4th April 1976 – Diamond-shaped UFO sighted over Portsmouth, Hampshire
7th April 1976 – *Liverpool Echo* – 'Flying Saucers scare solved'
8th April 1976 – *Liverpool Echo* – Chat show, 'Is there life in outer space?'
9th April 1976 – UFO over Bolton, Lancashire
12th April 1976 – Peter Hill of WATSUP on the move
20th April 1976 – Three UFOs in the sky over Louth, Lincs.
22nd April 1976 – Police Officer's close encounter with UFO
24th April 1976 – 'Square light' seen over Louth, Lincolnshire

### CHAPTER 5 – MAY 1976

May 1976 – Close Encounter, Yorkshire
2nd May 1976 – UFO over Gloucestershire
2nd May 1976 – UFO display over New Zealand
6th May 1976 – Glowing red cigar-shaped UFO
8th May 1976 – 'Martian spaceship to rescue Earth'
10th May 1976 – 'Flying Saucer' over Lancashire
11th May 1976 – Close Encounter, Manchester
13th May 1976 – Police chase UFO over Cheshire
16th May 1976 – Strange sighting over the coast
18th May 1976 – Presidential words about UFOs!
22nd May 1976 – Man from Mars will speak!
27th May 1976 – Talk of Aliens!
1976 – UFO over Kent, sighted by couple walking home

### CHAPTER 6 – JUNE 1976

3rd June 1976 – Motorist chases UFO
5th June 1976 – Cigar-shaped UFO hovers over Highway
6th June 1976 – Three cigar-shaped objects over Colchester, Essex
8th June 1976 – Cigar-shaped UFO

# CHAPTER 1 – JANUARY 1976

1976 was to see a huge increase in UFO activity from all over the United Kingdom, stretching in a great swathe across the Country that included Manchester, Aldridge, Banbury, Mildenhall, Sheerness, Southampton, and St Austell, in Cornwall, which was the scene of a number of 'Flying Saucer' sightings.

One of those witnesses was Gary Moore (then aged 13), who rejected the explanation given in the local newspapers, at the time, that what he and the other children had seen was refuelling of aircraft being carried out over St. Mawgan Airfield.

*"We used to play next door to the chapel in Bugle Street; most of the kids met up there. I remember there was talk about some of them having seen 'flying saucers', but I didn't believe them … after all, 'flying saucers' didn't exist – it was just their imagination getting carried away. This changed*

*when, one afternoon, somebody shouted 'There it is again', and pointed upwards. I looked and was shaken to see a silver saucer-shaped craft glowing from inside, with windows around it, flying low down parallel to New Street."*

## 6th January 1976 – Close encounter at Stanford, Kentucky

The February first issue of the *Kentucky Advocate*, published at Danville, Kentucky, carried an article about UFO sightings in the general area, among which was the story told by Louise Smith, Mona Stafford and Elaine Thomas, about their drive home to Liberty from a late dinner at the *Redwoods* restaurant, located five miles north of Stanford, when they encountered a saucer-shaped object.

[Although Mrs Smith and Mrs Thomas had known each other for many years, Mrs Smith had only been acquainted with Mona a few weeks previously.]

Stories like these are, once again, uncommon but not rare to the pages of our books. We cannot write this up without thinking of the similar experience which befell the three girls from Shropshire, England – two of whom we interviewed some years ago, and this was subsequently published.

### Huge disc-shaped UFO sighted

The newspaper described the journey taken by the three women, who said that at a point about one mile south of Stanford they saw a huge disc-shaped object, which was metallic gray with a white glowing dome. A row of red lights rotated around the middle, and underneath were three or four red and yellow lights that burned steadily. A bluish beam of light issued from the bottom.

### A familiar story – missing time

When the women arrived home in Liberty, it was 1.25am. Having left the restaurant at 11.15p.m, they should have arrived home by midnight, indicating that there was a time loss of about one hour and 25 minutes.

### The *Kentucky Advocate* article was forwarded to APRO by Field Investigator Bill Terry

After some consultation, he decided to make the necessary 60 mile trip to talk to the ladies. Mrs Coral Lorenzen, head of the group, along with her husband – Jim, felt it would be well worth the trip.

A few days later Bill called back and told Headquarters he thought it was a case of abduction, and that the usual hypnosis procedures should be utilized.

### Dr. Leo Sprinkle

Dr. R. Leo Sprinkle, APRO's consultant in psychology, was contacted and asked to travel to Liberty to interview the women and possibly use hypnotic procedures to relieve their anxiety and obtain any repressed information. A date was set for the trip on the weekend of the 6th and 7th March.

On the evening in question, Louse Smith – employed as an extension assistant for the Casey County Extension Office, where her duties consisted of visiting families in the county, counselling them in food preparation and preservation, nutrition and gardening – left work at the usual time and went home. After preparing a light meal, she got into her 1967 Chevrolet 'Nova', which she had just purchased that day, and drove to a service station to get gas/fuel in preparation for the next day.

### Mona Stafford – Happy Birthday!

While at the service station, Mona Stafford (who was driving by) spotted Louise's car and pulled her car into the station, whereupon Louise asked her if she would come home with her and help her put the collar on a jacket she was making, as she was having trouble fitting it. The two ladies, each in her own car, drove to the Smith trailer home and set about the task.

At about 8pm, Mrs Thomas dropped by and the three lapsed into conversation about their favourite subject: art.

Mona had planned to go to her sister's home to have her hair done and, at about 9pm, said she'd better call her sister because it was getting late and besides, it was her (Mona's) 35th birthday.

### Celebrating the birthday

When Louise learned about the birthday, she suggested they go to *Redwoods* for a late dinner and a sort of birthday celebration. Also, there was a painting on the wall of the restaurant which she had wanted to sketch. The restaurant, incidentally, is the only restaurant open at that time of night in that area.

The three drove the 29 miles to the restaurant, had their dinner and then pulled out sketch pads and went to work. A man at the restaurant asked Louise to sketch him – which she did – and then she realised it was getting late, so the three paid their cheques and left. Louise drove, Mona sat in the middle of the front seat, with Mrs Thomas on her right by the passenger window.

*Louise Smith, Elaine Thomas and Mona Stafford*

### Mona sights an object in the sky

Mona spotted the object, descending from their right to the left, and asked Louise (who had also seen it) to speed up as she thought it was a plane about to crash and she wanted to help any survivors, although at this point Elaine hadn't yet seen it, but saw it for herself when it stopped at treetop level, at what they estimated to be one hundred yards ahead of them.

All of the women said the object was huge, Louise describing it *"as big as a football field"*, while Mona Stafford said it was at least as large as two houses.

Louise said that the object rocked gently for perhaps two seconds, at which time she estimated its size, for it extended beyond the edges of the road and over the fields on both sides. The 'thing' then moved across the road to their left, circling behind and above some houses, and then apparently came back to the highway and swung in behind the car.

### Blue light illuminates the car

At a point in their journey, about a quarter of a mile beyond the houses, the inside of the car was lit up with a bluish light which came from behind. Louise thought it was a state trooper, approaching from behind, but realised almost immediately that it wasn't. At this point Louise and Mona were near panic. The car began to pull to the left and Louise screamed at Mona to help her control it. The speedometer was registering 85 miles per hour and both Mona and Mrs Thomas shouted at Louise slow down. Louise held her foot in the air to show them and said, *"I don't have my foot on the accelerator and I can't stop it!"*

Mona reached over and grabbed the wheel and they fought the force together. Then, quite suddenly, the women experienced a burning sensation in their eyes and Louise later described an additional pain which seemed to *"go right through the top of my head! It was almost unbearable!"*

The next sensation was that of some force pulling the car backward. In addition, they felt that the car was going over a series of *"speed bumps"* (raised ridges in a road, which are meant to keep the speed of automobiles to a minimum). Mrs Thomas began urging Louise to stop so that she could get a good look at the object, but Mona and Louise were too terrified. Elaine had only had a glimpse of the object as it had circled to their left and around behind her, and was later to comment about the object's beauty.

*"I can't describe it. I've never seen red that beautiful. I wanted to get out and look at it."*

### Engine begins to stall

The women then said that they saw a strange, wide, lighted road stretching as far as they could see ahead of them. At the same moment Mona noted a red light come on the instrument panel which indicated that the engine had stalled, despite the sensation that they were moving very fast. A split second later the women saw a street light ahead and realised they were coming into Hustonville, a full eight miles beyond where they had encountered the strange aircraft. They wondered among themselves how they had got there so fast – then became quiet while they proceeded on into Liberty.

### Physical discomfort – of the eyes, and strange marks on the body experienced

When they arrived at Louise's trailer, they all went inside. Louise went into the bathroom, took off her glasses and splashed water on her face, whereupon her hands and face began to burn with searing pain. All three had a red mark on the backs of their necks, measuring about three inches long and one inch wide, with clearly defined edges, giving the appearance of a new burn before it blisters. Louise and Elaine's marks were centrally located between the bases of their skulls and the top of the back, whereas Mona's was located to the left, behind her ear. They could not account for the marks, which disappeared two days later. All three were experiencing burning and tearing of their eyes, but Mona Stafford had a much more severe case of conjunctivitis (an inflammation of the conjunctiva membrane of the eyes).

### Hand of the watch moving at considerable speed

Prior to washing her hands, Louise had taken off her watch and was startled to see that the hands of her watch were moving at an accelerated rate of speed, the minute hand moving at the speed of a second hand, and the hour hand was moving also.

Upon experiencing the pain of the water on her hands and face, she forgot about the phenomena of the watch and does not recall when it returned to normal or when she reset it.

When Louise arrived home, the clock in the house showed 1.25am. (The ladies should have been home by midnight, i.e. 85 minutes of missing time.)

### Sketches of the object made

Concluding that something was wrong, the three ladies went next door to the home of Mr Lowell Lee, and told him what they had seen. He asked them to go into separate rooms and sketch the object and, when finished, he found the resulting sketches to be almost identical. Although all the women had trouble with their eyes, only Mona Stafford sought medical help, as her problem was so severe. The doctor who examined her found no explanation for the pain and tearing but gave her some eye drops, which helped very little.

### Background of the three witnesses examined – Louise Smith

Bill Terry found out that all three of the women enjoy good reputations. Mrs Smith is a tall, thin woman of 44 years, who was widowed when a young woman and brought up her son and daughter by herself. She has two grandchildren and busies herself in her spare time with painting and sketching and gospel singing. She performs around Casey County with the *Jubilee Echoes,* consisting of herself, a 14 year-old boy singer and a bassist, who is a police lieutenant in Danville. She is a lifelong member of the Baptist church and attends services regularly at the Poplar Springs Baptist Church in Liberty. Inquiries to such people as police personnel, her minister and employer, elicited only good comments. Several weeks after her experience she had lost 28lbs off her normal weight.

### Mona Stafford

Mona Stafford is 35, the former owner of an arts and crafts shop in Liberty and currently unemployed except for secretarial work which she does for her father, who owns a mobile trailer park. She was once married but has been divorced since 1970 and lives in a trailer home parked near her parents' home. She is a devout Christian, a member of the Hilltop Church of Christ near Liberty. She also lost weight amounting to 17 pounds but at this writing had regained 7.

### Elaine Thomas

Elaine Thomas is a 48 year-old housewife, who has lived in Casey County, Kentucky, all of her life. She

*Mona Stafford being questioned under hypnosis by Dr. Leo Sprinkle*

and her husband – Otis, live several miles out of Liberty. They have a grown daughter and three grandchildren. Mrs Thomas is also a lifelong churchgoer and is a member of the Church of Christ.

### Jim and Coral Lorenzen's assessment

*"The foregoing information indicated to APRO's staff that the women were of good reputation, sincere, honest, and had no motivation to concoct a story, so we proceeded with the investigation. It is at this juncture that we will explain the tardiness of the publication of this case."*

### Other interested parties arrive and start squabbling!

Bill Terry met Dr. Leo Sprinkle upon his arrival and the two proceeded to Mrs Smith's home. They were met with a conglomeration of investigators from CUFOS and MUFON, who felt that they were 'first' on the case and that APRO should not be allowed to enter. (They had preceded Mr Terry to the

**Jim and Coral Lorenzen**

Liberty site by only one day). Mr Sprinkle, under the circumstances, did not want to intrude and decided to call APRO Headquarters for advice on how to proceed.

*Dr. Leo Sprinkle of the University of Wyoming talks to the three witnesses about their night of terror onboard a UFO*

*Leonard Stringfield*      *Dr. Leo Sprinkle*

**A book – *Encounters with UFO Occupants***

Mr Jim Lorenzen talked to Len Stringfield of CUFOS and MUFON, who wanted to use the services of Dr. Sprinkle but didn't want the report to be sent to APRO!

Mrs *Coral Lorenzen pointed out that she had written a book – *Encounters with UFO Occupants* – [later volume was *Flying Saucer Occupants*] specifically so that the proceeds would furnish APRO with the wherewithal to conduct such investigations, and that not only was APRO's money (air fare and expenses for Dr. Sprinkle) wasted, but Dr. Sprinkle's time spent away from his family.

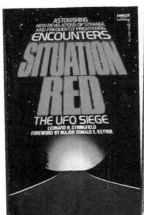
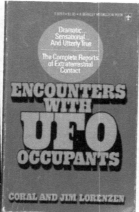
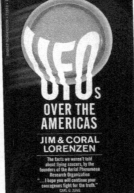

### Decision made

It was finally decided that Dr. Sprinkle would conduct the hypnotic sessions, but that there would have to be a mutual agreement concerning the release of the story.

Sadly, during meetings before Dr Sprinkle's arrival, a representative of MUFON or CUFOS had told Mrs Smith (she doesn't recall who) *"that the ladies should be careful about having anything to do with APRO, because they would call in the National Enquirer"* and they would receive much unwanted publicity.

Ironically, in a later letter from +Jerry Black – a MUFON investigator and, consequently, a CUFOS investigator – he suggested that the ladies contact the *National Enquirer* about their experience – which was a surprise, considering their reluctance to have anything to do with that paper if APRO was on the case!

### APRO unable to complete their investigation into the incident

It was for this reason, after the expenditure of several hundred dollars, that APRO felt they were unable to complete the case. Subsequently, the *National Enquirer* then contacted the ladies. Dr. Sprinkle, Ph.D., because of his participation in the *"Blue Ribbon Panel"* of National Enquirer experts, was called upon to go back to Liberty and use regression on the women involved.

### Reliable and sincere witnesses

His report of the weekend of March 6th and 7th is quite sketchy, except for his characterization of the three women as reliable, sincere, etc., because Saturday was largely wasted in quibbling about who should have *"control of the case".* Incidentally, the MUFON people wanted to make use of Sprinkle's expertise, *"as long as he was there".* However, they admitted they neither had the consultants nor the funds to send in someone expert in hypnotic techniques to carry out the trance sessions.

### Polygraph tests conducted

On the 23rd July, under the *National Enquirer's* aegis, a polygraph test was conducted on the three ladies, and James C. Young reported, in each case, that it was his opinion, based upon the polygraph examinations that the ladies believed they were telling the truth to the listed questions. This was conducted at the *Brown Motel* in Liberty, Kentucky.

In his report, Mr Young made the following pertinent observation:

> *"Prior to the examination of these three persons, it was determined by the polygraphist that these persons had been previously interviewed by Dr. R. Leo Sprinkle and the above-mentioned members of the Mutual UFO Network. How much or how little these previous interviews played a part upon what these persons now believe about this alleged encounter cannot be determined by the polygraphist. I cannot discount the fact that previous interviews with these persons could influence their personal beliefs as to whether or not this alleged encounter did or did not occur."*

### Sketches shown to witness at early stages

A very good point was raised, being that interviewers showing sketches of UFO types to a witness before they make their own renderings of what they saw, is highly suggestive, as is the display of any drawings of occupants. This apparently was done by MUFON representatives, prior to the polygraph test or the trance hypnosis carried out by Dr. Sprinkle on the next day, (the 24th July). APRO has a complete transcript of the trance sessions, which have been examined by the staff.

According to Coral Lorenzen, of APRO:

> *"While Robert Pratt of the National Enquirer, and Dr. Sprinkle, who has had extensive experience in this phase of UFO research, were careful not to lead the subjects, some very suggestive or leading questions were asked by Mr Stringfield and Mr Black of MUFON. It is just such errors that the sceptics will leap upon in attempts to discredit the investigative procedures or reliability of witness testimony in such cases".*

### Dr Sprinkle's findings (summary) from the hypnotic sessions –Louise Smith

> *"Mrs Smith suffered much as she relived the experience. The behaviours, e.g. weeping, moaning, tossing her head, shuddering, and shaking, etc., were evident to those of us who observed her – especially as she seemed to 'relive'* **an experience of a fluid material covering her face.** *Her smile,*

> *and evident relief in 'seeing the street light' at the end of her hour and one-half loss-of-time experience was dramatic and indicated that she was 'safe' in the car, once again, and returning home with her friends."*

Mr Sprinkle then goes on to recount Louise's claim that her pet parakeet which, according to her claims, and others who observed the bird, refused to have anything to do with her after the UFO experience. Others could approach the bird and it would not react wildly; however, whenever Louise came close to the bird, the bird would flutter and move away from her.

The bird died within weeks after the UFO experience. [Under hypnosis Louise said that the 'humanoids' were about four and-a-half feet tall and instead of hands had wingtips with jagged feathers]

### Dr Sprinkle's findings (summary) from the hypnotic sessions – Mona Stafford

*"Responded well to the hypnotic suggestions and she was able to describe impressions which led her to believe that she had been taken out of the car, **and that she was alone on a white table or bed. She saw a large 'eye', which seemed to be observing her.** She felt as if a bright white light was shining on her and that there was 'power' or energy which transfixed her and held her to the table or bed. She experienced a variety of physiological reactions, including the impressions that her right arm was pinned or fastened; her left leg forced back under her, with pain to the ankle and foot; pressure on the fingers of the left hand – as if they were forced or squeezed in some way; **a feeling of being examined by four or five short humanoids, who sat around in 'surgical masks' and 'surgical garments' while observing her.** At one point, she sensed that she was either experiencing out-of-the body travel, or else she was waiting outside of a large room in which she could view another person, probably a woman, lying on a white bed or observation table. She perceived a long tunnel or a view of the sky – as if she had been transported to an area inside a large mountain or volcano. Although she wept and moaned and experienced a great deal of fatigue as a result of the 'reliving' of the experience, she felt better the next day; she expressed the belief to me that she now had a better understanding of what happened during the loss-of-time experience."*

### Dr. Sprinkle's findings (summary) from the hypnotic sessions – Mrs Thomas

*"Mrs Thomas had been rather quiet during the initial interview in March, 1976, although it was obvious that she is perceptive and aware of other people's attitudes and feelings. **Like the others, she has lost weight,** but she has also experienced some personality changes. She dresses a bit more colourfully now, and she is more willing to talk and to share her ideas with others. She, too, experienced a similar reaction during the hypnotic techniques: she apparently was responding well to suggestions to go deeper; when she 'relived' the UFO experience, she experienced a great deal of emotional reaction. Her main impression was that she was taken away from her two friends, **and that she was placed in a 'chamber' with a window on the side. She seemed to recall figures which moved back and forth in front of the window of the chamber – as if she were being observed. Her impression was that the observers were four feet tall humanoids, with dark eyes and grey*

*skin. One disturbing aspect of the experience was the memory that she had some kind of contraption or 'covering' that was placed around her neck; whenever she tried to speak, or think, the contraption or 'covering' was tightened, and she experienced a choking sensation during these moments.***

*At first, Mrs Thomas interpreted the memories as indication that she was being choked by hands or that she was being prevented from calling out to her friends; later, however, she came to the tentative conclusion that an experiment was being conducted, and the experiment was to learn more about her intellectual and emotional processes. **She recalled a 'bullet-shaped' object, about an inch and one half in diameter, being placed on her left chest; she previously had experienced pain and a red spot at that location.***

*During the polygraph examination, and during the initial hypnotic sessions, each UFO witness was interviewed separately*

*Dr. Leo Sprinkle with psychologist and abduction reseracher Edith Fiore at a UFO conference.*

*from the other witnesses. After the initial description of impressions, the women were invited to attend the additional hypnosis sessions, so that each woman could observe the reaction of the other two women. During these sessions, there was much emotional reaction, which seemed to arise from two conditions: the compassion of the witnesses for their friend, who was 'reliving' the experience and releasing emotional reactions to the experience; also, it seems as if the description by one witness would 'trigger' a memory on the part of another witness, even if the experiences seemed to be similar or different.*

*Certain similarities were observed: a feeling of anxiety on the part of each witness regarding a specific aspect of the experience.*

*For Mrs Smith, it was the 'wall' and the 'gate' beyond which she was afraid to 'move psychologically'; for* **Ms. Stafford it was the 'eye'** *which she observed and the impression that something evil or bad would be learned if she allowed the eye to 'control' her; for* **Mrs Thomas, it was the 'blackness'** *which seemed to be the feared condition or cause for anxiety.*

*Each woman seemed to experience the impression that she had been taken out of the car and placed elsewhere without her friends and without verbal communication. For* **Mrs Smith, the lack of verbal communication** *was most distressing; although she had the feeling of 'mental communication' that she would be returned after the 'experiment'.*

*Differences were noted in that each woman seemed to have a somewhat different kind of 'examination', and in a different 'location'. Mrs Smith did not have a clear impression of the location, although she did recall a feeling of lying down and being examined; Mrs Stafford had the*

*impression of being in a 'volcano or mountainside', with a room in which a bright light was shining on a white table with white clothed persons or humanoids sitting around and observing her; Mrs Thomas recalled impressions of being in the dark chamber with grey light permitting a view of the humanoids who were apparently observing her."*

**In his conclusive paragraphs Dr. Sprinkle reports:**

*"In my opinion, each woman is describing a 'real' experience, and they are using their intelligence and perceptivity as accurately as possible in order to describe the impressions which they obtained during the hypnotic regressions session. Although there is uncertainty about their impressions, especially in regard to how each person could be transported out of the car and relocated in the car, the impressions during the 'loss of time' experience are similar to those of other UFO witnesses who apparently have experienced an abduction and examination during their UFO sighting.*

*Although it is not possible to claim absolutely that a physical examination and abduction has taken place, I believe that the tentative hypothesis of abduction and examination is the best hypothesis to explain the apparent loss-of-time experience, the apparent physical and emotional reactions of the witnesses to the UFO sighting: the anxiety and the reactions of the witnesses to their experiences which have occurred after their UFO sighting; an interesting subsequent event is the concern of the women that they were 're-experiencing' the physical symptoms which had been experienced for several days following the January 1976 sightings. . . . When I called them on July 26th, the women said that they were re-experiencing some of the same kinds of symptoms, e.g. fatigue, listlessness, sensitivity to skin, burning feeling on the face and eyes, fluid discharge, etc.*

*I tried to reassure the ladies that it is not an uncommon experience in hypnotic regression that persons — after 'reliving' earlier emotional experiences — may re-experience some of the symptoms which accompany those emotional reactions.*

*In my opinion, the UFO experiences of these women are a good example of the type of apparent abduction and examination which* **seems to be occurring to more UFO witnesses.** *I believe that the investigation could be continued with the hopes of obtaining further information about their experiences. However, the present evidence suggests to me that the women have cooperated sincerely and openly in describing their reactions to their UFO sighting and loss-of-time experience, and the polygraph examination and hypnotic regression sessions have been useful in uncovering their impressions of the UFO sighting and subsequent events.*

*I believe the case is a good example of UFO experiences, because of the number and character of the witnesses . . . and because of the results of further investigation through polygraph examinations and hypnotic regression sessions."*

### Dr. Sprinkle – interesting information obtained

Dr. Sprinkle alludes to 'subsequent events'. Conversations with Mrs Smith since the regressive hypnotic sessions took place yielded two very interesting bits of information:

Mrs Stafford had been having trouble sleeping, would not stay home, and would go to her parents' home or that of a friend, and curl up on the floor to sleep. She also has said repeatedly that she *"would not live to see another birthday"*. Hopefully this is only a fear and not a portent of things to come.

### Return to the scene – missing jewellery

In the fall of 1976, Louise Smith was overcome by an inexplicable urge to go back to the scene of the original sighting.

On 1st August, she returned to the site, got out of her car, and *"heard"* the words: ***"feel of your hands"***. When she did so, she realised that three rings, which she habitually wore – a small gold ring, a pearl ring, and a gold ring with onyx and a small diamond – were gone.

### Diamond ring is found

On the 26th September, Louise Smith walked out onto the stoop of her trailer home and found the onyx and diamond ring lying there. Inexplicably she picked up the ring, walked to the creek which runs by her home, and threw it in.

During one of her last contacts with Mrs Lorenzen by telephone, Louise intimated that she was beginning to have recall of the whole experience, and asked that Mrs Lorenzen not divulge the details as she was writing a book about the experience.

### Coral Lorenzen:

*"We appreciate Mrs Smith's desires, and will not comment on further information learned from her until such time as the book is published. However, we laud these ladies for their bravery; theirs is a very interesting and hair-raising experience and we feel sympathy for them in that their greatest ordeal may well still come."*

### *UFO Review* – interview with Elaine Thomas

An article appeared a few years later, in *UFO Review*, about this incident, written by Bob Allen, following interviews with Elaine Thomas.

**Elaine:**

*"One night after it happened, I told the girls that I had a feeling I could communicate with them and that I was going to do just that. They laughed at me. Still they agreed to go along with what I wanted to do, which was to go back to the Redwood restaurant. Nothing happened there, or on the way back, but when I was standing alone outside Leslie's house, I felt this trembling come over me."*

### Mysterious substance found on body

*"I went inside and I noticed that I had all these golden 'cobwebs' on me. I told the girls to look. I felt that this was 'their' way of symbolizing that they had communicated with me that night. I grabbed a strand of the mysterious substance and it squeaked between my fingers. Louise came over to look at it under the light; as soon as they touched it vanished. There were little golden strands over me, but they disappeared quickly. It was stiff to touch – like metal or plastic – and very shiny."*

### Promise made not to reveal all of the conversation

*"I feel that they know everything I do; it's a bad feeling, because there are so many things I remember about the incident that have never been said. I remember making a promise to 'them' that I would never tell, and if I did tell I would not know what would happen to me."*

The only mistake in the *UFO Review* article is the location given as Sanford. This should be Stanford – no doubt a typographical error.

According to a report in the *Ohio Sky Watcher*, Elaine's watch had stopped. Louise's watch showed 6am bur the minute hand was moving as fast as the second hand! Jim Miller, who wrote the article and talked to the women, saw for himself the remains of the burn marks on their necks, and also the blistered area on the vehicle. He confirmed that other UFO reports had been received during the same late night – although we have no details of those.

On the 7th July 1976, Mona – who had reported that every time she closed her eyes to go to sleep, she saw a strange vision of an **'eye'** which frightened her – was trying to doze off when she saw *'two eyes'*.

On the 19th July, as the last programme went off air, snowy patterns appeared on the screen. Mona felt as if she was being watched and, on turning away from the screen, caught sight of a man's face, about five feet away, staring at her. He had *"red hair and a red curly beard"*. When she jumped up, he disappeared from sight.

### Roberta Smith, State Director of MUFON

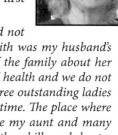

In 2013, we contacted Roberta Smith – a charming lady, State Director of the Kentucky branch of MUFON, hoping that she may have some additional information regarding the incident. Roberta told us she had no more than what was posted on the internet – other than Louise Smith (who was her husband's first cousin) had passed away several years ago.

*"I was not married to my husband when this abduction happened, and did not learn of it until years after the incident. I can tell you this. Yes, Louise Smith was my husband's first cousin, but she died several years ago. She never would talk to any of the family about her abduction. The last time we heard anything from Mona, she was not in good health and we do not know her personally. The other lady has passed away also. But these were three outstanding ladies in the community and just happened to be in the wrong place at the wrong time. The place where these ladies lived and were abducted is only about 30-35 miles from where my aunt and many relatives live. There are, what we call knobs between them. Knobs are taller than hills and shorter than mountains. After learning of this incident, I put 2 and 2 together, and remember that back at that time, there was a 'wave' of UFO sightings in this area. Everyone was seeing them. This went on*

*for over a week. It was the talk of the community; it is a rural area. Let me know how things go. I only wish there was more information I could give you concerning the Stanford Abduction, but as I said, I came into the Smith family after this happened.*

*I have asked several family members about it, and they all said she wouldn't talk about it and the only thing they knew was what they read from reports and newspapers. I am sorry, but I have never seen this drawing by Mona. I would assume that Mona has the copyright, but I do not know Mona personally and know of no way, at the moment, to contact her. I think there is something unusual about her drawing. As far as I know, the car was not taken into the craft – only the three women. I did not know that Mona was an artist, but Louise was a very good one. Someone in the family stated that Louise had several paintings she had done, but they had been stolen."*

An examination of the NICAP file on the internet reveals a staggering number of UFO sightings for this year. One is bound to wonder just how many other 'victims' there were, not only in the USA but the UK. This is quite frightening and makes a mockery of statements made, assuring us that the majority of UFO reports can be explained away rationally.

(**Source:** *APRO Bulletin*, **Volume 25, No. 4, October 1976**)

*Jim and Coral Lorenzen*

˙Coral E. Lorenzen was born in Hillsdale, Wisconsin, USA, on 2nd April 1925. She graduated at high school in 1941 and had a number of jobs, including proof-reader, newspaper writer and reporter, lathe machinist and ship fitter, during the Second World War, and a Project Mission Reporter at Hollowman Air Force Base in New Mexico, USA. In 1952, she and her husband – Jim Lorenzen, founded the Aerial Phenomena Research Organization (APRO). Together they share the opinion that UFOs are best explained by the extraterrestrial hypothesis (ETH). Coral witnessed several UFOs – the first at the age of nine, another in Arizona, during 1947, and another that was seen by over 300 people over the Door Peninsula, Wisconsin, in USA. Coral and Jim both passed away in the early 1980s. Coral's publications include: *The Great Flying Saucer Hoax* (1962), *Flying Saucers: The Startling Evidence of the Invasion from Outer Space* (1966), *The Shadow of the Unknown* (1970).

*Aerial Phenomena Research Organization*

3910 EAST KLEINDALE ROAD
602—326-0059
TUCSON, ARIZONA — 85716

12 October 1966

Dear Mr. Barrow:

The fact that summer is "vacation time" in this town, and a lot of our people are college personnel, contributes to our lateness in getting the bulletin out. The printer told me today however, that the Jul-Aug. issue will be ready Friday, so we'll be mailing Monday. We'll have our mailing session Sunday, and it takes a few hours to get it ready.

My "new" book is a revised version of the old one with more photographs, more cases, and up to date through June 1966. Published by SIGNET (New American Library), paperback, don't know the price. Title: Flying Saucers.

Sorry for the poor typing. I've been at this for 10 hours today and I guess I'm wearing out. You can expect to get your bulletin next week and we'll have the Sept-Oct issue out within one week either way of 30 October.

Sincerely,

*Coral Lorenzen*

---

*Aerial Phenomena Research Organization*

3910 EAST KLEINDALE ROAD
602—326-0059
TUCSON, ARIZONA    85716

21 July 1966

Robert Barrow

Dear Mr. Barrow:

Thank you for your letter of 1 July and the enclosed order for back issues. They are being mailed in book mailers (2 or 3 packets) under separate cover. We were out of July 1964 issues, and substituted an old March 1957 issue which we "dug up". I hope that is satisfactory to you.

Again, thank you- for your comments on the Editorials in the recent Bulletins. This, incidentally, is one of the big reasons that there are two large U. S. Research Organizations. NICAP is a pressure group dedicated to expending time and efforts attempting a Congressional hearing (which turned out just as we said it would) while we have concentrated on research, investigation, correlations, and interpretation of the results. Our theories are not generally popular at the time they are printed, but usually are adopted eventually. NICAP has been very unfriendly toward most of them, but we note that Frank Edwards is using considerable of our information, both from my book and the Bulletins (without asking permission, incidentally) and talking about the theories which were wholly rejected several years ago.

We have no pre-formed opinions, but do conjecture for we feel this is the life blood of research. We do not have the biased opinion, as NICAP does, that the UFOs are not hostile——we believe they very well could be and that the evidence does not support a non-hostile conclusion.

Another difference is that APRO is the oldest research organization in the U. S. and in the world. Also, we have always concentrated on GLOBAL information, for the UFO problem is global in nature. NICAP started out with the premise that an admittance from the USAF would naturally take care of everything. We can't agree. APRO is made up of people in all the free countries of the world who have an equal policy voice. There is no "titular" head of APRO- each staff member and representative enjoys equal voice along with the others. We might even be called the "United Nations" of UFO Research.

You may have heard or been told that there is "bad blood" between the two organizations and let me assure you that there is not, at least not on our part. We believe strongly that there should be as many groups as there are needs. The scientific community needs APRO and the enthusiastic community needs NICAP.

I hope the Bulletins prove to be valuable to you in your efforts, and ask only one thing, and that is that APRO be given equal emphasis along with NICAP in your lectures, etc. Good luck.

Sincerely,

*Coral E. Lorenzen*

Coral E. Lorenzen
Secretary

## FOOTNOTE

### Jerry Black

In *UFO Magazine* (June /July 2001) there is an interesting article about Mr Jerry Black – then aged 61, living in Blanchester, Ohio – by Christopher Kemp, a freelance writer from Cincinnati.

Christopher tells us that he met his wife in 1973, after she claimed to have been abducted by aliens. Of course, there was once a time when we would have treated such allegations as having no substance whatsoever – now the evidence points in the opposite direction.

The couple have collected thousands of eyewitness accounts from local people.

### Mr Black:

> "I am in the business of re-searching UFOs scientifically and objectively – just wish I had an answer for you people. I wish I could tell you that UFOs are nothing to worry about, but they've frightened a lot of people. Even so, there isn't a shred of evidence that UFOs are extraterrestrial, that they have landed on Earth,."

Mr Black's interest in the UFO phenomena began in the mid-1950s, while attending Hughes High School in Clifton – then aged 16. In 1988 he sighted some luminous objects in the sky, while driving along the highway with his wife. Since then, he has now thoroughly investigated as many as 20 sightings of alien abduction claims.

One such case was the Gulf Breeze photographs, taken by Ed Walters, which Jerry become involved in – costing him $4,000 without him leaving the house.

> "I spent over 4 years on this and also most lost my wife, because I spent so much time and money. I was obsessed with it." [Jerry discovered the photos were hoaxed.]

In 1976, after 20 years of researching UFOs, Jerry was to come across a case that could not be solved, involving Louise Smith, Mona Stafford, and Elaine Thomas.

> "I came into the case several months later, and contacted the women. At first they were reluctant to talk. They were finally convinced when my wife joined the discussion."

He accrued eight hours of tape-recordings, following the women being hypnotized. [According to Richard Hall's account of the incident, Elaine Thomas passed away two years later of an unknown cause.]

> "The abduction claims of the three ladies involved are unusual but not unique. There are still thousands of people on this planet – sincere people like yourself, like me – walking out on the street today, who sincerely believe they were abducted. Thousands of women sitting in their houses, housewives, looking out of their windows, seeing this strange object in the daytime sky approach their house. The next thing they remember is the food on the stove is burning, or the kids are home from school, and they can't account for the time."

### Authors' comments:

Our hearts go out to people like those concerned, who have had the misfortune to be involved in terrifying encounters like this while going about their everyday business. Those that have never experienced traumatic events like this cannot even understand the pain and long-term effects of what took place. While there is no direct evidence to suggest that the interaction was deliberate rather than being in the wrong place at the wrong time, it is obvious from examination of other close encounters brought to our attention, that such incidents are not, in all probability, beneficial to physical health – although most people who have been involved will, from a psychological point of view, feel their experience has been 'spiritually uplifting'. The greatest problem is that we all look for an answer as to why UFOs continue to be seen and where they come from. For a long time, Dawn and I have sensed that each and every appearance of a UFO can, in certain circumstances, lead to the frightening scenario which befell the three ladies involved.

## 10th January 1976 – Winged UFO over Essex

At 9.30pm, Donald Paul Sarjant (14) of Heathway, Dagenham, was in his back garden, along with Mr and Mrs T. Branch, when a most curious object was seen.

## 15th January 1976 – UFO over Isle of Wight

At 12.40am on 15th January 1976, Trinity House pilot's assistant – Rodney Ridell, was stood outside his home address at Elmfield, Ryde, Isle of Wight, checking the weather before going to bed, when he noticed an unusual cloud moving towards his direction, the interior of which appeared to be illuminated.

> "I shouted for my wife to come and have a look. As it passed overhead the light dimmed, allowing me to see a perfect silhouette. I estimated it was travelling at about 300 feet off the ground, and was a hundred feet in length by fifty feet wide. Suddenly, to my amazement, it shot up into the night sky at terrific speed and disappeared into the cloud."

*(Handwritten witness statement reproduced at right):*

"I was in my garden with my friend Mr G. Branch, we often go into the back garden to look for ufos, when 4 orange objects appeared. We watched for approx 5 minutes, when I went indoors to ask my father to come and see them, we came out to see them move away."

Location of sighting: Back garden of 9 White gardens, Dagenham. 4 objects gave off no sound, were coloured orange and were bird shaped.

The extreme edges of the objects appeared "blurred" or "fuzzy". Objects were about the size of a 5p at arms length.

The only familiar looking object, if transported to the sky would be a Mushroom.

Objects first seen in the Southwest, last seen in the Southeast. Objects passed directly overhead.

Total observation time: 10 minutes.
Objects angle of elevation above the horizon when 1st seen: 40°
Objects angle of elevation above the horizon when last seen: 50
Objects angular bearing from true north when 1st seen: 135°
Objects angular bearing from true north when last seen: 135°

Weather conditions: Clear sky, cold, dry, light breeze.

Formation (D.G.)

---

## UFO SPEED 'AMAZING' — RYDE MAN

Another U.F.O. has been reported over Ryde. At 10.30 p.m. last Sunday Mr. David Spicer, of 44, Great Preston Road, turned into his driveway after taking his mother-in-law and sister-in-law home.

He noticed a very bright and exceptionally white light in the sky in the direction of Ryde Airport at a height of about 2,000 feet.

Mr. Spicer parked his car and crossed the road to have a better look. "The light was motionless for four or five minutes," he said, "and then suddenly shot straight upwards at an alarming rate."

Mr. Spicer called his wife and together they watched the light move sideways about 200 yards and then towards them, travelling very fast.

When it was virtually overhead it stopped and the white light seemed to be switched off.

Mr. Spicer described what he saw as a spherical - shaped object with red lights "round a black mass" half-way up it, which looked like a cockpit area. Mrs. Spicer telephoned her sister, Miss Dorothy Buckett, who lives not far away in Lower Highland Road, and she also saw it.

Mr. Spicer served in the Royal Navy for ten years, spending three years on the carrier Hermes, and is familiar with all types of aircraft. He now works as a television engineer.

"I've never been interested in the subject of U.F.O.s before," he said. "I've never seen anything like this. It was too low for a star and too bright for an aircraft. Its vertical speed was amazing."

Earlier this year Mr. Rodney Riddell, from nearby High Park Road, also spotted a strange craft in the sky. His sighting was later confirmed by a meteorological officer at Portsmouth and was the subject of a Ministry of Defence inquiry.

### SISTERHOOD

Miss Higgs presided at a meeting of Sandown Sisterhood. Mrs. De Bank opened with prayer, and the lesson was read by Mrs. Pain. Speaker was Mr. Heywood, representing the Japan Evangelistic Band. Mrs. De Bank is the new president of the sisterhood.

---

## UFO riddle of lights seen over Orpington

*15/1/1976. Kentish Times*

TWO RESIDENTS who saw odd lights in the sky over Orpington last week are wondering if they saw a genuine unidentified flying object (UFO).

The two accounts, given independently by the two observers, are similar in several points.

THE TIME: About 7 a.m on January 6.

DESCRIPTION of the object: Two white lights too big to be stars and of exactly the same shape.

THEIR behaviour: hovering motionless, then slowly turning and moving off in a wide arc.

### MOTIONLESS

Mrs P. Webb, of Augustine Road, St Paul's Cray, looked out of the window and saw the two lights. She watched them for 10 minutes as they hovered motionless, so believes this ruled out them being on a plane or helicopter.

The objects then moved off in the direction of Chislehurst and as they turned she got the impression they were triangular, with a white light on each corner and one red light in between.

The other observer, a Green Street Green resident, was travelling along Glentrammon Road when he saw what looked like two large car headlights in the sky.

He continued along the road, glancing at the lights which seemed to be hovering motionless, before they slowly drifted off in the direction of the Crays, he said.

Shortly afterwards he saw a red and green light higher in the sky which he knew was a plane, and thought at that time that all the lights had been associated with the aircraft.

However later on, while crossing Hayes Common, he saw the lights again in the distance, somewhere over the Chislehurst area. He said he had never seen any lights of that kind on an aircraft, and was completely mystified.

A spokesman for the Ministry of Defence said that anyone seeing such objects could report the sightings with full details to the Ministry, who investigated for defence purposes.

Figures were no longer kept for these sightings, but the last statistics published showed an overwhelming majority of reports were of aircraft. Others were of balloons, satellite debris, flares, stars and other celestial objects, or strange effects caused by meteorological conditions.

From the descriptions given by the two observers in Orpington, he added, the most likely explanation would be that the sightings were of a helicopter flying by night using lights.

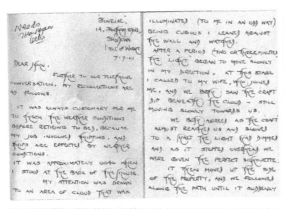

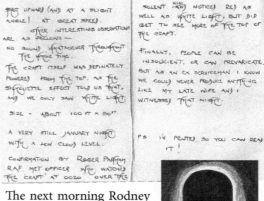

The next morning Rodney rang the Duty Controller, at RAF Thorney Island, and explained what had happened. Within a few minutes he received a telephone call from the MOD, who told him they would send somebody to see him shortly. He later discovered that RAF Meteorological Officer Roger Parham had seen a UFO displaying red and white light, over the Solent, heading towards Ryde at 12.25am, which he believes was the same UFO.

## 19th January 1976 – Strange phenomena over Kent

At 4.45pm, a strange 'length of light' was seen in the sky towards the north-west direction over Ramsgate, Kent, as the sun set.

At 6.10pm, the witness saw a small 'globe of light' in the same direction, accompanied by a yellow object, described as:

*"…about thirty times the size of a star, seen lengthways from the front one and widthways. It was apparently rotating and left at speed, before disappearing from sight at 4.35pm."*

## 19th January 1976 – Boomerang-shaped UFO over Heislerville, New Jersey

At about 7.30pm, witnesses saw an object with two bright lights hovering over woods, about 300 yards away. After about two minutes the object sped away, passing directly overhead, making a low whirring noise. It appeared to be boomerang-shaped (or more heart-shaped – something like an artist's palette, judging by the newspaper sketches). A semicircle of red lights was visible on the underside, near the front, where something like headlights was visible. Two of the witnesses reported seeing motion or 'figures' inside the apparent craft.

(Source: *The Press,* Atlantic City, New Jersey, 21.1.1976)

## 20th January 1976 – USO, Ventnor, New Jersey

At about 5am, Navy veteran – now New Jersey Police patrolman Frank Ingargiola (then aged 28), with five years service – was giving a lift home to newspaper columnist – Sony Schwartz. They sighted a 'bright light', roughly a mile offshore, and decided to investigate further.

They drove onto the beach, at 5.10am.

> **Frank:** *"All of sudden, the object came straight in towards us – that's when I backed up. I've been on many midnight watches at sea and trained in identifying different shapes. I've never seen anything like this before. It came in very close, just above the waves; say, 500 feet from the car. It was so huge that it seemed to fill the whole windshield. I couldn't see anything else. It had a very bright white light in the centre, with a yellowish haze twice the size of the light. When it got close you could see three small reddish-orange points in it in the shape of a triangle.*
>
> **Mr. Schwartz:** *It was enormous. I couldn't believe any light could be so bright. As we looked we became transfixed by it."*

By this time Frank had contacted the Atlantic City Police and asked if they could send officers out to confirm the sighting. Some 20 officers arrived and also watched the object. Two of them were patrolman – Daniel Conver, and his partner – Daniel Wilhelmy

> *"The light seemed to get dimmer and then brighter as we watched. We checked for helicopters; there wasn't any".*
>
> **Patrolman Henry Madanda:** *"It appeared to be a glowing light out over the ocean. As I gazed at it, it suddenly disappeared in front of my eyes. I was shocked."*

Enquiries, made later, revealed that earlier the same night, residents of nearby towns had also reported strange lights in the sky.

Mr and Mrs Wayne Tomlin of Heislerville (30 miles from Atlantic City) reported seeing:

*"...two enormous bright lights – like headlights – 300 yards away over some trees, at 7.30pm on the 19th January".*

Half an hour later at Dorothy, New Jersey, Mrs Morris sighted:

*"...a very brilliant red light – the most brilliant shade of red I have ever seen. I was really overawed by the thing."*

## 21st January 1976 – FOI re Cannon Air Force Base

Sometime before 3.55am. MST. NMCC Memo: The following information was received from the Air Force Operations center at 0555 EST: Two UFOs are reported near the flight line at Cannon AFB, New Mexico. Security Police observing them reported the UFOs to be *"25 yards in diameter, gold or silver in colour with blue light on top, hole in the middle and red light on the bottom."* Air Force is checking with radar, additionally, checking weather inversion data. Among other UFO researchers who arrived in Clovis were several members of the UFO Study Group, which has about 40 members, mainly employees of the Los Alamos Scientific Laboratories – the facility where the Atomic bomb was developed in World War II. Police said scores of sightings were reported between 6pm and 10.30pm Friday, an hour before the Los Alamos observers arrived. *(Las Cruces SUN News, Sunday Morning, Jan. 25, 1976)*

**(Source: FOIA document)**

### Town Marshall follows UFO

Town Marshal Willie Ronquillo, of Texico, said he followed a silent object about 300 yards over his car. Ronquillo said the object, which had green, yellow and blue lights, sped away at a high speed to the north. Lenore Hildebrand of the UFO centre in Wisconsin said Jim Epps of Valley Center, California, would arrive in Clovis. She said an Air Force officer from Clovis called the center on Friday night and told them he *"had a very close sighting and was able to witness a type of vehicle that did manoeuvre and that was unlike any type aircraft I had ever seen"*. **(Source: *Las Cruces SUN News*, same as above/NICAP)**

## 23rd January 1976 – Rotating object over Wembley, Middlesex

*"A large, rotating object"* was seen hovering approximately 1,000 metres in the sky above Watford Road, Wembley, Middlesex, at 12.15pm, by a woman, who wrote a letter to the MOD but never received any satisfactory answer. **(Source: Isle of Wight UFO Society)**

## 23rd January 1976 - Close encounter with UFO causes medical ailments

Another witness saw this at 3am, the following morning, over Watford.

Was there any connection with a terrifying incident that happened the same day, at 5.15 pm, involving 'Shelley' from Bolton, Lancashire? – without doubt one of the strangest and disturbing UFO encounters ever brought to our attention, involving the appearance of a *'spinning metallic 'disc', ablaze with lights, flat on the top, with sloping sides, three lights and three legs,* which swooped over her, while walking home past Rumworth Lodge Reservoir – causing a catalogue of various physical ailments.

They included crumbled dental fillings, burn marks on her arm and side, nausea and vomiting, and the discovery of a strange purple rash on her neck and shoulders.

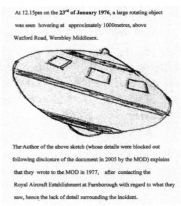

At 12.15pm on the **23rd of January 1976**, a large rotating object was seen hovering at approximately 1000metres, above Watford Road, Wembley Middlesex.

The Author of the above sketch (whose details were blocked out following disclosure of the document in 2005 by the MOD) explains that they wrote to the MOD in 1977, after contacting the Royal Aircraft Establishment at Farnborough with regard to what they saw, hence the lack of detail surrounding the incident.

*Artist's impression of the UFO over Watford Road, Wembley, Middlesex, January 23, 1976.*

### Received a telephone call

On 2nd February 1976, 'Shelley's' mother received a telephone call from a man who declined to identify himself, but told her he was *"an investigator of such things"* and asked her whether *"any marks had been left on the girl's body"*. She put the telephone down, declining to discuss the matter with him.

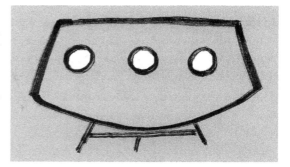

### Two men arrived at the house – threats made

At 7 pm, the same day, two men arrived at the home address of 'Shelley' and demanded to interview the girl, de-scribed as both being aged about 40 years, wearing crisp black suits, one of them tall and almost blonde. Although the father initially declined to let them in, the men persisted. One of them said, threateningly:

*"If you do not let us in now, we will come back later and make 'Shelley' speak to us".*

After making themselves comfortable the 'silent one' sat down, holding a black box – said to be a 'high-tech.' recording device, (although no visible parts were seen) – the other, who only had one arm, referred to himself as a 'Commander' in the RAF (a rank that didn't exist in the RAF), and conducted an interview that lasted three hours, following which the family were advised:

*"You must not talk to anyone about this matter. It is in your interests not to do so. Nobody will believe you in any case.*

*In particular, you must not talk to any UFO Investigator"* – then left.

The mystery men telephoned the family on a number of occasions over the following weeks, asking whether the girl had any unusual marks on her body. On the last occasion (in order to hopefully discontinue the harassment) they were instructed that she had, and this was the last time they telephoned the family again.

### Hypnotic regression

In a subsequent hypnotic regression, performed by Dr. Albert Kellar from Manchester, 'Shelley' reacted in absolute terror to the visit by the 'two men', and the Doctor was forced to abandon the treatment because of a dangerous rise in her vital signs.

We wrote to 'Shelley', hoping she would agree to an interview. She replied:

*"I am sorry, I cannot help. This is something I do not ever wish to discuss again. I am of the opinion that this kind of thing is best left in the past. I have children, who are at a very vulnerable and*

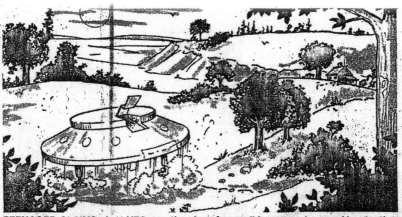

**TEENAGER CLAIMS** giant UFO was the size of a small house and caused her teeth to vibrate and crumble. Now she's afraid to have children.

# Terrifying encounter with UFO shatters teen's teeth

**A** GIANT UFO made a teenage girl's teeth crumble — and now she's afraid to have children.

Shelley ~~████~~ now 28, will never forget the day she encountered a spaceship near her home.

Recalled Shelley: "I saw a red and green light in the sky. The lights were about four or five times the size of a star. Then, the lights merged and the craft zoomed in.

"It was the size of a small house, flat on top, with sloping sides, and a trap door and tripod legs. It was spinning on an axis and then righted itself. I could see the portholes with lights shining through."

Suddenly, the UFO tilted toward the teen and there was terrible pressure on her head.

"My teeth seemed to vibrate," said Shelley. "There was a terrible taste in my mouth. When I tried to run it was like being in a nightmare. My arms and legs moved, but in slow motion."

The next thing she remembered was running

**BY EDWARD REYNOLDS**

home. Her mom thought she had been raped. Shocked Shelley took her mom outside and pointed to the sky, but the UFO had vanished.

Police in Bolton, England, filed a report, but didn't believe Shelley's story. Her local doctor said she was suffering from hysteria and investigators dismissed the UFO as a low-flying aircraft.

Two days later, 17-year-old Shelley became ill. A purple rash covered her body. Her joints and eyes ached. Then her teeth began to disintegrate.

And to make matters worse, two unidentified men came to her home and interrogated her for over four hours. They ordered her not to talk to the press or UFO researchers.

Said Shelley: "I was almost reduced to tears. These two men had a strange effect on all of us.

My father is normally protective, yet he sat by while they were tearing me to pieces."

She added: "They seemed to know about my rash, even though neither I or my family had mentioned it."

Now married and her teeth restored, Shelley vows never to have children. She feels it is unsafe to bring them into the world.

October 13, '87/EXAMINER **19**

*[handwritten note:] Mark Do you know if there is a grain of truth to this story? I am collecting medical injury cases & this one would be very interesting if true. Thanks [signature]*

Rumworth Lodge Reservoir

*critical period in their life, and I do not wish to be upset by any involvement with this. Please do not contact me again. I have managed to leave all this in the past, where it belongs. Your letter caused me great distress and anxiety. I want no further involvement whatsoever in this subject. Please do not identify me by name, or give my details to anyone regarding this subject."*

[We have honoured her wish, although her full name was published in a UFO book in 1990 by a UFO researcher]

### The trauma cannot be measured

No-one (unless they have had the misfortune to suffer what 'Shelley' went through) can adequately measure, or understand, the trauma involved with witnessing something clearly outside the parameters of normal everyday events, followed by threats and intimidation from visits by the two sinister men. No wonder 'Shelley' has adopted this attitude, although 'Shelley' was the subject of a newspaper article, in 1987, when she was only too willing to speak about her experiences, ending with a vow never to have children!

### Peter Hough

We spoke to Peter Hough, in 2008, about the incident. He said:

*"Yes – I only ever referred to her as 'Shelley'; interesting that you have tracked her down after all these years – I last spoke to her in 1988. At the time of the experience (1976?) she was only a 17- year-old receptionist. My feelings still are that this was a genuine example of the phenomenon and exhibited many of the key components; sighting of unusual object, missing time (although no full-blown abduction account), physical effects, subsequent visit by the MIB (verified to me by her parents) and post-experience paranormal abilities. This was at a time when details of the abduction phenomenon was not widely publicised, and therefore it was less likely that they had been fabricated."*

At about 6.15pm the same day, an unknown girl from Ladybridge, Bolton, contacted the Direct Investigation Group of Aerial Phenomena, after sighting a bright object over rooftops, which caused her great distress. (**Source: Bolton Evening News, 24.1.1976 - 'Girl spots UFO'**)

Enquiries with DIGAP to trace the source of this report, or any further details, were unsuccessful – a matter we found extremely frustrating, bearing in mind one is bound to speculate if this witness also suffered physical harm – unless this was 'Shelley', which doesn't appear to be the case.

(**Source: Jenny Randles, 1988/Peter Hough**/*Confrontations: A Scientist's Search for Alien Contact,* **Jacques F. Vallee**/*Australian Post,* **30.7.1987**/*Bolton Evening News,* **24.1.1976/DIGAP/Mr. Arthur Tomlinson**/*Flying Saucer Review,* **Volume 22, No. 1, 1976**)

### 25th January 1976 – 'Flying Saucer' over Lancashire

In the early hours, Christine Young from Slaters Field, Bolton, and her sister – Jillian, of Oriel Street, were on their way home from a club, when they saw:

> "...a 'thing' over some rooftops, near Sunnyside Mill, in St. Helens Road; it was really uncanny, and frightening. We thought it was a 'flying saucer', covered in bright lights – unmoving, silent, and about four feet long with jagged edges. After ten minutes, the object slowly changed into a smooth saucer shape."

In 2008, Jillian Bretherton (neé Newtown) contacted us about the incident after we had placed an appeal in the local newspapers.

> "It wasn't an isolated incident; there were others who also saw UFOs at that time. After we reported it we received many enquiries from UFO researchers, wishing to interview us. We even appeared on Granada TV. What I would like to tell you is that we also had a visit from a 'Man in Black' who interviewed us at the house."

Was this 'Man in Black' from a Government agency, or was he representative of something more sinister?

(**Source:** *Bolton Evening News,* **27.1.1976/DIGAP/Personal interview**)

### 27th January 1976 – Two UFOs sighted over Essex

At 4pm, Probation Officer – Mrs Bassten of Somercotes, Laindon, Essex, was with four others in her office, at 4pm, when she sighted two objects moving across the sky in the west direction, about two miles away.

> "The first object was disc-shaped with a flat bottom, and a dome on top and glowing white. This moved in a south to north direction and was lost in cloud, some 30 minutes later. The second one was cylindrical in shape but at an angle to us. This one was orange in colour and much closer to us. It then turned right and headed away northwards and faded into the distance. During the sighting we telephoned the Basildon Recorder, who took details from us."

## TWO UFO
27/1/76
## SIGHTINGS
## OVER
## CLEVELAND

UNIDENTIFIED flying objects were spotted over Cleveland twice at the end of last week.

Mr. Gwynn Williams, who lives at 8, Lorton Road, Redcar, was driving towards Stokesley after leaving the A19 when both he and his wife saw what they describe as a "green object" in the sky.

Said Mr. Williams: "I can't really say anything except that it was green and appeared to have a greenish tail like a comet. At first I thought it was a light on a low flying aircraft, but it couldn't have been because it did not blink.

### Disappeared

"I was travelling east to west and my wife and I watched it until it disappeared. It didn't fade—it just vanished as though someone had switched off a light."

"I honestly don't know what to think because I have an open mind on these matters."

A representative of the Unidentified Flying Objects Research Association confirmed that another very similar light had been seen the same evening over Redcar, flying out towards the sea.

# Mystery of flying objects

**SEVERAL** sightings of a mysterious bright flying object in different parts of Bolton are being investigated by UFO experts.

Three people have reported seeing an "uncanny" object hovering about ten feet over rooftops at night.

Now the Direct Investigation Group of Aerial Phenomena is looking into the possibility that the sightings were alien craft.

Sighting number one came on Friday night at about 6.15. A girl who lives at Ladybridge, Bolton, saw a bright object over rooftops.

"I saw it for about ten seconds and then I ran — it was terrifying," said the girl who wants to remain anonymous.

The second sighting was by two Bolton sisters who were on their way home from a club early on Sunday morning.

Miss Christine Young, aged 19, of Slater Field, and her younger sister Jillian Newton, of Oriel Street, say they saw the mystery object for about ten minutes.

### 25th January 1976 – Police Officer chased by UFO, Wyoming

At 8.09pm, a Sheriff's deputy was out driving with his family when an object was seen coming towards their car. The deputy immediately stopped the car and turned off the headlights. He described it as:

> "...the size of a semi-truck with rotating lights of many different colours, and a bright light in the centre. As the object came closer to the car, I felt it was trying to catch us and tried to turn the car around."

When unable to turn on the narrow road, he started backing away from the UFO. After travelling for almost a mile, he reached a point where he could then turn around. By this time the object was about 100 yards from the car and about 10 feet off the ground. As the officer was attempting to turn his car, the UFO was lost from sight.

Later, the witness went home and returned to the scene in a truck to search for the UFO away from the main roads. When he reached the valley where he had first seen the UFO, a *"bright light"* rose swiftly upwards and was soon lost from view. (**Source:** *UFO Investigator*, **May 1976, page 1**)

### 27th January 1976 – Three objects seen at Key West, Florida

Mrs Rosemary Heitmeyer was awake at 4.25am and happened to look out of her hall window. She saw three objects that looked like:

> "...upside-down soup bowls, with domed tops, bobbing and moving very slowly through the sky. Underneath the objects were square windows, glaring an orange-red colour."

Mrs Heitmeyer woke up her husband and he joined her outside the house. By this time the three objects were still moving slowly, but then began to increase their speed, heading rapidly away and soon out of sight. Mr Heitmeyer – a retired Navy chief petty officer and former employee of the Cape Kennedy Missile Test Center, confirmed his wife's observations. He estimated the objects were about one and-a-half miles away. (**Source:** *UFO Investigator*, **April 1976, page 3**)

### 29th January 1976 – UFO over Basildon, Essex

At 7.30pm, Jill Taylor (14) of Broomfields Place, Basildon, Essex, was on her way to the local keep fit club at the nearby school, accompanied by her friend – Doreen Moor (15). As they walked along Pitsea Road they noticed a strange object in the sky, which they brought to the attention of a passer-by, who told them not to be silly as it was probably *"a star, blowing in the wind"*. The girls kept it under observation until class started. When they came out at break time, it was still there *"but now bowl-shaped"*. After completing the session they walked home and watched it from their house, at 10.30pm, noting that ...

> "It occasionally sent out a ray of green light from what looked like a dumpy bowl-shaped object, with various lights flashing on the bottom and an orange band around the rim, showing a green light above. The outline of the object was very sharp when the lights were on; it looked shiny metallic in appearance. We watched it for over three hours as it moved silently backwards and forwards across the sky."

Jill (now in her 60s) told us that she still remembered it well.

> "It really freaked me out. When I arrived home and told my parents they didn't know what to make of it, but what made a lasting impression on me were the 'globes of light' which dropped out of the triangular-shaped object with a cylindrical top – like a half-moon."

We also contacted Doreen – now married for over 25 years, recovering from mental trauma associated as a result of major surgery – who (perhaps understandably) felt the matter didn't deserve a second glance, as she had moved on with her life. (**Sources:** *Evening Echo*, **9.2.1976**/*Basildon Recorder* – **'Truly this is what we saw'**/**East Anglian Paranormal Society, Brenda Butler/Andrew Collins, BUFORA**)

## TRULY, this is what we saw!

At 7.30 Doreen came round for me to go keep fit. I noticed this object in the sky we watched it all the time. When we got to the school we were early, and so we watched it again, We told some of the women to look but they told us not to be silly. It was probably a star blowing about in the wind. But there was no wind at the time. We then watched it again in our break and made it out to be a bowl shape. At the end of keep fit we got dressed and went home. we watched it all the way home. when I got home. I stood at the patio window and then I drew it.

→ It sometimes sent out green beams.
(GREEN RAYS WERE PARALLEL, AND SOME TIMES BENT DOWN.)

### Did you see it too?

TWO quietly-spoken teenage girls insist they saw a green flying saucer over Basildon last week. It stayed in the sky so long, they told the Recorder shyly, they even had time to sketch it.

Said Jill Taylor, 14, of Broomfields Place, Basildon: "We were going to our club on Thursday night (January 29) when we saw this thing in the sky.

"It was completely circular and we could see different colours on it. We told other people to look out but they told us not to be silly."

Doreen Moore, 15, of Broomfield Mews, said: "It was moving backwards and forwards in the sky and was quite silent."

"It was a greenish metallic colour with glowing globes in different colours at the bottom. When it came close it was about the size of a dinner plate. But when it moved away it could have been a star. "It was like nothing either of us has ever seen before."

We have reproduced the girls' sketch for readers. If you saw the flying saucer we'd like to hear from you.

● Basildon is becoming a popular tourist attraction for UFO's, it appears. In November a Laindon housewive claims she was followed by a UFO pear-shaped and the size of a jumbo jet. And a number of readers substantiated her claim.

Then in January five members of Basildon's probation office told the Recorder they had been watching two UFOs over Basildon for half-an-hour.

Now comes the green flying saucer. IS truth stranger than fiction?

**Jill (right) and Doreen, say "we feel daft, but we're telling the truth."**

# Third flying saucer sighted

BASILDON'S third flying saucer sighting was reported by two teenagers who spotted a plate-shaped object hovering over the town for more than an hour.

Jill Taylor, 14, of Broomfields Place, Basildon, and Doreen Moore, 15, of Broomfields Mews, say the UFO was a greenish colour with a collection of coloured lights at the bottom.

The girls watched the "saucer" long enough to make a sketch to show their friend who, they said, told them not to be silly.

Last November a housewife said she saw a pear-shaped object hovering over Laindon, and in January five people reported two bright discs in the sky for half-an-hour.

EVENING ECHO 9-2-76

*Impression of the Pitsea Road, Basildon UFO*

### 29th January 1976 – USA: Singer reports close encounter, Nevada

Johnny Sands (30) – a country and western singer – was living in Las Vegas, Nevada, and trying to promote his first recording.

> *"I had been out driving to the surrounding towns to check on how well my record was faring at the radio stations and on jukeboxes.*
>
> *I was driving on the Blue Diamond road, at about 10.30pm, some 22 miles out of Las Vegas, when I saw an unusual aircraft."*

He didn't pay much attention to it, although it appeared to follow him for about three miles. At this point, the car's engine began sputtering, so he pulled off the road and got out of the car. He walked around the car, removed the gas (petrol) tank lid (cap), and shook the rear end of the car to determine whether he had any gas. He could hear the gas splashing around in the tank, so he replaced the cover and went around to the front of the car and lifted the hood.

#### UFO sighted

> *"Looking up, I saw a 'craft' above me at what I estimated to be about 1,000 feet. It was about 60 feet long and shaped like the 'Goodyear blimp', with a large, round ring at the midsection, windows or portholes (round), about 10 feet in diameter, about five feet apart around the circumference of the ring or 'doughnut' section, with a light between each. The object was rusty-orange in colour with flashing red and white lights on the ends. It moved slowly over the mountain to the south of me, lighting up the mountain as it did so and appearing to land."*

#### Two 'figures' approached

Johnny turned his attention back to the car and started to take the air filter off. For some unknown reason, he turned and looked down the road in the direction that his headlights were shining (which were on low beam) and saw two 'figures' approaching. He could not make out any details and, at first, thought they might have been muggers. Then, he said, he 'froze' — he doesn't know why — he wanted to

*Tattler April 2, 1978*

# Singer takes lie detector test to prove he was quizzed by UFOnauts

A SINGER who claims he talked to UFO creatures in a frightening encounter on a lonely desert road has passed a lie detector test.

Country and western performer Johnny Sands said the two gray-skinned aliens used a strange force to render him immobile, and then asked him a series of questions.

He described them as humanoid in appearance with small, close-set eyes. Instead of ears, he said, they had vertical openings which pulsated like the gills on a fish.

He said the confrontation happened moments after he spotted a huge UFO with flashing lights while driving on a deserted road 15 miles south of Las Vegas. A mysterious force made his car stall, he said, and the two creatures approached him out of the darkness.

"I was scared to death," said the 30-year-old singer. "But I grew more calm as they talked to me and I realized they meant no harm."

Sands passed a polygraph test following the incident. Examiner R.L. Nolen of Las Vegas said the test showed no evidence of deception, and that Sands was truthful in his answers to questions about the encounter.

Leo Sprinkle, a psychologist from the University of Wyoming who is an investigator for the Aerial Phenomena Research Organization, witnessed the test.

Sands said the aliens were between five-feet-seven and five-feet-nine tall, and weighed about 145 pounds. They were completely bald and had no facial hair. They stared at him through close-set black eyes with white pupils.

"Their voices had a hollow sound," said Sands, "and their speech was slow—like a robot you see on television."

The aliens had small, wrinkled mouths which did not move, even though Sands could hear a voice clearly. They spoke to him in English.

Sands said the aliens asked him about eight questions, but he felt he could reveal only three of them.

"They told me not to discuss the meeting with anyone, and said they would see me again," Sands said.

"If they don't contact me

Johnny Sands: "I was scared to death".

## 'Gray-skinned aliens with slits for ears'

soon I'll reveal all the conversation. Right now I want to keep some of it secret to show good faith."

One of the aliens did all the talking while the other watched from about 10 feet away, Sands said. Occasionally, the creatures looked at each other silently and Sands believed they were communicating in some manner.

The questions revealed by Sands were "What are you doing here?" followed by "What are all these people doing here?" which Sands interpreted as a reference to Las Vegas, and "How do you communicate?"

Sands said that in answer to question one he stammered that he was an entertainer. In answer to the second question, he explained Las Vegas as a tourist town.

Sands said when he told the aliens he did not understand the third question they said: "Just answer the question."

"The alien spoke to me sharply," Sands said. "His voice changed. I could tell he was upset."

Sands said that when he maintained that he did not understand the question, the aliens looked at each other for almost three minutes without speaking. They then told him not to discuss the meeting.

Suddenly they turned and walked down the road until they disappeared.

Sands said the aliens were dressed in a one-piece uniform similar to a jump suit. The hands, although covered by the suit, had five fingers. The skin color was gray.

Flaps of skin stood out from the neck, partially covering the gill-like openings in the side of their heads and obscuring them from view when the aliens faced him directly.

"They seemed like they might have been 300 or 400 years old," Sands said. "It was just a feeling I had. I also had the feeling they didn't

have any trouble with heart attacks and the other things that humans have. All this just came to me while they were talking to me."

Sands, of Clarksdale, Miss., said the meeting took place soon after 10 pm on January 29. He was driving along the winding Blue Diamond Road when he suddenly saw flashing lights in the sky. Three miles further on, his car mysteriously stalled, he said.

While he was checking his engine, he said that he caught sight of a huge object directly overhead.

"It was about 1,000 feet above me," Sands said. "It looked like a blimp at first, with flashing lights at both ends and a bulge in the middle. It must have been 60 feet long or more."

It drifted silently behind a nearby mountain peak and was lost from view, he said.

Then suddenly Sands said he saw the two aliens in the beams of his headlights.

"They walked in slow motion, like they had balloons on their feet."

Sands said he was frightened and wanted to run, but suddenly felt himself unable to move.

Their uniforms sparkled brilliantly, he said. Both had a single black stripe running diagonally from the right shoulder to the left side, across a round white emblem bordered by gold buttons.

As the aliens turned to go, following their questioning, Sands said one reached out and brushed his fingertips lightly over Sands' right hand. "His suit was rough, like coarse sandpaper," said Sands. "I had the feeling they were from a very cold place."

Sands said the gesture seemed to free him from the immobility that had overcome him. He returned to his car and drove back to Las Vegas. The aliens walked down the road in Sands' headlights and vanished.

move, but he couldn't. The two 'figures' came towards him – one stopping about three feet away, while the other stayed about five feet beyond.

> *"They were perfectly bald with no eyelashes or brows and gill-like protrusions on either side of their faces which moved rapidly all the while they stood there. Their eyes were small, black, and the centres (or pupils) were white. The mouths were very small and never opened and their noses were 'pug' or 'flattened'."*

Sands estimates that the whole episode, from the time he spotted the two 'figures' until they walked away into the desert, took about 10 minutes. When they left, they walked about 150-200 feet away. Sands then said:

> *"A 'flash of light' came up, and they were gone".*

The road on which Sands was travelling is paved, but he says he only encountered four cars during the trip and that the last one passed by going toward Pahrump – just after he pulled off the road. He had jumped out of his car and tried to wave it down but, although the car slowed, it sped up again and continued along its way. After the encounter with the 'figures', Sands restarted his car with no trouble at all and drove on into Las Vegas.

### Police

Johnny Sands made his way to the police, who then referred him to the Office of Special Investigations at Nellis Air Force Base. The spokesman for that office said that the Air Force had stopped probing the UFO problem in 1969 and that their office only handles internal criminal matters. He also said the base's radar *"picked up nothing unusual"* that night, but admitted only the base's runway headings were being monitored.

A spokesman at McCarran Airport tower said nothing unusual was noted on their surveillance radar, which covers a 55-mile radius from the surface 'to infinity'. However, he did note that the radar was 'line of sight' and would not register craft beyond the mountains.

### Asked not to reveal what was discussed

Johnny disclosed that one of the 'beings' had asked him not to tell all of what had taken place – to which he agreed, saying that if he revealed the rest it would be a breach of trust.

[If one looks at the background of other incidents involving close encounters where a dialogue takes place between the human witness and the 'beings', whatever shape or form, it invariably includes a request to keep back some of the conversation. The purpose of this eludes us. Taking into consideration that to all intent and purpose, if the information was that important and of relevance, then why shouldn't the witness reveal it? However, common sense, logic and rationality, cannot be applied to situations like this. We sense, rather bizarrely, that loyalty towards one's 'captors' may be all part and parcel of a conundrum which continues to baffle us all.]

The humanoid (who was standing closest to Sands) asked him:

1. *What was he doing there?* Sands responded that he was an entertainer and in Las Vegas to do a show.
2. *Why were so many people in Las Vegas?* Sands said it was a tourist type town and that people came to Las Vegas from all over.
3. *What is your means of communication?* Sands replied that he didn't understand the question, because there are several different means of communication. The humanoid seemed to become irritated and said: *"Answer the question!"*

Sands repeated that he didn't understand, whereupon the humanoid turned to the other and the two just stood facing one another for two or three minutes – then his questioner turned to Sands, reached out his left hand and brushed Sands' left hand, and told him:

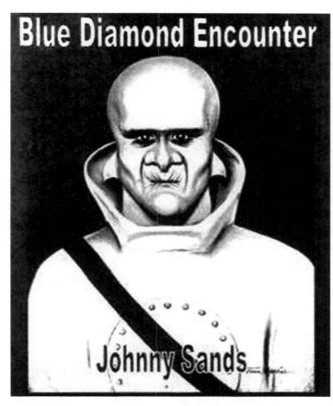

"Don't say anything about this meeting. We know where you are and will see you again".

The two then trooped off and disappeared in a flash of light.

Sands described the humanoid clothing as *"a black, 'silverish', all-encompassing overall with no visible seams"*. When the questioner brushed Sands' hand, it felt like *"rough, heavy duty sandpaper"*. Besides the white strap which ran diagonally from right shoulder to the left waist, there was a wide, white *"patent-leather-like"* belt, on which there hung capsule-shaped objects that were silver coloured and about one inch long. They appeared to be hanging on hooks and the *"man"* twisted one of them all the while that he talked to Sands, until he brushed Sands' hand and turned and left.

The *"men"* were about five feet, seven inches, or five feet, eight inches, about 140 pounds, and their gloved hands had a thumb and four fingers like normal humans. He also noted what appeared to be padding over the top of the feet, as well as across the back of the foot. The feet were covered by the same type of material as the rest of their *"bodies"*. They seemed to be very light on their feet and made no sound as they walked – as if they were off the ground, although Sands said they were definitely touching it.

Sands' description of the face of the one who *"talked"* to him:

> *"The face was wrinkled. Now, body wise, he looked as fit as a 21 year-old, but in his face, facial structure, I don't know. Something gave me the idea this guy was 300 or 400 years-old. It's a very powerful face, a very powerful set of eyes. He's not as ugly as he is powerful looking."*

A polygraph test administered by Robert L. Nolen, of Robert H. Nolen Associates, Las Vegas, indicates no deception.

**(Source: John Romero, APRO Field Investigator in Las Vegas/APRO Bulletin, Volume 24, No. 9, March 1976)**

[**Authors:** The description of the clothing worn by some of the 'beings' that we have come across, over the years, is often referred to as resembling 'sash' or belt, worn diagonally across the body. Sometimes physical ailments can follow after witnessing the appearance of something that is clearly out of the parameters of everyday normality.]

Here is the first example.

### 18th March 1972 – Humanoid figure seen, Wiltshire

Peter Mantell was cycling to Upton Scudamore, Wiltshire, accompanied by his friend – Ian, at 9.20am. Due to the extremely foggy conditions, Peter lost sight of Ian, who was, by now, well out in front.

**Peter:**

> *"I suddenly felt very dizzy, for no apparent reason, and decided to get off the cycle and walk. As I was doing so I glanced into a field on my right, and noticed nothing, to begin with, but was then stunned to see a humanoid stood about eight yards away, in a field of grass. It was about 9 feet tall and stood perfectly still, allowing me to see it had three fingers instead of five, the middle finger starting below what we would call the waist, an absence of any nose with markings on the face suggesting mouth and eyes. The 'figure' glistened, as though wet, and was wearing what looked like a tunic with a sash, and sock like shoes. The legs were short and stout, the arms reaching below the knees where the ankles would have been on a human. I shouted for Ian, being very frightened and unable to move. I watched in horror as the 'figure', whose left arm kept swaying to and fro, then touched its middle finger on the left-hand on a black spot, or lump, and completely vanished."*

In an interview conducted by Ken Rogers, the Warminster-based UFO Investigator, Peter told him:

> *"Throughout the whole experience, I had been unable to stop my own left arm from rising slowly upwards before returning to its normal position – almost as if, in some way, emulating the movements made by the 'figure'."* (**Source: Ken Rogers/The Dewey Museum, Warminster**)

Other 'entities' are now shown….

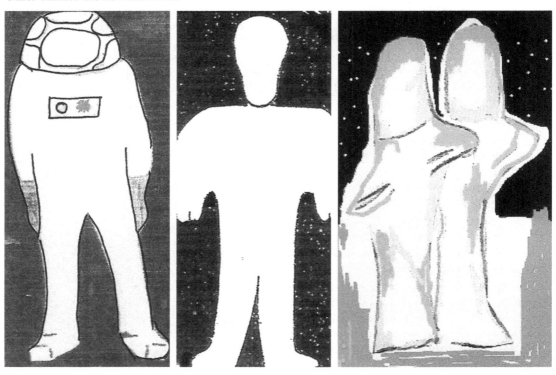

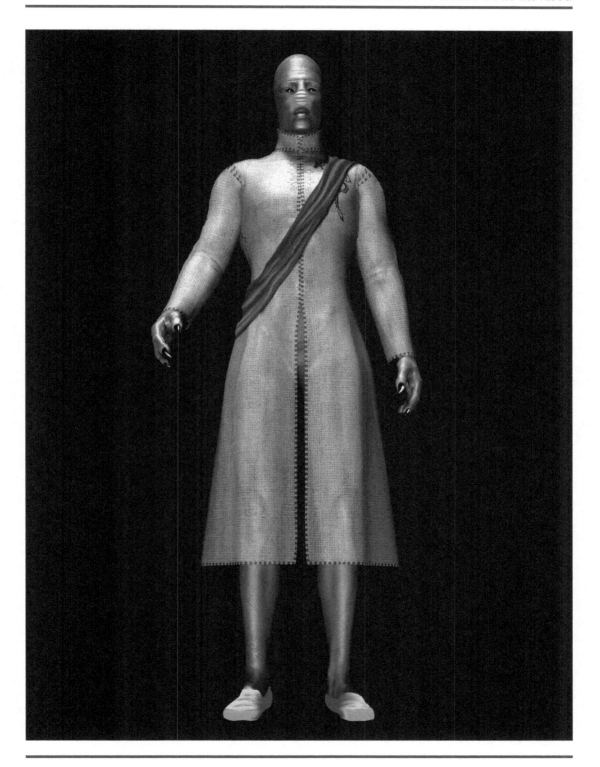

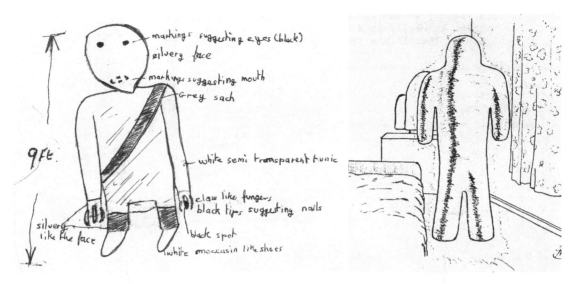

The drawing is annotated with the following notes:
- markings suggesting eyes (black)
- silvery face
- markings suggesting mouth
- Grey sach
- 9ft.
- white semi transparent tunic
- claw like fingers black tips suggesting nails
- silvery like the face
- black spot
- white moccasin like shoes

**1970s UFO over Basildon**

Mrs Sheila Masters wrote to us in 2007, regarding what her father had seen during the middle to late 1970s.

*"I can clearly remember him coming flying through the front door of the family house at Gaynesford, Basildon, shouting that he had just seen a UFO. I asked him what he had seen and he explained that while driving home along Stanway, from the direction of Laindon Link, near to The Knares in Basildon, at about 6.30pm in the winter time, he had seen what appeared to be a cigar-shaped object overhead.*

*He stopped his car and got out, after seeing that other drivers had also pulled up."* We were unable to confirm the sighting with Mr Masters but had no qualms, judging from the authenticity of the letter sent to us by his daughter, to question the events that had taken place.

# CHAPTER 2 – FEBRUARY 1976

### February 1976 – UFO display over the Peak District

David Bryant, ex-pilot, teacher and birdwatcher – well known for his website 'Spacerocks' and also for introducing the author John Hanson to Dr. Edgar Mitchell, Buzz Aldrin and General Charlie Duke, during a visit to the NEC at Birmingham, some years ago.

In addition, David has also written and published three books – 'one of which includes many private conversations with both US and Russian Astronauts – that are on sale on *Amazon.com*.

'*Our Forbidden Moon* has taken fifteen years of meticulous planning and research to write. During meetings with over thirty astronauts and cosmonauts, including seven of the twelve alleged Moonwalkers, the author gradually became aware of a number of major inconsistencies in their recollections of the Apollo program. Furthermore, in occasional unguarded moments, several space travellers have revealed personal experiences of the UFO phenomenon and

*David Bryant with his wife, Linda*

*Author John Hanson with Dr. Edgar Mitchell*      *Buzz Aldrin in conversation at a convention*

hinted at even more dramatic encounters. *Our Forbidden Moon* examines these revelations and considers whether there might be a link between UFOs, extraterrestrial races, and mankind's forty-year failure to travel beyond low Earth orbit. The author uses his knowledge gained during forty years as a teacher, lecturer and respected authority on spaceflight and meteoritics to ask controversial questions and provide convincing solutions.

He is known personally to the authors and told of an incident he and others witnessed, in February 1976, while walking in the Peak District.

*"At the time I spent as many weekends as I could, walking and climbing in the rugged hills of the Peak District. A friend of mine, called Robin, was a teacher of what are often euphemistically referred to as 'difficult' children: in reality, these were young thugs of fifteen or sixteen summers, who already had numerous convictions for crimes of violence and theft. Since I am (or, at least, was!) a physically commanding individual, Robin had no qualms about inviting me more than once to lead a group of his youthful recidivists on winter hikes and survival weekends in the Peak District. I will not bore you with the minutiae of these expeditions: suffice it to say that the young people learned much about real life while ploughing through waist-deep snow, ten miles from food and shelter!*

*On the occasion about which I wish to tell you, we had spent a gruelling day climbing up and crossing a high plateau, called Kinder Scout. The high tops were a metre deep in fine snow: here and there deep gullies posed extra problems for the unwary. As may be imagined, after seven hours away from our campsite, the boys were somewhat exhausted and chastened! We decided to build a fire, around which we could sit and enjoy a hot meal before retiring to our snow-heaped tents. The night was bright and star-lit, and held the promise of an intense frost. One of the boys, knowing of my interest in Astronomy, invited me to name the brighter stars: this I began to do, feeling quite flattered by the apparent interest of the group. I had, I recall, just finished naming the seven components of the familiar constellation of Orion, when an eighth and ninth slid in from the West to join them. Even the non-scientifically minded Robin sat up and took notice! The two new 'stars' were about as bright as Rigel: that is to say extremely bright and blue-white in colour!*

*As we watched, open-mouthed, a further five 'stars' moved in from the West to join up with the original pair. Then began an incredible light-show, as these strange visitors moved about the sky to form a variety of geometrical shapes: triangles, pentagons, squares, and even the unmistakable configuration of Ursa Major – the Plough!*

*After about an hour the display abruptly ended, as the lights scattered to the four corners of the sky. What was there to say or do? We retired to our tents in silence to reflect upon what we had witnessed.*

*Well that is the tale, perhaps not as impressive as some, but the feature that struck me then – and now – is that the strange lights were obviously intelligently controlled. I have never since questioned the existence of other life-forms in the Universe ... how could I?"*

## 5th February 1976 – Fort Shaw, Montana – UFO landing

A woman was caring for her neighbour's children while their parents were on a trip. She and her own two daughters were returning home from Simms, at 9.48pm, when they saw a 'bright light' behind the house and up on top of the hill. The woman stopped the car and they watched the 'light', which was very intense and pulsated when it was moving. It appeared to change colour from a dull glow to a bright reddish-orange. She described the object as:

*"...about 300 feet long, with rows of continuous lights along the top and bottom; the bottom lights pulsated alternately from left to right."*

One of the girls she was caring for (a 16 year-old) saw the glow from a second floor window of her home. After moving back and forth, the object left in a south-westerly direction, disappearing behind some buttes. Shortly after, officers arrived on the scene after having received a radio message from Sheriff Pete Howard, saying the lights were visible in the Sunny Slope area, near Fairfield, not far from where the rancher and his two sons had watched the UFOs. They were able to see the 'light', but because of the hilly terrain they could not get nearer to it. After two hours of trying to get closer, they lost sight of it entirely.

(Source: *Mystery stalks the Prairie*, Roberta Donovan and Keith Wolverton, pages 48-49)

## 7th February 1976 – Rectangular-shaped UFO over Farmersville, Indiana

At 5.15am, a middle-aged couple in a mobile home, one mile north of Mount Vernon, were awakened by their dog barking. The man looked out of the window and then went out on the porch and looked out onto a clear sky. He decided to investigate further and went to check the farm equipment when he noticed a glowing object, stationary in the sky, lighting up the whole area,

*"...like a dusk to dawn light that wasn't supposed to be there. It was less than 200 feet off the ground and 500-600 yards away, but then moved slowly east, climbing gradually towards a point south of my son's trailer, about 500-600 yards away, across the field and a gulley. The object was actually long, somewhat rectangular-shaped with blunt ends and flat on the bottom, with a strong yellow-greenish beam of light seen moving very slowly across the field – strong enough to light up the ground underneath. A short time later, just south of my son's trailer, was a round object. It was*

*a darker green than the rectangular thing and looked like it was right in the fence-row. This one looked like it might have been 8 or 10 feet in diameter and on, or very near, the ground. It changed colour from pale green to bright blue and back to pale green. When the larger rectangular object moved over into the area of the trailer, a little towards the south, the smaller sphere moved up to the bottom of the big object and went out like a light. The single remaining object departed, moving slowly eastwards – the whole incident lasting some twenty minutes."*

**(Source: Fran Ridge and Greg Ward)**

## 10th February 1976 – 'Flying Saucer' sighted over High Springs, Florida

A woman living near Lake City called the sheriff's office at 11pm, to report a 'Flying Saucer'. Sheriff Deputies were dispatched to investigate, and reported *"seeing a UFO hovering about 500 to 600 feet in the air. On it were coloured lights flashing from what looked like a glass dome"*. Florida highway patrol troopers also observed the object before it moved out of sight. **(Source: *UFO Investigator*, July 1976, page 1)**

### On the same day – this time over Hamden, Connecticut

On Denslow Hill, two 14 year-old teenagers – Grey and Barnet – reported having sighted:

*"...two very short humanoid 'beings', shuffle rapidly across a road. They wore purple coloured, luminous one-piece suits, and their waists were 20-22 inches above the ground".*

When the boys followed them, a bright white, lemon-shaped, UFO blinked on and took off into the air only 15 feet away from them. **(Source: James P. Barrett)**

## 10th February 1976 – UFO display over Peterborough

Mr J. Fry of Orton Longueville, Peterborough, wrote to Mr Malcolm Jay, in February 1976, who manufactured UFO detectors, about what he and his family witnessed after ironically failing to switch the machine on after arriving home from work.

*"At about 6.35pm, I was looking out of my bedroom window, facing south, when I saw two lots of 'light' moving silently through the sky. I kept them under observation and noticed that they extinguished their illumination before coming back on again. I went downstairs and called my brother and Mum. We watched the lights, the main colour of which was red with a blue green glow. Through binoculars they showed up as two red lights on the end and green-blue lights, which looked more like windows or portholes, as they started to circle around the houses in our locality – now making a roaring noise. My Dad arrived home, at 6.43pm, and he joined us while we continued to watch them. After they had circled, approximately six times, they slowly separated and one instantly disappeared, leaving the others to carry on their movement. They then changed direction to the south and shot upwards, at great speed, and that was the last we saw of them."*

Mr Fry telephoned the American airbase and spoke to the Commander, who said he would look into it and phone us back. He rang back later and said his jets were out there, but agreed from the description that it didn't sound like jet aircraft.

UFO sightings were not confined, of course, to the US or the UK. Many were seen over France, but we are (as always) limited with space, hoping that this volume would be shorter in length but just as condensed, realising how much space had been wasted during the construction of the first six Volumes of *Haunted Skies* – which were taken off sale by our ex-publisher, Mr Jon Downes, in September 2014.

A number of sightings attracted our attention, as published in a New Zealand magazine *EXNOLOG*, which we thought important enough to include because of the description and sketch of the object itself.

*Pakiri Beach holiday park*

## 7th February 1976 – Pakiri beach, north of Auckland

It involved Mr Peter Holman and his wife – Maureen, from Avondale, Auckland, who were on holiday at Pakiri Beach, north of Auckland.

**Peter:**

> *"We were situated about 150 yards from the beach. On the 7th February 1976, I got up at 4am and looked out towards the east. I noticed an orange glow, about four times larger than the brightest star. It was about eye level and definitely above the sand dunes. Now fully awake I awoke my wife, who came out to have a look. We watched it for 20-30 minutes, during which time it increased in size. We went back into the beach hut and sat on the floor in the dark, marking its progress on the window and frame. When it was halfway down the window, my wife panicked and threatened to gather up the two sleeping children and leave! We discussed what to do and decided to stay, as it was a pretty isolated spot. It looked like it was coming down and would land on the sand dunes, 65 yards away between us and the sea; we were really scared. We had heard of UFO stories in the Wellsford and Dome Valley areas, but never thought we would see one ourselves. Maureen awoke the children and, in doing so, knocked over an unlit kerosene lamp – which shattered. When we looked back at the UFO it was receding and decreasing in size, getting smaller and smaller, before disappearing. It was just an orangey-red oval light – diffused on the edges, with no definite shape. By this time dawn was breaking and we had been observing it for approximately one to one-and-a-half hours."*

### 10th February 1976 – White 'light' over the sea

Maureen had gone back to Auckland, leaving Peter with his daughter staying on at the beach hut.

At about 12.30am, Peter looked out to sea and observed:

> "...what I first took to be a boat, with its lights on, but this was a sort of white 'light' – not orange. Suddenly, it shot out of sight – one second it was there, in the middle of the gap over the sea between the dunes, and then gone. The 'light' then shot out to sea over by the Little Barrier Island, some 30 miles away. I woke up my daughter and we went down to the beach. We could still see it a long way out. It then shot away again, fast, and stopped in mid-air, appearing to travel backwards – so quick you could hardly see it do that. It appeared in a different position every time it made that movement. We watched if for 45 minutes, by which time, as Kim was getting cold, we made our way back to the beach hut."

### 13th February 1976 – Two glowing 'lights' seen

Maureen returned from Auckland. During the early hours of the next morning, incredibly, Peter was to find himself in the unique position of sighting yet another strange object.

> "I pulled back the curtains and looked out and saw, just over the sea, a large glowing 'light'. I asked Maureen if she could see – to which she agreed, telling me she could see what looked like framed glowing windows in the top, distorted not clear.
>
> I pulled my jeans on and ran out more excited than afraid. Maureen screamed, 'Don't leave me!' I ran down to the foot of the sand dunes and it was at the far end of Pakari Beach, near the camping ground, a couple of miles away from us. I saw two 'lights' moving out of sight, towards the south, reflecting in the water as they did so. Things are a bit hazy next; either one light or both went up. I do know that one changed into a perfect circle – then a change of colour, red to green. Both objects shot across the sky towards Barrier Island. It was now 4.30am.
>
> I made my way to a farmer's house to fetch a pair of binoculars; by the time I returned, they had gone."

### 14th February 1976 – UFO sighted through binoculars

On this night, the couple both took turns at watching.

**Peter:**

> "It came back again – the orange glow from behind the sand hills, at sea level, 50-60 yards out from the shoreline. It then went out to sea, towards Barrier Island – just taking its time. Through binoculars, there wasn't any bright glow; you could see a red light on top, and what looked like antennas. There was nothing else in the middle of it – just dark. There

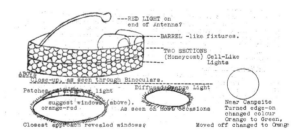

> were two sections to the bottom, of cell like honeycomb appearance. I don't know whether it was the back or front of the object, but there were two barrel like shapes on it."

Maureen confirmed the description given by her husband, and said how petrified she had been.

**(Source: As above/Mr Victor Harris of N.Z.S.S.R Auckland)**

### 17th February 1976 – UFO paces truck drivers

Three days later, on the 17th February 1976, the *Derwent Valley Gazette*, Tasmania, and the *Mercury* Hobart newspapers – outlined a report received from truck drivers. One of them was Ron Wilson, of the Midway Plat – a maintenance engineer with the Victorian Canning Company Industries – who complained of being 'buzzed' by a UFO, during the three hours journey from Wayatinah to Berrriedale.

*"I was coming down Nive Hill when I saw the object over Black Bobs. The UFO was a brilliant yellow-white light in the shape of a dome; underneath we could make out what appeared to be the shape of what resembled a sausage, bent down at each end. It kept pace with us, staying slightly to the front and left. It followed us through Ouse, and Hamilton. Near the Old Plenty Bridge on the Lyell Highway, I decided to stop to see if it would come any closer. I stopped, and the object – some 50 feet in diameter – shifted and flew away over the* River Derwent *and hovered in the air on the opposite side.*

*We stared the truck up. The UFO came back again. We tried to make a call on the radio, but all we got was static. By this time it was about 600 yards away."*

Between New Norfolk and Granton, the UFO could be seen clearly as it flew between them and the Dromedary hills.

Strangely, another 'light' appeared in the sky – which, like the first, also kept pace with them.

By the time the truck reached Berriedale, the object had began to climb up into the sky and was soon lost from sight. (**Source: Tasmanian UFO Investigation Centre**)

## 18th February 1976 – Alabama women followed by five UFOs

Alabama was the subject of media attention in this month, according to the *National Enquirer* (15.6.1976) – after being contacted by Sunday school teacher Mrs Geneva Carruth (33). She and her friend – Charlotte Staples – were driving from Gadsden to their homes in Talladega (some 4 miles away) when in the wood to their left they saw a strange orange object. Other similar objects appeared, making four in total, which moved southwards parallel to the car, about a mile away. Frightened, they switched on the citizens band radio. The light came on, but the radio was dead. Now there were five objects following them! They did so for 14 miles.

**Charlotte:**

*"They then turned, now behind the car – each the size of a car and oval in shape."*

At the bottom of a hill, the objects moved away. The radio then burst into life and the women continued on their journey.

(**Sources: CUFOS investigation file report, dated 17.5.1976/Mark Rodeghier**, *UFO Reports Involving Vehicle Interference*, **case 392, citing CUFOS**)

At 6.45pm, eight to ten 'flying discs' were sighted in a 'V' formation over Rancho Cordova, California. The objects were three to six meters in diameter, grey in colour, and made no sound. Afterwards, the witness saw ten aircraft circling that portion of the sky. (**Source: CUFOS investigation file, report dated 1.3.1976**)

## 19th February 1976 – Three red-orange glowing objects seen in triangular formation

At Marysville, Yuba County, California, Sutter County sheriff's office received a call, at 7pm, reporting a UFO being observed by two witnesses. Deputy Gerald Teplansky was dispatched to the scene and was able to observe the objects for about five minutes.

The deputy stated that he saw three red-orange glowing objects, hovering in a triangular formation. He soon saw another object streak northward across the sky, before all four objects disappeared.

(**Source:** *UFO Investigator*, **July 1976, page 3**)

## 19th February 1976 – Two 'balls of light' seen from aboard ship

In a letter sent to CUFOS from Warren Ballard, dated 4th March 1981, from the ship's log, we learn of the following which took place at Chesapeake Bay, Maryland:

*"At about 8.10pm, I went on deck for another check and saw two 'balls of light' moving very rapidly toward the eastern shore – altitude approximately 2,000 feet, heading due east. The starboard one went straight ahead, the one to port was bouncing around like a ball, moving directly up and down and to either side, estimated speed above Mach 1. It did not make turns but moved directly. Within seconds there were several military jets after them.*

[Apparently, from Patuxent River Naval Air Station]

*I followed them through binoculars, until they were out of sight over the Choptank River. I was laying off Point No Point; the vision was perfect."*

At 9.15pm numerous witnesses from Lake Hiawatha area, New Jersey, reported a strange object to the Parsippany Police Department, describing it as:

*"...a large, rectangular-shaped object, hovering in the vicinity of Jersey City Reservoir, estimated to be about 50 feet long with a small turret or dome-like top and a bright diamond-shaped light on the bottom. Two very bright lights were seen at each end of the object and in its centre."*

All of the people concerned reported seeing two separate similar objects. The first moved at a rapid rate of speed from west to the east. The second object followed the first but moved more slowly. It hovered over the reservoir for approximately four minutes, before moving out of sight at a high rate of speed. The hovering UFO made a sound described as a low fluctuating hum. Mr Walter Kahl observed the UFO with the aid of binoculars and could not observe any recognizable markings on the object.

(**Source:** *UFO Investigator*, **April 1976, page 1**)

## 20th February 1976 – Motorist encounters three triangular lights

A young man and woman out driving, at 7pm, saw some odd 'red lights' in the sky over Essex County, Massachusetts. This was followed by the appearance of two flattened disc-shaped objects, showing three triangular lights, which descended close to their car and manoeuvred nearby for about 10 minutes. The car's radio sustained heavy static during part of the incident, before the two objects finally flew out of view.

(**Source: Mark Rodeghier**, *UFO Reports Involving Vehicle Interference*, **case 394, citing MUFON case file**)

## 22nd February 1976 – Giant humanoid seen

At 10am, motorist Leonard Hegele (29) sighted a seven feet tall humanoid, with three feet wide shoulders, walking through a field about a mile from Interstate 15, south of Great Falls, Montana. Mr Hegele stopped his car and attempted to chase the 'being'. While doing so he saw a grey, oval, object hovering in the air nearby, about 10 feet above the ground, which periodically rose and fell back down. When within 700-800 feet, the 'being' turned around to face him. Hegele lost his courage and ran back to his car.

**(Sources: David F. Webb and Ted Bloecher, HUMCAT: Catalogue of Humanoid Reports, case 1976-41 (A1463), citing Jerome Clark; *Great Falls Tribune*, 23.2.1976)**

## 24th February 1976 – Domed 'disc' seen, with legs

At 9.27pm, a six meter in diameter domed 'disc' shaped object, with four legs on the base, was reported hovering silently over the road at Stratham, New Hampshire.

**(Source: Raymond E. Fowler, *Skylook*, May 1976, p. 3)**

## 25th February 1976 – Strange 'beings' seen by motorist

A woman motorist encountered two 'beings', described as *"very tall, with large feet and no necks"*, while driving on a country road north-west of Nashville. She reported that one of the 'beings' flashed a blue light at her before she drove away. **(Source: MUFON 100-7, CUFOS-AP)**

## 25th February 1976 – Pilot sights UFO over Essex

Barry Powling from Brays Lane, Rochford, Essex (then aged 30) – a flying instructor by occupation, based at Southend Aero Club – was instructing Mr G. Williamson (a pupil) at 7.15pm over Maldon, Essex, in a Cessna 150 plane (registration number GBBKV).

As they headed in a north direction, they heard Captain Philips – a Bristol Ferries Pilot – reporting an object over Sheerness.

**Barry:**

> *"We noticed a bright white light with a tinge of red, motionless in the sky, about ten miles away from us, flashing in bursts of light for five seconds at a time. Thirty seconds after, it disappeared from view. Later that day I told Captain Philips what we had seen."*

**(Source: Andrew Collins)**

## 26th February 1976 – Domed UFO sighted, Long Island, New York

At 6.15pm, Mrs Audrey Manny saw a large dome-shaped object hovering to the south of her home. A few minutes later it started moving towards her at a rapid rate of speed. As it passed overhead, Mrs Manny saw patterned lights set into the underneath of the very large object.

> *"There were four white lights in front and four red lights in the rear, each arranged in a diamond-shaped pattern. There seemed to be six to nine windows on the side of the object, through which a brilliant white light was seen."*

The height of the UFO was estimated to be between 1,000 and 1,600 feet. The object travelled northwards, before suddenly shooting straight up and disappearing into the sky.

**(Source: *UFO Investigator*, April 1976, page 3)**

## 26th February 1976 – Alabama Police Officers sight UFOs

James Curry – Alabama State Trooper patrolman of 16 years service – reported having sighted six or eight UFOs on this night.

> *"They were just round 'balls of light' – some orange, some white, and some pure red. One of them stopped in mid-air and went up and down like a Yo-yo."*

Patrolman Ralph Guyton (40) of Attalla, near Gadsden, also witnessed the phenomena. He spoke of seeing:

"...*three red objects, heading south-west*".

Other witnesses included patrolman Thomas Maltbie (31) of Boaz.

"*I saw a real bright orange 'ball' streak across the sky*."

In nearby Guntersville, Marshall County, Deputy Sherriff Larry Walden (24) said he saw a blue-green UFO on the 14th March. Rainbow City Patrolman Ernest Noreton described what he saw on the 28th March as a large, yellow, fiery 'ball'.

# CHAPTER 3 – MARCH 1976

LIGHT IN SKY PROBE:        (Evening Post 1.3.76 )

Nottingham UFO Investigation Society is today looking into a report that a resident from the Park twice saw bright lights in the sky last night. Several people, in fact reported seeing what appeared to be a distress signal from the River Trent in the West Bridgford area. Someone crying for help was also heard, and police mounted a search with tracker dogs. The search was called off after over two hours when nothing was found. Police have now appealed for any boatowners who were on the Trent last night or early this morning to contact them.

(2.3.76 )
Those mysterious lights in the sky which were spotted by residents in the Park, were probably either flares or distress rockets.That is the theory of the NUFOIS after an interview with the person who spotted the lights on Sunday night. Mr Syd Henley said " The groups sky watch co-ordinator said we are still making checks." He said they would be speaking to the East Midlands air port and Watnall Weather centre, to try and gather more information.

✦✦✦✦✦✦✦✦✦✦✦✦✦✦✦✦✦✦✦

Syd Henley and some images shown relating to investigations carried out by him and his colleagues from that time period.

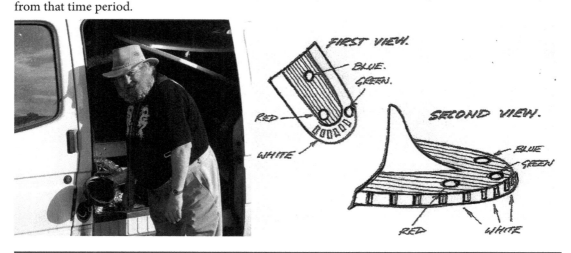

FIRST VIEW.
BLUE.
GREEN.
RED
WHITE

SECOND VIEW.
BLUE
GREEN
RED
WHITE

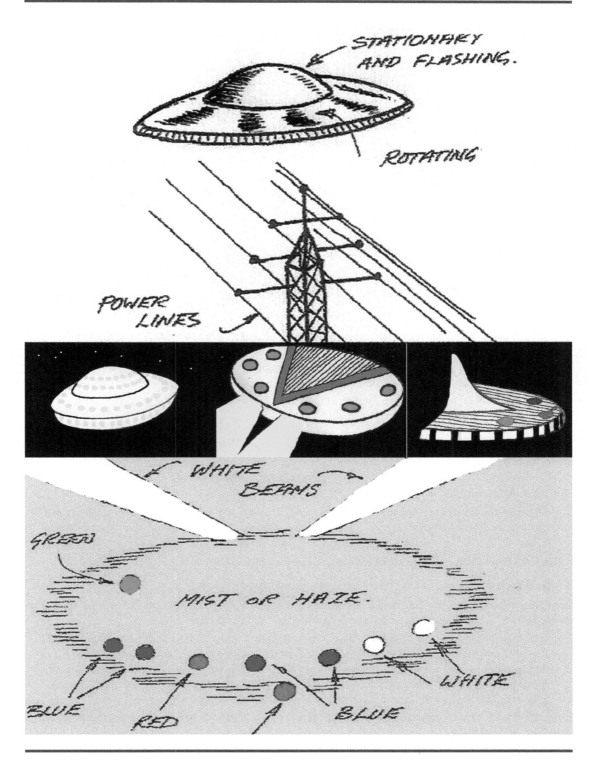

STATIONARY AND FLASHING.

ROTATING

POWER LINES

WHITE BEAMS

GREEN

MIST OR HAZE.

WHITE

BLUE

RED

BLUE

## 2nd March 1976 – Strange object over Essex

A small village called Butt's Green, near Chelmsford, was the source of apparent UFO interest at 11.15pm, involving Mr and Mrs Coleman, who had just retied to bed when an orange light lit up the bedroom. The husband looked out of the window, thinking the house next door was on fire. He saw:

*"...an orange circular object, moving out of sight."* (**Source: Andrew Collins**)

## 5th March 1976 – 'Flying Triangles' over Kent

At 6.45pm, bus driver Robert Cole was travelling along the Tonbridge Road, Kent, when he sighted a UFO hovering in the sky over Maidstone. Many others reported sighting a perfect 'triangle of white lights' moving east to west. Other witnesses included Dennis Puxty, from Lenham. He told of seeing *"a 'blaze of lights', quite low over Detling, while driving home at 6.30pm"*, while driving instructor Stan Oliver of Stockett Lane, Coxheath, was out with a pupil – Kevin Lumsden – when they noticed strange 'lights' above Detling.

*"The 'triangle' was almost stationary."*

(**Source:** *Kent Messenger,* **Maidstone, 19.3.1976 – 'Flood of calls on UFO lights'**)

## 5th March 1976 – Disc-shaped UFO over Oregon

At 9.25pm, a 23 year-old woman saw an object, high in the sky, which then dropped down to an altitude of only 75 feet, enabling her to see:

*"It was disc-shaped, about 26 feet in diameter, and had red and white lights revolving around its exterior. Two light beams were directed from the object to the ground."*

She reported that the radio in her car went dead as the object approached closer. Although the woman kept driving, the radio failed to function again until two miles down the road.

(**Source: Mark Rodeghier,** *UFO Reports Involving Vehicle Interference,* **case 395, citing CUFOS**)

## 8th March 1976 – Saucer-shaped UFOs seen

Marcus Hutson-Saxby (12), living in the Brendon Hills area of Somerset, was in his bedroom at 10pm, when he saw:

*"...two 'saucers', positioned facing each other, moving as one over the top of a nearby barn. They came close to the house.*

*I opened the window to listen, but heard nothing. I called out to my Mum – Sheila. She came upstairs and was just in time to see them – now whirling lights – fade and disappear into the distance."*

(**Source:** *Somerset County Gazette,* **12.3.1976 – Anyone seen a whirling UFO?**)

## 16th March 1976 – UFO sighted by Gatwick Airport worker

Fred Hargreaves from Eversfield Road, Horsham – a Gatwick Airport worker and Ex RAF man (22 years in the service) – was about to take his dog for a walk, at 9.35pm, when he saw:

*"...a huge orange object on the horizon. At first I thought it was a sodium lamp, but then realised it was moving slowly towards the east. A line of rooftops were, at times, obscuring my view and I had to move to keep up with it. The oval shaped object with a hazy outline continued eastwards. It stopped and moved backwards for a short distance – then stopped again. About twenty minutes later it suddenly accelerated at a speed I have never seen before, and was gone from sight."*

(**Source: P. Glover/***Crawley Advertiser,* **9.4.1976 – 'Riddle in the sky UFOs – Fred's a vital witness'/***Evening Argus,* **7.4.1976 – 'UFO sighting'**)

# Don't laugh at UFOs says Sgt Digweed

*12 MAR 1976*

**POLICE Sergeant Alan Digweed was disturbed to read in his local paper that people who spotted unidentified flying objects were being met with blank disbelief.**

He decided to come clean — and admit that he believed in them himself.

To make sure that everyone got the message he made his confession in a magazine which goes to every policeman in Kent.

'Don't scoff at UFOs,' he told his colleagues. And he backed up his message with the story of the night in 1965 when he saw one himself.

Sergeant Digweed, now 46, was stationed at Lydd, near Hastings. Going off duty one night, he saw a brilliant white light over Dungeness.

### Vanished

'I thought it was air-sea rescue,' he said. 'But I telephoned operations and found that nothing was going on.

The light vanished, and seconds later Kent radar were on the phone saying they had picked up unidentified traffic in the area.

'I'd always been sceptical up to then, but there was something in the sky and no one knows what it was.'

Sergeant Digweed, married with five children and now stationed at Tunbridge Wells, told his fellow policemen in the

**Daily Mail Reporter**

force magazine Patchwork 'We can all come up with answers of shooting stars or aircraft, but a moment's reflection on your stock answer should leave you wondering.

'Having questioned the witness and eliminated the obvious don't resign yourself to the thought "Another one of them"! If you can't spot an obvious solution let the person know that you accept that he or she has seen something that you can't explain.'

The official Kent police policy on UFOs? 'There isn't one,' said a spokesman. 'It's an entirely personal matter just like believing in ghosts. Some of our men may be sceptical but all incidents are reported.'

Six people have now reported seeing UFOs in the Tonbridge area. The sightings are to be investigated by the British UFO Research Association.

## 19th March 1976 – Letter sent to the newspaper

In a letter sent by Philip Odgers of High Street, Dovercourt, and published in the *Harwich and Manningtree Standard*, Dovercourt, **UFOs – facts and figures,** Philip tells the readers about a reference in Rex Dutta's book – *Flying Saucer Viewpoint*, about the landing at Lord Louis Mountbatten's estate, and that over 200 books on 'Flying Saucers' has been written over the last 25 years!

He also brings to their attention, quote:

*"Even now the sightings continue around the whole planet – at least 50-100 per week, every week. There is so much evidence now, despite the cover-up campaign by the four or five world powers, so why are the British people being kept in the dark? Local papers print UFO stories but never the Nationals (unless it is to smear and sneer). Why can't the British public be told that there are now the Governments of nine countries who officially recognise the reality of 'flying saucers' and that 28 astronauts have seen or filmed 'saucers' while in orbit. So much evidence and official Government reports from other countries which are never reported in the newspapers; there are at least 3,000 known contacts with 'saucer' crews, despite the hush campaign."* [Well said, Philip!]

## Police Sergeant's UFO sighting

On the same day the *Kent Messenger* newspaper, at Maidstone, published an article

relating to a UFO sighted by Police Sergeant Alan Digweed, in which Alan talks about his sighting that took place eleven years previously.

### 21st March 1976 – Film on UFOs

Italian Film Director – Mario Gariazzo, wrote to Mrs Margaret Booton – the Mayor of Kidderminster, West Mercia – asking her for details of photographs relating to UFOs and arrivals of 'ships' from outer space, as he wanted to produce a film on the subject.

A special UFO file was set up by Wyre Forest District Council Office under the direction of Dick Rogers. (**Source:** *Sunday Mercury*, 21.3.1976)

### 22nd March 1976 – UFO over Essex

William Ethel (60), and his wife, from Butt's Green, Sandon, near Chelmsford, in Essex, had just retired to bed, at 11.15pm.

After switching on the bedside light, they were stunned to see what they first took to be the next door house enveloped in flames. Jumping out of bed they looked out and saw a round orange object in the sky, projecting a powerful beam downwards. A few seconds later the object and light extinguished, and Mr Ethel telephoned the police. (Source: Essex UFO Study Group)

### 23rd March 1976 – The *Evening News*, Bolton – UFO photographed!

This newspaper told their readers of a UFO photographed by schoolboy Barry Yates (15) of The Avenue, Lilford Park, Leigh, after he had sighted a strange blue light directly above him in the sky, at 7pm – 'UFO man baffled by boy's picture'.

Unusually for Barry, when he took other photographs near Gin Pit, Astley, at 11am, two weeks later, following them being processed, he saw that he had captured the same image. The incident was brought to the attention of Mr Arthur Tomlinson – secretary of Direct Investigation on Aerial Phenomena, who said:

*"It is one of the weirdest I have ever seen."*

*Barry Yates*

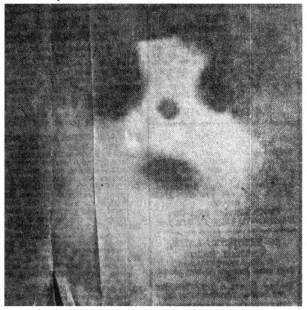

An *Evening News* photographer quite rightly remarked that without examination of the negatives, no explanation could be offered.

### 25th March 1976 – same account different newspaper

On the 25th March the *Leigh, Tyldesley & Atherton Journal*, published the same story, using the same banner grabbing headlines.

Unfortunately although the actual date when the photographs were taken is not known, it appears it could have been around the beginning of March 1976. What we found interesting is that if the image is representative of what he took in the sky, could this have been what is fast becoming an all too familiar background to the pages of these books – the three 'globes' which have been reported endless times, or is there another explanation?

## 27th/28th March 1976 – NUFORA Investigation at Highdown Hill

Members of this group – Paul Glover, Stephen Carter, Charles Walker, David Kay, David Stringer and David Wills – set up their observations at 11pm. According to the typed report, whistling noises were heard and Charles 'H' reported finding a footprint in the chalk pit which was similar to that found in Clapham Woods.

At 12.25am an object was seen in the sky which was moving in a strange way, up and down a lot. Shortly afterwards, the 'sky watch' was concluded.

# CHAPTER 4 – APRIL 1976

### 3rd April 1976 – Interview with Fred Smith

The *Isle of Wight County Press* published an interview with Fred Smith (a personal friend of the authors) about his role as secretary of the Isle of Wight Unidentified Flying Objects Investigation Society. Fred, Len Cramp, Kath Smith and Pat Smith, were also involved in the investigation and publication of a magazine, entitled *UFOLOG*, cataloguing UFO activity – Well done all of you. We are proud to have known you.

### 4th April 1976 – Diamond-shaped UFO sighted over Portsmouth, Hampshire

Portsmouth motor mechanics – Tom Sellence and Bob Jeram – were driving separately in the Portsmouth area, between 10.30pm and 11pm, when they saw something unusual in the sky.

Mr Sellence was motoring along Portsdown Hill, from Havant, with a passenger, when he saw a white 'light' travelling at speed over the east side of Portsea Island. The 'light' tuned green and appeared to stop in mid-air. He tried to take a photo, but the film was blank after processing. Mr Jeram was heading south, on Eastern Road, when he saw a 'light' pass from east to west.

"It then hung over Fratton Park like a star, for about five minutes – then turned red, green, and back to white, before heading off towards Portsdown Hill at speed."

Mrs E.M. Gates of Salcombe Avenue, Copnor, sighted what looked like a large star moving through the sky.

"I saw three distinct colours – blue, yellow, and red. After a few minutes, it lost its brilliance and headed away towards Copnor – now a long orange strip. As it passed overhead, there appeared to be four yellow circles of light. It disappeared silently towards Farlington."

(Source: *Portsmouth Planner*, 8.4.1976 – 'UFO')

#### Publicity in the local newspaper

As a result of publicity in the *Hampshire Telegraph and Naval Chronicle* (dated 15th April 1976) – 'UFOs over Hampshire?' a number of people came forward to confirm they, too, had seen the strange 'light' in the sky. They included David and Jocelyn Booth of Nutwick Road, who saw it as a red light passing over their house, heading northwards.

#### Four lights forming a square

As it did so they saw not one but four lights in a square formation, pointing forward, making it more like a diamond shape. The couple estimated it was several hundred yards away from them. Another witness was Graham Coleman and his father – Mr J.H. Coleman, living at Inkpen Walk, Warren Park. Their description was identical to that taken from Mr and Mrs Booth.

One man – Mr R.N Wensley of Dunbar Road, Milton, even tried to film it with his cine camera after having observed it for 30 minutes. Others also came forward to tell of what they had seen that evening.

(**Source:** *Portsmouth Planner*, 8.4.1976 – 'More reports of UFO sightings')

### 7th April 1976 – *Liverpool Echo* – 'Flying Saucers scare solved'

Although it appears that a number of residents living in the Merseyside area contacted the police reporting strange lights in the sky, during the evening of the 6th April 1976, it was later established that it had been a demonstration of eight red emergency flares set off by the Riversdale College at Grassendale, Liverpool.

(**Other sources:** *Liverpool Daily Post*, 7.4.1976 – 'Mystery lights just for show')

### 8th April 1976 – *Liverpool Echo* – Chat show, 'Is there life in outer space?'

Following an article in the *Liverpool Echo* (6.4.1976) asking for people to ring in to the office 'chat room' on 7th April 1967 – 'Your chance to ask about UFOs' – many did, asking various questions that ranged from *Dr. Who*, Is there a UFO base under the Merseyside? *The Bermuda Triangle*, and do 'Flying Saucers' exist? ... mostly offering, in the main, rational explanations for what was seen – not forgetting quips about *Dr. Who*, when asked the 64 million dollar question about what the occupants of the 'Flying Saucers' looked like! To be fair the lady on the panel was, of course, ˙Elisabeth Sladen, who plays *Dr. Who*'s assistant in the series.

*Elisabeth Sladen*

˙Elisabeth Clara Heath-Sladen (1st February 1946-19th April 2011) was an English actress best known for her role as Sarah Jane Smith in the British television series *Doctor Who*. She was a regular cast member from 1973 to 1976, alongside both Jon Pertwee and Tom Baker, and reprised the role many times in subsequent decades, both on *Doctor Who* and its spin-offs *K-9 and Company* and *The Sarah Jane Adventures*. Sladen was interested in ballet and theatre from childhood, and began to appear on stage in the mid-1960s, although more often as a stage manager at this time. She moved to London in 1970 and an appearance in the police drama *Z-Cars* led to her being selected for a part in *Doctor Who*. She stayed as a regular cast member alongside Pertwee and Baker until 1976. She subsequently starred in other roles on both television and radio, before semi-retiring to bring up a family in the mid-1980s. She returned to the public eye in the 2000s with more *Doctor Who* related appearances, which culminated in taking a regular lead role in *The Sarah Jane Adventures*. The show earned the Royal Television Society 2010 award for Best Children's Drama. She also made regular guest appearances on the main television series, and provided voice-over commentaries for its releases to DVD. Sladen died of cancer on 19th April 2011. Her death made national and international news headlines, and major television stations and newspapers paid her tribute. (**Source: Wikipedia**)

## 9th April 1976 – UFO over Bolton, Lancashire

Mrs Margaret Russell of Curzon Road, Bolton, was out with her friend (who declined to be named), walking along the top of Park Road, Bolton, when they saw:

> *"...an object like a blue 'ball', about half the size of the setting sun, showing a tail of red and green sparks, only visible for few seconds, heading northwards."*

(Source: *Evening News*, Bolton, 10.4.1976 – 'Low flying UFO shock for two')

This was later explained away as being a fireball, according to Andrew Collins of BUFORA

## 12th April 1976 – Peter Hill of WATSUP on the move

The *Southern Evening Echo* published details of a local UFO researcher who was moving to Edinburgh.

## 20th April 1976 – Three UFOs in the sky over Louth, Lincolnshire

Mr and Mrs Jean Blanchard of Harewood Crescent, Louth, and son – Perry, were returning home from Withern, at about 8pm, when they sighted three objects in the sky.

**Mrs Blanchard:**

> *"The object was quite visible, stationary, and had two lines of smoke trailing away from it. As we drove towards Louth I pointed it out to Perry (who was driving), and my husband, who was unable to obtain a clear view as he was in the back. About half way to Louth, we saw a second object similar to the first. As we drove into Louth along Church Street, I glanced up Queen Street and saw a shaft of pink light, split into two forks in the sky."*

(Source: *Louth Standard*, 30.4.1976 – 'Pink light mystery deepens')

Another witness was Robert Foster from 4, Eve Street, Louth, in Lincolnshire, who decided to go for a drive, at 8pm, with his girlfriend. While driving along the Louth to Market Rasen road, Robert noticed a pink light in the sky – like that given off by glowing charcoal. Curious, they turned off towards Binbrook and stopped near the old Kelstern Aerodrome.

> *"About half-a-mile away in the sky was a great shaft of pink light, beaming downwards from an object we estimated to be at a height of around 7-10,000 feet. Nearby were two other objects, both of which showed white vapour trails. Suddenly, the first one seemed to move closer to us. We felt frightened and I started the car up, anxious to get away. Without warning we were bathed in what appeared to be two separate beams of pink light. My girlfriend said she felt a sharp pain in her right shoulder and we drove away. The incident had now lasted 20 minutes, but did stop again to see if they were still there. There was nothing to be seen."*

(Source: *Louth Standard*, 23.4.1977 – 'Couples mystery of pink light in the sky')

## 22nd April 1976 – Police Officer's close encounter with UFO

George W. Wheeler (71) – Police Chief at Elmwood, Wisconsin, with 30 years in the Force and a combat pilot in the 2nd World War – was on duty when he saw an orange glow at the top of Tuttle Hill. Thinking it was a fire he reported it on the radio and made his way there. Police dispatcher – Gail Miley, received Wheeler's radio report and phoned Paul Fredrickson – a nursing home administrator, who lives in Tuttle Hill. Miley asked him what he could see out of the window.

> *"I saw a bright orange glow; it resembled a half-moon. I went back to the phone and by the time I returned to the window the object was gone."*

At about the same time Mrs Miles Wergland saw a bright orange object from her home, south of the hill.

> *"It was shaped like the moon, but was much brighter and coloured differently."*

In addition, according to the *Milwaukee Journal,* three people living near Tuttle Hill reported their television sets had gone off at 11pm, and came back on ten minutes later.

When George Wheeler arrived he saw . . .

> ". . . a huge object ... as high as a two-storey house, approximately 250 feet across. It was silver coloured and had a very bright orange light on the top. The light was so bright that I couldn't look at it. Suddenly it rose upwards and a blue flash of light shot out."

A few minutes later, David Moots (36) – a local resident and dairy farmer by occupation, who had been taking the babysitter home – saw the patrol car parked silently and unlit in the middle of a downtown street. He said:

> "He was trying to get out of the car and was kind of dazed. I asked him what was wrong and he said he had been hit. I asked 'by a car?' He said 'No, one of those UFOs'."

### Plugs and points of the police car burnt out

He was taken to Dr. Frank Springer, who had treated him for 25 years. He spent three days in hospital and then went home, only to return complaining of nightmares and headaches. He was treated for eleven days more, before once again returning home.

## UFOs Terrorize Wisconsin Towns

### ... Mysterious Glowing Objects Scare Families and Amaze Police

By BOB PRATT

A flurry of eerie UFO sightings has dazzled and terrorized residents of northern Wisconsin — and shaken even veteran law enforcement officers.

In one incident alone, at least a dozen police officers witnessed the astounding aerobatics of the Unidentified Flying Objects as they danced across the night skies along the shores of Lake Superior.

The wave of UFO sightings crested last March and April, slacked off during the summer, then picked up again in September.

"I think there is definitely something up there," said Sheriff Fred Johnson of Superior, Wis. "There are too many intelligent people who have seen them.

"I believe they are from outer space, not some mysterious type of vehicle that is manufactured here on earth."

Among the scores of reports:

• In March a glowing UFO landed on a road only 400 feet from a farmhouse in Mellen, Wis., badly frightening a family of six — then vanished with an ear-shattering roar.

• The same night, excited Ashland County, Wis., Sheriff's Deputy Peter Drolson called in on his car radio to report that a mysterious, blindingly brilliant object was whooshing just above the treetops — when suddenly his radio went dead.

• Veteran Police Officer George Wheeler of Elmwood, Wis., saw a gigantic fireball streaking straight toward him shortly after midnight April 7.

He slammed his brakes, leaped out of his patrol car and flung himself into a roadside ditch as the frightful fireball hurtled past.

"It was as big as a football field," said Wheeler, 70, still shaken by the incident. "I thought it was going to crash and wipe out the whole town."

Instead, said Wheeler, a former WW 2 fighter pilot, the mysterious object

**MAP** shows towns (shaded circles) where UFOs were spotted.

soared silently five miles southward, hovered motionlessly a few minutes — then disappeared.

On March 13 at 9 p.m., 15-year-old Jane Baker had just let her two cats outside when she saw a weird, object parked on the road outside her family's farmhouse near Mellen, Wis.

She screamed — and her father, Phil

**FRIGHTENED** by a gigantic fireball, veteran police officer George Wheeler leaped from his patrol car and took cover in a roadside ditch. "I thought it was going to wipe out the whole town," he said.

Baker, 37, rushed outside, followed by his wife and two of their sons.

"I didn't believe what I was seeing," Baker told The ENQUIRER. "It was circular, about 12 feet across, with red and bluish-green lights running around the outside.

"In the center was a door, with a brilliant light coming from inside. It made a high-whining sound — a sound I'd never heard before."

The family stared wide-eyed at the object for several minutes — then raced fearfully inside their home. "I no sooner called police when there was this loud explosion," Baker said. "I looked out and the thing had vanished."

The same night, seven sheriff's deputies spotted four different mysterious objects skipping and gliding through the skies in a four-county area around Lake Superior's southwest shore. Ashland Deputy Drolson, 24, was excitedly describing one such object zipping directly overhead when his police radio went dead.

"The object made a whooshing

sound — like a giant gust of wind roaring through the woods," Drolson recalled.

Ashland Undersheriff George Ree, listening on his radio 18 miles away, heard the rushing noise "and then Drolson's radio went blank." A few moments later, Drolson's voice came back on the air.

The strange sightings continued in April.

Mrs. Kathy Thompson, 25, of Superior, Wis., said she encountered a dome-shaped object with a pulsating red light, hovering directly over the roadway ahead of her car about 3 a.m. April 19.

"I thought: 'I've got to get away!'" Panic-stricken, she quickly made a U-turn and raced away in the opposite direction.

Douglas County Deputy Jack Hunker pulled her over for speeding, at 90 m.p.h.

"She was hysterical," he said. "She was a complete basket case. There was no way she could have made up that story."

*"I've been through all sorts of tests, but I seem to be 100 per cent ok now."*

The car was examined and Police Chief Gene Helmer discovered the plugs and points were burned out.

It is claimed on the Internet 2017 that, as his health rapidly deteriorated for causes his doctors could not determine, George repeatedly told them, to their disbelief, that he was dying from the mysterious effects of internal injuries caused by Alien beings. Within six months after his April encounter, Officer George Wheeler died of unknown causes. We cannot confirm this and if any of the garish, sensational, accounts published about the incident is anything to go on, then we should be careful about accepting anything at face value.

(Source: *The Enquirer* – 'Terrifying UFO attack ... knocks policeman unconscious, immobilizes his car and blanks out TV sets in the area')

## 24th April 1976 – 'Square light' seen over Louth, Lincolnshire

Miss Mary Lessenord-Kent – then living in a caravan off London Road, Louth – was out in her garden, at 7.30pm, when she saw what she thought was the sun coming through the cloudy sky.

*"I thought how odd that the sun was setting at this time – then I saw this 'square light' in the sky, heading slowly westwards.*

*I'm not easily frightened, but I was on this occasion and went back inside."*

(Source: *Louth Standard*, 23.4.1976 – 'Couple's mystery of 'pink light in the sky')

### 28th April 1976 – UFO sighted over Timaru, New Zealand

At 4.50am, a night shift worker stopped to purchase a loaf of bread at a shop opposite the Boys High School in North Street.

*"While talking, we heard a sound – like a ship, releasing steam. It increased in volume and we saw nothing over by the wharf but when we looked up saw, through the broken clouds, about 800 feet high, a luminous green object resembling a biro pen and about as long, moving through the sky at slow speed, say 60 miles per hour, directly overhead. It was heading towards the local Hunters Hill direction.*

*A dome on top appeared to have oblong slit like windows, from which white flare coloured light was shining out in a stroboscopic effect. The windows seemed to change position – almost as if shutters would come down and close them off, and then appear again.*

*A couple of minutes later, the object was out of sight."* (**Source:** *XENELOG*, **number 104**)

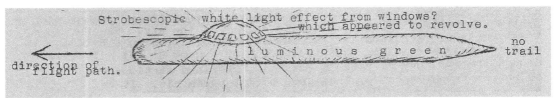

## CHAPTER 5 – MAY 1976

### Close Encounters of the Fourth Kind

Filming on what turned out to be a Hollywood blockbuster film began in May 1976, and was released in November 1977. The film received numerous awards and nominations at the 50th Academy Awards, 32nd British Academy Film Awards, the 35th Golden Globe Awards, the Saturn Awards and has been widely acclaimed by the American Film Institute.

In December 2007, it was deemed "culturally, historically, or aesthetically significant" by the United States Library of Congress and selected for preservation in the National Film Registry.

Bizarrely it was alleged that while making the film a series of terrifying events occurred which was to change the lives of many of the cast and crew members. According to *The Enquirer*, who launched an investigation, a ghostly presence frightened Steven Spielberg and his two associates, forcing them to flee from the hotel where they were staying. The set was lashed by at least a dozen storms. Eerie cloud formations, resembling precisely the one used in the film to hide a UFO, repeatedly

Elke Sommer's dining room was the favourite haunt of her household ghost. It eventually forced the 37-year-old star to move house

floated over the set. A *'real UFO, complete with four flashing and glowing lights'*, soared above the set while a scene depicting the landing of the UFO was being filmed.

Was this publicity just a ploy to advertise the forthcoming film or not? Not so according to Melinda Dillon, who reported having sighted a UFO herself at her California home two weeks before she was offered one of the star roles! She wasn't the only one – Elke Sommer herself reported having sighted a UFO.

## May 1976 – Close encounter, Yorkshire

Jan Molloy and her friend – Alison, were walking along the beachfront at Scarborough, Yorkshire, towards the pier, after finishing work.

**Jan:**

*"It was dark, at the time. We were chatting together, when we heard a deafening whirring noise coming from directly above our heads. Looking upwards, we saw a cone-shaped object – about the size of a small aircraft – with a flashing bank of lights beneath it, illuminating the ground as it approached us. We thought it was going to crash, so we started running towards the pier, noticing that although the noise was behind us, the lights had been extinguished. The next thing that*

# UFO CHASED US INTO A TIME WARP

## Jan Molloy and Alison Jones were pursued by a strange spaceship – into a graveyard and back to the 17th Century

A moonlight stroll for Jan Molloy and Alison Jones turned into a terrifying Close Encounters' experience when they were chased along a beach and into a timewarp by a UFO.

Ex-cabaret dancer Jan and her friend Alison claim they stepped back 300 years when they were pursued by a strange craft one night after their show.

'One minute we were on a beach in the 20th Century and the next we were being chased through a 17th-century graveyard. It was the most terrifying time of my life,' Jan, 36, told eva.

'Alison and I had been dancing in the evening show at Butlin's Filey Holiday Camp, near Scarborough. We were walking towards the pier, when we heard a deafening, whirring noise. Directly above us,

about 400ft up, was a cone-shaped object, about the size of a light aircraft, with flashing orange, red, purple and yellow lights.

'We ran towards the pier. It overtook us and then its lights went out so I couldn't see it any more, but I still heard the whirring.'

### 'I'll never forget the sound of the swishing skirts'

Before the girls reached the pier, they were hurled through a bizarre time warp.

'We must have gone back about 300 years because we were wearing long crinoline dresses and were in an eerie graveyard.

'I'll never forget the sound of the swishing skirts as we raced along. Then the lights appeared again through a swirling mist.'

Suddenly the girls were

back on the beach in their normal clothes.

'It was all over in a couple of minutes, but it felt like hours. Then Alison started screaming: "Jan, look, there's something beside you." But I couldn't see anything.

'She said there was a tall, thin person there. Later she told me it had a big head and a tiny body and was holding up a hand with just three fingers on it.'

Jan and Alison raced back to the camp. 'We were beside ourselves with fear, but no-one believed a word we said.

'But then, on the front page of the local newspaper the next week was the headline: "UFO lands in Filey."

'It wasn't a figment of our imaginations because other people had seen it, too. But I never want to experience anything like that again.' ■

happened was that we found ourselves running through an ancient churchyard – as if, somehow, we had been transported back into time. I vividly remember looking at the gravestones, which had an aged look about them. I couldn't understand what was happening. The locality was so unfamiliar to me.

As we ran along, I looked down and saw we were both wearing crinoline dresses, which made a 'swishing' *noise as we moved along the path. I could smell burning and had an impression that whatever it was that had been following us had landed nearby. I could hear Alison screaming and was aware of those coloured lights appearing through a swirling mist forming around us, before finding ourselves back on the beach wearing our normal clothes. The next thing I heard was Alison screaming out to*

12.1.97.

Hi,

Thankyou for the letter I recieved last week you have my permission to the Copyright, the incident is still very vivid in my mind, the swishing skirts were as real as any other clothes, because as we were running I looked down We were at that time running through an old grave yard but in Filey there is no grave yard The time Warp Must have Lasted at least 10-15 Seconds, there were no Helicopter the fact is the UFO did actualy land.

As Alison & Myself war still running we both smelt something burning, but our instincts told us not to go. Alison however did see two people standing in front of us, I can remember her screams; And told me to look! unfortunatly I couldn't see anything but She did Say that one of them were tall about 6ft. the other Small about 4ft.

But what Confused us that we throught we'd only gone about 1 hour, it turned out that we'd be gone 3 hrs - was it because of the time Warp that we lost the 2 extra hours,

*me, 'there's something beside you'. When I looked, there was nothing to be seen. Although the whole episode had lasted for only ten to fifteen seconds, we were shocked to discover that three hours had elapsed during the experience – something we found very difficult to believe."*

Alison later told me that she had seen a person in the churchyard, *"approximately six feet tall, thinly built, with a large head and three fingers on one hand"*.

It seems incomprehensible to accept that, in some way, the two women were physically transported back (or forward?) into another period of time, following the appearance of the UFO. However, one could not ignore those all too familiar patterns of behaviour common to so many other cases we were to come across, over the years, that included the presence of noise likened to that of a 'crinoline dress', or a cracking or whirring noise, and a burning smell – ingredients of not only UFO sightings but incidents often referred to as paranormal in nature.

### 2nd May 1976 – UFO over Gloucestershire

Retired farmer Ted Wheeler of Park Farm, Paganhill, sighted an object in the sky, at 9.45pm.

*"It was a dull glowing light, about half the size of the moon, moving slowly behind clouds."*

**(Source: The Citizen, Gloucester, 3.5.1976 – 'What was the light in the sky?')**

### 2nd May 1976 – UFO display over New Zealand

What they would not have known is that on the same day – this time over Temuka, New Zealand – the local residents were treated to a light display of strange objects. It began at 8pm, on the western outskirts of South Canterbury, when a farmer went out to check on stock in the paddock.

*"My attention was drawn to a large flame coloured object in the sky, and I called my wife and son to come and see it. At first it was round in shape and giving off a red orange glow. By 8.30pm it was half-moon shaped. Then it traversed on its axis 180° and moved to an upright position, slowly climbing upwards for a time. It then began to divide in the middle, forming two halves. The upper portion parted from the lower half to a gap about double the distance of its original length. It remained divided for about ten minutes – then the top half slowly sank to rejoin the bottom portion. It then took on an oblong shape and eventually diminished to a small circle. After a time the object began to drop behind the ranges. When out of sight the sky gave off a reddish glow, silhouetting the ranges in that glow. Later, the object rose up and 'reset'. A flare like object – brilliant white in colour, the size of a tennis ball – then shot upwards and vanished. This was followed by a few marble sized 'flares', at 9.45pm, which fizzled out like fireworks."*

**(Source: XENELOG, number 104)**

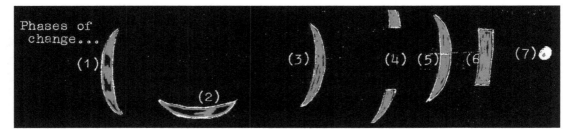

### 6th May 1976 – Glowing red cigar-shaped UFO

Mr Tony Jackson, of Redcar, was on his way home after visiting friends at Whitby, and about about five miles from Scaling Dam.

*"I saw a glowing red light in the sky; it seemed to be shaped like stubby cigar, or an elongated egg. I stopped to watch it for about five minutes, until it headed out of sight."*

David McGroarty – Cleveland representative of both the UFO Research Association and Research International – told the *Evening Gazette,* Middlesbrough – 'Two claim cigar-shaped UFO sighting' (7.5.1976) – that other sightings of what appears to have been the same object was reported to him.

### 8th May 1976 – 'Martian spaceship to rescue Earth'

… were the headlines in the *Evening News,* London, which related to information supplied by members of The Aetherius Society at Fulham Road, London, who claimed that the huge satellite packed with top Martian metaphysics is hurtling around the Earth in a fixed orbit, 1,550 miles up. Spokesman Ray Nielsen (40) – the Society's European secretary – warned that mankind was heading for materialistic disaster. *"The real energy is spiritual, not oil or gas or coal."*

## 10th May 1976 – 'Flying Saucer' over Lancashire

At 10.30pm, John (18) (family declined to be named) was walking home at 10.30pm along Broad Lane, St. Helens, Lancashire, when he saw a saucer-shaped object over Carr Mill. After arriving home he told his family what had happened. Fearing ridicule, John then decided to go to bed at 11. 30pm. The next thing which took place was that his family heard a clatter on the bedroom floor and rushed upstairs, where they saw:

> "...a round, brilliant white object, flat and darkish with a flashing light on top – like a police car – with a darker red light below.
>
> It was whizzing through the sky and seemed to hover over Billinge Hill, like it was pinned to a cloud, for about five minutes.
>
> We had time to look at it through binoculars."

(**Source:** *Evening Post and Chronicle*, 11.5.1976 – 'Flying Saucer shock for vigil family')

## 10th May 1976 – Leamington Spa

Mrs Diane Reader of Offchurch Lane, Radford Semele, Leamington Spa, was out in the garden at 10.50pm.

> "I saw this bright shimmering light suspended in the air, above Lillington flats. I called my husband to come out.
>
> We watched it for about five minutes. Suddenly it dimmed and headed away, at terrific speed, towards Birmingham."

(**Source: Leamington Spa Courier, 14.5.1976 – 'Visitors from outer space?')**

## 11th May 1976 – Close encounter, Manchester

Another sighting of a 'strange creature' took place at 6.15am, involving Mrs Kent – a middle-aged woman from Higher Folds estate, near Leigh, Greater Manchester, who was on her way to her daughter's house, a short distance away, when she saw:

> "...a strange 'figure', standing on top of the hill, wearing a brilliant silvery coloured suit, catching the sun's rays; it appeared to have a pointed hat and a cloak with sharply pointed lapels. By its side was a sphere of polished metal, beaming white light from its centre. The sphere came about halfway up the body of the 'figure'."

On her way back from her daughter's house, a few minutes later, she saw that the 'figure' was still there but by 6.40am it had vanished from sight. (**Source: Jenny Randles**)

## 13th May 1976 – Police chase UFO over Cheshire

In the early hours, two policemen from Lymm, in Cheshire, followed a series of 'lights' which appeared to be descending over trees, but soon lost sight of them. The matter was brought to the notice of the Press, who explained it away as likely to have been a helicopter, although the officers denied this to be the answer.

During spring/summer of 1976, *"a rectangular object, hundreds of feet long, showing bright lights set behind some form of grid structure"* was seen hovering over the Shell Refinery, at Carrington (which lies between Flixton, Partington, Daveyhulme and Sale), by a number of shoppers. A short time later, Police Sergeant Butts was travelling along Washway Road, Sale, when he and his colleague saw what appeared to be the same UFO.

## 16th May 1976 – Strange sighting over the coast

Eastbourne resident Mr Ronald Skelton (54) – a mechanical engineer by trade – was on the seafront at 2.15am, when he saw:

*"…two rows of six lights in the sky, at a height of about 3,000 feet. When the 'craft' was over the shoreline of Langney Point, I saw two searchlights from it, pointing out to sea. These lights were then briefly extinguished before coming on again. Immediately, a small dark object was ejected from the larger 'craft' and illuminated for a few seconds by the searchlight. The 'craft' then travelled in a wide arc over the larger object and moved towards Pevensey Marshes – the incident lasted about 25 seconds."* (**Source:** *Eastbourne Herald*, 29.5.1976 – 'Did Ron see a Flying Saucer'?)

## 18th May 1976 – Presidential words about UFOs!

The *Daily Express*, in their column written by Ross Mark of Washington – 'Jimmy's flying saucer', talks about Jimmy Carter and his bid to win the democratic nomination.

Quote: *"In this week, campaigning in stolid Nebraska, the peanut millionaire broke fresh campaign ground by asserting he had seen a 'Flying Saucer'."*

**Jimmy:**

*"I took a long and hard look at the object to convince me more serious investigation by the Pentagon."*

An aide for Ronald Reagan said:

*"Mr Reagan has good friends, whose word he trusts, who have seen inexplicable things racing across our sky, and he would like more inquiries made."*

(**Other source:** *Daily Telegraph*, 2.6.1976 – 'Carter saw Flying Saucer')

## 22nd May 1976 – Man from Mars will speak!

The *Esher News and Mail*, in its edition of the 20th May – 'UFO show at May Fayre' – told its readers about a forthcoming May Fayre, at Esher – which would also have an exhibition of unidentified flying objects, including photographs and models by BUFORA, who rather bizarrely also claimed to have a tape-recording of the voice of a Man from Mars! The event, organised by Esher Round Table, was to be opened by the comedian Jack Douglas, who would arrive in an open landau with Round Table chairman – Martin Moss.

## 27th May 1976 – Talk of Aliens!

The *Salisbury Journal*, in their edition of this date, headlined 'Saving Netheravon from the Aliens – its child play' with a story about rumours of strange unidentified flying objects over the plain and mysterious jamming of military communications… and so on. Fortunately, this story was concocted as part of the children's adventure workshop at Netheravon, forming part of operation DICE … normality returns.

## 1976 – UFO over Kent, sighted by couple walking home

Thelma Govier wrote to us, following an appeal in the *News Shopper* looking for any witnesses to the spectacular landing of a UFO in Bexleyheath, in Kent – as witnessed by Margaret Fry, in July 1955 (see Volume 1) – and told of walking home one night, with a friend, through Bexley, along Bourne Road (near to Hall Place), when they noticed a very 'bright light' heading towards them – which they took to be an aircraft.

*"To our great surprise it stopped above our heads, some 60-80 feet in the air. By this time, passing cars stopped the drivers getting out and pointing upwards with astonishment. It looked like the front of a cockpit, with a number of vertical 'windows' set into the nose – totally unlike the design of any aircraft or helicopter I've ever seen; out of these 'windows' streamed a dazzling light – so bright that it put the rest of whatever it was in the shade. I had the impression of 'figures', standing at waist-high consoles, looking downwards – then it moved away and was lost from view."*

(**Source:** Personal interview)

# CHAPTER 6 – JUNE 1976

## 3rd June 1976 – Motorist chases UFO

At 9.55pm a motorist and his passenger were travelling near Troy, Michigan, when they saw a silver or chrome coloured disc-shaped object in the sky moving nearby; curious, they followed it for some time as it changed directions and moved erratically about. Unusual static was picked-up on the car radio during the sighting. Eventually the object shot away at speed.

(**Source: Mark Rodeghier,** *UFO Reports Involving Vehicle Interference,* **case 398, citing personal investigation**)

## 5th June 1976 – Cigar-shaped UFO hovers over Highway

At 11.30pm over Merced, California, a glowing cigar-shaped object was reported hovering at a 40 degree angle over Highway 140; it appeared to have windows. It then made erratic manoeuvres in the sky.

(**Source:** *NICAP UFO Investigator,* **July 1976**)

## 6th June 1976 – Three cigar-shaped objects over Colchester, Essex

Later that evening, many people contacted the authorities after seeing strange objects in the sky over the Essex/Suffolk areas. These were later explained away as being a meteorite. Mr John Attree Poole (53) – then living in Hereford Road, on the Riverside Estate in Colchester – thinks otherwise.

> *"I was watering my garden, at 10.15pm, when an object appeared over the house. I looked up and saw three cigar-shaped lights, accompanied by a throbbing noise – like an aircraft in distress. It hovered overhead for 90 minutes, before heading away towards the coast at tremendous speed."*

For some days afterwards, he had a very sore tongue and found it difficult to swallow.

Despite attempts to attribute this sighting to being a Fireball, reported all over the UK at around 10.30pm, surely common senses dictates this was no Fireball, especially as the object was stationary for some seconds, and not forgetting the description taken.

(**Source:** *Evening Gazette,* **9.6.1976 – 'Gardner John says object in sky WAS a UFO'/***East Essex Gazette,* **11.6.1976 – 'UFO sightings may have been meteorite'/Andrew Collins & John Saville/***Leicester Mercury,* **7.6.1976 – 'Blazing UFO mystery'/***Evening Argus,* **Brighton, 7.6.1976 – 'Fireball lights up Sussex skies'**)

## 8th June 1976 – Cigar-shaped UFO

Mrs Bobby Madden was attending to her two week old baby Peter, as dawn broke over Goresbrook Road, Dagenham.

> *"I happened to look outside and saw a large, lighted cigar-shaped object, encircled with a halo – like haze. It was very high up and there for a couple of minutes, before it vanished from sight."*

(**Source: Barry King/***Barking and Dagenham Post,* **9.6.1976 – 'UFO report by Mum at dawn'**)

Meanwhile, over Katikati in New Zealand, a bright orange cigar-shaped object was seen by local farmers, during the early morning of the 8th June 1976, which hovered just above the horizon for about twenty minutes, until it vanished from view. (**Source:** *Sunday News,* **13.6.1976**)

## 10th June 1976 – Orange 'star' over Essex

Postman Mr G.R. Stewart (41) of Church Road, Braintree, Essex – an amateur astronomer – was looking into the eastern night sky with his telescope, at 10.15pm.

> *"I saw this orange star-like 'light', heading straight towards me. It stopped and hovered in the sky for a good two minutes and then shot away, at tremendous speed, before disappearing from view."*

## 11th June 1976 – Bright green object seen over Cumbria

Elsie Sanderson (58) of Cocklakes Cottage, Cocklakes, Cumbria, was about to retire to bed when she saw:

> *"…an object, shaped like a skittle, bright green in colour with fiery sparks coming from the back of it, moving slowly across the sky in a west to east direction. It seemed to land just at The Vicarage, at Cotehill."*

Another witness was George Jackson (48) of Glendale, Cotehill. He said *"it seemed more orange in colour"*.

The Vicar – David Wingate – had this to say:

> *"Sorry, but I haven't had any little green men to tea. Maybe that is an invasion but no-one has told me about it."*

**(Source: *UFOLOG/Cumberland News*, 11.6.1976 – 'Elsie's heavenly visitors')**

## 14th June 1976 – 'Flying saucer' over Essex

William Clarke of 62, Artillery Street, Colchester, Essex (58) – a casting and compound foreman – was outside at 1.30am, when he heard a noise – like a flock of swans – passing overhead. He looked up and saw a 'saucer' or circular-shaped object in the sky, with a dome on top showing an amber light, with a blue outer band of red metallic lights, in the south-west direction, heading north-west at a height of about 7,000 feet high, in a curious stop and start movement. **(Source: Essex UFO Study Group)**

At 10.20pm, Peter De'ath (14) and Gary Huntsman (15) from Basildon, in Essex, sighted a pale yellow 'bright light' – like a headlamp – moving slowly across the eastern sky. **(Source: *Basildon Recorder*, 25.6.1976)**

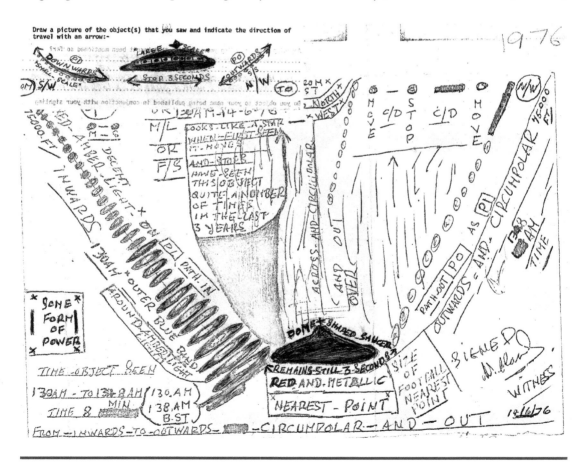

## 17th June 1976 – Orange glow over Dagenham

Robert Arthur Mathews (25) from Stamford Road, Dagenham, Essex, was looking out into the clear sky, at 9.09pm, when he saw:

*"…what looked like a vapour trail, but orange – then a banana-shaped object appeared with what looked like a 'hump' on its underside. It then shrank to a bright yellow circle in the sky, with a grey dot in the middle, before disappearing.*

*There were aircraft in the vicinity at the time, well behind the object."*

**(Source: Essex UFO Study Group)**

## 18th June 1976 – Pink objects seen to land in Berkshire

At 10.15pm, Paul Kerr (13) from Aldbourne Avenue, Earley, Reading, was looking out of his window on a hot summer's evening.

*"I saw a fluorescent pink object – like a glowing firework – go up and then land gently on the ground outside the University, near the Wilderness Road area, followed by another one which also came to earth."*

The sighting was reported to the *Reading Chronicle*. Paul wondered if, in fact, it could have been a firework rather than UFO. **(Source: Essex UFO Study Group)**

## 1976 Summer – UFO knocks out public transport vehicle

A very strange incident took place in the summer involving a peculiar white disc seen hovering over Liverpool City Centre. A bus stopped dead just about under the area of the sighting. All the lights and engine failed. Passengers could only sit there watching the UFO.

A relief bus arrived with jump leads, but before they could fix them to the power system, they completely failed. A third bus arrived and suffered the same fate.

Eventually a tow truck arrived and discovered the buses had been severely damaged and completely drained the heavy duty batteries. Other sightings were also included involving all manner of strange things seen in the sky according to the Liverpool bases chairman of the Unidentified Flying objects Research Council Alan Walsh.

## 24th June 1976 – Orange UFO over Essex

Mr A. Mathews of Stamford Road, Dagenham, was chatting to neighbours, at 9.10pm, when they noticed:

*"…a line or bar-shaped orange object, hanging in the sky at an angel of 45 degrees, surrounded by a brilliant glow. It then appeared to get smaller in length and width, until it was just a 'ball'.*

*Three minutes later, it had gone from view."*

At 10.30pm, Mr Allan R. Leigh (37) of Valence Wood Road, Dagenham, and his wife – Mary, sighted:

*"…seven white 'star-like' objects crossing the sky, at five minute intervals. Each one just appeared in the south-western sky, like a light bulb being turned on. All travelled in a straight line, except for one that zigzagged.*

*During this time a small propeller driven aircraft was seen in the same direction. As it did so, one of the lights switched off and failed to come back on.*

*This wasn't the end of it … a beam of light with clear defined parallel edges, orange-red in colour, hundreds of yards long, shot over the area in an east to west direction, only 20-30 feet off the ground."*

**(Source: Essex UFO Study Group)**

## 26th June 1976 – Classic Canary Island UFO sighting

Page 5 Canary Islands.

FLYING SAUCER REVIEW

fsr

Volume 23, No. 3, 1977                    70p

CANARY ISLANDS UFO

Maspalomas (Gran Canaria) June 22, 1976: UFO
departing after the landing in which occupants
were observed                    See page 4

# CANARY ISLANDS LANDING: OCCUPANTS REPORTED

## *J. M. Sanchez*

Señor Jesus Maria Sanchez, to whom we are greatly indebted for this contribution, is the director of the A.A. Ovnis Investigation Group* of Portugalete in the Province of Vizcaya in northern Spain. The report, first published by journalist J.J. Benitez, received the endorsement of the Spanish Government and was supported by photographs. It is a detailed report of the remarkable "onion phobia" affair which appeared in one of our "World Round-Up" columns (FSR Vol. 22, No. 4). Translation from the Spanish by Gordon Creighton

ON OCTOBER 20, 1976, acting in a personal capacity, a Lieutenant-General in the Spanish Air Ministry in Madrid handed to the Bilbao journalist Juan José Benítez a thick file bearing the label "Report on UFOs."

This most unusual document, while it does not constitute an *official* statement on the part of the Spanish Government — as has been somewhat precipitatedly claimed in some quarters — nevertheless represents a quite exceptional new development in the whole field of UFO research in Spain.

The 78 folio sheets which compose this Report contain the documentation drawn up by Spanish Air Ministry personnel on twelve UFO cases, the majority of which cases are also vouched for by Air Force personnel as witnesses. The documentation is backed by numerous pieces of photographic evidence and also by a number of pieces of film taken by pilots of Spanish fighter aircraft, as well as by details of certain cases in which the UFOs were registered on the radar.

The summarized account of the sightings begins with a case in the Province of Sevilla on March 20, 1964, and concludes with the case of June 22, 1976, in the islands of Fuerteventura and Gran Canaria, Canary Islands.

The last-mentioned of these twelve cases, in the Canary Islands, was already known in Spanish UFO research circles. A report on it appeared in issue No. 26 of *Stendek*, journal of the C.E.I. (Spanish Centre for Interplanetary Studies, Barcelona). In our present Report we confine ourselves to this particular case.

In that report published in *Stendek* No. 26 mention was made of the fact that "somebody" with sufficient "pull" had attempted, at the time when this case happened, to "request" the principal eyewitness to say nothing about the affair, as a result of which intervention the C.E.I's own correspondent in the Canary Isles had been prevented from reporting on the details of the case at first hand.

The divulging of some of the official documentation on this case, carried out as it now has been in pretty sensational fashion, has thrown fresh and

definitive light upon the case, namely in the conclusions reached by the Air Ministry. Among these documentary materials now made available are important new eyewitness statements — additional to those previously known — plus the revelation of the existence of a big series of coloured photographs of the UFO.

The features of this case, plus the large number of witnesses and the high qualifications of the latter, plus the other pieces of corroborative evidence, and plus the fact that we can guarantee that it emanates from the Ministry — all these factors go to make this Canary Islands landing case one of the most important ever recorded in the course of UFO investigation in Spain.

### Events of the night of June 22, 1976, over the Canaries

1. The Testimony

The UFO passed literally right across the whole of the Canary Island group, from East to West. The main concentrations of reports from witnesses who saw it come from three basic areas (See Map):—
  i) Area to S. of the Island of Fuerteventura.
  ii) Grand Canary, principally the northern part.
  iii) The islands lying further westwards: namely Tenerife, La Palma, Gomera, and Hierro.
Let us take them in order.

A: Here is a reproduction of the actual text of the despatch, file no. "01/76" dealing with this case, in the dossier handed to Sr. Benítez by the Lt. General from the Ministry. This relates to the first of the Canaries sightings (which had remained unknown until the Ministry released these documents):—

"At 21.27 (Z) hrs. on June 22, 1976, the corvette *Atrevida*, of the Spanish Navy, positioned at 3 NM, at 180 degrees from Punta Lantailla, on the southeastern coast of the Island of Fuerteventura, observed the following phenomenon, as described by the ship's personnel, including the Commanding Officer (Captain) and the Ship's Ensign (witnesses numbered B—07 and B—08 respectively):

" 'At 21.27 (Z) hrs. on June 22, 1976, we saw a

---

* UFO Investigation Group A.A. OVNIS, address: Martin F. Villaran 5, bajo C., Portugalete, Province of Vizcaya, Spain.

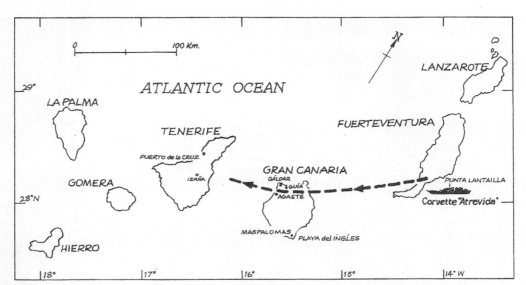

The flight path of the UFO from Fuerteventura Island westwards to Tenerife via Grand Canary

vivid yellowish-cum-bluish light moving out from the shore towards our position, and climbing as it did so. At first we thought it was an aircraft with its landing lights on. Then, when the light had attained a certain elevation (15—18 degrees) it became stationary. The original light went out and a luminous beam from it began to rotate.

" 'It remained like this for approximately two minutes. Then a vivid great halo of yellowish and bluish light developed, and remained in the same position for 40 minutes, even though the original phenomenon was no longer visible.

" 'Two minutes after the great halo, the light split into two parts, the smaller part being beneath, in the centre of the luminous halo, there a blue cloud appeared and the part from which the bluish nucleus had come vanished.

" 'The upper part began to climb in a spiral, rapid and irregular, and finally vanished. None of these movements affected the initial circular halo in any way, which remained just the same the whole time, its glow lighting up part of the land and part of the surface of the sea beneath it, from which we could deduce that the phenomenon was not very far away from us, but was close.

" '(...) The strange object which had been observed by the witnesses aboard the Spanish warship, to the south of the Island of Fuerteventura, covered the distance of 85 nautical miles between the sighting position and the north of Grand Canary Island in three minutes, at an estimated speed of some 3,060 km.p.h.' " (See Trajectory as shown on Map and in

**Right: The sighting from aboard the Spanish corvette** *Atrevida*, **at a point 3 sea-miles from the S.E. coast of Fuerteventura**

Appendix II of the official document issued by the Ministry).

B: A very few minutes later, at about 21.30 hrs. — so the official report states — the foregoing testimony as

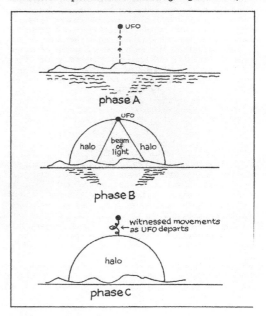

5

### 28th June 1976 – UFO seen near Snowdon, Wales

Mr Brian Guiver was on holiday in North Wales with his wife and child, driving down the A486 from Llanrug to Cwn-y-Glo, with Mount Snowdon in view, when they spotted a large black object in the sky moving towards the peak. After keeping watch on it for ten seconds, they lost sight of it due to their view being blocked by a hill on the right. Brian parked the car and saw the object heading back along the journey it had just taken. Before he could take a photo, it disappeared from sight.

**(Source: Personal interview)**

On 28th June, temperatures reached 35.6°C (96.1°F) in Southampton, the highest June temperature recorded in the UK. The hottest day of all was 3rd July, with temperatures reaching 35.9°C (96.6°F) in Cheltenham; one of the hottest July days on record in the United Kingdom. In the last week of August, severe thunderstorms brought rain to some places for the first time in weeks.

September and October 1976 were both very wet months, and the great drought of 1975-1976 had finally ended.

### 30th June 1976 – UFO over Eastbourne

Just before midnight an unidentified flying object was sighted over Eastbourne, by Mr and Mrs Ken Fielder of Upper Dukes Drive, who was accompanied by a group of foreign students – Abdullah, Giannandre, Raloh and Olivia.

*Mr Fielder (pointing), his wife Caroline (bottom right) and the students, Abdullah, Giannandre, Raloh and Olivia*

> *"It appeared to be just a shooting star and then it started to drop, as if it was a shooting star. We were all watching when it quite suddenly turned red, not brilliant but definitely red. It had stopped directly above Eastbourne College and was still red in colour. It must have stayed stationary for three minutes. We watched it turn from red to white again. It had an incredible luminosity and glowed above the college. It was like a theatre spotlight. The strange and uncanny thing was that there was no noise. We thought it might have been a helicopter. The thing seemed to increase its size by about three times. When we first saw it, it was about the size of Venus. Gradually, it started to move again and seemed to be coming straight towards us. It really was quite worrying. It then disappeared over the hills and we couldn't see it from the house or garden."*

**(Source: *The Argus*, 30.6.1976 – 'Eight people swear they saw the thing in the sky'/*Fountain Journal*, Number 3, 1976)**

### 30th June 1976 – UFO over Mount Snowdon

Brian Guiver was on Mount Snowdon, when he was surprised to experience another sighting – this time at 3pm, while following the Pyg Track leading to the top of Mount Snowdon.

> *"On this occasion we had stopped halfway up the mountain, near to the Miners' Track, and were eating our lunch, when some seagulls swooped down overhead, causing us to look upwards. I saw three dark 'discs', set into a triangular formation, heading towards us in zigzag movements. I stood*

*still, watching, as they passed overhead. One of them seemed to tilt, showing a red glowing centre, surrounded by a shining light that obscured the other two objects from view. Whether this was caused by reflected sunlight, I cannot say."* (**Source: Personal interview**)

---

19th February 2002

Mr J. Hanson
P O Box 6371
Birmingham
B48 7RW

Dear John,

Further to our telephone conversation I have made the following notes, which I hope will give you all of the information you need. If you require any further information about anything, please do not hesitate to contact me.

NOTES REGARDING UFO SIGHTING IN SNOWDON

While we were on holiday in North Wales (Llanrug) from the 26th June 1976 to 2nd July 1976, my wife (CHIRSTINE) and I experienced two separate sightings of unidentified flying objects.

On Monday 28th June 1976 at about midday, I was driving with my wife and child ( Laura aged 4) down the A4086 from Llanrug to Cwm-y-glo, we had Mt Snowdon in view, which was actually six miles away. It was whilst looking at Snowdon that I spotted a large black object in the sky. It was moving towards the peak of Snowdon from the rounded mountain to the left of Snowdon's peak. I said "What's that it's huge and shaped like a UFO". After seeing it for ten seconds, Mt Snowdon on the right blocked it from sight. It took us about fifteen seconds whilst still travelling to get it back in view. I then parked the car on the corner to take a picture of the UFO, which was last seen travelling behind the peak of Snowdon. I expected it to come into view on the other side of Mt Snowdon's peak, but it did not. Instead, by the time I had hold of the camera, it was travelling back towards the round mountain and disappeared behind it. It vanished before I had time to take a photograph.

On Wed 30th June 1976, at about 3.00 pm. We experienced our second sighting. We were following the Pyg Track which is a path that leads to the top of Mt Snowdon. We had climbed about halfway and stopped just before the Miner's Track to have some lunch. While we were eating, a few seagulls swooped down, and my daughter Laura threw them some bread. When we had finished lunch and were ready to set off, I looked up at the sky once more to watch the seagulls and saw three dark discs in a triangle formation. They had come over the top of the mountains and started to zigzag towards us at high speed. At this time Laura ran off down the mountain and my wife went after her. I kept my eyes firmly fixed on the objects, which stopped overhead. When they had stopped moving, one of the discs seemed to tilt, which is when I saw a glowing red centre surrounded by a silvery white light that blocked the other two objects from my view. This could have been due to the sun reflecting on the object, but I am not sure about this.

While I was watching the objects I was trying to get my camera, which was strapped to my belt. I eventually managed to free it, but by the time I had adjusted the lens to infinity, the objects had darted off and vanished. My wife had retrieved Laura by this time and also witnessed the objects disappearing. We carried on our journey and reached the top of Mt Snowdon.

N.B.  Electricity failure during the early hours of the morning of 30th June, which lasted until 9.15am.
The length of this holiday was supposed to have been from 26th June 1976 to 4th July 1976, but due to the affect that this sighting had on us we went home two days early.

---

We did not hear any noise during either sighting

I enclose a copy of an article entitled "Mystery of the exploding mountain" by Jenny Randles, which I thought you might find interesting, and also a poem I wrote called "Summer of '76". I do not often write poetry but felt it appropriate due to the magnitude of this experience.

I would be pleased to hear from you again in the near future.

Yours sincerely

Brian.C.Guiver

Signed_____ Date 26/2/02.

LAURA AND MYSELF ON THE SUMMIT OF MT SNOWDON.

Both sightings witnessed by Mrs Christine.M.Grove (formerly Guiver)

Signed _____bMGrove_____ Date 26/2/02

NOTES AND DRAWINGS MADE AT THE TIME
BY CHRISTINE AND MYSELF

NOTES AND DRAWINGS MADE AT THE TIME
BY CHRISTINE AND MYSELF

SHAPE OF OBJECT
NOT TO SCALE.

SHAPE OF OBJECT

CHRISTINE          BRIAN

SHAPE OF OBJECT.

KIND 219-205 NS ALL OVER THE PLACE BUT STATED IN FORMATION.

## 30th June 1976 – UFOs over Cradle Hill, Warminster

Many miles away on the slopes of Cradle Hill, Warminster, Peter Paget, his wife – Jane, Arthur Shuttlewood, and several others, were stood talking amongst themselves, when at 10.30pm on 30th June 1976, an object came flying in from the direction of the north, described (through binoculars) as:

> *"...five white lights, arranged in a square on the underside, a fifth being in the centre. The object's body was metal-grey in colour.*
>
> *It then flew silently over the copse at Cradle Hill, about a quarter of a mile away, and banked westwards, showing just a body devoid of any wings, or windows. A faint sound – like a turbine – could be heard."*

This was not the end of the story. After returning to Star House, several bright pinpoint lights flashed on in the sky.

Barry Musselwhite flashed his torch, a number of times. The signal was returned!

**(Source: Peter Paget, *Fountain Journal*, No. 3, 1976)**

Kevin Goodman was one of those who spent time in the Warminster area, and got to know Peter and his wife – Jane.

> *"It was the time when admitting to being interested in this area of interest became more acceptable, mainly in part to the huge success of a certain Steven Spielberg film. I remember being excited when the news broke that Spielberg was creating the ultimate UFO film, and queuing to get my ticket – such was the public interest and fervour in the offing. Overnight, being interested in UFOs suddenly became no longer the preserve of a few 'oddballs' and 'cranks', but slowly began to become a more socially accepted interest.*
>
> *Between 1976 and 1979, the famous or infamous 'Warminster Mystery' was fading from the general public's consciousness. Warminster had been a hotbed of sightings and paranormal events since late in 1964. I was first exposed to it when I read Arthur Shuttlewood's – The Warminster Mystery – in 1973, and until then, in my naive young mind I had thought that UFOs were mainly a phenomenon that occurred in the United States. That blinkered opinion was soon to change.*
>
> *I lapped the book up, reading it in one day, and I became determined to visit this town as soon as I could ... but my pleas to have a family holiday in Wiltshire fell on deaf ears, and it was not until the long, hot summer of 1976 that I first visited the town, and saw the 'Thing' for myself. For the next few years, along with like-minded friends, repeated visits followed. We soon became seasoned sky watchers, and knew when a satellite went over, or a car came over a distant hill-top road. And did we see and experience anything strange? Oh yes, we did! Warminster has always held a fascination for me from that day on. Since then, my Warminster experiences will always be with me.*
>
> *I was one of the first people to visit and stay at 'The Fountain Centre', run by Peter and Jane Paget, which opened its doors in the spring of 1976 and became the main point of contact for people visiting the town, keen to see the infamous 'Thing' for themselves. The Pagets, along with Arthur Shuttlewood, aimed to publish a magazine – The Fountain Journal. This kept those 'in the know' appraised of events happening in the town.*
>
> *However, it's a sad fact of life that politics between groups, as always seems to happen in Warminster, can shatter an ideal, and the infighting between various groups ended any research into the town's enigma in late 1980. But, it's interesting to note that many of today's respected researchers and authorities actually cut their young teeth in Warminster during this period.*
>
> *Arthur Shuttlewood, over the years, has come into some criticism for his very sensationalist style of writing and reporting. Arthur only chronicled the events in the town, albeit diligently, but it has*

*to be remembered that he was a newspaper reporter with an interest in the town's strange phenomenon. Arthur began to suffer from ill-health during the years this book covers; some say that this was due to the long hours he spent on Cradle Hill. Possibly due to his lack of commitment, during the later period of the 1970s, when Warminster was considered to be old news by the press, sightings became less frequent.*

*Sadly, until now, the events at the end of the Warminster Mystery have been largely ignored or forgotten. The work put into this volume speaks for itself, as there are nuggets in here that even I had no knowledge of. For those of us touched by Warminster, and I know there are many of us, I can say only this: 'Keep the flame burning.' So sit back, and enjoy another meaty slice of UK UFO history."*

**Kevin Goodman** (Author of *UFO Warminster: Cradle of Contact*)

# CHAPTER 7 – JULY 1976

## 1st July 1976 – UFO over Canvey Island, Essex

Mr Victor Arthur Charles Lee – an AA Patrolman (34) – with his wife and their two small children, from Rugby Road, Dagenham, were visiting relatives at Canvey Island. While driving along the seafront, at 9.30pm, they saw a bright red/orange elongated oval object in the northern sky.

*"It had a flattish top and tapered end; there was a hazy effect along the top and underneath. After about four minutes it appeared to get smaller, as though receding, and was lost from sight." (Source: Andrew Collins)*

## 2nd July 1976 – Cigar-shaped UFO over Essex

Dagenham residents – Mr and Mrs Irene Florence Varney, and their daughters, Maxine and her sister – had left East Ham swimming pool, High Street South, and were talking outside the premises, when one of the daughters caught sight of:

*"…an orange or red 'cigar' or bullet-shaped object, motionless in the sky; it was blunt at one end, rounded at the other".*

The whole group watched it until it moved away silently and out of sight, five minutes later.

**(Source: Andrew Collins)**

## 4th July 1976 – Close encounter, California

At Montrose, California, a woman was walking down the driveway of her home with her 9 year-old granddaughter, at 9pm. She saw:

*"…a dark lilac coloured, glowing, round object, about 25 feet in diameter, hovering just above the ground, with orange flames at the edges."*

Something impelled the woman to walk down the road and look down a side street, where she saw another object hanging low in the sky over a church, 75-100 feet away. This second UFO had *"no colour, no lights, and a strange appendage in the back."*

She watched the purplish object, which hurt her eyes, for 4-5 minutes.

During this time, strangely, there were no cars on the street and no other persons around except her granddaughter, who did not observe the UFO. The next day she examined the site where the purplish object had been, and saw *"a lot of brown oil"* on the fence and bushes; the oil stains remained for months.

The witness later remembered that she saw *"a man, sitting at a table inside the purplish object; he was human looking, brown haired, and was watching a screen of some kind."* She felt he was contacting her mentally, warning her not to tell anyone what she was seeing. [Authors: Another instance where the witness is warned to keep quiet about what she encountered. The frustrating thing about many of the US incidents is the need for witness anonymity, understanding many people have no objection to their names being used. No doubt the reader will accept there is far more to these accounts than we shall ever know…not forgetting important evidence, such as photographs taken of the scene and analysis of the 'oil'. Maybe these were done, but where are the original files? They may well exist somewhere – but where?]

**(Source: Ann Druffel and Vince Uhlenkott for MUFON)**

## 5th July 1976 – Children sight UFO and strange 'being'

At Gitchie Manitou Park, Iowa, brothers, eight-year-old Andy and six-year-old Joel Rygh, were out playing, at 9am, when they heard: *"…strange noises, followed by a grunting sound and then a whistle"*.

When they looked in the direction of the noises, they saw:

> *"…a seven feet tall man standing behind a bush, wearing a shiny blue uniform"*.

When the whistling sound became louder, the boys ran to fetch their brothers – Chris, age 11, and Tom, age nine. All four boys then saw a pulsating, glowing, domed, object emerge from behind a large tree, 50 yards away, *"about the size and shape of a large haystack"*. It hovered with a humming sound for five seconds, and then sped away. Small oak trees that the craft hovered over were later found defoliated.

**(Source: Pat Miller, Sioux Falls, South Dakota, *Argus Leader*, 15.8.1976)**

## 7th July 1976 – Orange bar-shaped UFO sighted

Mrs Maureen Sackett (then 40) of Edgehill Gardens, Dagenham, was in her back garden, at 9.30pm, when she saw:

> *"…a long, thick, bar-shaped object – orange in colour – heading across the sky in a straight course, at the speed of an aircraft. It then reduced in size until a small globe, disappearing in the north-west direction one minute later." (Source: Andrew Collins)*

## 9th July 1976 – Schoolchildren sight UFO over Cornwall

# UFO sighting sets school a mystery . . .

FOR about five minutes on Friday, three adults and at least 90 children at Treleigh CP School, Redruth, watched a spherical object cross high in the midday sky . . . and what exactly it was is a complete mystery to them.

Most of them—they watched from the school yard—agreed that it resembled two dinner plates face to face.

"It was white and spinning," said Miss Deborah Foster, a teacher. "It appeared to be very high up, and came from the Truro direction. We lost sight of it over Carn Brea. It was saucer-shaped and seemed to have an aura or halo."

Another teacher, Mr. Sam Hawkins, said he clearly saw silver and yellow flashes at 90 degrees to the object's direction.

He said it was travelling very slowly. "It went through high cloud, yet we could still see it," he added.

Mrs. Sylvia Harris, school secretary, agreed it was round and whitish. She also saw flashes from it. "They were like lightning and were spasmodic," she said. "I have never seen anything like it before."

Miss Foster added: "It was a little frightening. I do not like anything I cannot explain."

Pupils said there was no sound, and the sphere changed to a green hue when it went behind high clouds.

They agreed it was spinning and say they saw flashes from it. They were certain it bore no markings.

Mr. Sidney Thorne, headmaster—who is interested in unidentified flying objects— missed the sighting. He said it could not have been a weather balloon, as the object's journey included a distinct manoeuvre.

He added that unexplained objects had been sighted at the school and by parents at Northcountry, Redruth, in March and November, 1973.

At 8.30am, pupils and teachers from Treleigh Comprehensive School, Redruth, Cornwall, watched a white cigar-shaped object, resembling *"two spinning plates in the sky, pulsing spasmodically with light"* as it crossed the sky from the direction of Truro, heading towards Carn Brea, giving off 'puffs of smoke'. We spoke to Sydney Thorne – a man of considerable intelligence, well travelled, with a dry sense of humour (then Headmaster at the school) – who was to take great interest in the incident, although he had not personally seen anything on the morning concerned.

"*I was invited to attend the Television Studios, at Plymouth, to tell the viewers about the incident. The producers asked me to bring along some of the illustrations, drawn by the pupils under strict supervision. I have to say I expected a lively, sensible, debate on what, after all, had been an extraordinary sighting. Imagine my surprise to discover the complete opposite attitude, reflecting an obvious unwillingness to even consider that matters such as this should be taken seriously, rather than treating the subject with ridicule.*

*During the same year I was at home and asleep, when my wife disturbed me at lam. She told me about a luminous object she could see hovering in the sky. I went to the window and saw something – about the size and shape of a harvest moon – that tilted and changed into a 'cigar'. Out of this exited a smaller object which shot off across the sky, heading out over the Atlantic.*

*I prepared a report and sent it to the MOD, who sent two investigators around to see me. After explaining what we had seen, one of them said to me, 'off the record, what you saw was an example of a Mother ship, releasing some form of scout craft or probe'.*"

(**Source: Personal interview/***Flying Saucer Review*, **Volume 22, No. 3, October 1976**)

## July 1976 – Allegation of interactions with UFOs and their occupants!

The version of events which follows took place at Oakenholt – a small village surrounded by farmland, close to the Clwyd coast, adjacent to the *River Dee*. These were first brought to the notice of Mrs Marion Sunderland (then in her 30s), who lived in Oakenholt with her five children, during March 1978, following considerable publicity in the UK shortly before the film – *Close Encounters of the Third Kind* – was released.

Marion was reading a story about the forthcoming film in the local newspaper, when Darren (10) asked her what a 'close encounter' was. Marion explained and Darren told her he had, in fact, had something like this happen to him. He then mentioned something which had occurred in July 1976. Gaynor (11) came into the house and, after overhearing some of the conversation, then made light of the conversation. However, after Darren had left the room, Gaynor admitted she had also experienced some strange happening in July 1976 but had decided not to tell anyone about it, fearing ridicule. Marion, unsure what to do next, called Darren back inside and interviewed him further, during which time he sketched what he had witnessed.

### Terry Bellis

The incident was originally investigated by Mr Terry Bellis – a local investigator – following a radio 'phone-in' program for *Radio City*, Liverpool, in April 1978, after Marion telephoned with brief details and then sent a detailed statement of what Gaynor had seen to him.

### Jenny Randles and Paul Whetnall

This matter was the subject of an investigation by Jenny Randles and Paul Whetnall and was later published in *Flying Saucer Review*.

It is a fascinating and quite complex account pertaining to a number of reports of strange lights in the sky and manifestations on the ground of what appeared to be non-human beings. Whether they were, in fact, the occupants of the craft concerned can only be speculation.

### Darren's version of what happened

Darren told of walking down a quiet deserted lane, known as Coed Onn Road, during the mid-afternoon in mid-July 1976, just after the school holidays had began, when he saw a glint of silver in a nearby field and went to take a closer look. He saw:

*"...a silvery, oblong, object on four tall metallic legs, resting on the field. It had a large, round, dome on top – apparently made out of dozens of tiny square windows. There appeared to be some black writing on a silver rim. Five or six wires came out of the object and seemed to stick into the ground."*

### Six 'beings' seen around the craft

Six 'men' were also seen clumsily walking around the object, and appeared to be in an angry mood. They carried gun-like objects, which had a blue button that would release a red beam of light when touched. The men were described as four feet, 10 inches tall, human-like, but with sparse hair sticking up. They wore silver tops with green pants. The men proceeded to strike some coloured bulbs that were stuck on the ground at the end of the wires.

### Ramp comes out of the object

At this moment a central ramp came down from the 'craft' – then a bizarre creature appeared; it was described as reptile-like, with a green body and a red neck. It appeared to have long floppy cheeks. It then

*Gaynor Sunderland's July, 1976 encounter as illustrated on the cover of* FSR, *Volume 25, No. 3.*

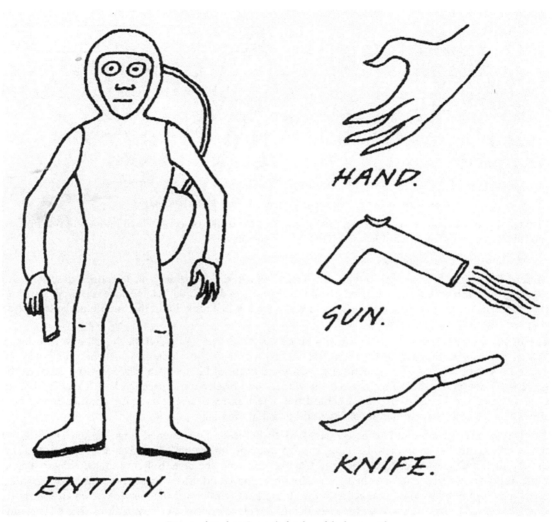

HAND.

GUN.

KNIFE.

ENTITY.

*Drawing based on Gaynor's sketches of the humanoid*

went back into the object, after one of the men growled at it. A human-like figure now appeared inside the dome. He had a rosy pink complexion with abundant black hair, and appeared to be wearing a white T-shirt. He had five fingers; unlike the other entities, who had four.

He seemed to be operating some controls and, according to Darren, glanced at a picture on the inner wall of the object that resembled the man who lived next door. He smiled, then hid behind a wall and disappeared. Darren thought that everything looked smaller inside the 'craft'. Moments later the object left, silently.

### What Gaynor saw

About the same time of the previous incident (the time given as 1.50pm), Gaynor Sunderland, was riding her bicycle along a secluded stretch of the same road, at a different location, when she caught sight of a silvery cigar-shaped object behind a nearby hedge on a field. She hid behind the hedge and, looking

*Sketches based on Darren's alleged sighting. Left: The UFO. Right: 'Man' and 'gun'; 'animal'.*

through a gap, was able to see a narrow rim along the base of the object – which had a dull red 'box' on top, and three rectangular windows along the side of the object.

### Human-like 'figure' appears

Minutes later a five feet, five inch, human-like 'figure' appeared from behind the object. She describes him as being very thin with an angular body, walking clumsily in a stiff manner. His face was long, thin, and very pale. He had very large round eyes – white in colour with a pink dot in the middle, and a few sandy wisps of thin hair.

The 'being' wore a silvery one-piece suit and boots with thick black soles. On his head he wore a silvery helmet with a glass bubble on the front. He carried a gun-like instrument, which he pointed to the ground several times – each time emitting a wavy red beam of light, which made cup size holes in the ground. At one point, the 'being' noticed the witness and briefly stared at her; she felt cold and dizzy at that point. The 'being' disappeared behind the object and was not seen again; another 'being' now appeared – described as similar but shorter, and possibly a female.

This 'being' carried a knife-like object attached to her side, and seemed angry when she noticed the witness. The 'being' then walked up a ramp into the object and disappeared. The red 'box' on the top of the object began to pulsate and Gaynor ran from the area, noticing that the cigar-shaped 'craft' angle (skywards) had vanished into a low hanging cloud. The witness noted a burning smell. The aliens continued to make contact with the Sunderland family over the next few years and, at times, Gaynor seemed to be possessed by the visitors and unable to control her own actions. The girl's claims were backed up by her family, who all gave matching descriptions of the aliens.

(**Source: Jenny Randles and Paul Whetnall,** *Flying Saucer* **Review, Volume 25**)

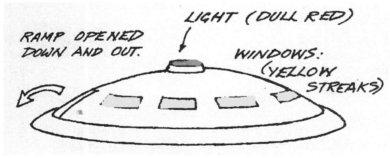

*UFO allegedly seen by Gaynor on the ground*

*Gaynor Sunderland*

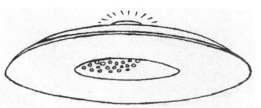

*Gaynor's UFO on take off*

*Gaynor looking at a hole in the hedge at approximately the position from which, lying down, she watched the UFO and the humanoid*

*The view from the point where the domed object is said to have stood, looking towards the gap in the hedgerow, by which Gaynor was lying prone*

*Gaynor looking towards the landing site through the gate further along the hedge*

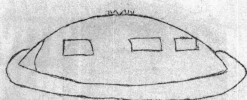

SPACECRAFT: "Like a saucer with windows and a flashing Light." Drawing by Gaynor from the STAR newspaper.
Credit: DAILY STAR, Friday March 9th 1979, by Neil Moran.
TALK of outer space and these could be the drawings any youngster dreams up...
A funny looking man with a weird helmet, a flying saucer with windows and flashing lights. All in a child's imagination --or is it? For little Gaynor Sunderland who drew these pictures is an exception. She says she came face to face with aliens of another planet, and UFO experts believe her. They say the sighting is "a most incredible breakthrough."
Eleven-year-old Gaynor has twice been questioned under hypnosis. One UFO expert, Miss Jenny Randles, of Flying Saucer Review, said yesterday: "It is probably the best encounter ever documented in Britain."
Gaynor's close encounter of the frightening kind happened in July 1976, when she says she watched a silver saucer-like craft and two silver-suited people for half an hour.
She lay terrified, peering through a gap in the hedge after it landed in a field a mile from her home in Julius Close, Oakenholt, near Flint, North Wales. Yet it was another 18 months before she spoke openly. Said her mother, Mrs. Marion Sunderland: "Gaynor was frightened of ridicule. Her story has been studied since last April. "It is extremely detailed and tallies with sightings in other parts of the world," said another UFO expert.
Gaynor describes the space craft as being half the size of a house, and its occupants--a man and woman-as short and angular with large pink eyes. Both were silvery suits and helmets.

### HUMMING

The ship, about 35 feet across and nine feet high, had a row of yellow windows along the side and a flashing box on top.
Gaynor says the aliens probed the ground with equipment before taking off with a loud humming noise.
Then she dashed home too scared to speak. Said Gaynor: "I was cold and frightened-I was sure both of them had seen me.
Added Jenny Randles: "Her description is among the most detailed recorded. We shall be asking her many more questions."

## Sir Bernard's being stupid—UFO expert

**From NIGEL NELSON in New York**

THE world's most respected authority on UFOs accused Britain's top astronomer, Sir Bernard Lovell, of stupidity yesterday.
Dr. Allen Hynek, president of America's Centre for UFO Studies said it was ridiculous for Jodrell Bank Director Sir Bernard to suggest that a UFO filmed over New Zealand last Christmas was nothing more than a burned-out meteorite.
The UFO, tracked on radar and captured on film from a light aircraft by Australia's Channel 10 television network, has been care-

*Sir Bernard... and the UFO he 'shot down'*

fully studied by 20 of America's top physicists and astronomers.
Yesterday the scientists declared that the film was the first-ever verified footage of an unidentified flying object.
Dr Hynek went on to attack Sir Bernard 'or dismissing the object as just a meteorite. 'That was one of the more stupid explanations,' he said, 'it's completely unfeasible.
'This is scientific irresponsibility. He should examine the data before pontificating.

*CNK said in issues 20 and 21 something to the above effect that Sir Bernard was acting out of his depth, although we would have liked to use vehemently the strong words above—we didn't. but this is what we meant. Seems like we wasn't far wrong in this summing up. We said: "Sir Bernard should go out and get first hand experience of such a happening, before opening his mouth to the press". Seems like he's put his foot in it at last!

*From the pages of Cosmology Newslink relating to the incident at Oakenholt, in 1976*

*Marion Sunderland (right) with Darren and Gaynor*

LANDING WITH ENTITIES IN CLWYD          Investigation: Paul Whetnall, & UFORA
                                         Jenny Randles, WUFOS

July 1976      Oakenholt, Clwyd       Level A      CE 3a (L) T ,Psycho

This case was originally discovered by WUFOS,who completed an initial report
and then left the matter in abeyance.Paul Whetnall and Jenny Randles persued
it for a further six months,and Martin Keatman (UFORA) is presently undertaking
a detailed site analysis for UFOIN.

It is now believed that the incident took place on Saturday,July 24 – during
a hot,sunny day.At around 13.50 9yr old Gaynor Sunderland was riding her bike
on a lane near her home when she saw over a hedge in a field (below the road)
a metalic object.Thinking at first it was something from a carnival she got
off and crouched in the hedge to watch.

The object was a silvery dome with a rim around the bottom,about 10 feet high
and 35 feet wide.It had a row of square windows (four) that were different
shades of yellow blended in.She saw a dark shape pass across one 'window' and
stayed hidden,frightened she might be scared away.

After a few minutes a figure appeared from around the back.'He' was dressed in
a one piece silver suit with a balaclarva type helmet and thick soled boots
(like divers).He was about 5'5" tall and had an angular body with the knee
joint high up.He also had just four fingers (three pointed and a thumb) a.
pale thin face with large white eyes with tiny pink pupils.

Gaynor obtained a close-up view as the man came within ten feet carrying an L
shaped cream 'gun' that fired a red ray to the ground.He made a series of 5~
little holes in the grass and bent stiffly to feel them.

Presently the man returned to the side of the craft where a 'ramp' came down
and he seemingly communicated with a 'hand' that came out.He then went in and
.oments later a 'woman' came out.She was similar to the man but about 4 inches
smaller and carried a long jagged dagger that she used to solve the holes.
Presently she returned to the craft too,upon hearing a whimpering noise from it,

Gaynor felt that both entities had detected her presnce and had physiological
sensations of dizziness and nausea when they looked at her.She was rooted to
the spot.When the woman was back in she fled,gashing her leg badly on the
hedge.She saw the UFO take off at an angle into the one cloud in the sky.It
made a hum, she smelt a burning and the leaves on adjacent trees trembled.It
did not come out of the Cloud.The next day she returned,with her brother,to
the field and found a circular
area of silver tinted grass.The
holes had been 'filled in' but
the grass was noticably greenr
around them.Gaynor was recently regressively hypnotised.She added a few more
details but there was no significant change in her testimony (which is far
more complex than this summary presents).The hypnotist was positive she was
relating an experience that had genuinely taken place..... 45T-(S) (Pending)

Here is another contemporary newspaper article (date believed to be in 1976) relating to a frightening ordeal for a schoolgirl.

# RIDDLE OF STRANGE ENCOUNTERS
# GIRL RELIVES UFO NIGHT OF TERROR

**A TEENAGE girl has relived the evening she ran terrified and crying through the street with a friend — convinced they were being chased by a UFO.**

Caroline Muncey (15) said they were shadowed until she went to a house for help and the "craft" disappeared.

The girls' ordeal began as they were walking home from a disco at Wellingborough on Saturday. It was one of a series of mysterious sightings in the area.

Caroline and Mandy Dooley (16), who both live in Vicarage Farm Road, Wellingborough, saw bright lights in the sky.

After a few minutes the lights vanished and the friends continued walking home along Queensway.

Caroline said: "We started talking about something else, then Mandy looked behind and started running. I looked back and saw the lights bathing the road, and ran.

"I tripped and fell. It was right behind me, gliding over the bridge. It was getting so near.

"I knocked on somebody's door and the UFO turned way up into the sky."

Caroline, a pupil at Wellingborough's Breezehill school, added: "I was terrified and crying. I came out in rash, all over my hands nd arms."

Caroline explained that he object turned upside own, with the dome facing wards the ground, and the ghts went out.

The man whose door she nocked on, Mr Les Stainer, ld her it looked like an old artime bomber as it disapared.

● Caroline Muncey with her drawing of the UFO she claims terrorised her.

Caroline went home and drew a sketch of what she had seen.

The incident occurred at about 9.30 pm — and an Irchester man saw an object in the sky in the same area at 9.15 pm.

Mr Martin Batley said he was driving along the Finedon to Wellingborough road when he saw it.

"It was delta shaped — like a 'V'. It was enormous and had two huge white searchlights at the front with a green light behind," he said.

He got out of his car and several motorists behind him did the same.

Mr Batley added: "One woman was really panicking and I was terrified.

"The object was making a

thin whining noise. It was stationary for about five minutes and then zoomed off."

Taxi driver Mr Victor Angers is also convinced he saw an alien craft on Saturday evening.

He was travelling from Higham Ferrers on the A45 towards Sanders Lodge with a fare, Malcolm Young, when they spotted something in the sky.

Mr Angers, of Milton Street, Higham, said they pulled into the side of th road opposite Skew Brie Ski Club to look at the object hovering three or four hundred feet above.

"We wondered why it wasn't making any noise. We thought at first it might have been a jump jet or something

but it would have been making a horrendous noise if it had been a normal aircraft," he said.

The UFO then moved off, accelerating towards Higham.

This is the second time in less than two years that a UFO has been seen near the ski club. Staff there reported a sighting in December, 1976.

Members of Corby's Kingswood Community Association football team were just finishing a training session on Friday evening when they claim they saw a UFO.

According to team member Mr Jimmy Middleton they saw a line of different coloured flashing lights.

"It was far too big to be an aeroplane," he said.

"The object moved very slowly from Weldon towards Beanfield. It took at least seven minutes to disappear. There were 16 of us who saw it at about 7 pm."

Several sightings were reported the previous weekend — but they turned out to be nothing more sinister than four light aircraft from Sibson airfield, near Oundle.

However a spokesman for the airfield said there was no night flying on Saturday.

He dismissed all talk of UFOs and said sightings were more likely to be shooting stars.

The spokesman said: "There are a lot of cranks about and many people imagine half of what they see," he said.

## 11th July 1976 – UFO landing, Wisconsin

At Egg Harbor, Door County, Wisconsin, Dean Anderson was cutting grass on a golf course under the bright full moon, at 3.30am, when he noticed two round 'discs' *"coming off the moon"* side by side. One flew off; the other dropped down and landed 200 yards away. A ladder appeared at the side and three 'figures' ran quickly down it, after which Anderson, heard *"pounding coming from under the 'ship', toward the back"*.

A few minutes later, the 'figures' ran back up the ladder – which was hauled back in. The 'men' were five feet, eight inches, to six feet tall and very agile. Three landing 'balls' or spheres on the UFO left depressions 2two feet deep and 15 inches wide, 20 feet apart.

The witness took photographs of these indentations. (**Source: Keta Steebs,** *Sturgeon Bay Advocate*)

## 13th July 1976 – Two silver UFOs over Dagenham

Irene Georgina Howard (58), of Fanshawe Crescent, Dagenham, was walking along Halbutt Street, at 11.20am, when she saw a helicopter passing overhead. Nothing unusual about that – except that in another part of the sky was two unmoving, silver cigar-shaped objects. Five seconds later, they vanished from sight. (**Source: Ron West**)

## 15th July 1976 – Three black triangular UFOs sighted – witness intimidation

A family was travelling on Freeway 84 at Cave Junction, Oregon, during the afternoon, when they noticed what at first they described as *"funny looking airplanes"* north of their location. The father described the objects as:

> *"...three black triangular-shaped craft above the other side of the river gorge, heading our way."*

Suddenly the car engine stopped working, including the dash lights, radio, CB, etc. The driver then coasted to the side of the road, curious as to what was going on. His next memory was of standing in front of the car, wondering what he was doing there.

> *"My wife and kids were looking at me from inside the vehicle with a confused look on their faces.*
>
> *I got back into the car and everything was now working fine."*

### Mysterious stranger appears

The family, dazed and disorientated, stopped at a roadside diner. While the father sat down eating a hamburger, the hair on the back of his neck stood up – as if someone was behind him. He turned around and saw a man sitting two tables away, not eating but just staring at the family.

Sensing danger, the father stood up and walked over to the stranger – who was described as thin, with olive-brown skin, coal black hair, and beady eyes framed by bushy-black eyebrows, and pointed chin, wearing black shoes, suit and a white shirt.

He asked the stranger: *"May I help you with something?"*

He shot back crisply: *"Where are you going?"*

Feeling very uneasy, the witness answered: *"I am going to take the family down to Fossil and see the sights"*.

The stranger then replied in a low but distinct voice: *"Do not go down there … things bigger than houses come in over the tops of the trees."*

### Three hours of missing time

With that he stood up and went out of the door. Stunned, the witness went back to his table and discussed the events of the day, when it dawned on him now that somehow they were unable to account for three hours of time, followed by the encounter with this weird stranger.

### Drove away in a black car

They all then saw him drive very slowly by the side glass door of the diner, in a very black, highly polished utility truck, just staring at them as he passed by. Afraid, the family drove quickly on Highway 97 when, suddenly, a large black car passed them – like if they were standing still – with the same face looking at them as he passed (the witness was driving at 65 miles per hour) and the strange black car was quickly out of sight.

Everyone in the car became quite upset again. The witness then accelerated up to 80 miles per hour to leave the area, but the strange black car with the stern face passed by them again. In a panic, the family went looking for a place with other people around and drove towards Deschutes State Park, just ahead.

As they made a quick right turn they saw, standing on the side of the road, the same strange man. They camped at the location overnight, but never saw the stranger again. Their car never functioned correctly after the incident. (**Source:** NUFORC)

## 17th July 1976 – Curved UFO over Kent

During the afternoon of 17th July 1976, Mrs Hedge – a resident of Bexleyheath, in Kent, and a neighbour of Margaret Fry – saw what she took to be an aircraft, moving over the suburb. Suddenly, 'it' exploded in mid-air. Frightened, she ran into the house to alert her husband and telephone the authorities, fearing the worst. When she came back outside, she was astonished to see what she regarded as:

> "…one of the strangest things I have ever seen in my life – a long curved 'arm', salmon pink in colour, motionless in the sky, one side of which was the same width along its outer edge, attached to a regular box-like grid; the other side of the 'arm' ended in another box-like section. It then began to rotate slowly, allowing us to take note of the 'revolutions' every 15 minutes – until it finally moved away, some hours later."

## Mr Michael Knighton … Message received telepathically

Another high-profile witness to inexplicable phenomenon, during 1976, was former Carlisle Football Club Chairman – Michael Knighton, who kept quiet about his UFO sighting for twenty years, until appearing in a programme organised by *Central TV* about UFOs with former British Airways Pilot – Graham Shepherd, on 21st November 2003, when he admitted to having received a message telepathically to the effect – "*Don't be afraid, Michael*".

## Soccer chief who saw UFO is under the moon

By Nigel Bunyan

A MILLIONAIRE soccer club chairman threatened to resign yesterday after being "publicly humiliated" over his bizarre account of a UFO sighting.

For 20 years Michael Knighton, 45, who owns 90 per cent of Carlisle United, thought he had kept the lid on the most astonishing event of his life.

True, he and his wife, Rosemary, had watched an apparently alien craft perform a range of "impossible" aero-gymnastics as they set off from their Yorkshire home one afternoon in 1976.

And, also true, as the glowing UFO disappeared into the stratosphere, he believed he had received a telepathic message urging him: "Don't be afraid, Michael." But, as a

businessman, he realised how he might be treated if the press ever got hold of the story.

Unfortunately for Mr Knighton, he hinted at his close encounter while at a meeting of the Aetherius Society, an organisation dedicated to studying metaphysics.

A local reporter questioned him in more detail and a front-page report duly appeared in the *West Cumbrian News and Star* under the headline, "Knighton: Aliens Spoke To Me."

Mr Knighton was not so much glowing as incandescent. Despite the newspaper's assertion that he was sufficiently co-operative to draw a sketch of the craft in the reporter's notebook, he

**KNIGHTON: ALIENS SPOKE TO ME**

The front-page article that upset Mr Knighton

*... Close encounter of the third*

maintains that the disclosure was made during an off-the-record conversation.

"I feel deeply betrayed," he said. "This was a very private story and I made it perfectly clear to the reporter that it was not for publication.

"The damage has been done now and so I've decided to resign at the end of the

season. I have a nine-year-old son and it's not fair for him to be ridiculed."

He still cannot explain his "wonderful" UFO experience. "It was quite extraordinary," he said. "This object fell out of the sky, starting off as a tiny dot like a shooting star but it was unbelievable.

"It changed from an inverted V to a huge metallic disc the size of half a football pitch. We watched it perform the most unbelievable aero-acrobatics in silence."

Mr Knighton and his wife watched the display for 30 minutes, watching with "two men walking their dog". Although they later read reports of a similar sighting, they decided against informing the authorities.

"My wife was quite overawed by what we saw and she

would not like to experience it again. I was totally enthralled."

The *News and Star* has now followed its "Aliens speak" story with a campaign to persuade Mr Knighton to stay.

In a front-page article, Keith Sutton, the editor, tendered an "unreserved" apology. He said: "Just because Michael Knighton has seen a UFO doesn't disqualify him from being a football club chairman."

Last night Mr Knighton said he would re-consider his decision.

"Perhaps it has been an overreaction on my part, which is a bad sign. I don't get uptight about things but I did feel betrayed," he said.

Mr Knighton hinted that he might stay as chairman but appoint a new chief executive.

East

*19 NOV 1997 DAILY TELEGRAPH*

The Times - London

19 NOV 1996

# Aliens cause downfall of soccer chief

### BY PAUL WILKINSON

THE chairman and chief executive of Carlisle United Football Club is stepping down after a newspaper disclosed his belief that aliens spoke to him from their spacecraft above the M62.

Michael Knighton thinks that no one will take him seriously after details of what has since been dubbed "a close encounter of the Third Division kind" were published in the *Carlisle News & Star* under the headline "Knighton: Aliens spoke to me". He said: "I am not prepared to have my nine-year-old son Rory taunted with, 'Your dad speaks to ET.' I can see the funny side to it, but there is also a serious side and it is a great shame."

Keith Sutton, editor of the *News & Star*, said he was now starting a campaign to keep Mr Knighton at the club. "The fact that he sighted a UFO on the M62 doesn't disqualify him from being the chairman. He has done a lot for the city and the club."

The newspaper said that Mr Knighton, who counts David Icke, the sports presenter turned mystic, among his friends, made the claims at a conference of UFO experts in Carlisle. But he claimed that he had told the story in the strictest confidence. Its publication was the latest in a long-running dispute with the newspaper. "This story was the last straw. I know they are going to say there is no campaign or hidden agenda, but they were completely out of order." he said.

The sighting happened in 1977 as he was driving on the M62 with his wife, Rosemary, and saw strange lights in the sky. The paper quoted him as saying: "The bright dot became a triangle and shot down from the sky at an incredible speed. It then turned into a glowing disc which hovered above a petrol station at about the height of Nelson's Column. It was amazing." They watched the light for about 30 minutes.

Then, moments before the shape sped off, he heard a voice inside his head which told him: "Michael, don't be afraid." He said: "I was so excited. It was just the most incredible experience. For seven years after that I spent time UFO-spotting. I just wish I could come in contact again."

Mr Knighton, 45, a property millionaire, was previously known for his unsuccessful attempt to buy Manchester United in 1989, when he was photographed juggling a football on the Old Trafford pitch. He failed to secure backers for his £40 million bid.

Mr Knighton has received dozens of messages from Carlisle supporters asking him to reconsider. One, Karen Reay, said: "It is unbelievable that he is leaving over this. I hope he will change his mind when he cools down. I'm pretty sure we are the only club in history to lose a chairman to aliens."

But Mr Knighton said the newspaper story had been "one headline too far". He added: "I have said I am leaving and I will leave. Maybe it is time for a change. I have turned this club around. My own company, Knighton Holdings, has invested £3.5 million in Carlisle United." The team, which is at home to Cambridge United tonight, is fourth in the Third Division.

Knighton showing his ball-juggling skills at Old Trafford in 1989

Unfortunately for Mr Knighton (rather naively), he allowed himself to be interviewed by a journalist on the promise that it would be 'off the record'; hence the front page spread, published the following day in the *West Cumbrian News & Star* – 'Knighton Aliens spoke to me'.

Mr Knighton felt betrayed and decided to resign at the end of the season, being concerned about the effect it would have on his then nine-year-old son, fearing the inevitable ridicule that would be directed against him and his family.

However, following an apology published by the *West Cumbrian News and Star* on the front page editorial, unreservedly apologising to Mr Knighton, he said he would now reconsider his decision to resign.

Sunday Express
Nov. 17. 1996

**NEWS 3**

THREAT: Knighton

# The soccer chairman who talks to aliens

### by REBECCA HOLMES

MILLIONAIRE football club chairman Michael Knighton has spoken of the night he came face to face with a UFO.

The Carlisle United boss claims aliens communicated with him telepathically and that he was overwhelmed with a sense of well-being.

And he admits that he longs for the day when his UFO returns.

"It was so utterly fascinating, so inexplicable, such a wonderful piece of technology that I wanted to meet the creators."

Mr Knighton, 45, first disclosed his secret encounter during a private conversation with a local journalist. He claims his words were off the record and says he was disgusted when the paper printed the story.

Now he is threatening to resign as chairman of the club because of the breach of confidentiality.

Last night father-of-three Mr Knighton spoke freely to the Express of his experience, which happened in 1977 as he and wife Rosemary were driving to Edinburgh.

"We must have just stood there watching it for about 30 minutes. We were enthralled."

And it seems that something magical touched his whole team yesterday.

Carlisle romped to a 6-0 FA Cup win against Shepshed Dynamo.

## Pass Notes

# No 924: Michael Knighton

**Age:** 45.

**Appearance:** Ian Beale after years of steroid abuse.

**Job:** Chairman of Carlisle United, the most northerly football club in the English league. Notorious self-publicist.

**Why is he in the news?** Claims he made contact with extra-terrestrial creatures, none of them a football manager.

**Is he serious?** He was when he spoke to a reporter off the record after attending a UFO conference at a Carlisle hotel. He claimed that he and his wife Rose-mary-Anne saw the spaceship as they were driving along the M62 to Edinburgh in 1977.

**And what happened next?** A local paper — not the Daily Planet — splashed the story under the headline "Knighton: Aliens spoke to me".

**I think this needs a bit more explanation . . .** According to the Carlisle News & Star, Knighton said he spotted strange lights from the spaceship. A bright dot became a triangle, and shot down from the sky at an incredible rate. It then turned into a glowing disk which hovered above a petrol station at about the height of Nelson's Column. Then the aliens made contact via a strange voice within his head.

**And said what?** "Michael, don't be afraid".

**In which language?** Soccerspeak.

**Has it left a lasting impression?** Yes. Michael has spent the last seven years UFO-spotting. Well, there's not much else to do in Carlisle.

**How did he react to his hobby being made public?** Not exactly over the moon, Brian. "I'm not prepared to have my nine-year-old son taunted with: 'Your dad speaks to ET'." Has threatened to quit the club. Even more bizarrely, he confirmed that the story was true: he *did* see an alien craft and he *did* hear voices. It was just that headline. Made him out to be some sort of nutter.

**Previous history?** Another voice once told him he could take over Manchester United amid huge publicity. He even juggled a ball on the pitch at Old Trafford before a game. Unfortunately, there was a slight liquidity problem.

**You mean he didn't have the dosh?** More a temporary funding shortfall situation. There he was, looking under the mattress for the spondoolies to take over the biggest club in the country, when someone pulled the plug on the deal. He claims he provided the blueprint for Manchester United's phenomenal commercial success.

**So he went off and ploughed all his money into Carlisle?** Yup — £4.5 million, he says.

**Pound notes or Dalek dirhams?** You'd better ask his accountant.

**Not to be confused with:** Homer Simpson (abducted by aliens).

**Most likely to say:** "Beam us up Scottie, we're fed up with life in the Third Division."

**Least likely to say:** "Hello, is that the News & Star? I've got a scoop for you . . ."

## The sighting

In 1976, Mr Knighton and his wife – Rosemary, happened to stop off to make a telephone call near the M62 Pennine Motorway. While doing this they noticed a tiny 'dot' – like a Shooting star in the sky – which suddenly dropped downwards.

> *"It changed from an inverted 'V' to a huge metallic 'disc' – the size of a football pitch and-a-half. We then watched it perform the most unbelievable aerobatics in silence."*

Mr and Mrs Knighton and their colleague were not the only witnesses. Two men, out walking their dogs, also watched the UFO 'display' for over 30 minutes.

Mrs Knighton said she was quite overawed by what they had seen and didn't want to experience it again.

The *Halifax Evening Courier* (22.11.96), published a report by Geoffrey Smith of Claremount Road, Halifax, who told of sighting a UFO over 20 years ago, which he believes may well have been the same evening as the sighting made by Mr Knighton.

> *"I was on my way to work, as a maintenance engineer at the former Crosrol factory in Pellon Lane, Halifax, when I saw this 'thing' hovering over the* Golden Pheasant *Public House, in Pelton New Road. It looked just like a cross – then it disappeared.*
>
> *I kept quiet about what I had seen until I read about Mr Knighton's sighting, and decided to come forward."*

**(Source: Personal interview)**

28 NOV 1996    Cumberland Evening News & Star

# Terrestrial show out of this world

**CHIP'S CHAT**

THANKS to my ring of spies, I have watched a video of Michael Knighton speaking on Central TV on Friday night about UFOs. (Thanks for taping it, mum!)

Michael Knighton started the show by telling the studio audience about his close encounter, as reported in the *News & Star* a couple of Saturdays ago.

The host Nicky Campbell, a Radio One presenter, asked Michael Knighton if what he saw was natural.

**Michael Knighton:** "I am not a sci-fi buff at all. I am the most cynical, rational person you would hope to meet."

**Nicky Campbell:** "You are a multi-millionaire, so you must have a few brain cells."

**Michael Knighton:** "I had this wonderful feeling of well-being. I wanted to be with it and know more about it. I did hear in my mind the words, 'Michael, don't be afraid'."

Next, Nicky Campbell brought in Professor Heinz Wolff, the bloke off *The Great Egg Race* on BBC2 – you remember?

The Prof put it to Michael Knighton that the human mind can make up almost anything. Michael Knighton replied that his wife and another man saw the UFO too, at 4pm in summer.

"I believed it was a different realm of physics. For me it was an inter-galactic machine."

Then came ex-pilot Graham Sheppard who saw a disc-shaped craft in 1967, and Dave Davies of the Kinks, who, on tour in America in 1982, had an experience in his hotel room. He did not help his case by adding that he had not taken drugs since the 1970s.

### MESSAGE

Alas, some berks in the audience got a look in. One man asked why aliens showed themselves to Michael Knighton: why not the Queen? (Yes, her majesty is really going to devote her Christmas message to the day she had a Martian to tea!)

We had a man insuring people against alien abductions ("our aim is to separate the feeble-minded from their money") and a man who reckoned he had been kidnapped by aliens, "I saw a brief glimpse of an alien," he said.

**Nicky Campbell:** "What did it look like?"

"A typical alien," he replied. Everybody laughed. Dave Davies put another word in – that he is sure aliens are on the planet, among us.

**Nicky Campbell:** "The last word has got to go to Michael Knighton."

"Are you happy, are you relaxed about the fact that you are going to go through the rest of your life knowing that certain people accept it, but others say, you're a nutter, mate?"

**Michael Knighton:** "Absolutely. The point is, for me, the experience was real. I don't know what it was. I believe the only logical explanation – it was something out of this world, completely. (Talking faster all the time.)

"I felt privileged, I would love to have another experience."

(Talking about some other speakers) "I have heard a lot of unbelievable arrogance. I would ask those people to simply open their eyes to the 10,000

billion galaxies out there – and to say that we are the only intelligent life forces in this entire universe is, frankly, absolutely outrageous."

Michael Knighton came across well, when he could easily have looked a fool (and plenty of people on that show did.)

You notice that Michael Knighton kept saying it was what he believes. It does come down to belief – are we alone, is there a God?

Not all that long ago you got laughed at if you doubted the earth was flat.

**Diary dates:** Carlisle United supporters' club is running two more forums: tonight at Stanwix Holiday Centre, Greenrow, Silloth; and tomorrow at Penrith Cricket Club.

Each meeting starts at 7.30pm. Entry is £1 for club members, £1.50 for non-members.

**Chip's chips:** In the Tesco restaurant at Rosehill fish and chips are £3.49. Yet in June I reported fish, chips and baked beans and a pot of tea there were £2.78!

If anybody wants to watch the Michael Knighton video, send me your address and I will pass it to my mum. Feel free to tape over it.

**CHIP ROWE**

**I saw UFO, too!**

Nicky Campbell: Studio date with Knighton

Dave Davies: Experience in a hotel room on tour

Picture: ALAN BARTON

*Looking out ... Mr Geoffrey Smith and inset: A sketch of what he saw*

**By NICK DRAINEY**

A HALIFAX man has spoken of his own extraordinary extraterrestrial experience after soccer chairman Mr Michael Knighton saw a UFO above Calderdale.

Mr Geoffrey Smith, 62, of Claremount Road, Halifax, described today how he had spotted a strange shape in the sky at the same time as the Carlisle United supremo 20 years ago.

Mr Knighton threatened to resign earlier this week following newspaper reports of his sighting which he said had ridiculed him.

On his way to work the night-shift as a maintenance engineer at the former Crosrol factory, Pellon Lane, Halifax, Mr Smith saw the unexplained phenomena above the Golden Pheasant pub, Pellon New Road, Halifax.

"I saw this thing hovering around above the pub, it looked like a cross," he said.

"It just disappeared fast. I do not know what it was but it wasn't a shooting star, definitely."

Mr Smith said he had kept quiet about his sighting since but decided to speak out now in support of Mr Knighton.

"What I would like to do is put this chap's mind at rest because everybody thinks he is

going round the twist. If somebody else has seen it, it will look good for him."

A woman was also reported in the "Evening Courier" seeing a similar object in November 1976 above Hanson Lane, Halifax.

"I should have reported it then as well. At least if two people had seen it, it would have been more believable," said Mr Smith. "But when I got to work and told the lads they said it was a load of rubbish."

Mr Smith said he had not seen any other UFOs since the eerie moment 20 years ago.

## July 1976 – Saucer-shaped UFO over Lancashire

During the English heat wave of July 1976, a housewife from Lancaster Road, Hindley, was unable to sleep and stood at her bedroom window, watching a 'star' that seemed bigger and brighter than the others.

*"Suddenly, a beam of light shot out of the 'star' and a bronze coloured saucer-shaped object – as big as two houses – appeared and hovered above the houses across the road. As quickly as it appeared, it vanished in a second beam of light – back towards the same 'star'."* (**Source: Bill Eatock**)

## 22nd July 1976 – Hexagonal UFO over Germantown, Wisconsin

At 10.50pm, a hexagonal object with a flat bottom was seen hovering over the highway, for five minutes, showing a red flame coming from its base. Four or five lights were seen on the front and a green light on one end, red on the other. (**Source:** *CUFOS News Bulletin*, **September 1976, page 6**)

## 26th July 1976 – Bell-shaped UFO sighted over Kentucky

Jimmy Hooper (13), Max Hooper (12), Joe Hooper (8), Mike Braswell (13), and Gary Januchowski (14), decided to camp out on Sunday night in a wooded area, about a mile from the (Jim) Hooper home on Route 1, Reynolds Station, which is situated a mile and-a-half south of Patesville.

After arriving, at 8pm, in a small valley located in the 200 acre forest as their campsite, they found an open area, some 30 yards in diameter, and built a large fire to cook their evening meal. The supper was finished some time later, then the fire was banked and the teenagers retired to bed. Ten large hickory trees, estimated to be fifty feet tall, ringed the camping area.

There was no moon and no light visible in any direction. The stars were out and shone brightly, so they started looking for various constellations – Orion, The Hunter, in particular. The youngest, Joe Hooper, observed at least two "shooting stars", which cut white trails across the night sky.

### Bell-shaped UFO sighted

Around 11pm, one of the boys glimpsed a bright, glowing, bell-shaped object, travelling at fantastic speed in an east-to-west direction, at an estimated altitude of about 450 to 550 feet. He called the attention of the other campers to the object sighted. Five to eight minutes later, the 'craft' was seen again, going in the opposite direction from west-to-east. After a time lapse of equal duration, the object made still a third pass over the camping area.

By the third time, every one of the boys had seen the object at least once. They agreed it was a glowing, golden colour, that it maintained an altitude of 450-500 feet, and travelled at incredible speed. They described it as emitting *"sparkles"* from the rear as it traversed the sky. It was in a flat trajectory – almost horizontal in flight rather than an arc, as most meteorites follow when falling.

All the boys admitted they were frightened at the sight of the bell-shaped object. One of the older ones said they seriously considered breaking camp and going home. The youngest said he was so scared after the third appearance that he burrowed under his sleeping bag so he wouldn't see it if it came back.

They returned to the Hooper home on Monday morning, at 10:30am, and recounted the story to their parents, who encouraged them to contact the *Clarion*.

In the course of a subsequent interview, Mike Braswell recalled that he and Natalie Rosenblatt had sighted an identical object at Windward Heights, four nights before, on Wednesday, 21st July. Its direction was toward the country club – a westerly course.

The group remembered later, that all the insect noises – (crickets, Katydids, etc.) – in the camping area ceased, as the object passed overhead. Gary Januchowski's mother, Pat, on Tuesday morning, declared that her family had observed a similar object to what the boys reported for the past 18 months. She said they had spotted it three times, and the description given matched the one her family members gave. (**Source:** *Hancock County Clarion*, **Kentucky, 29.7.1976**)

## 28th July 1976 – Domed 'disc' over Blueberry Mountain

Fourteen boys and their camp counsellor – Mr Leifer, from Camp Delaware, were out hiking, at 3.45pm on July 28th on Blueberry Mountain, three miles south-west of Winsted, Connecticut. They were astonished to see:

*"...a shiny, metallic domed 'disc', hovering over their heads, making a high-pitched whine – like the feedback from a loudspeaker".*

A second 'whine' was accompanied by a high-speed vertical ascent. Within seconds, the UFO had vanished by shooting straight up in the sky. (**Source:** *International UFO Reporter,* **November 1976, page 6**)

## 30th July 1976 – Three oblong UFOs sighted

### Location: Fort Ritchie, Maryland.

The National Military Command Centre in Washington DC put out this memo, at **0545 EDT: 1.**At approximately **0345 EDT** the ANMCC (Alternate National Military Command Center) called to indicate they had received several reports of UFOs in the vicinity of Fort Ritchie.

The following events summarize the reports (times are approximate).

**0130** – Civilians reported a UFO sighting near Mt. Airy Md. This information was obtained via a call from the National Aeronautics Board (?) to Fort Richie Military Police.

**0255** – Two separate patrols from Site R reported sighting 3 oblong objects with a reddish tint, moving east to west. Personnel were located at separate locations on top of the mountain at Site R.

**0300** – Desk Sgt. at Site R went to the top of the Site R Mountain and observed a UFO over the ammo storage area at 100-200 yards altitude.

**0345** – An Army Police Sgt. on the way to work at Site R reported sighting a UFO in the vicinity of Site R. 2. ANMCC was requested to have each individual write a statement on the sightings. One individual stated the object was about the size of a 2 1/2 ton truck.

(**Source: FOIA document**)

## Summer 1976 – UFO over Tilbury- medical ailments follow

Mrs S. Muirhead of Thunderley, Essex, was living at London Road, Tilbury Essex. One of her memories, apart from having to endure the exceptionally hot summer, involved her mother – Mrs Ethel Gatward.

*"My mother was having trouble sleeping, because of the heat in August, and awoke in the early hours of the morning. She went to the window for some air and saw a large silvery coloured cigar-shaped object, flying slowly at some height across the playing fields.*

*As it moved away from her she had a good view and told me it had a ring of blue flames coming from the rear, fanning out into a circle. In an attempt to obtain a better look she opened the window and leant out to watch, as it disappeared over the tops of buildings.*

*She then went back to bed. When she awoke in the morning, she discovered her arm and face were itchy and inflamed. The skin that had been exposed to the air was red, blotchy, and sore for several days."*

(**Source: Personal interview**)

## Summer 1976 – UFO display over Cley Hill, Warminster ... Three orbs seen

David Kingston (now deceased) – a former RAF serviceman, whom we occasionally spoke to over the years, spoke of his sighting of something highly unusual, while 'sky watching' for UFOs on Cley Hill, Warminster, during the summer of 1976.

We appreciate that we have not included any Warminster/Wiltshire reports, as they have been published in the Wiltshire book; having said that, this is an important sighting which illustrates a possible association between UFOs and the creation of a simplistic formation in the crop.

**David:**

*"I saw three separate orbs – approximately six feet in diameter – of coloured light, weaving around and above us for some three hours, on the top of Cley Hill. On occasion they would merge into a single globe and then separate again. Suddenly, one of the orbs descended to some thirty feet above us and then flew down into a field at the base of Cley Hill. As dawn broke, I noticed a flattened circle in a field of wheat. On inspection, there were no broken stalks – just a perfectly flattened circle, some thirty feet in diameter. At that particular point in time I had seen and had knowledge of the famous 'Tulley UFO Nests' in 1966, at Australia, but had not heard of anything of a similar nature in this country"* (**Source: Personal interview**)

David Kingston

## Summer 1976 – Ghostly Quaker, Basildon, Essex

In the summer of this year, Mrs J. Seymour (67) was working in the greenhouse at her family home at 184 Great Gregorie, Basildon, in Essex.

*"I was kneeling down when I heard a voice behind me say, 'Can I help you?' I said 'no thanks' and stood up, expecting to see my husband. Instead I saw a tall thin man, wearing Quaker dress, narrow dark trousers and round, flat, felt hat. This shook me up so I returned to the house, passing my husband, daughter and granddaughter working on the fish pond. I had a smoke – then made a cup of tea. It was several months before I plucked up the courage to go into the greenhouse. Even today [1989] I do not feel at ease in that part of the garden."*

## Summer 1976 – UFO over Worcester

Ian, from Worcester, contacted us some years ago, wishing to bring our attention to something he had witnessed over Hadzor Woods, near Droitwich, during summer 1976:

*"I was watching the TV, when I had a strong feeling I should look out the window. I looked out and saw an object underneath a large cloud formation, travelling at speed, which would have stalled a conventional aircraft. This circular 'disc' appeared to float beneath the cloud formation before changing course and gaining altitude, rotating as it did so, but at an incredibly slow speed. It then disappeared into what looked like an invisible slot in the sky underneath the cloud, rather than entering the cloud."*

## 1976 – Two triangular objects sighted over Wigan school

In October 2017, Mike Gorman contacted Steve Wills – head of the Warminster sky watching website – about his UFO sighting, which took place in 1976.

*"I don't know the month, but I was 8 years-old and in the second year of St. Cuthbert's Junior School, Pemberton, in Wigan. It was a Games lesson and I think we were playing football on an overcast day with a few not a great deal of cloud.*

*Someone called our attention to the sky above us. We observed, and I saw what looked like two silver coloured, triangular objects (on their sides) very slowly moving toward each other. We called this to the attention of our teacher – Mr Dean. He took one brief glance and said that it was simply two planes refuelling. For some reason this didn't seem right to me or, from the looks on their faces, the other pupils. We continued to watch as the objects very slowly moved toward each other. When the tips of the objects seemed about to touch, there was a very brief flash of light and the objects had vanished. We were all amazed by this, except for Mr Dean – who had gone inside and missed the objects' disappearance. I have no idea of the height of the objects, but it seemed to me to be very high."*

### Summer 1976 – UFO over M11 Motorway

Mr Ray Hendy (22) was travelling back in his friend's car down the M11, at 8pm, when they saw an object moving in the sky from the direction of Stansted Airport.

*"We thought it was an airplane but then it swung around and, after circling, dropped down in front of us on the Motorway – low enough to have struck a bridge, if there had been one there in that location. It was a rectangular object with a red light on one corner and four legs, with row of framework in the middle. We observed it for 15 minutes and the other peculiar thing was that we didn't see one single car on our side of the carriageway, or the other side, during the incident."*

**(Source: Dan Goring)**

## CHAPTER 8 – AUGUST 1976

### 2nd August 1976 – Glaring UFO over Essex causes irritation with eyes

Raymond Hammel (13), and his brother – Darren (10), were out playing near their homes at The Upway, Basildon, when they saw a sphere or 'globe' crossing the sky in a westerly direction, at an angle of 30 degrees. A minute later, it shot off towards the north-west, changing colour to red as it did so, leaving a faint trail. Afterwards the boys claimed their eyes watered considerably, due to the glare given off by the object.

### 5th August 1976 – Dome-shaped UFO frightens Essex motorist

Mr Christopher Hines – a farm worker of Lexden, near Colchester – was driving his scooter along Halstead Road, at 10.45pm, when he saw a circle of 30-40 lights in a line, hovering some distance in front of him.

*"As I continued on my journey, I saw they were candle-shaped, pale blue in colour, and on top of them was what looked like a large dome. When only some 200 yards away from them, I panicked and drove into someone's front garden and hid there for a few minutes. When I returned to the road, the lights had gone."*

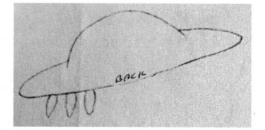

**(Source: Bob Easton, RIC for BUFORA)**

### 7th August 1976 – UFO over London

Mrs McLaughlin (37) of Hartington Road, London, was in the back garden, burning rubbish, at 11pm, when she noticed:

*"…a half-moon turned upside-down object, with a beam around, hanging motionless over St. James Park, some 900 feet away."*

Excited, she called her husband – John, who came running out, by which time it was still in the same position but tipping slightly from side-to-side. The UFO then moved towards the house and passed overhead – last seen heading along the High Street, before vanishing from view minutes later.

## 10th August 1976 – UFO over Southsea

At 10pm, Mrs C. Parker of Dunsmore Close, Southsea, opened the back door to let the dog out when she saw:

*"…a very bright orange 'light', moving across the sky at speed. Five or ten seconds later it disappeared, followed by an explosion or bang. I then saw a trail of smoke in the sky in the direction the object had taken.*

*I telephoned my mother and was telling her about it, when my sister arrived home and told me she had also seen it.*

*I contacted the police, at Havant, who told me I was the eleventh person to notify them about this. They reassured me it wasn't an aircraft which had crashed."*

**(Source: Nick Maloret, WATSUP)**

## 14th August 1976 – Three objects sighted

Gillian Goring (20) – the sister of our esteemed colleague, Dan Goring, living at Carlton Terrace, Great Cambridge Road, London N18 – was sat in the front room, listening to the record player, when she saw:

*"…a bright 'light' out of the window. It rose up and suddenly became three brilliant lights. They rose higher and then went out. The object moved a little way, before disappearing near to a street lamp."*

Apparently, her mother also witnessed this incident.

5/8/76

### Special day for UFO watchers

UNIDENTIFIED flying object enthusiasts are keeping their fingers crossed that Saturday will not be the day extra terrestrial beings decide to land in Cleveland in large numbers …

For all the county's UFO fans will be crammed into Middlesbrough's Dorman Museum for the first ever seminar on their studies organised by Middlesbrough Borough Council's Recreation and Amenities Department.

The seminar, entitled "Phenomena of Earth and Sky", has been organised to coincide with the only public showing in the North-east of an exhibition of prehistoric Peruvian ground drawings which have baffled scientists despite 35 years research by a German woman, Maria Reiche, who has become a living legend.

The drawings stretch for miles over flat desert, 250 miles south of the Peruvian capital of Lima, in straight lines and outlines of animals, birds and plants.

One theory is that they were constructed before the Birth of Christ to guide in visitors from other planets.

Museum curator Mr. Cliff Thornton said the exhibition of photographs, will open for two weeks before returning to its base in Munich.

"We have organised the seminar because increasing public attention is being focused on these unexplained phenomena and we want to give people the chance to come and see, listen and ask questions" he said.

Among those taking part in the day long seminar organised with the help of the Cleveland UFO Research Group will be Redcar UFO watcher, Mr. Dave Mc-Groarty, and Mr. E. S. Hay, of Eston, who has made a study of geometrical patterns involved in tumuli or ancient burial sites on the North York Moors.

## 15th August 1976 – UFO over creek bed, Indiana

At 10.55pm a woman living in Connersville, Indiana, heard a noise like a vacuum cleaner sound, for a couple of minutes' duration. Curious, she and her family went to investigate and saw a wide band of white light in the creek bed under trees off Harrisburg road.

A glowing white, oval, object was seen to slowly rise up and fly away to the north-east, changing to dark oval – now displaying white, green and red lights, revolving around its edge or middle. The woman told of seeing a 'hump' on the top. (**Source: Lucas Worley files**)

## Other sightings for the middle of August 1976

Although the actual date is not known, we were to come across a number of sightings that took place around the middle of August 1977. The first involved Mr T. Robson of Ambleside Crescent, Enfield, Middlesex. He was lying out in the back garden on what was a very hot night, at 11.15pm, when his wife shouted out – *"Look at that falling star!"* He said:

*"I looked up and saw an object zigzagging through the sky. Suddenly it stopped and turned red, carried on a little way, zigzagged, changed to red again, and headed off at great speed towards the east 30 seconds later."*

In conversation with Mr Robson, he admitted that he had seen a UFO once before, in November 1950, while in the Army.

> *"There were about 200 of us working outside the cookhouse at Bicester, near Oxford. It was 4.30pm, when we looked up to see a cigar-shaped object – the size of an airship – glowing in the sky, hovering over us at a height of about 2,000 feet, as if observing us.*
>
> *It then made off at great speed. This was reported to the Army."*

Ray Hendy (22), was driving through Walthamstow High Street, near Coppermill Lane, at 11pm, in the middle of August 1976, with a Mr Richardson, when he saw two strange 'lights' over a building, but lost sight of them. A short time later, on his way back, he saw what appears to be the same 'lights', hovering about 50 feet off the ground, over the pumping station at Warwick reservoir.

### Three UFOs sighted

Roy Edwards (38) of Daventry Gardens, Harold Hill, Romford, Essex, was in is garden getting some fresh air, after wrestling all day with a plumbing problem, when at 11.30pm he saw:

> *"...three blue and dark silver egg-shaped 'discs', with grey centres, motionless in the sky very close to each other. By the time I had run into the house to fetch binoculars, they had gone."*

Some of the sightings appeared to have been centred over Coppermill Lane, Walthamstow. It was said that a number of people gathered there nightly, armed with telescopes and binoculars, hoping to catch sight of the UFOs that were plaguing the area.

(Source: Essex UFO Study Group, Dan Goring)

## 1976 – UFOs over Kent

In August of this year, Miss Clare Miller – a nurse by occupation from Orpington Hospital, Kent – was being driven over the Medway bridge (towards the direction of Rochester), by her boyfriend – Paul Whittaker, at about 6.30pm, when their attention was drawn to a peculiar object hovering close to the top of a nearby building, close to Rochester Town Hall.

> *"At first I took it to be an airship, but as I couldn't see any means of propulsion, portholes, or identification mark, I asked my boyfriend to stop the car so I could get a closer look. I leaned over the side of the bridge and saw a dull grey coloured object, metallic in appearance – the body of which was covered in lots of bolts and rivets."* (**Source: Margaret Fry**)

## 16th August 1976 – 'Ball of white light' over pylon

Ex-RAF flight crew – George Foster (64), of 29 Southbourne Grove, Southend-on-Sea, was driving along the A127 road, returning home, at 8pm.

> *"I saw a 'ball of white light' – the size of a tennis ball – travelling very slowly through the air on my right-hand side. I stopped and saw that the 'ball of light' was now stationary in the air over a pylon. I was about to get back in the car when it suddenly glowed brighter, with an orange tint, and then shot straight upwards in the sky and was lost from sight."* (**Source: Ron West**)

## 18th August 1976 – Object over Middlesex

Stephen Robert Delaforce from Kettering Road, Enfield, in Middlesex, was travelling home from East Finchley as a passenger in a car being driven by his friend – Richard Hall, of Carnarvon Avenue, at

11.10pm. As they turned into Creighton Avenue, East Finchley, they noticed a cluster of red and white lights in the sky, around an object low down in the sky.

*"As the car proceeded on its journey, we seemed adjacent to the lights. I first thought it was a helicopter on account of its shape.*

*The lights seemed stationary in the sky. We decided to stop the car and pull into a small lay-by. By this time it had moved and was heading westwards."* (**Source: Essex UFO Study Group**)

## UFOs over Worcestershire

During the same year, Mr Trevor Jones from St. Johns, Worcester, was getting ready for bed when he was disturbed by the sound of cats fighting outside.

*"I opened the window to look out and was astonished to see one of the strangest 'craft' I had ever seen in my life, slowly moving through the night sky, just above rooftop level. The exterior of this UFO appeared solid and was a dark brown rusty colour, showing a distinct circle of white lights constantly changing in colour from white, yellow, red, orange, to purple, on its underside. The main 'body' of the craft had a flat end, curling inwards. Within a few minutes, the whole of the 'craft' became transparent – although the outer edge could still be seen before it became lost from view, as it headed over the town."* (**Source: Personal interview**)

Rachel Smith was a pupil at Chase High School, Malvern, during the late 1970s. She contacted us, after learning we were looking for people who had witnessed sightings of UFOs in the Worcestershire area.

*"I was in the playground when I saw an orange 'ball of light' with a distinctive matt finish, rather than gloss. It rolled across the sky, as you would roll a ball along the ground. It had a number of flat edges around its perimeter and was segmented in the middle.*

*I last saw it heading towards the Radar Establishment, before losing sight of it."*

Rachel was not the only pupil at the school to see something unusual. We were contacted separately by two other people, who told of sighting a *dome-shaped object*, hovering over the Radar Establishment at Malvern, one particular afternoon. Both of them individually described the exterior surface of the UFO as looking like the *old-fashioned 'grainy' effect,* similar to the swirled finish on stainless steel pans.

A few miles from Malvern, Susan Meredith – a young housewife from Tunnel Hill, Worcester – was fetching in the washing, at about 9.30pm, when she became aware of coloured lights flashing behind her.

*"Puzzled as to where this source of illumination was originating from, I turned around and was staggered to see a bright silver saucer- shaped object, with a 'hump', or 'dome' on its top – about the size of a small car – hovering close to the roof of a nearby house.*

*I stood watching, mesmerised – not knowing what to do for the best, as the object began moving very erratically, as if struggling to keep itself up in the air. To my horror it slowly moved towards me, slid past into the wall of the house, and completely disappeared. The following morning, I plucked up the courage to go outside and have a look. I inspected the brickwork, expecting to see burn marks. There was nothing. It was almost as if it had never happened."*

### 18th August 1976 – Family sight 'Flying Saucer'

At 8.30pm, a family of four were motoring about 30 miles outside of Orlando, in Florida, when they noticed a saucer-shaped object, hovering silently, approximately 1,000 yards away over their vehicle. The driver – an amateur pilot – stopped his car and opened the windows to obtain a clearer view. The UFO appeared to have a *"dome-shaped red light on the top and white window-like lights around it"*.

They were unable to transmit or receive on the CB radio, as it malfunctioned – only static was heard.

The UFO was seen to perform movements and turns that would be impossible for conventional 'craft' to perform. They observed the phenomenon for about thirty minutes, before losing sight of the 'craft' behind the tree line.

They drove directly to the nearest town and reported their experience to the local police. The officer told the witnesses that there had been several other reports describing similar craft.

(**Source:** *UFO Investigator*, **September 1976, page 2**)

### 23rd August 1976 – Strange orange 'star'

At 9pm, Joan Smith – 50 from Cheshunt Chalvedon, Basildon, Essex, was leaving her friend's house with her young son. As she did so, she saw what she took to be a star in the sky.

> *"It was bright orange and moving fast. I watched for a few minutes and then it did a semicircle. The 'light' was lost from view as it dropped silently down behind houses."* (**Source: BUFORA**)

### 24th August 1976 – Three UFOs sighted

At 10.05pm, Mrs Angela Stearn (26) of Donald Way, Chelmsford, in Essex, was with two neighbours – Mrs Chunn and Mrs Parker, in Mrs Chunn's back garden (at number 30), when Mrs Stearn told the other two women that she had just seen:

> *"…three 'balls', joined to a rod, float across the sky."*

This was followed by hilarity with comments about a pawnbroker's sign.

As a result of her sighting, she later contacted the Essex UFO Study Group and spoke to Doug Canning – and then later, Bob Easton.

### UFO over Catterick Army Camp

David Pritchard contacted us in October 2017.

> *"I was in the Army, based at Catterick Army Camp, Cambrai Barracks, 5th Royal Inniskilling Dragoon Guards, at the time Royal Armoured Corps Training Regiment.*
>
> *On the afternoon of the sighting, I had returned to my barrack block, which was right on the perimeter of the camp looking over the moors. "I had the urge to look out of the window – not just out, but to twist and look upwards to the roof. As I did this a huge, silver, self-illuminated object appeared. The 'cigar' must have been 30 to 40,000 feet up and it was leaving a 'vapour trail'.*

*David Pritchard*

> *Suddenly, about 30 degrees from the horizon, the 'vapour trail' shot back inside the 'cigar' – which then disappeared in a blinding flash.*
>
> *I felt elated that I'd seen a UFO and thought to myself … I'm going out onto the moors to see if I can see anything else … but then had this internal voice saying … 'Don't bother – they are gone'.*
>
> *As a bit of an aftermath, I was working at that time in the officer's mess. One of the jobs was to dish out the daily newspapers, first thing. All the local papers were full of sighting reports from all over the region. This sort of confirmed that my sighting was genuine."*

## August 1976 – Close encounter at Leeds

Encounters with UFOs still continue to excite the imagination of the public right up to the present day. We have lost count of the incredible number of stories and sightings we were to come across over the years, which took place in and around the British Isles.

### 'Our Jessie'

In 2011, we spoke again with our long-term friend, Jessie Roestenberg – a fantastic lady, in her mid 80s, with an infectious sense of humour – who David Sankey and our respective partners, visited a few years ago. She remembers, with great clarity, that monumental experience in October 1954 (see *Haunted Skies Revised Volume 1*) when she saw a 'craft' hovering over a remote farmhouse, which contained human-looking occupants.

This is an incredible story from an incredible woman. It was a privilege to have known Jessie and we certainly had no qualms in accepting her version of events as being absolutely truthful.

## Disc-shaped UFO seen at Leeds

Somebody else who reported a similar experience but with one vital difference – where he entered the 'craft' after being invited in by the occupants – was Leeds garage man, Jan Siedlicki (then aged 65) of

Polish descent, who came to Britain shortly after the Second World War and obtained employment at Brydens Garage, Wellington Road, Leeds – his house being a few hundred yards away.

In August 1976 – a hot and humid month, with England still in the grip of a heat wave – Jan, who had been working late, finished at 1am and locked up. As he did so he noticed heavy summer clouds, which were slightly orange, suggesting the onset of stormy weather.

*Garage*

After arriving home he made himself a cup of tea and went to bed, but found it difficult to sleep – although his wife was fast asleep.

At 2am Jan became aware of an intense light in the bedroom, far brighter than the glow from nearby streetlights. Thinking that his place of work was on fire, Jan ran to the window and looked out across the deserted road towards his garage, and was stunned when he saw:

> "...*a disc-shaped object, moving backwards and forwards, about 15 feet above the ground with lights pouring from underneath the object.*"

*Generator building fence*

### Strange 'figure' seen

Jan dressed and ran across the road towards the object. By the time he had reached a nearby generator building, the dark blue object had apparently landed. Jan crouched down behind a fence, some 75 feet away, and saw that the object was supported by three 'legs'.

> "*Suddenly a brilliant white glowing 'tube' came out from beneath the object. I felt full of fear but remained watching. Two 'figures' appeared, dressed in what appeared to be*

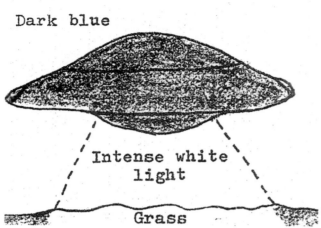

Dark blue

Intense white light

Grass

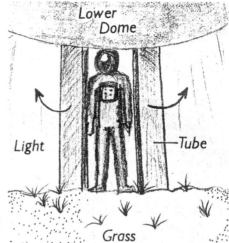

Lower Dome

Light

Tube

Grass

yellow space suits, without any joins (apart from a slight line above the necks) and what I presumed were boots. They also had what looked like two slightly rounded 'square boxes' attached to their chests, covered with several switches (both square and round). They appeared from inside the 'tube' and stood outside.

They sighted me and waved their arms at me, beckoning me to approach closer. I walked towards them. They started to talk in a language completely unknown to me."

### Told that the 'craft' needed repairs

"One of them started to press several switches on his chest and said – in a voice that sounded tinny, like a child's:

'We are in trouble with 'ship'. As soon as repairs are finished, we will be on our way.'

I summoned up my courage and asked them how the 'ship' works. One of them said:

'If you want to come, come' – at which point they entered the 'tube' and rose up into the object. A few seconds later it lowered down again and I entered the 'tube' which rose upwards into the craft, as I felt (although still fearful) that they were not going to harm me. The 'tube' appeared to be made of some kind of hard, very shiny, metal – not unlike highly polished steel. An unusual white light was flooding out of the

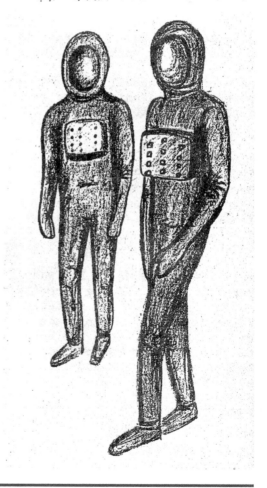

*metal. The 'tube' doors then opened and I stood on what I presumed was the first level and entered the room.*

*A white light poured from all sides of the wall and floor; it was not harmful to my eyes. I realised I was towering over the two 'figures'.*

*I am five feet, six inches tall; they would have been about four feet. I could smell a strange smell, similar to rotting grass. The 'figures' led me up a spiralling ramp; the light was now slightly blue. We entered a room. 'This is a cooling system', one of the beings said. I looked around* the room and saw, around the edge of the room, a two feet channel of flowing water; in the water was what looked like weeds – some two feet tall."

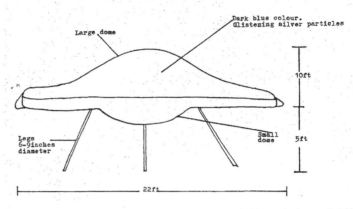

Diagrams projected from witnesses original sketches. Note the seemingly same height from ground level - in relation to the overall height of the object.

**Jan asked:**

*"How did the 'ship' fly?"*

They made no comment. At this point Jan believed they were taking him to the engine room. He asked:

*"How fast could the ship travel?"*

One of the 'figures' replied,: '*B13*'.

Jan was then led into a room without any door. In its dim half light he saw four or five crouching 'figures', with brown hair, wearing black suits. In front of the 'figures' lay a circular pool of fluid (which Jan thought to be oil) from out of which red sparks leapt out.

*"I didn't go inside this room but looked directly above my head and saw a large dome, which I took to be the ceiling. Suddenly, an orange 'ball' began bouncing from side-to-side above my head."*

At this stage Jan heard many footsteps and apparent panic. He turned around to see one of the 'figures', who approached him and said:

*"We have got space bug."*

Jan returned to the first floor and quickly entered the door which led

*The scene of the incident in 1976*

to the tube, left the 'ship', and made his way towards the safety of the electricity generator, where he watched as the object (making a slight whistling sound, which increased in volume) tilted at an angle of 45 degrees, and then moved away at very fast speed. Within seconds it reached the cloud cover. As it did so, a blast of red fire spilled out from its underside.

Jan then went over to where the object had been and noticed how warm it was, and then decided to go home to bed where he tried to wake up his wife – who told him to come to bed.

The matter was later reported to The Yorkshire UFO Society, who published their findings in the *Quest Magazine* (July/August 1984), following an excellent investigation by Mark Birdsall, Mr William Tree, and Mr Paul Swallow. Philip Mantle was also involved in taking photographs of the scene.

YUFOS considered this to be one of the strangest cases they had ever come across, culminating in a 14 pages long file with an additional 23 pages of investigation. Thanks go to Phil Mantle for assisting us in this matter.

We never met Jan. We didn't even know of the incident until a few years ago, when details of the case were found on the internet – which included his real name and correct location, as opposed to the pseudonym and slightly different location published by the 'team of researchers' in the YUFOS magazine. However, time has flowed on and Jan would have passed away by now, but at least his record is preserved for posterity.

### August 1976 – UFO hovers over Essex cornfield

At 7.20pm, towards the end of August 1976, Wendy Barham (20) of Brian Road, Chadwell Heath, Essex, went out into the garden to check on her pet pigeon. While doing this, she casually looked up into the sky and saw:

> "...a large, dull grey spherical object. After about a minute, what looked like a yellow burst of flame came out of the base and formed a horizontal line – like a glowing strip – along the bottom of the UFO. I shouted my brother – Philip, and sister – Christine (29), to come out and have a look. Philip had one look at it and declared it was a balloon and went back inside."

Wendy and Christine continued watching. Over the course of the next few minutes, the object emitted further 'bursts of flames' while remaining stationary; the time was now 7.30pm. The girls then decided to approach the object closer, and ran down Eastern Avenue – where they watched it again, noticing it appeared to be hovering over a cornfield at the side of the road.

> "Every minute or so a bright glow would appear from the bottom of the object and form a glowing horizontal strip. We ran back home to fetch our cameras. By the time we got back, the object was no longer there." (**Source: Barry King**)

## CHAPTER 9 – SEPTEMBER 1977

Early September revealed a flurry of sightings over America. They included a report of a UFO sighted at 12.39am, on the 1st, showing two red lights on the top and a silver base, over Montana.

A disc-shaped 'domed' UFO, making a vertical accent on the 5th over Cape Girardeau, Missouri, at 10.30am.

Five UFOs – apparently picked up on radar at Port Austin, Michigan, on the 6th.

This was followed by a sighting on the 8th September, of a white triangular object showing three red lights, over Montana.

### 3rd September 1976 – UFO sighted over County Durham

# UFO LANDING AT FENCEHOUSES, COUNTY DURHAM

#### Close Encounter of the third kind in the North East of England

## William D. Muir

THE first intimation that there had been a UFO landing in Co. Durham, with occupants observed, came to me through Ken Phillips of BUFORA. He had received a brief letter giving some details of the incident from the son-in-law of the elderly eye-witness. An interview was arranged, and this is what was revealed...

At 2100 hours on the evening of September 3, 1976, two ladies were walking home from a friend's house in the small colliery village of Fencehouses when they had an amazing experience.

It was a dry, cool evening with a slight breeze. As they walked past a piece of wasteland they saw a very strange object. Both women stopped, then walked towards it. They said that they felt "attracted towards it," and it was disclosed that "It" was an oval shaped object about three feet high and five feet long, standing on chrome or steel runners. The main compartment was glasslike with an orange section on top (see diagram). The whole thing was resting on a mound of earth.

When they reached the object the elderly lady stated that the wind and traffic noise appeared to stop. She then touched the glasslike sides of the object and it felt warm. At this point two strange looking beings appeared inside the glasslike structure. They had long white hair parted down the middle, large eyes and claw-like hands. Both beings appeared to be frightened at the sight of the two ladies. Their size was that of a large doll.

In their turn both ladies became frightened at the appearance of the entities, and they hurried away. Once they had moved away from the object all the normal street noise re appeared. The object then took off at great speed, with a humming noise.

The entire episode only lasted about ten minutes, but it seems that both witnesses were so badly shaken by this encounter that they are unwilling to co-operate any further. The elder of the two is suffering from "nerves" and is being treated by her doctor.

One odd result that is claimed of the encounter is that the elderly lady could not plug her vacuum cleaner into the electric socket the next day. Each time that she tried there seemed to be a force pushing the plug out. In the end she managed to get her daughter to put the plug in for her.

The wasteland is now being reclaimed and built upon.

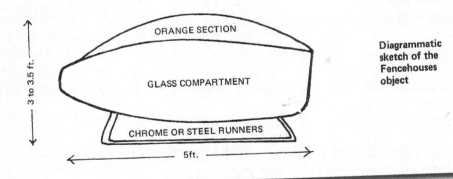

ORANGE SECTION

GLASS COMPARTMENT

CHROME OR STEEL RUNNERS

3 to 3.5 ft.

5ft.

Diagrammatic sketch of the Fencehouses object

### 10th September 1976

A disc-shaped object, showing a rotating rim and bright lights, was seen hovering low in the sky over Colusa, California, shining beams of light downwards – which apparently caused power outages.

## 19th September 1976 – Tehran UFO incident

This was a radar and visual sighting of an unidentified flying object (UFO) over Tehran, the capital of Iran, in the early morning hours of 19th September 1976. During the incident, two F-4 Phantom II Jet interceptors were reported to have lost instrumentation and communications as they approached, only to have them restored upon withdrawal; one of the aircraft also supposedly suffered temporary weapons systems failure, while preparing to open fire.

### Four-page US Defense Intelligence Agency

The incident, recorded in a four-page US Defense Intelligence Agency (DIA) report, distributed to at least the White House, Secretary of State, Joint Chiefs of Staff, National Security Agency (NSA) and Central Intelligence Agency (CIA), remains one of the most well-documented military encounters with anomalous phenomena in history, and various senior Iranian military officers directly involved with the events have gone on public record stating their belief that the object was not of terrestrial origin.

### Civilians report a strange 'star' in the sky

At approximately 12.30am, the Imperial Iranian Air Force command post at Tehran received four reports by telephone, from civilians in the Shemiran city district, of unusual activity reported in the night sky – described as an object similar to a star, but much brighter.

### General Yousefi contacted

When the command post found that no helicopters were airborne, which might have accounted for those reports, they called General Yousefi – assistant deputy commander of operations. General Yousefi at first

# NOW YOU SEE IT, NOW YOU DON'T! (U)

### Captain Henry S. Shields, HQ USAFE/INOMP

Sometime in his career, each pilot can expect to encounter strange, unusual happenings which will never be adequately or entirely explained by logic or subsequent investigation. The following article recounts just such an episode as reported by two F-4 Phantom crews of the Imperial Iranian Air Force during late 1976. No additional information or explanation of the strange events has been forthcoming; the story will be filed away and probably forgotten, but it makes interesting, and possibly disturbing, reading.

\* \* \* \* \*

Until 0030 on a clear autumn morning, it had been an entirely routine night watch for the Imperial Iranian Air Force's command post in the Tehran area. In quick succession, four calls arrived from one of the city's suburbs reporting a series of strange airborne objects. These Unidentified Flying Objects (UFOs) were described as 'bird-like', or as brightly-lit helicopters (although none were airborne at the time). Unable to convince the callers that they were only seeing stars, a senior officer went outside to see for himself. Observing an object to the north like a star, only larger and brighter, he immediately scrambled an IIAF F-4 to investigate.

Approaching the city, the F-4 pilot reported that the brilliant object was easily visible 70 miles away. When approximately 25 NM distant, the interceptor lost all instrumentation and UHF/Intercom communications. Upon breaking off the intercept and turning towards his home base, all systems returned to normal, as if the strange object no longer regarded the aircraft as a threat.

DECLASSIFY ON: 4 Dec 81
by: ACS/I HQ USAF

32

CONFIDENTIAL

A second F-4 was scrambled ten minutes after the first. The backseater reported radar-lock on the UFO at 27 NM/12 o'clock high position, and a rate of closure of 150 knots. Upon reaching the 25 NM point, the object began rapidly moving away to maintain a constant separation distance while still visible on the radar scope. While the size of the radar return was comparable to that of a KC-135, its intense brilliance made estimation of actual size impossible. Visually, it resembled flashing strobe lights arranged in a rectangular pattern and alternating blue, green, red, and orange. Their sequence was so fast that all colors could be seen at once.

As the F-4 continued pursuit south of Tehran, a second brightly-lit object (about one-half to one-third the size of the moon) detached from the original UFO and headed straight for the F-4 at a high rate of speed. The pilot attempted to fire an AIM-9 missile at the new object but was prevented by a sudden power loss in his weapons control panel. UHF and internal communications were simultaneously lost. The pilot promptly initiated a turn and negative-G dive to escape, but the object fell in behind the F-4 at 3-4 NM distance. Continuing the turn, the pilot observed the second object turn inside of him and then away, subsequently returning to the primary UFO for a perfect rendezvous.

The two UFOs had hardly rejoined when a second object detached and headed straight down toward the ground at high speed. Having regained weapons and communications systems, the aircrew watched the third object, anticipating a large explosion when it struck the ground. However, it landed gently and cast a bright light over a two-three kilometer area. The pilot flew as low over the area as possible, fixing the object's exact location.

Upon return to home base, both crewmen had difficulty in

DECLASSIFY ON: 4 Dec 81
by: ACS/I, HQ USAF

33

CONFIDENTIAL

SECRET CONFIDENTIAL

adjusting their night vision devices for landing. The landing was further complicated by excessive interference on UHF and a further complete loss of all communications when passing through a 150 degree magnetic bearing from the home base. The inertial naviga- tion system simultaneously fluctuated from 30 to 50 degrees. A civil airliner approaching the area also experienced a similar communica- tions failure, but reported no unusual sightings.

While on a long final approach, the F-4 crew noted a further UFO. This was described as a cylinder-shaped object (about the size of a T-33 trainer) with bright steady lights on each end and a flasher in the middle. It quickly approached and passed directly over the F-4. In answer to the pilot's query, the control tower reported no other air traffic in the area, although they subsequently obtained a visual sighting of the object when specifically directed where to look.

The following day, the F-4 crew was flown by helicopter to the location where they believed the object had landed. This turned out to be a dry lake bed, but nothing unusual was noticed. As the helicopter circled off to the west, however, a very noticeable beeper signal was received, and eventually traced to a nearby house. They immediately landed and asked the inhabitants if anything strange or unusual had occurred the previous night. Yes, they replied, there had been loud noises and a very bright light, like lightning. The helicopter returned to base and arrangements were made to conduct various tests, such as radiation checks, in the vicinity of the house. Unfortunately, the results of such tests have not been reported.

DECLASSIFY ON: 4 Dec 81
ACS/I, HQ USAF

34

SECRET CONFIDENTIAL

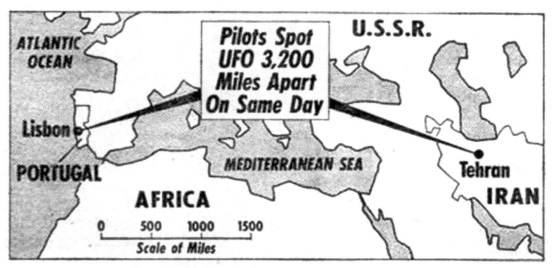

ATLANTIC OCEAN

**Pilots Spot UFO 3,200 Miles Apart On Same Day**

U.S.S.R.

Lisbon

PORTUGAL

MEDITERRANEAN SEA

AFRICA

Tehran

**IRAN**

0    500    1000    1500
Scale of Miles

*Map pinpoints UFO sightings only 45 minutes apart*

said the object was only a star, but after conferring with the control tower at Mehrabad International Airport, and also looking out into the night sky himself, decided to order a F-4 Phantom II Jet fighter from Shahrokhi Air Force Base, in Hamadan, approximately 175 miles (282 km) west of Tehran, to have a look.

### Captain Mohammad Reza Azizkhani

At 01:30 hours the F-4, piloted by Captain Mohammad Reza Azizkhani, proceeded to a point 40 nautical miles (74 km) north of Tehran. [It was noted that the object was of such brilliance that it could be seen from 70 miles (110 km) away.]

### Aircraft suffers malfunction

When the aircraft approached to approximately 25 nautical miles (46 km) from the object, the jet lost all instrumentation and communications capabilities, prompting Azizkhani to break off the intended intercept and turn back toward Shahrokhi. As he did so, both systems resumed functioning normally.

### Captain Azizkhani:

*"The UFO was travelling somewhere between two and three thousand miles per hour. The object was beyond my speed and power. The [later] F-4... also could not catch up to the object. That's when I thought, this is a UFO. No country had this type of flying object, so I was thinking ... this craft is from another planet."*

### Lieutenant Parviz Jafari and Lieutenant Jalal Damirian

At 01:40 hours, a second F-4 was scrambled, piloted by Lieutenant Parviz Jafari and Lieutenant Jalal Damirian. Jafari's jet had acquired a radar lock-on the object at 27 nautical miles (50 km) range. The radar signature of the UFO resembled that of a Boeing 707 aircraft. Closing on the object at 150 nautical miles (280 km) per hour and at a range of 25 nautical miles (46 km), the object began to move, keeping a steady distance of 25 nautical miles (46 km) from the F-4. The size of the object was difficult to determine due to its intense brilliance.

### Lights on UFO were arranged in a square pattern

The lights of the object were alternating blue, green, red, and orange, and were arranged in a square pattern. The lights flashed in sequence, but the flashing was so rapid that they all could be seen at once.

### Smaller second object seen to emerge from UFO and approach jet fighter!

While the object and the F-4 continued on a southerly path, a smaller second object detached itself from the first and advanced on the F-4 at high speed.

### Aircraft attempts to fire on UFO

Lieutenant Jafari, thinking he was under attack, tried to launch an AIM-9 Sidewinder missile, but he suddenly lost all instrumentation, including weapons control, and all communication. He later stated that he attempted to eject, but to no avail, as this system, which is entirely mechanical, also malfunctioned. Jafari then instituted a turn and a negative G dive as evasive action. The object fell in behind him at about 3 to 4

nautical miles (7.4 km) distance for a short time, then turned and rejoined the primary object.

Once again, as soon as the F-4 had turned away, instrumenta-tion and communications were regained. The F-4 crew then saw another brightly lit object detach itself from the other side of the primary object and drop straight down at high speed.

The F-4 crew expected it to impact the ground and explode, but it came to rest gently. The F-4 crew then overflew the site at a decreased altitude and marked the position of the light's touchdown. Jafari would later comment that the object was so bright that it lit up the ground and he could see rocks around it.

### Lietenant Parviz Jafari:

*"After trying to fire a missile and failing, we feared for our lives and tried to eject, but the eject button also malfunctioned. The main object emitted four objects – one that headed towards him and later returned to the main object, a short while later, one which he tried unsuccessfully to fire on, another which followed him back, and one which landed on the desert floor and glowed."*

### Object lands gently near Rey Oil Refinery

The object had touched down near Rey Oil Refinery on the outskirts of Iran. They then landed at Mehrabad, noting that each time they passed through a magnetic bearing of 150 degrees from Mehrabad, they experienced interference and communications failure.

### Civilian airliner also experiences loss of communications

A civilian airliner that was approaching Mehrabad also experienced a loss of communications, at the same position relative to Mehrabad. As the F-4 was on final approach, they sighted yet another object, cylinder-shaped, with bright, steady lights on each end and a flashing light in the middle. The object overflew the F-4 as they were on approach. Mehrabad tower reported no other aircraft in the area, but tower personnel were able to see the object when given directions by Jafari.

Years later, the main controller and an investigating general revealed that the object also overflew the control tower and knocked out all of its electronic equipment as well.

### Helicopter flies out over site of UFO landing

The next day, the F-4 crew flew out in a helicopter to the site where they had seen the smaller object land; in the daylight it was determined to be a dry lake bed, but no traces could be seen. They then circled the area to the west and picked up a noticeable 'beeper' signal. The signal was loudest near a small house, so they landed and questioned the occupants of the house about any unusual events of the previous night. They reported a loud noise and a bright light – like lightning. Further investigation of the landing site, including radiation testing of the area was apparently done, but the results were never made public. Since this event occurred before the fall of- the Shah, any records in Tehran may be lost.

### Control Tower supervisor

The control tower supervisor – Hossein Pirouzi, confirmed that the pilot was in a panic with the large UFO on its tail. According to Pirouzi and other controllers, the UFO performed a low-altitude flyby over Mehrabad at about 2,200 to 2,500 feet (760 m). It was described as a cylinder-shaped object, as large as a tour bus, with bright steady lights on each end and a flasher in the middle. During the flyby, the control

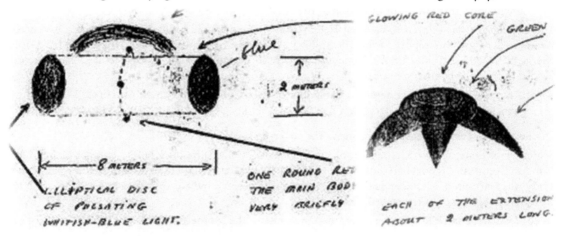

tower lost all power, although other parts of the airport were unaffected. After the flyby, the UFO took off to the west and was spotted 25 minutes later over the Mediterranean by an Egyptian Air Force pilot – then again over Lisbon, Portugal, by the pilot, crew, and passengers of a KLM flight, reporting that it was speeding westward over the Atlantic Ocean.

### Investigation held in Tehran

The following day, an investigation was held in Tehran. The Iranian Air Force Deputy Commander, Lieutenant General Abdollah Azarbarzin, conducted interviews with all of the principals and wrote up a report. General Jafari, the second F-4 Pilot stated he was among those interviewed and an American Colonel sat there and took notes. This information later appeared in a DIA account of the incident.

### Iranian Air Force Deputy Commander, Lieutenant General Abdollah Azarbarzin

Azarbarzin independently confirmed Pirouzi's statement. He said:

*"We concluded that the UFO had deliberately jammed both the aircraft and control tower electronics." [About the objects that seemed to shoot out of the UFO] "The pilots called them fireballs, but we all thought that they were very powerful waves of electromagnetism, which jammed all the electronics starting from VHF, UHF, fire control system, gun radar, gun communications – everything. Everything was gone. The co-pilot got a good look at the UFO when the second F-4 came out of its emergency dive and passed underneath it. I believe in UFOs. I cannot ignore their existence. They want to find some way of contacting the people of Earth. They are trying, and they are going to do it."*

He told researcher – **Dr. Bruce Maccabee:**

*"The co-pilot could see the shape, which he said was round – like a plate, or just like a saucer – with a canopy or cockpit that looked like half a ball, bathed in a dim orange or yellowish light, but with no visible crew."*

### Tower controller Pirouzi

Tower controller Pirouzi was also among those interviewed. He recalled a discussion by Azarbarzin's panel at the conclusion of the meeting.

*"When they heard our report and the report of the pilots, they concluded that no country is capable of such technology, and all of them believed it was a strange object from outer space."*

### Conclusions brought to the attention of the Shah

This conclusion was relayed to General Hatemi, the Shah's personal military advisory, who instructed Azarbarzin to give his report to the US Military Assistance Advisory Group, in Tehran (MAAG); in charge of MAAG and chief US Air Force military advisory to the Iranians was General Richard Secord. Secord declined to be interviewed.

**Amir Kamyabipour** – former deputy commander of operations in the Iranian Air Force:

*"UFOs are trying to find some way to make contact with our world. I am positive of this."*

### Secretary of State, Henry Kissinger ... The cover-up begins

Secretary of State, Henry Kissinger, took the official US policy line on UFOs. Kissinger claimed the Condon Committee report had shown that all UFOs could be attributed to natural causes and no further study was warranted. Kissinger said people had probably seen a meteor or a decaying satellite part, for which there was no re-entry record.

In 2012, amateur satellite observers identified the cause of the Moroccan sightings as the re-entry of the "BOZ ullage motor assembly ejected from the third stage of the Molniya rocket that orbited, Molniya 1-35". They produced a ground track plot that shows that the re-entry trajectory passed within sight of all locations from which UFO sightings were reported.

## 20th September 1976 – UFO display, Hampshire

Another Hampshire resident to witness something out of the ordinary was Neil Landimore, and his brother, who were out walking over Hayling Island, at 7.15pm. While stood talking on the 'Fort' – an open space, close to the nearby Golf Links – watching a thunderstorm in progress over The Solent, suddenly, amidst the flashes of lightning, appeared a small 'red light' which began to perform a series of fantastic movements across the sky, over Southsea – home to the nearby Naval Base.

It then lit up and flew horizontally over Eastern Road, below Cosham – now glowing even brighter, showing a central red light, one larger white light, and a cluster of smaller lights equally spaced around its edges, scattering beams of light across the night sky. (**Source: Personal interview**)

# CHAPTER 10 – OCTOBER 1976

### 1st October 1976 – UFO seen near the Dartford Tunnel

Richard John Day (24) from Rainham, in Essex, had this report to convey:

> *"At 5.30am I first sighted a round grey object moving across the sky from the direction of the Dartford Tunnel, towards Rainham village direction. It wasn't any aircraft and hovered silently in the sky for a couple of minutes – then, just before it moved away, it went brilliant white and disappeared into the clouds."*
> **(Source: Ron West)**

## 2nd October 1976 – UFO lecture

## 7th October 1976 – Three 'lights' seen over Essex

Mark Draper (13) was in his back garden at Rushes Mead, Harlow, Essex, at about 8.30pm, when he noticed three 'lights' moving across the sky; the first red, the second white, the end one red. No shape could be seen, but the 'lights' seemed to be rotating. They were seen to halt over Willofield Tower for a minute, before heading westwards.

**BUFORA LTD. LECTURE PROGRAMME 1976-77**

**Saturday, 2nd October, 1976, 7 pm**

*Michael Davies (Police officer with the West Mercia Force)*

**" THE UFO EXPERIENCE—THE POLICE OFFICER'S VIEWPOINT "**

Mike Davies has been investigating UFO cases for many years utilising the special knowledge and expertise gained from his training with the Police Force. He contributes serious UFO articles to the " Police Review " which is distributed all over Britain and he is also a frequent correspondent to Flying Saucer Review. Mr. Davies will be describing some of the more remarkable cases which he has investigated and will be suggesting ways in which Police practice and procedure can be used to advantage by other investigators, as well as giving advice on fostering good relations with local Police forces.

Mark rushed into the house and told his parents, who didn't seem very interested. **(Source: Andrew Collins)**

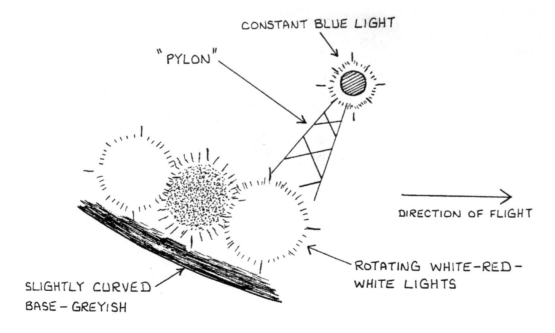

CONSTANT BLUE LIGHT

"PYLON"

DIRECTION OF FLIGHT

ROTATING WHITE-RED-WHITE LIGHTS

SLIGHTLY CURVED BASE – GREYISH

THE UFO WHICH PASSED LOW OVER THE WITNESSES' HOUSE

## October 1976 – Triangular UFO seen over Canvey Island

Mrs Gillian Cadman, from Canvey Island, had just left her house, at 6.30pm, when she became aware of a soft humming noise, accompanied by what she took to be a Shooting star travelling towards her.

> "As it moved closer, I could see quite clearly that it was oval in shape with three distinctive 'bumps' on its underneath. As it passed over the top of me, it seemed to be more oblong than oval. Whatever it was had lights all around the underneath – a bit like disco lights … red, blue, and mauve. All I could do was just watch, as it headed off towards the direction of the Thames Estuary, taking ten minutes to do so." (**Source: Personal interview/Ron West**)

## 11th October 1976 – UFO display over football match

During a football match held at Ilford, Goodmayes, Dagenham, spectator – Mr Gerald Douglas Sprought (23) of Blackborne Road, Dagenham, noticed that at 8pm many people were looking up into the sky, rather than on the players. Curious, he saw three white lights manoeuvring about in the sky. This went one for about 90 minutes! (**Source: Bob Easton**)

At 11pm on the same evening, Mr Keith John Stour (44) of Crescent Road, Dagenham, Essex, was travelling along Seven Kings High Road, towards Chadwell Heath, approaching the traffic lights at the junction with Barley Lane.

> *"My attention was caught by a very bright white 'light', passing through the sky from the south-east direction, about 60 degrees off the horizon. As I stopped for the traffic lights, the 'light' in the sky halted and dropped downwards a few degrees in the sky. After the lights changed to green, I drove into Barley Lane, stopped, and got out – just in time to see the luminous object accelerate away into the distance, north-westwards."*

When Keith arrived home he rang the *Dagenham Post*, who sent a reporter out to him.

## 12th October 1976 – 'Globe of orange light' seen, West Midlands

At 8.30pm, a mysterious 'globe of orange light' was seen crossing the sky over Dudley, West Midlands, followed by a later sighting of a similar object, which began a number of intricate manoeuvres over the town. Enquiries made by the Birmingham-based group – UFOSIS with Air Traffic Control at Birmingham Airport, ascertained that although no civilian flights were flying in the area, Military helicopters were operating in the Midlands on that day.

## 13th October 1976 – *Barking & Dagenham Post* – 'Landing strip for a UFO'

Mrs Hatch of Cedar Road, Dagenham, describes what she saw on the 26th September 1976 – *"...a huge 'star', static in the sky for 20 minutes, before veering away"*.

(**Sources:** *Barking & Dagenham Post*, 6.10.1976 – 'Did you see the star' article, re UFO sighting by Mr Keith Stone)

## 14th October 1976 – Aircraft paced by mystery 'light', Essex

One week after the sighting of three objects over Willow Field Tower, Essex, Mark Draper's mother was outside in the garden, hanging out the washing, when she saw:

> *"...a white and red rotating 'light', similar to what my son had seen. I ran indoors and told Mark. By the time he came outside, there were now three 'lights'. A short time later they began stacking in the sky, before all moving away towards the west – once again taking up a position over Willow Field Tower. To the right of the tower block appeared an aircraft; you could hear it audibly and you could see the difference between this and the strange rotating 'lights'. Suddenly, the end light broke formation and paced the aircraft for about five seconds, before rejoining the other two."*

Mrs Draper telephoned Stansted Airport about the incident. They told her that they had received other sightings.

On returning to the garden she was stunned to see that there were now eight objects visible – the last five in the south direction.

Mrs Draper took ten photographs, using a Hanimex 126 Instamatic camera. (**Source: Andrew Collins**)

Other witnesses to strange objects seen in the sky were Eileen and Charles Patience of Rushes Mead, Harlow, Essex. They were called out by Mark Draper.

> *"We saw 6-8 objects in the sky that had red and white rotating lights. We watched them for 15 minutes and then they faded away."* [The sketch shows three objects. See p119]

### 16th October 1976 – UFO over Ipswich

Bread baker delivery man – Roy Simpson, from Ipswich, was employed to deliver bread to Norwich, during 1976, working alternate shifts – either starting at 4.30am on the early shift, or 10pm on the late.

> *"These past eight weeks or more I can say that there has hardly been a journey which passes without the sighting of brilliant flashes of light seen in the sky outside Long Stratton, near Norwich. When I spoke to my colleagues at the bakery about this, they told me it's been going on for years!*
>
> *At 4.40am, my mate – Bruce Carter, told me about an object moving across the sky, about a mile away. I went to the side door with another workman, called Herbert, and looked out and saw a star-shaped, hazy 'disc', showing a red light and blue light – as if suspended in the sky. Bruce told me it had been there since 10am. It was still there when I finished at 5.15am. I felt, in some way, that I was being observed."* (**Source: Letter to MAPIT**)

At 11am, the same date, two metallic looking objects were sighted in the sky over a small village on the outskirts of Bath, by a van driver and his companion. (**Source:** *Fountain Journal*)

### 16th October 1976 – Red glowing 'ball' over Essex

On the same day, State Enrolled Nurse – Vivian McLaughlin (25) was on the playing field opposite Elizabeth Way, Harlow, in Essex, at 7.30pm.

> *"I saw a small 'light' in the north-eastern sky. At first I thought it was a star, but it increased in brightness and appeared to be moving towards my position – now a glowing red 'ball'. It suddenly changed its course to north-west, turning to white and blue, before completely vanishing from sight."*

(**Sources: Doug Canning/Ron West**)

### 19th October 1976 – Luminous objects over Essex

Mr Bernard Peter Perry (then 54) – a keen astronomer from Betchworth Road, Ilford, Essex, with his sister, Ann Mary Berry – was out studying the night sky, at 7.30pm, using his German 11 x 80 Beck Kassel 'Tordalk' binoculars. Within a few minutes he saw:

> *"...five or six pale orange or amber 'patches of light', arranged in a straight line, travelling from west to east, before being lost from view five seconds later, as they moved over rooftops. It reminded me of a fuselage of an aircraft, with the interior being fitted with gas lamps – no wing or tail section in evidence."* (**Source: Bob Easton, BUFORA**)

### 21st October 1976 – UFOs return!

Mark Draper and his mother, who had been watching the skies since the 14th October, were rewarded at 8pm, when the couple saw a total of six objects. One of them approached closer, allowing them to see:

> *"...a greyish curved underneath, and a pylon structure that appeared to be protruding from the front upper surface with a blue light on top of it."*

This matter was investigated by Doug Canning and Tony Gough, of the Essex UFO Study Group. Of some concern was that the photographs sent to Mr Canning were lost in the post! Stansted Airport was not able to confirm that any of their officials had spoken to Mrs Draper, and denied admitting other reports had been received. Enquiries made, revealed that aircraft which had been paced was a British Airways Tri-Star on a training flight.

### 23rd October 1976 – Domed 'disc' seen by motorist

A couple, out driving through Winchester, Massachusetts, at 7.15pm, saw a row of very bright rotating lights rising above the trees. They stopped the car to investigate, and saw that the lights were on a dark, elongated object. They watched for about five minutes and then commenced on their journey. As they did so, the object began moving away to the south. (**Source: Walter N. Webb investigation report**)

## 23rd October 1976 – UFO sighted over Cradle Hill, Warminster

```
Date: Saturday 23rd October 1976          Bridget Chivers - Melksham

Place: Cradle Hill                                   B2

Time: 11.02 - Red light travelling along Battlesbury horizon from right
to left.  There was also a plane in the same area of the sky and the lighting
cannot be compared with that of the first light, which seemed to stop and
occasionally flashed.

11.15 - White light on Battlesbury dismissed as an army arc light until
a party of skywatchers (4) who were up at the copse reported an identical
light coming up from Battlesbury, flying across the valley and disappearing
behind the second copse.  Due to identical time and description it is feasible
to log these lights as one and the same.

11.25 - Large amber coloured ball was sighted flying along the horizon to
the right of the golf club house.  As the UFO neared the copse on the top
of Cradle Hill it sank below the horizon, it had up till then been flying
at approximately 7½° above the horizon. Two skywatchers ran up to the copse
when they came back they reported the object hovering in the next valley for
a short time before it flew off in the Westbury-Trowbridge direction.  There
was no noise from the object but it did cause a malfunction of a U.F.O.
detector.  When the object was first sighted, the detector was checked and
though the needle was swinging wildly between the loop the buzzer was not
working.  When the object dropped below the horizon the buzzer went off and
when tested later worked perfectly.

A number of white flashes were later seen in the sky in the area of last
sighting.

There were 9-12 skywatchers and good visibility.
```

## 24th October 1976 – Square-shaped UFO sighed over Gateshead

On the same day, just before darkness fell, Thomas (15) – a schoolboy from Low Fell, Gateshead – was called outside by his friend Andrew, at 6.10pm. A few minutes later, Thomas came back in and told his mother he had been watching a UFO and that he had switched-on his battery operated tape recorder. He showed his mother the tape recorder and switched it on. As he did so, the recorded speech was garbled and speeded up. This was followed by the tape spilling out of the machine into little pieces; prior to this it had worked normally. The mother asked the boys to draw independently what they had seen. The UFO was seen for a couple of minutes' duration. Andrew said he had heard a 'sucking sound' – as if air was being displaced, while Thomas said it was silent. (**Source: William Muir**)

## 24th October 1976 – Cigar-shaped UFO sighted, Essex

Andrew Moakes (21) and his girlfriend – Ingrid Carter (19) were on their way home, after been visiting Ingrid's mother. Driving along School Lane, Orsett, at around 9pm, they noticed:

> "...a cigar-shaped object, orange in colour with a black aura around the outside, motionless in the night sky."

Curious, they stopped the car and wound down the window. No sound could be heard, so they decided to continue their journey.

They kept the object in sight of a couple of minutes, before vision was lost due to the street lamps of the A13.

## 24th October 1976 – Black 'ball' seen in the sky

At 10.30pm, six miles away in Upminster, Mrs Mary Louisa Strand (52) of Rosemary Close, South Ockenden, was heading east along St Mary's Lane, when in the north-eastern part of the sky she saw an orange spherical object in the sky, with a black aura around it. It remained in view for ten minutes, before she lost sight of it. (**Source: Andrew Collins**)

## 27th October 1976 – UFO over Guildford Surrey

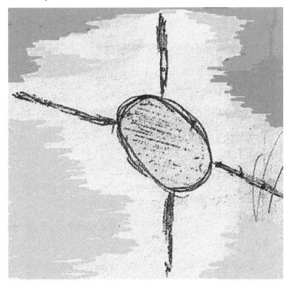

Mrs Jessie Cleghorn living in Spalding, Lincolnshire, proudly described to us, in 2011, her brother – Alexander Cleghorn's role in the Second  World War. As a RAF Sergeant serving with 550 Bomber Command, his heroic action was in clearing the beaches at Dunkirk on D-Day – for which he was later awarded The Croix de guerre. She also told of having completed a book on her own traumatic experiences in just surviving the Second World War – all brought back, ironically, while watching the *BBC News* on the 3rd March 2011, which showed some film footage of the War following the recent disclosure of UFO documents from the Public Records Office.

This lady wrote to the MOD, after sighting a most peculiar object in the sky over Guildford, in Surrey, at 3am, which she described as:

"...*having circular lights running down its sides, and what looked like four 'legs' sticking out of it – apparently following the course of the railway line, heading towards the direction of Guildford. As it moved away I heard a droning noise, followed by a flurry of air or cloud around it.*"

### MOD reply

She received the following reply from the MOD:

"*Dear Mrs Cleghorn,*

*I am writing to thank you for your letter of the 9th December and the detailed account of the unidentified flying object which you saw during the night of the 29th November 1976. As I explained, we cannot undertake to pursue our research beyond our defence interests. You may, however, wish to know that over the past number of years sightings are considered to originate, in the main, from aircraft or the lights of aircraft being seen under unusual conditions, balloons, and various meteorological phenomenon, as well as astronomical sightings, space satellites and space 'junk'. I am sorry that I cannot assist you any further with any account of what you actually saw.*

*Signed, J. McBlane, MOD Main Building, London – 23rd December 1976*

(**Source: Personal interview**)

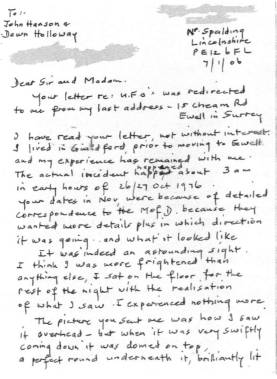

To:-
John Hanson &
Dawn Holloway

Nr. Spalding
Lincolnshire
PE12 6FL
7/1/06

Dear Sir and Madam,

Your letter re: U.F.O.'s was redirected to me from my last address - 15 Cheam Rd Ewell in Surrey

I have read your letter, not without interest. I lived in Guildford, prior to moving to Ewell and my experience has remained with me. The actual incident happened about 3 am in early hours of 26/27 Oct 1976. Your dates in Nov, were because of detailed correspondence to the MofD. because they wanted more details plus in which direction it was going.. and what it looked like

It was indeed an astounding sight. I think I was more frightened than anything else, I sat on the floor for the rest of the night with the realisation of what I saw. I experienced nothing more.

The picture you sent me was how I saw it overhead - but when it was very swiftly coming down it was domed on top, a perfect round underneath it, brilliantly lit

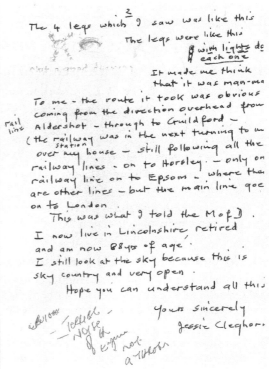

The 4 legs which I saw was like this
The legs were like this
with lights de each one

It made me think that it was man-made

To me - the route it took was obvious coming from the direction overhead from Aldershot - through to Guildford - (the railway was in the next turning to us over my house - still following all the railway lines - on to Horsley. - only on railway line on to Epsom - where there are other lines - but the main line goes on to London.

This was what I told the MofD.

I now live in Lincolnshire, retired and am now 88yrs of age. I still look at the sky because this is sky country and very open.

Hope you can understand all this

Yours sincerely
Jessie Cleghorn

## 28th October 1976 – Rectangular UFO over Indiana

Evansville, Indiana resident – Lee Golden, was one of six people that saw this UFO at 7.05pm. He said:

> "This was no hallucination. This thing came right over the top of the house, 50 feet away – I'd say a 100-150 feet over the top of the house – rectangular on the top, showing a big light at the bottom. I couldn't see how the bottom was made, but it was totally noise proof … wasn't any noise at all.
>
> As it passed overhead it appeared to be the size of an automobile and was gaining altitude, heading north. When higher up, something shot out from the bottom of it. Later on, something shot out from the side."

The object had come from the south, before heading north, at low altitude (180-150 feet), then turned and headed north-east, gained altitude, and finally shrank to the size of a star. Duration of observation was 15 minutes. It moved slowly at first, then seemed to stop – then moved quickly away and out of sight.

(**Source:** *Regional Encounters: The FC Files,* **Fran Ridge, page 66**)

## October 1976 – 'Flying Cigar' over Essex

Nigel Brunning contacted us, wishing to bring to our attention what he and his friend – Trevor Schlosz – saw, while riding their motorcycles past Harold Hill, in Essex, one afternoon.

> "We were riding our Yamaha 250cc bikes down the hill, when we both independently stopped our machines and got off, after having seen this 'flying cigar' passing overhead, slowly – definitely not an airship – like nothing I had ever seen before. We got back onto our machines and tried to keep up by riding up the hill. Suddenly, it accelerated away at tremendous speed and was gone."

When Nigel contacted the police to report the matter, they told him they had received other calls from the public of what appears to have been the same object.

# CHAPTER 11 – NOVEMBER 1976

### 5th November 1976 – Two objects seen in the sky over Essex

Gary Clifford Draper (22) of Harlow, Essex, was outside his house, at 3am, when he saw:

> "*...two objects in the sky, showing red and white revolving lights – much brighter than aircraft lights. One was at 45 degrees, the other at 60. Both disappeared towards the south-west. I tried to contact Greenwich Observatory, without success.*"

**(Source: Doug Canning and Tony Gough, Essex UFO Study Group)**

At the same time, Joe Wilson (43) from Norwich, Norfolk, was waiting for a lift to work, on what was a cold and rainy morning.

He glanced upwards into the sky and saw three star-like objects, forming a triangle in the sky. A short time later three more objects appeared in the sky, at which point his colleague arrived and that was the last he saw of the phenomena.

### 5th November 1976 – UFO over Huntingdonshire

David Pointer from Norfolk Road, Huntingdon, was out walking his dog in the Sapley Playing Fields area, at about 6.20am, when he spotted an object in the sky, followed by the extraordinary sight of an unusual flying object hovering above the ground, with the letters **VAWCON** marked on the side, described as being:

> "*...a dome-shaped structure with coloured lights on the top, hovering above the playing field; it had a telescopic probe, which appeared from its metallic dome structure. I was petrified and ran home.*"

A police spokesman added:

> "*We do get some calls about UFOs. We had one last Christmas from a woman in Fenland, who had seen bright lights above her house. We wondered whether it might have been Santa in his sleigh.*"

**(Source: Declassified MOD records/Joe McGonagle)**

### Train guard sights UFO during the same month

Although we cannot connect this sighting and an incident which took place in the same month, at 2am, involving then train guard – Mr 'K' (22), who had applied for a high security job with the ˙Police, from Pitsea, in Essex, we learned that he was on a train pulling into Basildon, when he saw an object (showing six green lights at the bottom and six red lights on the top) in the sky towards the western direction.

We have been told that two men from London came to interview Mr 'K' – who declined to be fully named, as his father was then a civil servant in the MOD.

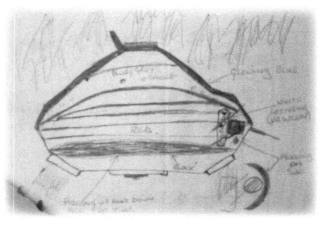

---

˙Presumably he had applied to join the police – unless it was with a civilian department (L10 Internal affairs).

## 5th November 1976 – UFOs over Hadleigh Castle

At 7.34am, Mr John Bannon (22) of Fairfax Drive, Westcliff-on-Sea, Essex, caught the 7.34am train from Chalkwell to London.

The train passed through Leigh Station without stopping, and then passed into the countryside south of Hadleigh Castle.

> *"After a few minutes on the train I looked out to see two spherical shiny objects, joined together, in the western part of the sky, about a mile away and 1,000 feet high, over Hadleigh Castle. I watched them for a minute, before they suddenly accelerated to hundreds of miles an hour towards the west."*

As a result of John contacting Graham Lowing of the *Evening Echo*, after reaching work at 9am about the incident, the newspaper published an article on the 8th November 1976 – 'Probe into UFOs sighting'.

Enquiries with the MOD revealed that while they had no reports for that time, they were told of a flashing blue and white 'light' seen at 6.21am on the same day. **(Source: BUFORA)**

## 7th November 1976 – UFO over Surrey

On the 7th November 1976 (time not given), a 'globe of white light' was seen to drop vertically downwards through the sky over Wednesbury, West Midlands, and eject a silver 'square'.

At 7.25pm, a local resident – Jacqueline Bradshaw – was walking towards the bus stop in Bromfield Road, when she heard a 'buzzing' noise. Looking upwards, she was astonished to see:

> *"...an oval object, with a band around the middle, which housed a number of lights around the*

*circumference that appeared to stick out of it. The domed top section was dull white silver, showing vertical slatted lines. The third section (base) was a smaller dome that was brighter that the rest of the 'craft', though it did not appear a as a light."*

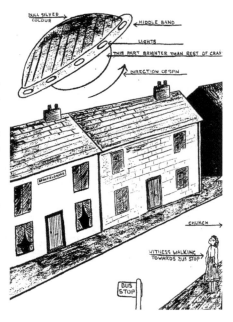

The whole thing was tilted at an angle and remained tilted until it moved, when it dropped its 'tilt' and moved to a horizontal position.

It then travelled around the sky and passed over and behind a church, where it was seen to revert to its original position. **(Source: UFOSIS/M. Pritchard)**

## 8th November 1976 – Strange UFO over Norfolk

Janet Smith (39) of Avon Road, Norwich, in Norfolk, was working in her kitchen, at 12.45am.

*"I glanced out of the window and was astonished to see a strange dark object, showing a central red light – the size of a coffee table – hovering in mid-air. I watched for about ten seconds – then made my way to the back door and was about to go out, but inexplicably changed my mind. When I went back to the window and looked out, it had gone."*

## 11th November 1976 – Three 'lights' seen over Worthing

At 5.15pm, three 'lights' were seen travelling westwards, over Worthing, by Miss Lawrence of First Avenue, Charmandean. She then made her way to Worthing Police to report the incident.

Another witness was *Gazette* reporter – Liz Jones, who was in her car at the time.

*"They looked to me as it they were three pairs of lights, travelling in a line – too close to be aircraft. I must say I wondered what they could have been."*

**(Source: Gazette, 28.1.1976 – 'UFO goes west')**

## 14th November 1976 – Close encounter with UFOs

What should one make of an extraordinary incident that took place, involving Joyce Bowles, from Winchester, and her friend – Edwin Pratt, who found themselves confronted by the appearance of a 'silver-suited man', while travelling along Chilcombe Road, Hampshire? (Map reference SU 505290)

The matter was first brought to the notice of Leslie Harris, a UFO researcher from the Bournemouth area, responsible for the investigation of numerous UFO reports in the Hampshire area, during the 1970s – many of which were published in an excellent booklet, entitled *SCAN* Magazine.

### Interview arranged with Joyce

Leslie told us that he contacted Mrs Bowles and arranged to interview her, after watching a BBC television news report on the *'Today' News* programme (15th November 1976). In company with John Ledner, the two men visited Mrs Bowles at her family home in 45 Quarry Drive, Winchester.

### Joyce Bowles:

*"I left my home just after 8.50pm, accompanied by Mr Pratt, with the intention of collecting my son – who had been visiting his girlfriend at Chilcomb Farm, some three miles away. While driving*

Joyce Bowles

Edwin Pratt

*along the A272, we noticed an unusual orange glow in the distance, but when we looked again a few seconds later, it had gone – although I noticed it again, a short time afterwards. We turned left into the Chilcomb road – a narrow lane, bordered on the right-hand side by a grassy area, about 15 yards in width, then bushes – when the car began to shudder and shake – the engine roaring with increased revolutions, despite my foot being off the pedal. The next thing that happened was the car slewed across the road and came to a halt on the grass verge, with its headlights blazing – much brighter than I've ever seen them before."*

### Cigar-shaped UFO seen – three heads appear

### Joyce:

*"We noticed the alarming sight of a glowing orange cigar-shaped object, about 15 feet in length, hovering 12-18 inches off the ground, about five yards away – then Edwin reached over and switched the ignition off ... the engine died. There seemed to be some sort of window set into the top left part of the object, out of which three heads could be seen peering out from the 'craft', which appeared to have jets of 'vapour' issuing beneath it. A 'man' emerged from the object. Although no door was evident, he just passed through the side of the object. This silver-suited man was not a human being; he was about six feet tall, slimly built, and wearing clothing resembling domestic cooking foil, and some sort of garment with a zip-like device all the way up to his chin. The garment was flapping about, though there was no wind to have caused this effect."*

### Description of the alien

*"His hair was long, blonde, brushed straight back from his forehead and curled at the back, with a dark beard reaching to his sideburns. He strolled over to the Mini Clubman, accompanied by a whistling noise (not heard by Edwin) and after placing what I presumed was his 'hand' onto the car roof, leaned over and looked in on us. I was so alarmed I clung tightly to the clothing of Mr Pratt, which seemed unusually hot. After a couple of minutes of apparent scrutiny, he moved towards the rear of the car – at which stage both he and the 'craft' disappeared."*

The couple then continued on the journey to collect Joyce's son, arriving there at 9.02pm. Joyce reported that she was unable to eat for three days after the incident, occasionally suffered from a rash on the right-hand side of her face, and was unable to wear her eternity ring because of soreness of the finger.

This was not the last time Mrs Bowles and Edwin Pratt were to become involved in UFO encounters with entities; enquiries into Mrs Bowles' background provided evidence of a number of strange incidents more in keeping with psychic phenomenon.

FLYING
SAUCER
REVIEW

Volume 22, No. 5    1976                    50p

# WINCHESTER ENCOUNTER

UFO landing, EM effects and occupants
See page 3

### Healer and psychic energy

During interviews with Leslie and John, she disclosed she was a healer and that her psychic energy, built up over a passage of time, was often released through healing.

> "Since childhood I have been accompanied by physic manifestations that have taken place at the family home in Quarry Road, Winchester, and also at my place of employment – Winchester Railway Station – where I work as a powder room attendant.

> These psychic outbreaks usually involve the movements of objects hurtling through the air. I have chips in the paintwork, caused by candlesticks coming off the mantelpiece, and sometimes I have seen the ghostly 'figure' of a white robed nun (also seen by others, but not as clear).

> What I saw with Edwin at the side of the road was no ghost; he was far more substantial than the nun. My experiences have given me a renewed inner strength and made a new woman of me."

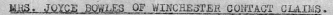

MRS. JOYCE BOWLES OF WINCHESTER CONTACT CLAIMS.

Despite their anomalies, these 'men' are friendly to the human race. (Although we have heard nothing from Mrs. Bowles since her fourth contact, it is probable that she has had <u>other</u> humanoid contacts)

The first humanoid seen by Mrs. Bowles & Mr. Ted Pratt at about 8.50 p.m. on Sunday, 14th November, 1976. The incident took place in Chilcomb Farm's access lane, nr. Winchester. The humanoid approached to within a few feet of Mrs. Bowles, who was seated in the driver's seat of her stalled mini-car.

Mrs. Bowles & Mr. Pratt were abducted by this humanoid and others of his kind on Thursday, 30th December, 1976, at 6.30 p.m.

# OUT OF THIS WORLD 4-PAGE PULL-OUT
# MYSTERIES OF THE UNKNOWN

### TIME LIFE REVEALED...PUZZLES OF SPACE AND TIME

● CAN there really be strange forces which affect our lives from beyond the world, from within it, and from its dark and mysterious past? Few scientists or rational people believe that it does. Yet equally few would deny that there are many things in the world which are unexplained.

● This world is inhabited by tantalising possibilities. Of invisible ley-lines which converge and produce powerful energies. Of a frightening vortex which swallows voyagers, even

in the 20th century. Of sightings of strange objects in the sky which can neither be dismissed as hoax nor natural phenomena. Of psychic links with the past.

● Here in special extracts from Time-Life's series of books, Mysteries Of The Unknown, we explore these intriguing but often frightening possibilities. There are no certainties. No concrete proofs. But there is doubt, mystery . . .and The Unexplained.

WERE ALIENS TRYING TO MAKE CONTACT? An awesome figure with piercing pink eyes and silver jumpsuit approached the car and peered inside at Joyce and her neighbour Ted

# Close encounters of the weird kind

**A** REMARKABLE number of supernatural experiences are believed to occur on or near "leys" – amazing alignments of pre-historic grave mounds, altars, stone circles and mediaeval churches.

Some visitors to these sites - Stonehenge being perhaps the best known - have had visions of historic figures re-enacting deeds of past lives.

Others say they feel the physical presence of a strange

force that they cannot see or identify, but which lifts them from the ground, strikes them, shoves them about, or suffuses them with inexplicable moods.

No-one seems able to explain the reasons for these things, though statisticians, engineers, dowsers, UFO enthusiasts, psychics, and astro-archaeologists have all had a hand in trying.

Some researchers believe that 'ley-lines' are located along channels of geophysical power. *They suspect that ancient people sensed a pulsating energy coursing through the earth, and that they built their monuments at sites where the energy was strongest.*

Modern investigators believe that these points are where two or more ley-lines intersect, form-

### By ROBERT WILSON

ing so-called nodes, and are therefore points where the energy is particularly strong and capable of setting off psychic phenomena.

Though rational explanations remain elusive, many documented psychic episodes have occurred on these ley lines.

Joyce Bowles, of Winchester, Hampshire, was driving towards the nearby village of Chilcomb on a Sunday night in November 1976, with her neighbour Ted Pratt.

They were on the way to collect Joyce's son Stephen when

**J** OYCE and her passenger looked out of the window and both saw a cigar-shaped craft of glowing orange hovering above the road. And through its windows they could see three heads lined up like passengers on a bus.

As they sat in awe, one of the figures emerged from the craft and approached the car. It was a being with piercing pink eyes but without pupils or irises, dressed in a silver jump suit. "He

suddenly the car shook violently and careered on to a grass verge. The headlights went out and the engine stopped.

peered through the window at the dashboard controls," Joyce recalled.

And at that, the dead engine burst into life and the headlights flared back on. "Then he and the cigar-shape simply vanished."

*Though Joyce was completely bewildered by the experience, some experts have pointed out that ley-lines often attract alien beings.*

And it is true that at the very point where the car stopped two alignments of ancient burial mounds intersect.

They radiate from that point between mounds nearby towards others in the direction of Old Winchester, crossed by another ley-line starting further north of

● Continued on Page 11

# The Bishop of Winchester

The Rt Revd Michael Scott-Joynt

Wolvesey, Winchester SO23 9ND
Telephone: 01962 854050  Facsimile: 01962 897088
Email: michael.scott-joynt@dsl.pipex.com
www.winchester.anglican.org

The Diocese of
Winchester

THE CHURCH
OF ENGLAND

15th March 2010

Dear Mr Hanson

**Haunted Skies**

Thank you for your letter.  I have asked the Diocesan Convenor of Deliverance Ministry and neither of us have any recollection of ever having heard about an exorcism carried out in a house called Quarry Bank in Winchester.  I am sorry that I cannot help you.

I expect that you may already have been in touch with the Hampshire Records Office, which is based in Winchester.  They may be able to help you locate the whereabouts of the property.  Their contact details are:

Hampshire Records Office
Sussex Street, Winchester, Hampshire SO23 8TH
tel 01962 846154, fax 01962 878681

With my best wishes.

+ Michael Winton

Mr John Hanson
31 Red Lion Street
Alvechurch
Worcestershire
B48 7LG

*Dawn Holloway with Lionel Beer*

### Lionel Beer and his investigation

From Lionel Beer's just as thorough investigation into the matter, we learn that Mrs Bowles (then aged 42) had four sons and lived in a semi-detached house on the eastern side of Winchester. Mr Pratt was then approximately 60 years of age and came from the small hamlet of Nether Wallop. It is said he and his wife were visiting the Bowles family on the evening of the incident.

### Examination of vehicle made

The matter was also brought to the attention of BUFORA representative – Mr Frank J. Wood from Broadstone, Dorset, whom we spoke to with regard to his initial visit to see Mrs Bowles and examination of the white Mini Clubman, Car Registration number SAA 749P, showing 3,500 recorded miles on the 17th November 1976, followed by a another visit some weeks later.

### Conversation between the witnesses prior to incident

From a detailed account, submitted by Frank to BUFORA, we were to learn of the various conversations that transpired between him and Mrs Bowles during an examination made of the vehicle electrics and mechanics, after Mrs Bowles claimed the car had come to a stop while in third gear driving down the hill. (Gradient of 1 in 20)

**Joyce:**

> *"I saw, ahead of me and to the left, high in the sky, an unfamiliar orange light. I said to Ted, 'Good God, whatever is that?'*

*The car engine then cut out and the car vibrated violently before coming to a halt. The car moved again, diagonally forward and to the right – as if floating through the air. Ted grabbed the steering wheel and said, 'Watch out where you are going, girl!' (or words to that effect) and then switched off the ignition and put the gear into neutral."*

Mr Wood pondered on this and wondered, perhaps in the excitement of what was occurring, whether Mr Pratt had accidently turned the ignition back on with the car in gear, causing it to move again, a short distance, after ascertaining he owned a large Vauxhall with the ignition switch on the far side of the wheel – which he put to Mrs Bowles. However, she was adamant that the ignition had not been switched on again. An examination of the ignition switch revealed it was faulty, as the barrel could be depressed at least an eighth of an inch downwards into the housing and, accordingly, he advised Mrs Bowles to get it repaired under guarantee, believing that if this had been the cause, the next time it happened could have been far more serious – especially if travelling down a road filled with traffic.

He also discussed the point of the headlights being brighter after the car had come to a stop, and suggested to Joyce this could have been caused by a wisp of smoke or fog passing across the front of the headlamps. Joyce insisted this was not the case and that the headlamps had increased in brilliance (four times as strong, without burning out any bulbs) – strong enough to illuminate the road ahead, rather than throwing back illuminated light. Checks were also carried out on the fuel system, heating and wiring, with no apparent signs of damage or burning being discovered.

### Visit made to locality

A visit was made to the locality, from which Frank made the following observation:

*"Mrs Bowles had been driving downwards at the time of the incident, after having left the main road some 150 yards (approximately) behind her, and now 50 feet above her on a 45 degree slope, which means her vision would have been restricted due to hedgerows and undergrowth – although if a double-decker bus or tall vehicle had driven by, she would have seen the tops. I asked her about the size of the object, but she was vague. I asked her if it was as large as a car. She said 'smaller'. I asked her, 'What about a baby's pram?' She said, '...smaller; the windows were at the side, the occupants were sat one behind the other – as if on a bus. I have no recollection of when it departed, because the stranger had moved to the rear of the car; we looked back to see him, and then forwards, by which time the object had disappeared'."*

Frank asked her about previous knowledge of UFOs. She replied:

*"I know nothing about UFOs. I hadn't the slightest clue they contained people".*

Asked if she was sure the occupant was human, she replied:

*"Oh yes, he was human all right. He was no ghost. Although human, they were unlike any humans I had seen before, especially with those penetrating pink eyes."*

Frank mentioned about a forthcoming visit from Dr. Cleary-Baker, who he understood was known to Mrs Bowles. She told him:

*"He (Dr. Baker) used to work at Winchester Railways Station, where he was known as 'Curly' and that whenever he heard of a UFO being seen, would drop his tools and rush off to investigate."*

### Unusual occurrences at family home

She also told Frank about an unusual occurrence which happened on the 29th November, at lunchtime, after having received a telephone call from a Guildford resident, who told her:

*"I have read about your experience in The Sun newspaper, on Thursday morning, and I can tell you the Government is very displeased with the publicity you are getting. You will be getting a visit from some officials who will be visiting you, and you are not to talk about it to anyone."*

The caller rang again, half-an-hour later, and repeated the warning – this time threatening her by saying they would take her away and connect her up to wires! During the afternoon the same man rang again. Once more he repeated the threats, despite Joyce telling him in no uncertain terms that *"it was a free country and she would speak to whom she liked"*.

Frank advised her to tell the caller she had telephoned the police, in the hope that this would stop the calls being made. Coincidentally, on the same afternoon, Joyce received a visit from a man who identified himself as Richard Lawrence, from Fulham, who claimed to be interested in UFOs but 'sceptical', and asked Joyce to describe what had taken place.

### Roman roads and Ley lines

While they were talking, the phone rang and the caller identified himself as Richard Lawrence. Amazingly, both men from the London area had decided to visit her on the same afternoon – which they did, not having met previously before. Frank, in his 'write up' of the investigation carried out by him, wondered if there was any connection with the close proximity of six Roman roads which converge on Winchester – the original alignment of four of these roads missing the City Centre and passing along the City boundaries, suggesting they existed as track ways before the Romans came to England.

> *"Three of them meet at a point half-a-mile north, near Winchester, and, if this point is also joined by a straight line to Old Winchester Hill, we find on this line the following: a tumuli, two and-a-half miles away from Old Winchester Hill, four and-a-half miles away, connected by a footpath, another tumuli, six and-a-half miles away, another tumulus, eight and-a-half miles away, another ten, and half-a-mile away another tumulus, eleven and-a-half miles away the junction of three Roman roads (from which the previous group of tumuli are visible).*
>
> *Nine and three-quarter miles away, on the same dead stretch of road on which Mrs Bowles had her experience, is exactly aligned with and is on the same line, with tumuli on either side (which should be visible).*
>
> *I have seen good alignments on maps, but never one more striking that this one. I doubt whether there is another piece of road in Hampshire with a more obvious association with a Ley line."*

### Authors:

We believe there are strong links between the sightings of UFOs and Roman roads/ancient Ley lines, and have noted the nearby profusion of place names such as Fawley, Crawley, Brockley, Eastliegh, Downleaze, Hursley, Baddesley, Ropley, Hattingley, Summerley, Ashley, Botley, Oakley, Dursley, Lockerley, Tytherley, Netley, and many more. Do they provide a clue as to why manifestations like this occur?

Frank also pondered on the possibility that the 'orange glow' seen by Mrs Bowles may have been the product of a mirage, caused by the reflection of over a hundred sodium street lamps, situated about half-a-mile away from where the incident happened, reflected from cloud cover – something Joyce disagreed on, saying it had been a clear night.

### Frank:

> *"I pondered whether it was possible (bearing in mind Joyce had mentioned about a frost developing on high ground, earlier, which had thawed by 8.45pm) that a stream of warm air had come in over the hills and left a layer of cold air in the valley, causing an image of the lights to be thrown up into the clear sky, causing an illusion (even shining through the hedgerows) and forming an impression of 'bow windows' and 'people sitting in them'."*

We do not believe this was the answer, but remain impressed with the painstaking investigation carried out by Mr Frank Wood – a credit to the BUFORA organisation.

### Professor John Taylor

Another person who became involved with researching the claims made by Joyce was Professor John Taylor, from King's College, London, who had allegedly witnessed for himself a number of manifestations taking place at Joyce's home address (a guest speaker at the BUFORA Conference, organised by BUFORA's Tony Pace, Charles Lockwood and Roger Stanway, on the 10/11th May 1975, which was also attended by Leonard G. Cramp).

Although we eventually traced Professor Taylor, after several letters and emails sent to King's College were ignored, we were not allowed the opportunity to talk to him personally, but were told, during a telephone conversation with his wife, quote:

> *"The Professor has finished with all of that, many years ago, but if you care to obtain a copy of his book – Science and the Supernatural – it will give you some information relating to a scientist's view of the Supernatural."*

We obtained a copy of this now out-of-print book, but were disappointed to find no reference to Joyce Bowles, or any information pertaining to the Professor's involvement in this case, and could take this matter no further. What a pity he had adopted this attitude – but, of course, did we really expect anything else? (**Source: As above/Lionel Beer, BUFORA**)

It appears the couple weren't the only ones to see UFOs. On the 14th November 1976, an orange glow was seen in the sky over Hampshire, by Mr P.J. Baker from Shirley, Southampton, who was in Curbridge when he noticed:

> *"...a disc-shaped orange glow, just above the horizon, at 7pm – which disappeared, seconds later".*

### BUFORA Liaison Officer

According to Mr Richard Nash – Cosham BUFORA Liaison Officer – he told of having received at least ten separate reports of UFOs seen over Southern England since Sunday night (14th November 1976). They included a report from Mrs Marion Taylor, who was on her way home, when she noticed a bright orange object hovering in the sky, with a trail of fire coming from the end of the object.

> *"I watched it for about 20 minutes, before it vanished behind clouds. I have never seen anything like this previously. I realise people will laugh at the idea of a UFO, but I am certain that what I saw was not an ordinary airplane. Many people might say I was mistaken, as I had been working all night, but I know what I saw."*

## 16th November 1976 – 'Flying Wotzit', Hampshire

Alan Shipsey (then aged 12) from Rowner, was out buying some sweets, just after dark, when he noticed an orange object, low down in the sky, surrounded by a 'ring of light'.

(Source: *Portsmouth News*, 19.11.1976 – 'The Flying Wotzit and you')

## 19th November 1976 – Fireball passes overhead in Wales

At 5.20pm, Brian Jones (aged 16) of Llanerch, Llanelli, observed a very bright white 'light', moving overhead in the sky.

> *"It varied in brightness as it moved. I realised that what I was looking at was definitely not an aeroplane, a helicopter, or any other aircraft, because it travelled low and made no noise. I began to get so excited about the object that I ran to my house, and as I came to our side entrance I looked up behind my shoulder and there, closer to where I was standing, I saw that the 'light' had brightened to a yellowish, round fireball, with underneath a bright emission of sparks. As I was excited and a little frightened about it, I ran in at our backdoor and told my mother about the 'light', for her to see it, but when she came outside it had completely disappeared."*

(Source: *The Welsh Triangle*, Peter Paget, 1979)

### 21st November 1976 – What lay behind this incident?

At 1.30am, 'a huge round mass of dark red light' was seen flying at speed over Maidstone, Kent, before coming to a halt in the sky.

It then projected a dark red ray of light onto a nearby farmer's field, before continuing on its flight – now orange in colour. (**Source: Mrs Valerie Martin**)

### November 1976 – Close Encounter on Surrey Downs

A short distance from the old Roman road, near Epsom Downs, in Surrey – the home of the famous 'Derby' – was the venue for a different type of meeting, that formed the subject of conversation while talking with Peter Leather (then in his twenties), from Marlborough, Wiltshire – an ex Jockey, whose career included a notable win on Leuven at Brussels, Belgium, on 15th June 1979.

*"One November evening in 1976, my companion and I were walking home to the training stables, along a quite country road that was originally a roman road. We noticed an unusual blue haze forming over the tops of nearby trees, a short distance from the racecourse itself, and stood stock-still, watching, as this 'mass of light' – now shaped like a saucer – began to descend groundwards, about sixty feet away from where we were standing. Then, to our amazement and fear, in front of us, appeared a humanoid 'figure' – very athletic in build, about six feet tall, dressed in some type of tightly fitting apparel – apparently holding a small red light on 'its' chest.*

*My companion started to scream and became hysterical, shouting out 'He's got a gun', and ran across the road nearly colliding with an oncoming vehicle. When I looked back, the 'saucer' was taking off; there was no sign of the 'figure'. Suddenly, with a huge burst of speed it had gone, leaving me to try and calm down my friend – whose health was to suffer as a result of this incident. In fact, he was never the same after this.*

*I went to Epsom Police Station and reported the incident. The following evening I received a telephone call from a man, who refused to identify himself. He advised me that 'I had seen a weather balloon' (in what I took to be quite a threatening tone), so I kept quiet about it for many years."* (**Source: Personal interview**)

### 23rd November 1976 – Egg-shaped UFO sighted

Gary Simpson (15) of Beambridge Place, Chalvedon, Essex, had just finished band practice and was walking across the field of Barstable School, at 9.45pm.

*"Glancing upwards, I saw a silvery-yellow egg-shaped object in the east of the sky – as bright as the moon – with a yellowish haze around it. It was travelling in a straight line and just below cloud cover. I watched it for a minute, before it was lost from view behind the school block. The weather was bad, at the time, with heavy cloud and a strong wind."* (**Source: Andrew Collins**)

### 27th November 1976 – Pink UFO sighted over Essex

Mrs Rosemary Longmure of 72, Deidre Avenue, Wickford, in Essex, and Mrs Stella Howell of 42, Elder Avenue, Wickford, in Essex, were employed as night attendants at the Chaplain Lodge residential care home in Nevendon Road, Wickford.

At 7.15am, they had just finished taking tea to some of the residents, when Mrs Longmure – who was in the kitchen – happened to look through the window and see:

*"...a crescent-shaped, or shrimp coloured object, moving across the sky in an eastern direction".*

She alerted Stella and the two of them watched the object manoeuvring about in the sky for about five minutes, before it moved upwards and disappeared into cloud cover.

### Bob Easton, of the Essex UFO Study Group

Later, following the matter being reported to Bob Easton, of the Essex UFO Study Group, he interviewed both of the women – for which he obtained the following information:

Mrs Longmure said she had seen the saucer-shaped object, emitting a soft pink/shrimp coloured glow. It appeared to have a 'bubble' on top, which flashed red every few seconds. The other side had what looked like some form of power unit, which projected a glow similar to that seen on jet aircraft.

Mrs Howell thought it looked like a 'fat cigar', projecting a soft pink colour, and that it could have been discoid in shape, although she has no recollection of any power unit. During conversation with Rosemary, she told of having sighted *"a rocket or church door- shaped object in the sky over Schlesien, in Germany, in 1949"*. She said she had read many books on the subject, including those of Erich Von Daniken.

(**Source: Bob Easton**)

## 28th November 1976 – 'Bright light' over Gravesend, Kent

At 2am, Susan Smith of Brook Road, Gravesend, Kent, was awoken by a 'bright light' streaming into the bedroom, coming down from the sky. The next thing she knew was that she felt tired and went back to sleep. Curious as to what it could have been, she wrote to the local UFO group to report the matter.

### Four police officers arrived at the scene

What she did not know was that there were other witnesses to this. Neighbour – Susan Gillingham (52) had just arrived home with her husband, when they noticed the 'silver light' in the sky.

> *"It was very high up and moving slowly – not in a straight line, but moving about all over the place. It would go to the left, then right, then back to the left and return to its first point, before repeating the manoeuvres – as if looking for something. There was no noise. After about 45 minutes, we telephoned the police. Four police officers came out and watched it with us for over 30 minutes, until it went out."* (**Source: Ron West**)

## 29th November 1976 – Multi-witness UFO sighting, Texas

A group of ten Lockhart, Texas, women – who had gathered for a bridge party, at 1.30pm – were astonished to see an oval object in the sky, followed by a rocket-shaped fragment shooting out of the object and streaking across the sky. Seconds later, the UFO vanished from sight. The matter was reported to the local newspaper – the *Lockhart Post Register*. The Editor – Louis Mohle (49), said:

> *"Theirs is one of the convincing reports of a UFO sighting that I've heard before."*

### Like a saucer on its side

First to spot the object was Mrs Norma Jean Burchill (47) – owner of a restaurant. She was driving to the bridge party, when she happened to glance up at the sky and see

> *"a white, oval object – like a saucer on its side – moving slowly southwards."*

When Norma arrived at Mrs Scott's house, she called the four women outside to come and have a look.

A few minutes later, Mrs Martha Blake and Mrs Nan Patton, with three other ladies, arrived.

> *"Suddenly, a black part at the bottom of the UFO burst away from the main body and headed away eastwards. The UFO then vanished. After the bridge party had finished, I made my way home. As I did so, I saw the same UFO again but travelling much faster – now yellowish in colour, then turning pink and orange. Finally, two reddish-yellow lights flashed and the UFO disappeared for the second time. Seven of us saw this."*

Mrs Onita King (77) – a rancher's wife – said:

> "It was an eerie feeling. The thought that someone is up there, watching you, is a frightening one".

Mrs Jessie Scott – the wife of a retired Army Colonel, and a Mrs Blake, all described seeing the same thing.

At Bergstrom Air Force Base, Major John Slevin said their radar had not tracked anything that afternoon.

> "We don't have any explanation."

*Pointing to where UFO hovered: Mrs Onita King showing where she and (from left), Mrs Norma Jean Burchill, Mrs Martha Blake, Mrs Josie French, Mrs Josie Gambrell and Mrs Bonnie Scott saw the UFO*

## Winter 1976 – Norfolk woman's chilling encounter with a UFO

Mrs Bertha Humphries – a retired Solicitor's clerk – living in North Walsham, Norfolk, decided to take her dog, 'Sooty', for its evening walk, just after 7pm. As it had been snowing heavily, with the ground thickly covered with snow, she decided to take a short walk down one side of the road and up the other.

> "I crossed Mundesley Road (near to Crow Road) and, while glancing ahead to the top of the road, near the bend, I noticed a dull red glow moving above the ground, from side-to-side. At first, I thought it was the rear lights of a car reversing. I was stunned into disbelief when an object emerged, floundering along the road. It was jet black, oblong in shape, and bat-like in appearance, with a centre showing a circle of dull red light.
>
> It began to move towards me, taking up the complete crown of the road. Still floundering, until near the Orchard Garden public house, it slowly rose into the air, reached housetop level – the red circle glowing, the black shape flapping and billowing like a cloak dragging behind it (like the tail of a kite, a miniature version of itself) – before moving upwards into the sky and disappearing.
>
> I later wrote to the Astronomer Royal, explaining what I had seen, but never received any explanation."

(**Source:** *Fountain Journal,* **Number 2, 1976/Gordon Creighton,** *Flying Saucer Review*/**Ivan W. Bunn,** *'The Lantern' Series*/**North Walsham – 'Batmobile')**

## 1976 – UFO over RAF Abingdon, Berkshire

Hilda Lister telephoned us, in September 2010, wishing to bring our attention to a UFO she had seen while living in married quarters at RAF Abingdon, during 1976.

> *"It was one of those quiet days; my husband was watching television and I was outside, during the late afternoon. Suddenly, I looked up and saw this long cigar-shaped object, flying across the sky. I was frightened and stumbled back into the house to tell my husband, but he didn't even bother to come out and have a look."*

Hilda told us it was something that has always been at the back of her mind, despite the years having slipped away, and still remains puzzled by what it was that she saw all those years ago.

# CHAPTER 12 – DECEMBER 1976

### 3rd December 1976 – Talk on UFOs

### 4th December 1976 – Triangular UFO over Essex

William Foley (59) of Mare Street, Hackney, London:

> *"I was leaving my friend's house in De Beauvoir Road, North London, at ten past midnight, when I sighted a large orange light, very low in the sky – as bright as the sun – just stationary there. I watched it for five minutes – then my taxi arrived."*

**LOOK OUT!**

WATCH IT, Dagenham! According to the vigilantes of the Essex Unidentified Flying Object Group you're the centre of increasing UFO activity over the last four years. And to prove it, the group are discussing more than 100 sightings, supported by slides, tonight at Harts Lane Hall, Barking. The session starts at eight (non-members, 30p).

EVENING NEWS (LONDON) 3 DEC. 76

Other witnesses to the sightings of UFOs on this day were Mr and Mrs Iris Jennings (32) of Dewsgreen, Vange, Essex, and their two sons (7) and (5), who were travelling along Clay Hill Road, towards their home, at 5.15pm, when at a distance of approximately one hundred yards, an 'array of lights' appeared. They continued watching the phenomena, until they seemed directly over the top of the 'lights'. They stopped the car and got out, and saw:

> *"…a delta or triangular-shaped object, motionless overhead; on its left-hand side were three large red lights, spaced far apart.*
>
> *On the other side was a large blue light and on its rear were three white lights, close together, flashing in a set pattern.*
>
> *A few minutes later, the object slowly and gracefully moved away towards the Chelmsford area."*

(**Source: Ron West/***Basildon Recorder***, 13.12.1976/Andrew Collins**)

## 6th December 1976 – UFO over Essex

On the 8th December 1976, BUFORA investigator – Andrew Collins, was told about a UFO sighting which had taken place on the 6th December 1976, involving John Bailey of 21, Larkswood Walk, Wickford, Essex, by Sylvia Knight of the *Basildon Recorder*.

### The incident

At 5.45pm, John Bailey (then aged 10) left his home in Larkswood Walk, Wickford, in Essex, to purchase some tobacco (as you could in those days!) from a shop in Nevendon Road, about a quarter of a mile away. As he was about to walk along Park Drive he noticed, at an elevation of some 50 degrees in the sky:

> *"…a white disc-shaped object, showing a large red, glowing, dome in the centre of its underside. On each side of the rim were two red lights, and around the object itself was a shimmering effect. The 'disc' was spinning on its axis, and I could see what looked like short and long lines underneath it. These seemed engraved into the surface."*

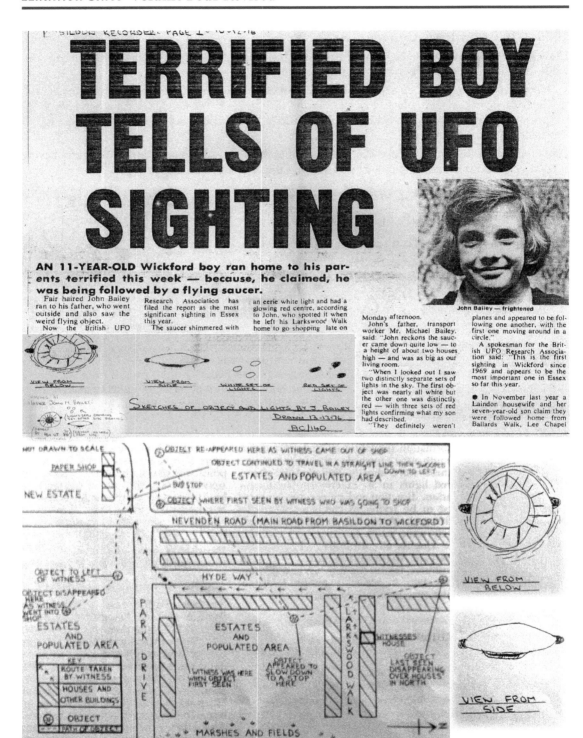

BILDON RECORDER PAGE 1 10.12.76

# TERRIFIED BOY TELLS OF UFO SIGHTING

**AN 11-YEAR-OLD Wickford boy ran home to his parents terrified this week — because, he claimed, he was being followed by a flying saucer.**

Fair haired John Bailey ran to his father, who went outside and also saw the weird flying object.

Now the British UFO Research Association has filed the report as the most significant sighting in Essex this year.

The saucer shimmered with an eerie white light and had a glowing red centre, according to John, who spotted it when he left his Larkswood Walk home to go shopping late on Monday afternoon.

John's father, transport worker Mr. Michael Bailey, said: "John reckons the saucer came down quite low — to a height of about two houses high — and was as big as our living room.

"When I looked out I saw two distinctly separate sets of lights in the sky. The first object was nearly all white but the other one was distinctly red — with three sets of red lights confirming what my son had described.

"They definitely weren't

*John Bailey — frightened*

planes and appeared to be following one another, with the first one moving around in a circle."

A spokesman for the British UFO Research Association said: "This is the first sighting in Wickford since 1969 and appears to be the most important one in Essex so far this year.

● In November last year a Laindon housewife and her seven-year-old son claim they were followed home from Ballards Walk, Lee Chapel

VIEW FROM BELOW

VIEW FROM SIDE

WHITE SET OF LIGHTS

RED SET OF LIGHTS

SKETCHES OF OBJECT AND LIGHTS BY J. BAILEY

DRAWN 12-12-76

AC/140

NOT DRAWN TO SCALE

PAPER SHOP

NEW ESTATE

② OBJECT RE-APPEARED HERE AS WITNESS CAME OUT OF SHOP

OBJECT CONTINUED TO TRAVEL IN A STRAIGHT LINE THEN SWOOPED DOWN TO LEFT

BUS STOP

ESTATES AND POPULATED AREA

① OBJECT WHERE FIRST SEEN BY WITNESS WHO WAS GOING TO SHOP

NEVENDEN ROAD (MAIN ROAD FROM BASILDON TO WICKFORD)

OBJECT TO LEFT OF WITNESS

OBJECT DISAPPEARED HERE AS WITNESS WENT INTO SHOP

ESTATES AND POPULATED AREA

HYDE WAY

PARK DRIVE

ESTATES AND POPULATED AREA

WITNESS WAS HERE WHEN OBJECT FIRST SEEN

OBJECT APPEARED TO SLOW DOWN TO A STOP HERE

LARKSWOOD WALK

WITNESSES HOUSE

OBJECT LAST SEEN DISAPPEARING OVER HOUSES IN NORTH

VIEW FROM BELOW

VIEW FROM SIDE

KEY

| | |
|---|---|
| ROUTE TAKEN BY WITNESS | |
| HOUSES AND OTHER BUILDINGS | |
| OBJECT | |
| PATH OF OBJECT | |

MARSHES AND FIELDS

The object, which was moving slowly in the same direction as John, then suddenly swooped to his left and continued on its journey.

John turned into Park Drive and, the next time he looked up, whatever it was had gone.

After purchasing the tobacco he left for home, but after seeing the object – now on his left in the sky – began to run.

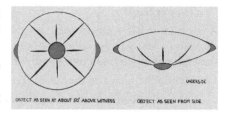

> "I crossed into Park Drive. The object swooped again to my right, and appeared to follow me all the way back to Hyde Way, where it almost seemed to stop spinning – now motionless in the sky – before it began to spin fast and then move out of view, towards the North."

John rushed into his home in a state of agitation, and no doubt excitement. His father – Michael, after hearing what had transpired, ran out into the garden with his son, just in time to see three white 'lights' in the sky.

(Sources: Andrew Collins, BUFORA/*Basildon Recorder*, 10.12.1976 – 'Terrified boy tells of UFO sighting')

## 6th December 1976 – UFO over Basildon

At 6.30pm on the same date, Mr McDonnell (65) of Sparrows Herne, Kingswood, Basildon, was taking his dog for a walk when he was to sight something so strange that he wrote to the MOD and the local TV Station.

## 12th December 1976 – Flashing object over Pontypool, South Wales

Tony Heare, of Pontypool

> "I saw a blue/white light at the front of an object with a red/orange light flashing directly above, and three or four blue/white lights behind the first. It gave the impression of being vaguely similar to the size of a single-decker bus. No noise was audible at all. A car moved off nearby, but soon all was quiet again. The object was seen from the car park of Llandegfedd Reservoir, facing towards Newport. The object travelled on a seemingly straight line. It reached a mountain to our right, seeming to hover – then turned on its axis and travelled back towards our left."

(Source: *UFO-UK*, Peter Paget, 1980)

## 18th December 1976 – Police sight UFO

At 12.55am, three police officers sighted a 30 feet diameter oval UFO, while on patrol on the Soda Springs road, Caribou County, Indiana. They described it as:

> "...devoid of any seams or windows – the size of three to four cars – emitting a light green light, hovering silently, only 60 feet away from us, but made a whistling 'wind' sound when in motion."

(Sources: J. Allen Hynek Center for UFO Studies case investigations file, December 1976/*International UFO Reporter*, February 1977, page 6)

## 21st December 1976 – Spectacular UFO display of triple light formations, over Essex

Mr Arthur Newbold (then aged 31) of King Edward's Road, Barking, Essex, was in the back garden at 5pm. The sun had set about an hour ago and it was dark. Something caught his eye above the church, which lay a little distance away from his house. He looked out and saw:

> "...moving in different directions, were three groups of lights. Each group was made up of two fuzzy white ones and a pulsating red one, which lay between the latter. Two of the three groups were moving to the right, while the other moved to the left between the two groups. They then flew slowly away and merged into one brilliant white light, circling the area of Barking Park and Mayesbrook Park – then were lost from sight. I was awestruck by what I was seeing."

### They're back!

A few minutes later, now accompanied by his wife – Hilary, they saw the objects return from the northern direction – all three, travelling in a straight line. At some stage Hilary became distraught, as she thought they were going to crash into nearby trees.

This did not happen and they were seen to fly over the church in individual groups of three lights.

*"As they passed over the church, a fourth light shot out of the middle group of three lights at great speed. This object/light slowed down and began its own circling movement over Barking. It was larger than the others and had five small brilliant lights – a red pulsating one in the middle; the others, white. Finally the three groups of light passed over the roofs of nearby houses and disappeared over Beckton Marshes in the south-west.*

**(Source: Ron West/ Doug Canning/ John Saville)**

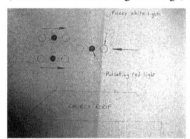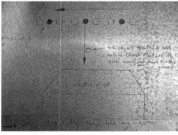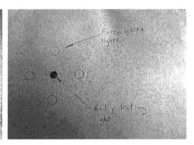

## 22nd December 1976 – UFO over Walthamstow

Coppermill Lane, Walthamstow, was again the subject of apparent UFO interest. Carol Ann Smith (then aged 30) of 4, Haroldstone Road, Walthamstow, was walking home along the High Street.

*"There were still stalls open when I saw this object in the sky. I naturally thought it was an aeroplane, to begin with, but why wasn't it moving? It looked like a wartime barrage balloon, with lights all around it. I watched it for about five minutes – then turned the corner and thought no more of it."*

She was not the only one – Harlow, Essex, bus driver – Mark Draper (then aged 26), was to find himself once again witnessing further examples of UFO activity. While motorcycling home, he noticed

*"a Swiss cheese-shaped object in the sky. I stopped and saw that it had red and white lights spinning around the centre, clockwise, as it moved silently at approximately 5-10 miles per hour through the sky, at a height of about 2,500 feet".*

## 23rd December 1976 – Red object over Chingford, Essex

Hungarian lady – Mrs Mucsi, of Larkshall Road, was taking the dogs for a walk in Endlebury Road, when she noticed a red object passing across the night sky.

*"It then increased in size, and stopped for a few seconds in mid-air, before disappearing. I was very alarmed by what I saw."*

**Source: Dan Goring)**

## 25th December 1976 – Saucer-shaped object over the London area

At 1am, Mrs D. Chapman of Hoddesdon, in Hertfordshire, and her husband, saw a bright pink circular object, flying silently through the sky over rooftops. Mrs Chapman thought it had what looked like an antennae on it, while her husband described a tail.

Thirty seconds later, it was out of sight.

At 1.15am, Mrs Iris Eagliner (then aged 45) of Latymer Way, Edmonton, was on her way to bed.

*"I saw an object in the night sky – a white 'light', sending out flashes of bright light before dimming – allowing me to see a reflection of some sort of shape. It was making this zigzagging movement. I called my daughter into the bedroom; she watched it for a while and then left. I watched it until 2.30am, by which time it was much smaller in size."*

Tina Marie Eagliner (then aged 20):

*"At 1.30am, I saw a strange 'light' in the sky; it was dimming and then growing brighter as it zigzagged through the air, left and right. When the light went dull, I saw a saucer-shape in the middle. At one stage it floated towards the window, stopped for a few seconds, and then moved back to its original position. I observed it for a while longer and decided, after about ten minutes of watching, to go to bed. The 'light' was so bright that it made my eyes water."* (**Source: Dan Goring**)

## 26th December 1976 – Rectangular object over Enfield

At 1.30am, Irene Ingles (then aged 41) of Westmoor Road, Enfield, was enjoying the Boxing Day festivities, with friends, when her daughter – Lorraine Ingles, noticed:

*"...an object in the sky towards the south-east, moving from side-to-side. It resembled a distorted rectangle, showing white and yellow lights (possibly red ones) – gone, moments later."*

(**Source: Ron West**)

## 26th December 1976 – Two orange 'lights' over Portsmouth

Just before midnight, two small orange 'lights' were seen flying across the sky over the Portsmouth area. According to the witness:

*"The 'light' stopped moving and one of them began to circle the other. A short time later, they left – one behind the other – and then out of sight."* (**Source: Stanley Nelson Pitt, WATSUP**)

## 26th December 1976 – UFO paces ambulance

The ambulance service in Whitehorse, Yukon Territory, received a call to rendezvous with an out-of-town ambulance and transfer a patient. The driver and attendant drove off along the Alcan Highway, towards Haines Junction, near Whitehorse. While en route at 6.30pm, they noticed a strange object which:

*"...buzzed us several times on the way out, causing me to loose complete control of the electrical system of the ambulance".*

(**Sources: RCMP Report File on the incident [5.4.1977] Janice Hamilton & Andrew Hume – 'UFO Chases Ambulance', *Whitehorse Yukon STAR*, 5.1.1977**)

## 28th December 1976 – Egg-shaped UFO seen over Stafford

Mr R. Wooley, from Birmingham, was staying overnight at a friend's house in Stafford. He happened to look out of the window, at 4.30pm, when he was surprised to see an oval object,

*"...like an egg, with a bright white light at the front, moving rapidly and silently across the moonlit sky".* (**Source: UFOSIS**)

## 28th December 1976 – UFO over Yakima, Washington

During the evening, a ranching family – husband, wife, and child, living near Toppenish Rise, Yakima – sighted a 'bright white light' moving off the nearby mountain, towards their home. It then settled between the house and the corral, several hundred yards away, but its exact distance couldn't be judged.

*"It seemed the size of a large beach ball and hovered there, sputtering and sending off sparks – like a fourth of July sparkler."*

# It's the 5.30 flying

Halifax Evening Courier

# saucer

## 31 DEC 1976

THE GLOWING balloon-like object seen over Norland on Wednesday night was similar to about 40 others reported in the same area at the same time, it was claimed today.

Mr Allen Hornby, of High Lee Head, Midgley, said the most recent sighting of the blue object at about 5.50 pm followed a similar pattern to the others.

"It is about half the size of the moon, varies in colour, and has been travelling the same course," said Mr Hornby, a keen sky watcher.

"It moves slowly across the sky, suggesting that it is not an aeroplane or a star."

The only difference was that the other reported sightings had been on Tuesday nights.

"It must be regarded, like the others, as an unidentified flying object," said Mr Hornby.

Last night Mr Johnathan Bissell, of 123, Dudwell Lane, Halifax, telephoned the "Evening Courier" to say that he had seen an object near the horizon.

"It was about 5.15. It was white and moving slowly. When I looked through my binoculars I was almost certain it was a helicopter," he said.

Although generally staying in place, it 'oscillated' back and forth in a horizontal plane, in a rough manner. It remained in this mode for several minutes, during which time the family picked up a huge amount of static on their radio. The 'light' finally left the area, returning to the top of the mountain ridge by the route it had come. The family turned in for the evening.

The next morning, they discovered that all of their electric clocks were running three hours slow. Several of their neighbours corroborated having also seen an unusual 'light' that evening, but none of them experienced any electrical anomalies.

**(Sources: Mike Swords – 'Yakima Indian Reservation Incidence Report', W.J. Vogel, investigator, 4.1.1977 / J. Allen Hynek files, CUFOS)**

## 29th December 1976 – Unusual 'star'

At 3.30am, Mrs Margaret A. Waddell (then aged 32) living in Bellamy Road, Highams Park, London, was having trouble sleeping and decided to make herself a cup of tea, while the rest of the family were asleep.

*"I was looking out of the window, at the time, when I saw an orange-yellow 'light' – bigger than a star – moving across my vision to the right. It then stopped and was stationary for a short time, before moving back along the same direction. I'm sure it wasn't an airplane or star".*

**(Source: Essex UFO Study Group)**

Lesley Scotting (then aged 62) was on her way home from bingo, with a friend, at 9pm, when they heard a humming noise overhead. Looking upwards, they saw:

*"…what looked like an electric light bulb, sideways on, with flames coming out of the back, about 500 feet high. Seconds later, it had gone."* **(Source: BUFORA)**

| UB/ | Date | Time | Location | | | Size |
|---|---|---|---|---|---|---|
| | | | Unidentified Flying Object Studies Investigation Service, U.F.O.S.I.S. | | | |
| UB/20 | 29-2-76 | 7.15pm | West Bromwich | W/B | | 1m |
| ONE/16 | 23-1-76 | 1.35pm | Redditch | S | | 1½m |
| ONE/18 | 14-2-76 | 5.45am | Hamstead | H | | 1m |
| ONE/19 | | 8.00am | Stechford | O | | 2m |
| UB/22 | 22-3-76 | 10.20pm | Hall Green | Y | | 8s |
| UB/23 | 22-3-76 | 8.50pm | Harborne Golf Course | W/R | | - |
| UB/24 | -9-72 | 8.30pm | Hamstead | W/B | | 20m |
| UB/26 | 4-4-76 | 7/8.00pm | Erdington | W | | 35m |
| UB/27 | 20-4-76 | Pm | Hamstead | R | | 2m |
| UB/28 | 31-12-76 | 7.00pm | M6 Cheshire | Amber/O | | 3m |
| UB/29 | 7-11-76 | 7.20pm | Wednesbury | W | | 2m |
| UB/31 | 12-10-76 | 8.30pm | Dudley | O | | 20m |
| UB/31a | 12-10-76 | 9.10pm | Dudley | W | | 2½m |
| UB/32 | 7-11-76 | 7.30pm | Wednesbury | W/S | | 5m |
| UB/33 | 12-10-76 | 8.00pm | Dudley | W/R | | 1½m |
| UB/34 | 27-11-76 | 1.30pm | Cookley,K'minster | Bl | | 3m |
| UB/46 | 27-8-76 | Late | Hopwas Wood,Lichfield | W | | 5s |
| UB/80 | 9-1-76 | 5.50 | Kidderminster | W/R | | 15s |

# THE
# FOUNTAIN JOURNAL
## (WARMINSTER UFO SIGHTINGS)

No. 4, 1976 Vol. Price 30p UK Illustrated. Contents on page 3.
Cover: "You are already a member of an inter-planetary race."Artist concept

*A late addition*

## Investigations of Anomalous Aerial Phenomena

John Hanson: In November 2017 I spoke to retired physics teacher Denis Martin after he contacted me following a letter sent to the *Milford Mercury* asking if any of the readers could assist us with reports of strange events around the Pembrokeshire area.

Denis told me that he been interested in UFOs for over 50 years and for a short time had undertaken some investigations himself, having met Randall Pugh, Pauline and Billy Coombs.

**Denis:**

*"Since the 1960s I have had an interest in anomalous aerial phenomena, or unidentified flying objects (UFOs) as they were referred to until a few years ago by most people who undertook a serious interest in them. They are now often termed UAPs – Unidentified Aerial Phenomena. In 1974 I soon began to hear reports from students who claimed they had seen UFOs, so I took it upon myself to undertake some basic investigation and interviewed them in what I believe was an impartial and unbiased way. I also began to receive reports from other people. I did not normally seek out witnesses of these phenomena but acted only when individuals, or a mutual friend, came to me because they knew of my interest."*

## December 1976 – Malvern. UFO sighted over Malvern Hill ,Worcestershire

At 5.30pm two sixth-form students saw an unusual object near the Malvern Hills in December 1976. The information was reported to Denis and has been on file now for 40 years.

*"Whilst walking on the fields to the rear of the Spring Lane industrial estate one weekend – weather conditions cold with some snow and ice on ground – they noticed an object, stationary, over the hills, slightly East of the range and to the North – approximately no more than two hundred feet directly above the hill to the left of the moon and about the same size."*

### Blurred outline

*"It had no distinct edges and appeared firstly to be rectangular, luminous blue with even illumination over all its area. At no time could it be said it was truly three dimensional because of its blurred outline."*

*After about ninety seconds it gradually, over the course of about the next twenty seconds, seemed to change shape until it approximated a circle of the same colour with edges still indistinct. It then (moved) very slowly towards the West and sank down behind the hills, in much the manner of a sunset, but taking perhaps another thirty seconds to do so. We waited for about two minutes, during which time the object did not reappear, after which we continued."*

### Could it have been Venus or a UFO?

**Denis:**

*"No specific date was given in the report but using a software planetarium was able to obtain the relative configurations of Venus and the moon for December 23rd. I have superimposed on the star map a picture of the Malvern Hills as seen from the Spring Lane area. Could the 'object' they saw have been Venus viewed under unusual atmospheric conditions?*

# 1977

## THE QUEEN'S SILVER JUBILEE AND THE WELSH UFO WAVE

### CHAPTER 13 – JANUARY 1977

1st January 1977 – Essex Police officers sight UFO

2nd/3rd January 1977 – Cigar-shaped 'light' over the Malvern Hills, Worcestershire

4th January 1977 – Orange 'lights' over Bishop's Stortford Hertfordshire

5th January 1977 – UFO sighted over Suffolk by MOD official

7th January 1977 – A disturbing close encounter from Surrey

7th January 1977 – Triangular UFO over Middlesex

9th January 1977 – Expression of concern about the UFO subject

9th January 1977 – Erratic 'light' over Stansted, Essex

10th January 1977 – Views held by Dr. Allen J. Hynek

11th January 1977 – 'Flying Saucer' over Coulsdon

13th January 1977 – Schoolboy photographs UFO

15th January 1977 – White object sighted over Dagenham, Essex

16th January 1977 – UFOs over London

17th January 1977 – UFO over Hertfordshire, Poole and Dorset

20th January 1977 – UFO over Evesham, Gloucestershire

21st January 1977 – Close Encounter, Bridlington

21st January 1977 – Cigar-shaped UFO, Sheffield

24th January 1977 – Smoke ring over Wiltshire school

25th January 1977 – UFO over Chingford, Essex

27th January 1977 – Kentucky close encounter

27th January 1977 – Over Tasmania

### CHAPTER 14 – FEBRUARY 1977

3rd February 1977 – UFO over Swansea, South Wales

3rd February 1977 – Strange 'figure' seen at Seven Mile Beach, Tasmania

3rd February 1977 – UFO sighted by schoolchildren in South Wales

4th February 1977 – UFO landing at school, Broad Haven, Dyfed

7th February 1977 – Berkshire Motorist followed by strange light

9th February 1977 – Schoolboy sights UFO

10th February 1977 – UFO sighted by Police Officers, Mississippi

10th February 1977 – Elliptical UFO in the sky over Essex

12th February 1977 – UFO over Fulham, London

12th February 1977 – 'Strange lights' over Geilston Bay, Tasmania

13th February 1977 – UFO over Essex

13th February 1977 – UFO knocks youth off moped at Worcestershire

16th February 1977 – UFO over Lancashire

17th February 1977 – UFO over Llandudno Junction

17th February 1977 – UFO sighted over Broad Haven School South Wales

18th February – Mystery lights and cigar-shaped UFO sighted over UK

19th February 1977 – Large glowing object at Warminster, Wiltshire

21st February 1977 – Green 'star' over Boston, Lincolnshire

23rd February 1977 – Three 'lights' seen over London

24th February 1977 – Report of a UFO seen by motorists over Somerset

24th February 1977 – UFO over Little Haven South Wales

25th February 1977 – Hampshire schoolgirls sight UFO

26th February 1977 – Brilliant 'red lights' seen in the sky over Croydon

27th February 1977 – Strange object over London

28th February 1977 – Ex RAF man sight UFO over Worcester

February 1977 – UFO sighting at Lancashire

February 1977 – Close Encounter – Huyton, Liverpool

### CHAPTER 15 – MARCH 1977

1st March 1977 – Norfolk Schoolchildren sight UFOs

2nd March 1977 – *Lancashire Evening Telegraph*, 'Hilda's flying saucer appeal'

2nd March 1977 – UFO sighting over East Sussex

2nd March 1977 – 'Double star' over Essex

3rd March 1977 – UFO and 'aircraft' seen circling over Essex

Early March 1977 – UFO over Pendle Hill, Lancashire

7th March 1977 – Close Encounter, Winchester, Hampshire

8th March 1977 – UFO over Hampshire

9th March 1977 – UFO over Lancashire

11th March 1977 – Strange blue 'light' over London

13th March 1977 – UFO landing and occupant seen in South Wales

17th March 1977 – Heart-shaped UFO over Kent

18th March 1977 – Five glowing 'discs' seen over South Wales Estuary

26th March 1977 – 'Flying Saucer' over Little Haven South Wales

27th/28th March 1977 – UFO over Glasgow Airport, Scotland

28th March 1977 – Mystery 'ball of light' in the sky over Tasmania

Spring 1977 – 'Flying Saucer' over Hampshire

30th March 1977 – Landed UFO sighting, Birmingham

Spring 1977 – Close Encounter, Worcestershire

1970s – Strange 'beings' seen, Farnham, Surrey

## CHAPTER 16 – APRIL 1977

7th April 1977 – Welsh children chased by green 'ball'

7th April 1977 – Close encounter with Alien 'figure', Milford Haven, South Wales

8th April 1977 – Police officer reports strange 'light' over West Yorkshire

10th April 1977 – Strange 'being' seen on Cradle Hill

12th April 1977 – Close Encounter near Milford Haven, South Wales

12th April 1977 – Landed UFO, Penrith, Cumbria

15th April 1977 – Three UFOs sighted over Staffordshire

17th April 1977 – Huge 'ball of light' with 'winged structure' seen at Lowestoft, Suffolk

19th April 1977 – UFO landing, Haven Fort Hotel, Little Haven, Pembrokeshire

22nd April 1977 – Giant 'figure' seen at Ripperston Farm, South Wales

30th April 1977 – Oval-shaped UFO sighted over Essex

## CHAPTER 17 – MAY 1977

1st May 1977 – UFO over York Hill, Loughton Essex

3rd May 1977 – Police officers sight landed UFO, Essex

3rd May 1977 – Motorist sights 'strange light'

8th May 1977 – 'Strange figure' reported in the Hainault area

11th May 1977 – UFO, Leicestershire

15th May 1977 – Silver suited 'figure' seen at Ripperston Farm South Wales

15th May 1977 – Crop Circles discovered at Bristol, after UFO sighting

17th May 1977 – UFO crash-lands, West Yorkshire

17th May 1977 – UFOs sighted over East Lothian, Scotland

18th May 1977 – UFO over Surrey

19th May 1977 – UFO over Cheshire

20th May 1977 – UFO display over Bournemouth

21st May 1977 – Three UFOs seen by motorist on the M1 Motorway

22nd May 1977 – Strange object over London and Top Secret file

24th May 1977 – 'Flying Saucer' over Yorkshire

26th May 1977 – UFO over South Humberside

28th May 1977 – Pulsing 'red light' seen over Birmingham

28th May 1977 – Saucer-shaped object sighted over Clacton-on-Sea

30th May 1977 – Nottinghamshire schoolchildren sight UFOs

## CHAPTER 18 – JUNE 1977

1st June 1977 – UFO over Wales

3rd June 1977 – Diamond-shaped UFO seen over Essex

5th June 1977 – 'Bulbous light' over Essex

6th June 1977 – Close encounter by Durham motorcyclist

6th June 1977 – A frightening visit by the 'Men in Blue' to Welsh UFO witnesses

7th June 1977 – Three lights seen over Middlesex

8th June1977 – UFO over Hertfordshire

9th June 1977 – UFOs over County Durham

11th June 1977 – Misty UFO at Stone, Staffordshire

12th June 1977 – UFO over Brecon Wales

16th June 1977 – Close Encounter, Worcestershire

21st June 1977 – Motorcycle paced by UFO over Lancashire

26th June 1977 – Essex motorist sights 'ball of light'

28th June 1977 – Large sphere in the sky

29th June 1977 – Strange object seen in the sky

30th June 1977 – UFOs over Nottinghamshire

June 1977 – Cylindrical UFO over Holyhead, Anglesey, North Wales

## CHAPTER 19 – JULY 1977

July 1977 – Randall Jones Pugh (interview)

3rd July 1977 – Strange phenomena, Northumberland

5th/6th/7th July 1977 – UFO over Cheshire

9th July 1977 – UFO over junction of A128 and A13 Middlesex

17th July 1977 – Essex Police officer sights UFO

18th July 1977 – UFO over Essex

20th July 1977 – Disc-shaped UFO seen, Wiltshire

23rd July 1977 – Hampshire couple disturbed by two UFOs

25th July 1977 – UFOs over Somerset

26th July 1977 – RAF chase UFO over Warminster

July 1977 – Schoolchildren sight UFO over Hartlepool

July 1977 – 'Flying Saucer' over Northumberland

30th July 1977 – UFOs over RAF Boulmer

July 1977 – 'Flying Saucer' landing near Bradford

## CHAPTER 20 – AUGUST 1977

3rd August 1977 – UFO over Derbyshire

4th August 1977 – UFO over Truro

6th August 1977 – UFO over Chester

6th August 1977 – Close encounter with Aliens in Georgia, USA

7th August 1977 – Triangular object over Enfield, Middlesex

9th August 1977 – Triangular UFO over Stoke-on-Trent

10th August 1977 – Domed object near chemical plant

14th August 1977 – UFO over Warminster

14th August 1977 – 'Flying Saucer' reported over Wales

21st August 1977 – Police officer sights UFO

24th August 1977 – UFO over Cheshire

24th August 1977 – UFO over Bournemouth

25th August 1977 – Strange sighting over Middlesbrough

27th August 1977 – Close encounter, Dyfed

28th August 1977 – UFOs over the Lake District

30th August 1977 – Mystery light seen over Warminster

31st August 1977 – Illustration of UFO

## CHAPTER 21 – SEPTEMBER 1977

1st September 1977 – Bell-shaped UFO frightens couple over Essex

2nd September 1977 – Three UFOs sighted over Peterborough

3rd September 1977 – UFO seen over Barking, Essex by Tony Steel, UFO investigator

4th September 1977 – UFO seen over Surrey

7th September 1977 – Flashing light over Motorway Yorkshire

# LETTERS — FORUM & ARTICLES

## A LETTER FROM BUCKINGHAM PALACE.

In this Jubilee year, CNK took this opportunity to write to the Royal family the following letter:-

5th July 1977

Dear Madam,

To show honour in this Jubilee Year of your rein, my amateur publication wishes to produce a Silver Jubilee issue. I can only do so by asking your Royal Highnesses, yourself and your husband, where your beliefs lie in regard to matters not of this world, but others.

Therefore to ask both of you a direct question of the following: Do you consider it a possibility that, in your opinion only, that there are other life forms in space, other than our own? Please note that I have never written to a Royal Person before and it would therefore be the first time I could get the views of yourselves on these matters, since I have not read of any such views held privately by yourself or his Royal Highness Prince Phillip.

If you both hold any beliefs, I would like to know what they are, and if these would have to be private or for publication. I am sure however, that all persons on earth, whatever their status, must hold some beliefs of this nature-it's just that, we don't know for sure, if you have them. Can you tell me if you do. I'm sure your reply would be very interesting, if you feel this, of course warrants such a reply.

I wish to thank you for your time in reading this, and feel sure that I shall not be sending any more requests, at least, for the next 25 years.

God Bless you all at Buckingham Palace, Long may you look after us all. Yours sincerely, Edward Harris, Editor

THE REPLY:

BUCKINGHAM PALACE

11th July, 1977

Dear Mr Harris,

I am commanded to thank you for your letter of 5th July asking for an opinion from The Queen and The Duke of Edinburgh about 'other life forms in space'.

I fear that it is not possible to do as you ask.

Yours sincerely

Heselltine

# CHAPTER – 13 JANUARY 1977

## The Silver Jubilee

More than one million people lined the streets of London to watch the Queen and Prince Philip, in the golden state coach, make their way to St Paul's at the start of the Queen's Silver Jubilee celebrations, held on the June 6th/7th, 1977.

How many of them would have suspected, in their wildest dreams, that behind the enormous groundswell of public enthusiasm for The Royal Family, headed by a much loved Queen (then celebrating 25 years on the throne), the existence of a veritable 'blitz' of UFO activity, sweeping the length and breadth of the Country, involving the sighting of all manner of inexplicable aerial phenomenon and their even occasional stranger occupants? – Matters many of us will have no knowledge of until now, when we peel back the calendar of many previously forgotten breathtaking UFO events, which would alter so many lives – some for the good; others, the opposite.

Sadly, some of the 'tongue in cheek' banner catching headlines, calculated to entertain rather than raise awareness in this Jubilee year, were hardly helped by story lines, such as 'Mysterious men, who fly around in upturned jelly moulds', 'Wife is chased by UFO', 'Unidentified Football', 'Beautiful People from Space', 'What our little Earthlings saw', 'Earth calling Spaceship'….. to name just a few of the headlines which denigrated issues of real concern, to become the inevitable butt of public humour, and poking fun at those courageous few, whose eyewitness accounts were often dismissed as flights of fanciful imagination, or worse.

## 1st January 1977 – Essex police officers sight UFO

Police Constable Ronald William Rowley, of the Essex Constabulary (then 23) of Poynings Avenue, Southend-on-Sea, was on patrol driving a Ford Cortina Mk3 along Belton Way West, in Leigh, at 8.15am, in company with PC Bowler, when he saw a yellow-white flame coloured cigar-shaped shining object in the easterly sky, which he first took to be an aircraft.

> *"After watching it for a short time, I realised it was not leaving the usual vapour trail and moving very slowly. I watched it for five minutes and then continued on to Leigh Broadway – where, between gaps in the hedge, I could still see it. By that time ten minutes had elapsed."*

Policewoman Marion Annette Young (then 25) of Ringwood Drive, Eastwood, in Essex, was driving a Mini, southwards, down London Road.

> *"I saw a shape in the clear blue sky, which I thought was the vapour trail of an aircraft. Perhaps it was a cloud, I wondered? Strange, as there were no other clouds in the sky, apart from one or two small ones on the horizon; it was stationary.*
>
> *When I arrived at the police station, I saw my husband and another PC who had also sighted it."*

Police Constable Malcolm Young (then aged 39) was driving his police car east, along Belton Way, Leigh, and corroborates what his colleagues described. The total duration of the sighting was some fifteen minutes.

## 2nd/3rd January 1977 – Cigar-shaped 'light' over the Malvern Hills, Worcestershire

Mrs Patricia Hobson, of 21 Victoria Walk, Malvern Link, was inside, ironing, on Sunday night, when she saw:

> *"...a bright 'star' in daylight, hanging downwards, about three times the size of a star – had it been darker I would have taken it for that. I watched it for a couple of hours with my daughter – Melanie (13), and three neighbours. It moved very slowly over North Malvern Clock Tower in a west direction. It seemed to be dipping slightly."*

Mrs Hobson told the reporter that her daughter had seen a *'flying saucer.'*

On Monday night, when conditions were described as cloudier, Jean Hudson of the *Star* public house, Cowleigh Road, was shown the 'light' again, by Patricia Hobson – who both agreed this was not the North Star, as it was in the wrong place. One explanation was that it could have been rays being reflected from a high flying aircraft, or reflection from a meteorological balloon – or model aircraft!

The matter was reported to the *Malvern Gazette & Ledbury Reporter*, who ran the sighting under – 'Mysterious light over Hills puzzles watchers' on the 6th January 1977.

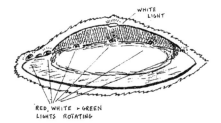

**Disc over airfield**

WHITE LIGHT

RED, WHITE & GREEN LIGHTS ROTATING

# 'Sky cigar' that baffled bobbies on the beat

MINISTRY of Defence experts are investigating claims by three Leigh policemen that they saw mystery objects over Southend.

The arresting sight mystified the policemen and they stopped their patrol car and watched the glowing cigar-shaped object for five minutes.

Then they saw it again 15 minutes later lumbering across the sky above the town. Pc Richard Rowley, on only his second day of duty, said: "It was very bright with an orange tint."

Meanwhile WPc Maureen Young — patrolling alone — also saw the orange light. Her husband, Pc Malcolm Young, was in Mr. Rowley's patrol car.

Pc Rowley, 24, of Poynings Avenue, Southchurch, said: "Malcolm first pointed it out and we stopped the car to look at it. We watched it for about five minutes and then drove back towards the station.

"We thought first of all it was an aircraft. It was cigar-shaped and very bright with an orange tint.

"When we got back to the station Malcolm's wife said she had seen it too."

The sighting was reported to Mr. Andy Collins, researcher for the British UFO Research Association, who has already logged three other sightings in South-East Essex in six weeks.

One of the other sightings was a silver disc seen over Southend by aircraft spotter Tony Shaw, of Honiton Road, Southend.

Mr. Shaw, a former RAF storeman, glimpsed the object dropping through clouds — but within seconds it had vanished.

Within the past two weeks there have been sightings by a Brentwood family who spotted a ring of flashing lights and reports of a strange flashing light that "buzzed" an aircraft over Heathrow Airport.

### Radar

Last year there were 46 confirmed reports of strange objects in the sky above Essex, including a spate of six sightings in Basildon and 13 over Dagenham.

Mr. Collins, of St. David's Way, Wickford, said: "This object was seen by policemen at two different locations. They are convinced they saw something that cannot be explained.

A spokesman for the Ministry of Defence confirmed that they had investigated the sightings by the three police officers, but said he could not comment on the findings.

"We are only interested with UFOs seen on or over military installations and the like. We did investigate this sighting, but there are no reports available."

A spokesman for the Ministry's Proof and Experimental Establishment at Shoebury said nothing unusual had been reported on radar.

"It's unlikely we would have seen anything as the rad-

## 4th January 1977 – Orange 'lights' over Bishop's Stortford Hertfordshire

Mr Paul Exon of Clayton, Staffordshire an AA engineer was driving along the A500 towards the junction with Basford. A colleague was driving behind him and communication was by means of a radio on a frequency of 72.3MGHz.

At 2.25am their conversation suddenly became swamped with static. This was composed of two definitive levels of noise, a general background hiss and a high pitched noise.

Looking out to the side of the road one of the men saw an orange light over the Shelton Iron and Steel plant, -a few seconds later it began to movie parallel with the road. As it did so the noise increased on the radio sets. The light ws last seen heading westwards towards the M6, as it did so the noise gradually faded away. Enquiries made later by Derek James of NUFON revealed the Police radios operating on 102MHz at Stafford HQ had sustained very bad static between 2.15am and 2.25am. They were unable to discover the cause.

Robert Luck (then aged 31) of Stansted, Essex, and his wife – Beryl, were travelling home from Widford, Hertfordshire, at 6.45pm, along the Great Hadham Road, Bishop's Stortford, and heading north.

> *"We sighted an orange 'light' in the sky and slowed down the car to nearly a stop, when my wife sighted another orange 'light'.*
>
> *I suggested that I observe the one ahead to the north, while Beryl the one in the east.*
>
> *After about ten minutes it was difficult to see the one in the east, because of trees obscuring our vision.*
>
> *We watched it head slowly towards the north-west and decided to give chase, but within a few minutes it was lost over the horizon."*

The couple reported the sighting to the police and local airbase, at Suffolk. (Source: Essex UFO Study Group)

On the same day, at 7.30pm, Brendon, Laindon woman – Leslie Scotting (then 62) not surprisingly (for people that have experienced a fairly close UFO sighting) found herself witness to something else in the sky. While in the process of collecting the washing off the line, she observed:

> *"...a huge yellow 'ball of light' in the sky – about the size of the moon – approximately fifty feet in diameter. I watched it for five minutes – until, in the blink of an eye, it disappeared."*

## Early January 1977-'Flying Saucer' over Glamorgan

In early January 1977, a motorist and his family were driving from Llantwit Major to their home in Bridgend. While passing the disused 'RAF Llandow airfield, about two miles from Wick, they saw a flashing light in the sky, which they presumed was connected with nearby Rhoose Airport and St. Athan RAF base.

**Liverpool Daily Post**

Planner No: 67-370

Daily - 92,749

E'6 JAN 1977

# Sightings indicate UFO 'pattern'

IT APPEARS that during the past couple of months, Britain has been visited by alien beings from outer space, who have dropped in on the world at ten-year intervals.

Another spate of UFO sightings, similar to the ones which recently stunned people in the South of England, have been reported to the British Unidentified Flying Objects Research Association, based in North Staffordshire.

The sightings come as no surprise to the association's 36-year-old research director, Mr Tony Pace, of Eccleshall.

He said yesterday: "These latest visits seem to be part of a general pattern of visits to the world by UFOs.

### Seriously

"Experts have anticipated this latest spate of sightings before they happened and if we can start to predict visits, then we are on to something. People will take us as seriously as scientists."

Mr Pace, a GEC office supervisor, explained that every ten years there had been a massive increase in UFO sightings in various parts of the world. In 1947, it was the USA, in 1957 France, 1967 and 1977 Britain. Nearly all the sightings had been within about two months either side of Christmas.

During the past twenty days, over a score of people in North Staffordshire have reported sightings to local newspapers and radio stations.

In the latest sighting, 65-year-old widow Mrs Nellie Richardson saw a yellow shining object over Bignall End, near Stoke-on-Trent.

*"Suddenly a brilliant orange flash lit up the ground; our first thoughts were that a plane had blown up. We then realised an object was moving across the road in front of the car. It was silver-grey in colour, the shape of a round 'disc' and was out 200 yards away from us; we estimated its diameter to be 30 feet. By this time we had stopped the car by the hedgerow and watched the object, now about 60-80 feet above the road, showing flashing red, green, and white lights – which were rotating. It then silently headed away over the disused airfield, and circled back towards the south, before turning eastwards – where it rose upwards and disappeared into the sky at a fantastic speed."*

## 5th January 1977 – UFO sighted over Suffolk by MOD official

What lay behind a startling claim, made by a Senior Civil MOD employee to Journalist – Michael Hellicarr, who told of a domed-shaped craft seen by them, while walking through rural Suffolk, on 5th January, 1977?

We spoke to Mr Hellicar, hoping to glean further information concerning this matter, but were told:

*"The man's identity and location were not divulged, as he had requested anonymity, but I can tell you that I had no reason to doubt his version of the events".*

It all started when the couple took their dog, 'Flop' – a Springer Spaniel – for a walk, on a bitterly cold evening, but decided to cut their journey short because of the freezing temperatures.

Suddenly the dog slipped its lead, which was completely out of character, and ran away. Glancing around, the couple were astonished to see:

*"...a huge, saucer-shaped object, hovering about 80 feet off the ground; we stood holding each other in sheer terror, noting an absence of any lights, markings or supporting structure on the object, which cast a shadow.*

*Twenty minutes later, it took-off in a blur of light and was gone".*

When the couple arrived home, they discovered (during conversation with their son) he had experienced a complete loss of signal to the TV, for a short time, until it stabilized itself.

'Flop' was found, two days later, in a village four miles away, in an exhausted state, and since the incident, refused to go anywhere near the field where the object had been seen.

Incredibly, while watching television, the following evening, the family noticed a number of zigzag lines were showing on the TV screen and guessed 'something was up'.

### Dome-shaped craft seen

When the husband rushed to the window, he saw an identical dome-shaped craft, hovering in the same place as the previous evening, before it flew upwards and vanished.

According to Michael, the incident took place in the locality near either Mildenhall, or Lakenheath United States Air Force Base.

The reason why the man chose anonymity was because he feared a backlash from his superiors.

(**Source: As above**)

## 6th January 1977 – Close encounter, Winchester

Winchester housewife – Joyce Bowles, was to report another 'close encounter', while driving back to Winchester with her companion – Edwin Pratt, at 6.30pm. As they drove past a cemetery on the A31,

Alresford to Winchester Road, Edwin directed Joyce's attention to an orange glow, moving in and out of the clouds.

**Joyce:**

*"The car then began to go out of control, accompanied by this piercing, whistling, noise. The next thing I became aware of, was finding myself standing inside a rectangular chamber, with rounded corners".*

In a tape-recorded interview, (a copy of which was sent to us by Leslie Harris and John Ledner), we heard the following conversation:

**John Ledner:** *"Did you see the car when you were in the UFO?"*

**Joyce:** *"No I did not. Ted said he can remember getting out of the car, but I am talking about my version of it. I can't speak for Ted."*

Joyce stressed that her memory of the entire event was clouded with gaps, although she was able to describe:

*"...a number of lights seen on one wall of the chamber, that I took to be part of an instrument panel, flashing on an off, displaying the spectrum of colour like a diamond. Standing in the centre was an artefact of graceful lines that had bands of yellow and black around it. Between these 'bands' were symbols, looking like horoscope symbols."*

The couple found themselves confronted by three 'beings', humanoids in form – two of whom were dressed like the entity seen by them previously; the third wore different apparel.

Leslie asked Joyce what they were wearing.

**Joyce replied:** *"Like a white Mac, as before, but it was long."*

**John:** *"So it was like a boiler suit?"*

**Joyce:** *"No – like a white Mac, but it was long stockinet stuff, tight to their legs."*

**John:** *"I don't see why you call it a Mac."*

**Joyce:** *"Because it was very much like these trench Macs – the colouring of it – where they've got these markings."* (Pointing to the chest)

**John:** *"But it was still trousers?"*

**Joyce:** *"Oh yes, but up here* (indicates shoulders) *it was the shape of a Mac."*

**John:** *"Were there any pockets?"*

**Joyce:** *"No, but it had different coloured markings; I don't mean seams, but like a beige thing across there* (indicating epaulettes) *one of them had on."*

According to Joyce, one of the entities was recognised as being one of the 'persons' involved in their first encounter.

*"His dress was the same and he wore a two or three inch belt sewn into his suit, with a square buckle, on which was mounted a white stone that he kept touching. He stepped forward and looked at Ted and he looked at me and said: 'We are not enemies, we are friends'. I replied: 'That's what Hitler said'. He replied: 'You have a strong tongue', so I shut up. Edwin was asked to take seven strides forward and then seven back. He was asked by the entity whether he had noticed anything. He replied, 'Yes, it's warmer there'. There was a map on the wall of the chamber consisting of lines. Edwin asked them what they represented. They told him, 'These are our fields'. Edwin thought he meant agricultural fields. The entity said, 'No, this is our fields.' The entity then turned to me and*

*said, in broken English, 'You are one of us. We will be back'. The next thing I remember was a 'beam of light' shining into the car and finding ourselves at the side of a river. We hadn't got a clue where we were, but after driving around came across a place we knew, called Chilworth, and arrived back at my house at 8.20 pm."*

Mrs Bowles told John and Leslie she had been plagued by psychic manifestations, going back to when she was 16 years of age. They included sightings of 'ghostly figures' and, more recently, the teleportation of a plastic swan from the mantelpiece at home, which landed in her lap while driving the family car, witnessed by her friend and neighbour – Miss Shears. (**Source: As above**)

## 7th January 1977 – A disturbing close encounter from Surrey

Mrs Mills from Camberley, in Surrey, was in conversation with her daughter – Carole (then aged four) when she said: *"Mummy, have you seen a man in my bedroom?*

Mrs Mills asked her, jokingly: *"What man?"* Her daughter replied, *"A shining white man".*

Further questioning revealed,

*"He was dressed in a shiny one-piece suit with a polo neck and belt, showing a torch light in the centre. He had a long face, a head like 'Kojak', pointed ears, large eyes, and a shining 'ball' in one hand. He sat on the bed, watching me, and then walked around the bedroom looking at the other five sleeping children. He picked up a teddy bear and then touched me on the tummy with the shining 'ball' and then threw the shining 'ball' into the air, before disappearing."*

Bearing in mind that similar experiences involving curious 'globes of light' and the appearance of 'nocturnal visitors' seem to form part of the background found in people who allege they have been abducted, one is bound to wonder if there is any connection with what took place, or should we dismiss the events as a dream or the result of a vivid imagination? What a pity we are unable to speak to Carole, who would now be in her early 40s. What other stories would she have to tell?

(**Source: *Fountain Journal*/Peter Paget**)

## 7th January 1977 – Triangular UFO over Middlesex

At 5.45pm, John Pain (then aged 64) of 103, The Chase, Enfield, in Middlesex, was on his way home when he sighted:

*"...three large white lights – one on top of the other two – forming a triangle. They were the size of cricket balls and were completely silent. I estimated they were 100 to 150 feet apart and about 1,000 feet high. I watched them for about 30 minutes, before they vanished from view."*

(**Source: BUFORA**)

## 9th January 1977 – Expression of concern about the UFO subject

As the New Year came into being, the *Sunday Sun,* Newcastle (9.1.1977) – 'Will 1977 be known as the year of the Flying Saucer –UFO Mysteries and the big cover up' – published a refreshing article by Peter Bibby, based on common sense, in contrast to the usual way in which the media ridiculed reports of UFOs. He looked back at what was already then an astonishing number of UFO reports, quoting that more than 250 UFOs had been sighted in the north-east between 1973 and 1976.

## 9th January 1977 – Erratic 'light' over Stansted, Essex

Robert Luck (then 31) was to find himself witnessing further examples of strange phenomena – this time while at home in Bentfield Green, Stansted, Essex, who went outside, at 6.30pm, to collect some coal for the fire. Something caught his attention in the sky.

*"I saw this bright white 'solid light', moving fairly fast across the sky. I called my wife – Beryl, to*

*come out and see. It was completely silent – no navigation lights and moving in a very erratic manner. We saw it climb at 90 degrees from the parallel and then vertical, without altering course or speed. No such aircraft exists on this planet, as far as I know, that has those capabilities."*

**(Source: Essex UFO Study Group)**

## 10th January 1977 – Views held by Dr. Allen J. Hynek

The *Herald Express*, Torquay (Alison Becket), published an article relating to the views held by Dr. Allen J. Hynek – 'Evidence about UFOs being shamefully suppressed'.

Dr. Hynek is an American astronomer, professor, and investigator into reports of UFO activity, and acted as scientific advisor to UFO studies undertaken by the US Air Force under three consecutive projects: Project Sign (1947–1949), Project Grudge (1949–1952), and Project Blue Book (1952–1969). In later years he conducted his own independent UFO research, developing the "Close Encounter" classification system. He is widely considered he father of the concept of scientific analysis both of reports and especially of trace evidence purportedly left by UFOs.

He cited an incident which took place in the Blueberry Mountains, Connecticut, involving a group of 13 American schoolboys, who had hiked to the top and were looking over the valleys below, when they saw a strange object in the sky – *"Like a flat bottomed saucer, 20 feet in diameter, silver metallic in colour, with a glowing red dome on top surrounded by a purple haze."* There was a high-pitched whine and the object vanished vertically into space.

Next day, the excitement and rumours abounding the camp died down after the camp authorities, fearful of harassment by the press and investigators, clamped down on it.

**Dr. Allen Hynek:**

> *"...an attitude typical and shameful; therefore it had not happened.*
>
> *Any question of it was closed. Stacks of evidence are being suppressed, through fear of scorn, ridicule, interference and disbelief.*
>
> *I know from personal contact with many airline pilots that under no circumstances would they officially report their experiences.*
>
> *They know better. Some have informed me that they wish to forget the whole thing ever happened."*

### Blue Book – UFOs do not exist!

The Blue Book report was prepared at the request of the US Air Force, conducted by Dr. Edward Condon of the University of Colorado. It took two years to produce and contains 140,000 pages and $200,000 to prove that 'flying saucers' do not exist!

**Dr. Hynek:**

> *"I set out as a disbeliever in UFOs and am the first to admit that at least 90% of the sightings are explainable. Many are honest mistakes, flocks of birds, distorted images of the sun, moon and planets. Weather balloons, meteors, and falling satellites have all been mistaken for strange craft. A few sightings can be attributed to mischievous hoaxers and sheer invention. Yet a weight of detail of something beyond normal scientific explanation remains among the 'quagmire of nonsense'. How can such evidence be dismissed as 'taradiddle'?"* **...so it continues....**

### 11th January 1977 – 'Flying Saucer' over Coulsdon

A Coulsdon woman saw something unusual crossing the sky, at 8.20am.

*"It looked like a plate, bright red in colour, and it left a red trail behind it which gradually cleared afterwards – like a vapour trial."*

The woman, who declined to leave her name (fearing that her friends would think she was a crank) probably did the right thing, bearing in mind the unnamed reporter who printed her sighting on the 14th January 1977, from the *Coulsdon and Purley Advertiser*, said:

*"I'd like to hear about any local UFO sightings – so, please, if you think the Martians have flown over the area, please contact us."*

Ignorance can be bliss.

At 10.30pm, James H. Trench (then 58) of 16, Blenheim Road, Walthamstow, London, was looking out of his window with his wife when:

*"We saw a thick cloud in the sky, and noticed a circle of white light shining through the clouds. I picked up a pair of binoculars and, looking through them, saw a 'circle of lights' with a cross in the middle of it. Seconds later, it immediately vanished from view."* (**Source: BUFORA**)

### 11th January 1977 – Tim Good lectures on UFOs

Later that day, Tim Good appeared at the William Temple Church, Abbey Wood, Eltham (admission free) to lecture on the UFO subject.

### 13th January 1977 – Schoolboy photographs UFO

Schoolboy Martin Paul Greaves of Lansdowne Road, Walthamstow, London, (then 14), was upstairs looking out of his bedroom window, at 5.30pm, as light snow fell, when he saw:

*"...something out of the ordinary in the west-south-west direction. I dashed downstairs for my Polaroid camera and took a photograph of it. The object (two elliptical objects side by side, standing upwards some 20 meters in diameter) had appeared from behind cloud cover. Just under a minute later, 'they' or 'it' moved in a straight path downwards, westerly, in a left to right action. The whole thing was over in about a minute."*

The photograph was later handed over to Douglas Canning, of the Essex UFO Study Group. Its present whereabouts is not known.

### 15th January 1977 – White object sighted over Dagenham, Essex

*Timothy Good*

Mr Arthur Sidney Toms (then 51) of Canberra Crescent, Dagenham, working for British Railways, was driving home from work at 7.45pm, along the A13 new road, towards Dagenham, when he noticed a white cigar-shaped object moving slowly across the sky, before it went into a bank of cloud. Although he later picked out a saucer-shaped image (shown to him by Barry King), the general consensus of opinion was that it might have been a misidentification of a natural phenomena. However, this was not the only sighting recorded for this day.

## 15th January 1977 – Silver 'disc' seen over Worcestershire

Later that evening, Geoffrey Westwood and his wife, Margaret, Head of the Birmingham UFO Group – UFOSIS – received a number of UFO reports from the Kidderminster area. They included the sighting of a silver 'disc', seen silently moving just under cloud, heading towards the Malvern Hills – possibly the same object reported over Ronkswood and the St.

*Margaret and Geoffrey Westwood*

John's areas of Worcester, on the same evening – now showing a red flashing light.

**Source: Derek Lawrence, SKYSCAN)**

## 16th January 1977 – UFOs over London

A couple were in Hyde Park, London, at 4pm, watching a flock of birds. They noticed a black 'boomerang' shaped object in the sky and realised it was no bird. A short time later, a second one was seen – possibly higher up and further away. After watching them for ten minutes, they became bored and left.

**(Source: Mr J. Shaw, BUFORA)**

## 17th January 1977 – UFO over Hertfordshire, Poole and Dorset

At 6.30am, Pamela Jones (then aged 24) of Brookside South, East Barnet, in Hertfordshire, opened the curtains in her bedroom and looked outside.

> *"I saw a huge object, shining like a star, motionless in the south-east part of the sky. I watched for a couple of minutes. It began to head north-westwards, stopped, travelled back to the original south-east position, then north-west again, before suddenly shooting upwards, at terrific speed, and vanishing from view six or seven minutes later."* **(Source: Ron West)**

Poole, Dorset, newspaper girl – Karen Beeston – was delivering newspapers, at 7am, when she noticed a large, unusual, prominent cloud in the sky, and felt a curious sensation that *"somebody or something"* was watching her.

As she walked along Buccleuch Road, she saw an unidentified flying object moving across the sky, resembling:

> *"...a streamlined car – about the size of a helicopter – showing red flashing lights around the centre, with white flashing lights on the end, accompanied by a buzzing noise – like an electric razor – before being lost from view as it entered a cloud."*

She was not the only witness. Mrs Joan Power was walking up her garden path, at 7.15am, when she sighted a cluster of 'bright lights' moving through the air,

> *"...just as you would imagine a 'flying saucer', saucer-shaped, with portholes – to look like, hovering over the rooftops of Heckford Road – then, as if someone realised I was watching, the lights went out. The next day I suffered from earache, which I never had before."* **(Source: Rachel Dear)**

## 20th January 1977 – UFO over Evesham, Gloucestershire

At 8.30 am Andrew Hyde (then aged 14) – a pupil at a local school in Evesham, Worcestershire – was walking to school with a friend, when they saw something white in the sky, travelling over the town.

> *"It was bullet-shaped and glowing, with a pointed tail. We thought it was going to land, so we rushed over to where we believed it had descended, but on looking upwards, were surprised to see it now low down in the sky, a few miles away. When I asked around at school, I found out that other children had also seen it."* **(Source: Personal interview)**

Dear sir/madam,

I was watching with interest, your article tonight on U.F.O.s, asking for reports on recent sightings, and I decided to write to tell you of my personal experience three months ago. It was on the morning of January the 21st at around 8.25 when my friend and I were walking along a road in our village and we spotted a white object moving rapidly across the sky in front of us. Suddenly it slowed down and we thought it was going to stop. At once we ran towards it to investigate, but by the time we had got to the spot where it had been, it had completely disappeared and the next time we saw it, it was miles away in the distance. There were quite a few witnesses and later on, in the day, we discovered that some pupils from another school had also spotted this unusual object. Since my own sighting I have seen a film of an identical object taken by someone 20 years ago! I have also reported it to the 'Sky Scan' group

at Malvern.

This object was white, glowing and very. Its front end was rounded and the rear was pointed. At the presumed front was a very faint yellow streak or dash. The other strange point about this object was that it made no noise as far as we could hear. I hope that this information is of use to you in the future.

Yours faithfully — Andrew Hyde (1

## 21st January 1977 – Close Encounter, Bridlington

This case was originally featured in *Flying Saucer Review*, Volume 3, Number 23, in 1977, following an investigation by members of the Nottingham UFO Investigation Society – John Cree, Sydney Henley, Robert Morrell and Philip Fargus. If it wasn't for the article having been published in *Flying Saucer Review*, it is unlikely there would be any reference to it – understanding, from conversation with the late Sydney Henley, that the records for this group were lost from history owing to the demise of one of the researchers.

At the time of the investigation, the three witnesses (who were not named) were employed as factory cleaners at the Britax factory, Bessingby Industrial Estate, located in an area of open ground on the outskirts of Bridlington. It is flanked on one side by a railway track, on another by one of the main roads out of the town, on another open land, and on the fourth side by a housing estate – this side being rather hilly.

The three women were aged in their late 20s to 50s. Two of the ladies cooperated, the third declined – her reason being of a domestic nature.

The Bessingby Industrial Estate consists of several small factories mainly situated on the side do the road, which turns into the estate.

Paul Sinclair – a highly respected man within the UK UFO organisation and a good researcher – told us about the Leslie Buttle experience, which was published in his book *Truth Proof*, and after obtaining

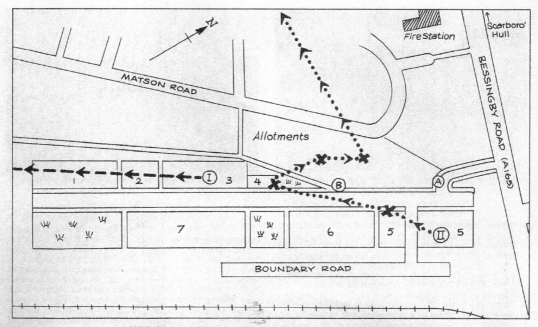

UFO flight paths at Bridlington, based on a sketch by John Cree

Key to above:—

| | | |
|---|---|---|
| 1. Adcock Shipley, Ltd. | Approx. length | 200 yds |
| 2. Turner Bros. Candlewick, Ltd. | " " | 75 yds |
| 3. Britax (PMG), Ltd. | " " | 200 yds |
| 4. Pickering & Bull, Ltd. | " " | 50 yds |
| 5. K.B. Dixon, Ltd. Woodyard & factory | " " | 200 yds |
| 6. Rig Holdings. | " " | 200 yds |
| 7. Britax (PMG), Ltd. | " " | 250 yds |

A Position of witnesses when they first observed the objects.
B Position of witnesses when objects last seen.
(I) Position of first object throughout the sighting.
(II) Position of second object when first observed.
x. Position of second object when hovering.

### Effects

The woman claims to have been physically affected by what they saw. The two interviewed claim to have developed bad throats and to have had "odd sensations." On arrival at work they were in a state of fright and "had a cry." They said this was also true of the eyewitness who refused to be interviewed. Mrs. A. said her watch stopped at 16.52 hrs. Both witnesses stated that the day after the event they developed bad colds, and Mrs. B. also added that her whippet dog, which was usually quite affectionate, refused to go near her for three days after the sighting. The women also asserted that a machine at Britax

First object first seen from here. Woodyard to the left, allotments to the right

Second object first seen from this point as witness looked over woodyard

Position of UFO and "telegraph pole" over Dixon's factory

Point over allotments where UFO took up bag

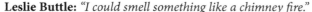

a copy we read about what was, and still remains to this present day, a fascinating but chilling encounter with something completely out of the ordinary.

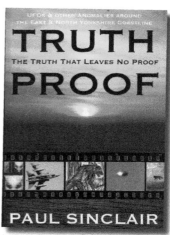

### Hazy object seen above a factory

The three women were walking to work, as dusk fell, when they observed a hazy object hovering above the factory to which they were going, but were unable to make out any details.

### Second object seen

They then noticed a second hazy object hovering above K.B. Dixon Ltd. wood yard, about 100 yards ahead of them. This second object started to move off, almost as soon as the women saw it, halting over first the timber merchant's office and then the factory part of the timber merchants. Just above the halted object was a ventilation pipe; this came out of the factory wall, which had a built-in air pump and was the only source of noise.

**Leslie Buttle:** *"I could smell something like a chimney fire."*

### Rugby ball-shaped UFO – cylindrical structure seen

As the object hovered over a vapour discharge chimney, the vapour disappeared and the object became distinct in appearance.

It appeared to be a Rugby ball shaped object – larger than a double-decker bus – with a dark grey top and bottom, and a flat central section with a row of portholes, through which could be seen a corridor and its wall. These portholes emitted a brilliant light.

On the back of the object was a cylindrical structure, shaped like a telegraph pole (according to Leslie). As the object moved away,

LESLEY BUTTLE'S ENCOUNTER

this projection was leading; in effect the object was moving backwards.

### Hovered over nearby allotment – sucked up waste

The object moved over the premises of Pickering and Bull (Fruit Merchants), and then came down to within six feet of the ground over some allotments; it then lowered what looked like a 'telegraph pole' and appeared to suck up a polythene bag, which allotment users held to store waste material. The object then moved rapidly away towards the West Hill housing estate and was lost to sight.

The observation lasted between five to 10 minutes.

### Bad colds – and malfunction with watch worn

Both witnesses who were interviewed developed bad colds after the incident, and this was believed to be the case with the third witness. One reported that her normally affectionate dog refused to go near her for three days following the incident; another that her watch stopped at the time. A claim by the witnesses that machinery at the factory had stopped at the time of the incident and took days to put right was emphatically denied by the management.

As the second object was said to have appeared to take something from one of the allotments (known as Hilderthorpe Allotments), the Nottingham Investigators went to see the chairman – Mr H. Morris. He told them that he knew of no thefts, interference or damage at that location on the day concerned. Mr Redshaw, who cultivated the allotment over which the object had been seen, was spoken to. He confirmed nothing was missing from his allotment, or any damage seen. This was more or less the same case with staff at Dixons, who sighted nothing unusual – but to be fair, they hadn't been looking. The older lady (Leslie Buttle) contacted *Radio Humberside* but, due to their sceptical attitude, she decided not to take it any further.

### Conclusions – 1977

In summing-up the very strange version of events, the organisation had this to say:

> *"We could establish no reason for doubting that the women had seen something unusual. However, we feel there are grounds for treating their claims with a healthy measure of caution."*

## 21st January 1977 – UFO sighting, Bridlington

[Authors: With the hindsight of now 40 years of UFO reports, including many that parallel what took place at Bessingby, no caution is needed in this instance!]

Our colleague Paul Sinclair, now author of books on the UFO subject, spoke to us about this particular matter in 2017. Like us, he remains intrigued about what took place there all those years ago.

**Paul Sinclair:**

> *"On Monday, 20th April 2014, I interviewed a lady from Bridlington – named Lesley Buttle. She wanted to tell me about a close encounter she and two other women had with a UFO back in 1977.*
>
> *Lesley told me that she worked as a cleaner for a manufacturing company named Britax PMG, on the coast at Bessingby. She was on her way to work that day with two other women, named Liz Jennison and Margaret Mooney. It was winter and about 4.30pm in the afternoon. Lesley said that it was starting to get dark when they noticed a patch of low white cloud or mist, over some nearby gardening allotments. The rest of the sky was clear so they stopped, as they were puzzled by this fuzzy cloud. They stood to watched it for a short time, trying to make sense of what it was, when it slowly began to clear. To their amazement they could now see a huge oval-shaped craft, hanging low in the sky over the allotments."*

#### 'Wave' of fear

> *"Lesley says their instant reaction was extreme fear. For some reason the three of them were so terrified, but to this day Lesley cannot understand why this 'wave' of fear came over them. The object was very close and making a strange humming sound. This made the hair on their arms and bodies stand up and their skin feel tight and prickly. 'It was not a nice feeling', remarked Lesley.*
>
> *She told me the craft was white or light-grey, with a darker band around the middle, which she was sure had seven illuminated windows. It was also spinning very fast but the windows were not spinning. This is something that still confuses Lesley even now, but they all agreed that the object looked huge as it hovered above the allotments."*

#### Big as a double-decker bus

The three women estimated that close to it, the craft would have been as big as a double-decker bus, although from where they were standing it looked no bigger that the size of a family car. Lesley thinks that if they had stood beneath it, the object would have been circular. Her reasoning for this was that the windows were small and seemed to curve towards the edges, as though the whole thing was round. As they stood there watching the object, they all began feeling sick and dizzy – which heightened the fear they all felt.

#### Green luminous tube appears – sucks up material from ground

Then – without warning, the spinning and humming sound stopped and a green luminous tube began to descend from the middle of the craft.

**Paul:**

> *"I asked Lesley if she thought it could have been a green 'beam of light' rather than a solid structure, but she confirmed it looked like a tube. The fact that the sound and spinning had stopped when the*

*tube descended is an interesting observation, which may indicate that the sound was associated with the spinning – yet the craft remained in the same position and did not need to spin to remain in the air. Leslie said the green tube was very close to the ground and, if they were closer, she thinks they would have been able to reach up and touch it. They saw material from the allotments rising up into the tube – which, after a few minutes, began to slowly retract back into the craft. The three women were observing all of this as it happened but were glued to the spot, as though trapped in fear. Once the tube had retracted, the humming noise started up and the object began to spin once again.*

*Moments later, the entire craft vanished into nothing more than a tiny speck of light and was gone"*

### Left shocked by the incident

All three women were shook up by what they had experienced. They were shaking and crying as they made their way back to the factory. The three of them discussed the incident in hysterical tones. Looking back now Lesley thinks the object affected them all, both mentally and physically, for weeks and months after the sighting.

### Watches stopped at 4.45pm

The first thing they had to do when arriving at work was 'clock in' to begin their shift. As they did do the three of them realised all their individual worn watches had stopped at 4.45pm. These were wind-up analogue watches, so whatever they had been through earlier had affected the mechanics of their watches.

Once inside the factory it was clear things were not right. The factory clock had stopped at 4.44pm and the machines on the factory floor had all stopped working too. They began to tell everyone at the factory what they had just seen and experienced, but no one would believe them. They were laughed at for suggesting that everything had stopped because there was a 'spaceship' in the sky near the factory.

**Paul:**

*"Lesley told me that when an engineer finally got the machines back up and running, they ran backwards (?)"*

*For days and months after their encounter, all three women suffered from severe head pains and bouts of dizziness. Leslie remembered that people came out to interview them about what they had witnessed. She also said that Bridlington Town Hall was open, the following Sunday. She thinks this was something to do with finding out who owned the allotment where the object had appeared to take things."*

### Men arrived to take samples from the area concerned

A short time later the women learned that some men had arrived, who took samples of earth and did tests on the area where the object was seen. A few times afterwards the three of them were questioned further but, due to the traumatic effect the experience had on them, they decided not to talk about it anymore. The ridicule they endured from friends and other factory workers was bad enough, without added pressure from unknown outsiders.

### Green glowing UFO seen in the same month

**Paul:**

*"I was able to track down two witnesses who saw a green glowing UFO, in January 1977. One of them, at the time, was an eight year- old boy named Tim. Now in his mid-forties, Tim told me about seeing a green oval object as he was playing with friends, close to the golf course on Bridlington's*

*south side. The distance between the Britax women's encounter and Bridlington golf course is only approximately half a mile. I do not have the exact dates for the two encounters, but I do know they were seen in the same month.*

*Tim told me that at first, he and his friends were puzzled by the green glowing object hovering in the sky – then, for some unknown reason, a kind of fear came over them and they began to run. He swears that the object followed them home and was there in the sky above his house when they arrived.*

*Another report from January 1977 came from a young man, who had been walking home from a night out at the time. Phil Morris told me of how he observed a green glowing UFO, close to where Bridlington fire station now stands. He told me that back in 1977 the area was an open field, over which he was making his way in the early hours, when the object slowly passed him. He said that it was very low in the sky and about the height of a first floor window. Phil also remembers other people talking about seeing the object and said it was reported in the Bridlington Free Press, the following week. This would have been the Britax women's encounter.*

*Phil said he was relieved to find that others had seen it at the time, even though he never spoke of it back then for fear of ridicule.*

*It is unfortunate that back in 1977, no one was able to fit all three of these sightings together. It might have helped Lesley Buttle and her two friends come to terms with what they experienced, rather than them having to be the target of ridicule and sarcastic comments."*

## 21st January 1977 – Cigar-shaped UFO, Sheffield

At 5.40pm, John Rothwell of Intake, Sheffield, was walking home when he sighted an object in the sky. Fetching a pair of binoculars, he looked through them and saw:

*"...a cigar-shaped object with blunt ends, moving slowly across the sky, from out of which a bright yellow flash was emitted, with no discernible sequence. Sometimes they followed immediately; other times there was an interval of ten seconds. I could see smaller, more rapid flashes, apparently above and behind the object. I watched it move northwards, before it halted over some trees – then lost sight of it."*

**(Source: Mr J. Whitlam, *BUFORA Journal*, Volume 6, Number 2, July/August 1977)**

**Sheffield ' flashing cigar '**

*Inv J Whitlam*

LARGE WINDOW-LIKE OPENING EMITTING, ON &OFF, A BRIGHT YELLOW FLASH.

## 24th January 1977 – Smoke ring over Wiltshire school

Pupils and staff waiting to go into Steeple Ashton School, near Trowbridge, Wiltshire, sighted something resembling:

*"...a huge, dark grey smoke ring travelling, at speed, across the sky".*

From the children's descriptions, they said they could see white clouds passing through the outside but not through its centre.

Others spoke of seeing a black/grey 'ring', with one side dark and a thin line running through it.

In February 2010, we were contacted by the daughter of Michael Green (her father, who had been the headmaster at the school at the time of the incident) – following which we received a telephone call from

WOMANS OWN 20 NOVEMBER 1989.

# It happened to me

## 'I saw a UFO fly past'

**Julie Goddard didn't believe in life on other planets, and certainly not in little green men. But one day she saw a very strange light on Salisbury Plain . . .**

There we were, in an ancient part of England, standing in a field, gazing up at something very strange and dazzling. It was like being in a time warp. For a few moments, it was as if two separate time dimensions had overlapped. I and about 20 other mothers and children just stood there with our mouths open, watching while a strange phantom circle bowled silently past our 14th-Century church. To this day, I couldn't say what it was. All I can say, is that it was something unidentifiable, and it was flying. So I suppose it was a UFO.

Up until then, I'd never even thought about the possibility of life on other planets and certainly not human life. I was very much a believer in Patrick Moore's theories, as I used to watch The Sky At Night. He maintained that human life was an unusual development, unique to Earth, and couldn't be found on any other planet. I thought that perhaps plants or animals could exist on other planets, but that was about it. I certainly had no ideas about little green men and have never even been faintly interested in science fiction films or books. In most ways, I was a total non-believer in unearthly goings on.

I didn't believe, even though I was living very near Salisbury Plain, an area well known for strange sightings of things in the sky. In fact, anyone who has visited Wiltshire knows it's a place full of mystery. Stonehenge dominates the area, refusing to give up any of

### 'Suddenly it disappeared into the clouds'

its supposed secrets. And every summer I was used to hearing about mystery circles appearing in the corn, baffling farmers. The most unusual circle appeared, like clockwork, every year, directly below the massive white horse that is etched on the chalk hillside near Westbury.

In many ways, Wiltshire could strike one as an eerie place. But I was never bothered. I did read about sightings in the paper occasionally, but thought nothing of them. A UFO society had been set up in the area, but I was so sceptical, that I always thought they spotted things because they had nothing better to do!

But all my views and beliefs were completely overturned the morning I saw something inexplicable fly past my very own eyes—in broad daylight. That morning I had decided to walk my two children, aged seven and eight, the short distance to school. I didn't have to take them, but it was a lovely day, and I always enjoyed chatting to the other mothers in the school yard. The sky was clear blue and there was a slight nip in the air, which made us glad we had our warm coats on. We closed the back garden gate, crossed the road, and went into the school field through another wooden gate.

As we skirted the field, avoiding the football pitch, I was aware that a small group of parents and children were standing still, looking up. Some of them were pointing. Soon we were standing next to them. "What's going on?" I asked. "Look!" someone said, and we all looked towards the sky. There, moving from the Westbury direction, was a large circle.

The village of Steeple Ashton, where we were living, lies in a very flat area at the foot of the steeply rising escarpment of Salisbury Plain, so the sky is very open and you can see for miles around without anything obstructing your vision. What we saw was in clear view. And it was extraordinary.

I can only describe it as looking like a band of transparent plastic. It had grey edges and the ends were fastened together, making it look like a hoop. It seemed to me to go over and over like a hula hoop rolling along—and the thickness of

**Eye-witnesses—these children saw the UFO on their way to school**

it wasn't all the same. It made absolutely no noise at all, no buzzing like an aircraft. I'd never seen anything like it before. All I can remember is that it seemed to bowl along in front of our eyes, and then, suddenly, it disappeared into a bank of clouds towards the south east. It was hard to judge how far away it was, how big it was, or what substance it was made of. It didn't look very solid—I couldn't imagine it being full of inter-planetary invaders or little green men. But it was unearthly.

After it passed, we all just stood still. I can't remember if anyone had said anything during or after the sighting. We were all too flabbergasted to speak, I suppose. But when it had gone, the school's headmaster, Michael Green, who was with us, simply said, "Come on then, it's school time," and we all followed him along the path towards the school. But we all kept looking at each other, wondering if we really had seen the flying object. It was strange to carry on as if nothing had happened, but what else was there to do?

One of the mothers with us was a local reporter, and she went off to ring the local paper immediately, so the newspaper rang the headmaster for his comments. Then, some television people came round and interviewed local people. The UFO society also came to the school and asked people to draw what they had seen, but it was very hard to put it down on paper.

When I went home afterwards, I just did the washing and continued life as usual. I did tell my husband when he got home that evening, but he's a very matter-of-fact, down-to-earth sort of man, and he just said, "Oh. When's dinner, then?" To this day I haven't been able to convince him that we saw something strange. He thinks we saw a big smoke ring blown over from the nearby cement works. But it would have been the equivalent of a hurricane blowing for a smoke ring to have travelled as fast as the thing we saw.

I've told this story to people many times, and sometimes tell the children I look after at the local school. People are always fascinated to hear about it. But even though it's a story I tell others, about something I saw with my own eyes, I still don't really believe there are little creatures living in outer space travelling around in flying saucers. But I did see something very unusual—and it was a UFO. I saw something odd, something that can't be explained. That's how I'd sum it up. ■

### TELL US YOUR STORY

Has anything extraordinary happened to you or to anyone you know? If so, we want to hear about it! Your story can be happy or sad, touching or funny. It can be about a happy event, a dramatic incident (however scary it seemed at the time), a never-to-be forgotten moment.

Whatever your experience, we'd like to hear about it. You must be prepared to use your real name and to be photographed for the magazine—and we'll pay £150 for every story we print. (Your story must not have appeared in another magazine.) Send a brief summary to us at Room 482, Woman's Own, King's Reach Tower, Stamford Street, London SE1 9LS, marking your envelope "It Happened To Me". Sorry, we cannot return your letters.

MICHAEL GREEN: "It looked like a big smoke ring"

## The whole school saw the thing that flew away

Michael, wishing to put the record straight.

*"We were in school. It was only a small school. I was upstairs when a girl came into the office/classroom and said:*

*'Have you seen what they are all looking at out there?'*

*I looked out, but couldn't see anything; she suggested I go downstairs to have a look properly, so I went out onto the landing and saw this 'thing', by which time it was nearly 9am, so I went out and got the children in.*

*One of the mothers contacted the newspaper, as she was worried about it. I think they put her in touch with Arthur Shuttlewood, who I had met before. My only regret is that I didn't stand and watch it, at the time, to see what happened to it in the end.*

*Did it just disappear or what? If it hadn't been for the lady concerned, I don't suppose we would have heard much more about it. I remember someone ringing us up, suggesting it was smoke coming from the Westbury cement factory chimney. We had so many people that came to school, expressing an interest in talking about the UFO seen. It just built up and up. The News of the World even covered the story with me on the front page. People even rang us from America."*

During an interview by the local television station about the incident, Michael firmly rejected the suggestion put to him that they had seen an aircraft.

**Julie Goddard, one of the 'young mothers' at Steeple Ashton School, and a witness to the incident, had this to say:**

*"As we skirted the football pitch with my two young children on the way to school, I noticed that some of the children and their parents were looking upwards into the sky. I asked what was going on. Somebody said, 'Look', and I saw this large circle moving across the sky from the Westbury direction. It looked like a band of transparent plastic, with grey edges and ends fastened together, like a hoop, and was going over and over – like a Hula Hoop rolling along – before disappearing into a bank of cloud in the sky, towards the south-east. The headmaster, Michael Green, arrived and asked us to go into school. One of the mothers, a reporter, contacted the newspaper and, following publication, the television company came around to see us – then members of a UFO group. I told my husband, when I arrived home, what I had seen. He suggested it might have been a smoke ring from the cement factory."*

(**Source: As above/Michael Green/*Woman's Own* Magazine, 20.11.1989/Personal interviews**)

## 25th January 1977 – UFO over Chingford, Essex

Master Gordon Jackson (then aged 13) of Laurel Way, Chingford, Essex, was in Mansfield Park, Chingford, at 7.30pm, when:

*"I noticed a 'bright light' in the sky. It seemed strange, so I watched it for a little while and it seemed to change colours – then went back to being a 'bright light' and faded into the distance, fifteen minutes later."* (**Source: Douglas Canning, Essex UFO Study Group**)

## 27th January 1977 – Kentucky close encounter

At 1.05am, Lee Parrish (then 19) of Prospect, Kentucky, a high school graduate, employed by his father's firm – 'Parrish Supply', had been around to see his friend, Kathy Johnson. He left as the TV programme went off air, at about 1am. He fed the dog on his way out and then got into his 'Jeepster' (a 1970 model with a V6 engine), and headed home – normally a seven minutes journey.

The weather was cold and partly cloudy, with quite a bit of snow on the ground. The roads were relatively clear. Lee drove west on *Highway 329* heading towards US 42. He was four miles short of that junction when he saw an object, hovering silently, just above the tree line, between 1-200 feet away.

> *"It appeared to be about ten feet tall and forty feet long. Its shape was perfectly rectangular. Its colour was like the setting sun, but much brighter. I felt compunction to look at it and was unable to remove my gaze, but at the same time it was too bright to look at the object. I felt frightened and wanted to leave but couldn't do it. I don't even remember how I stayed on the road. About 15 seconds later the car radio failed. I kept up my observations on the object until I was directly underneath it. Suddenly, it shot away – faster than any jet – towards the north-west."*

When Lee arrived home, his mother met him at the door and asked him: *"What's wrong with your eyes"*?

Lee looked into the mirror and saw that his eyes were entirely bloodshot, and he was in considerable pain. He looked at his watch and saw it was 1.45am, which meant that he had been en route from Kathy's house for 45 minutes, on a journey that should have lasted seven minutes!

As a result of this incident, Kentucky researchers – Don Elkins and Carla Rueckert – received a telephone call from Lawrence Allison – a hypnotist who had worked with them before on Close Encounter UFO cases. He had been contacted by Lee's mother, who was very concerned about what had taken place.

### Story under hypnosis (extract)

Subsequently, Lee was regressed. Under hypnosis, he tells of seeing the rectangular UFO and thought it was a fire – then rejected that, feeling scared, asking himself over and over, *'What is it?'* Eyes hurt from looking at brick-red object – cannot remember driving car, is not sure if craft had actually moved over road or whether car had entered field part of the flat land the UFO was hovering over – increasing scared – *"It's not moving"*, he says in a puzzled tone. Suddenly couldn't see anything – split-second before craft had changed colour to black and then white – felt something in his eye – when he could see again, he was no longer in a jeep but in a circular, all white room. No knowledge of the transition. Before him stood three objects, which he felt or sensed were sentient 'beings', although they were not human.

**A black one:** To his left, as high as the ceiling, roughly the shape of an army silhouette target – jug shaped, with a relatively small 'head'. It had a flat bottom and one 'arm', a handless, jointed appendage – arm was rough skinned; the rest of the 'entity' rough in patches, smooth in patches – with featureless head – moved slowly towards Lee and touched him on the left side and back, hurting him quite a bit and terrifying him. **Lee:** *"No, not the black one."*

**A red one:** *"...on my right, about my size, a little smaller and rectangular in shape – like a 'coke machine' – it had one arm or probe un-jointed and handless."* Lee felt that this one was scared and reluctant to touch him, but it came over and touched him on the shoulder and on the right temple above the ear – felt like a needle and stung briefly. Didn't terrify him, and didn't hurt long.

> *"The whole ship was rocking like a boat on the water."*

**The white one:** about six feet tall, sat in middle of room, watching Lee – its body solid and blocky, its head square on the sides, flat at front. In profile, the head sloped towards the body at a 45 degree angle with no features. Whole 'being' glowed. It had arms, but did not use them, remaining stationary. Lee knew it was the 'ruler' of the two.

### 27th January 1977 – Over Tasmania

Of course, the UK wasn't the only country to see an upsurge in reports of 'strange lights' seen in the sky. One of the first was reported to Launceston Police Station and brought to the attention of John C. Dean, Northern representative for the Tasmanian UFO Investigation Centre. John was able to confirm that the 'strange light', observed between 11.30pm and 4am, at the farm located 25 kilometres north-east of Launceston, was, in fact, Venus. The same could not be said for what Peter Damon saw, while staying with friends at another farm in the same area.

*"About 11.30om, two 'lights' were seen in the western direction, accompanied by a humming noise, which set the dogs off barking. Clearly they were frightened. One of the 'lights' – a red one – was situated in the Den Range of hills and was seen to move up and down in the sky. The second 'light' was more intriguing. This was larger and elliptical in shape, showing red and silver colours. This was closer to the farm, about half a kilometre away and apparently stationary over a ploughed paddock. It would occasionally phase out and then reappear. A couple of the group went over to have a closer look but returned back to the farm, clearly disturbed after it appeared in the sky again."*

**(Source: UFO 1978, *Tasmanian UFO Investigation Centre*, No 23)**

## CHAPTER 14 –FEBRUARY 1977

### 3rd February 1977 – UFO over Swansea, South Wales

**Mrs Jessie Morris, of Swansea:**

*"I had a phone call from a relative, at 10.15am, telling me about a strange bright object below the clouds, a couple of hundred feet up. The glow was blinding and vanished after seven minutes. His wife also saw it, but a strange thing happened while the UFO was visible – his legs and feet became numb, and afterwards he could not walk for three hours. It was above Ystradgynlais, Powys, just over the Dyfed border, and there are reservoirs not far away – also, a high tension electrical installation."* **(Source: *UFO-UK*, Peter Paget, 1980)**

Later the same evening, Mr and Mrs Whiting, and their two children, were driving along Shepherds Hill, Romford, towards Brentwood, Essex, when they saw a yellowish oval object, quite low in the sky, showing a number of red flashing lights on its one side. As they continued on their journey towards Gallows Corner,

*"...a little red spark came out of the object and went from one side of the road to the other."*

Mr Whiting wondered if it could have been some sort of parachute exercise over a nearby Aerodrome.

By now they had been keeping watch on it for 45 minutes and it hadn't moved.

As they turned down the A12, they felt it was now moving and following them.

They arrived home in Wingletye Lane and rushed upstairs. They were stunned to see the object, motionless in the sky, above the right- hand side of the house. Through binoculars,

*"...a bright bulb-shaped object was seen, showing red lights, which on one occasion changed to blue. At 9pm, it began to fade and was gone by 9.30pm."* **(Source: Barry King)**

### 3rd February 1977 – Strange 'figure' seen at Seven Mile Beach, Tasmania

A group of children staying at a youth camp, including Michelle Russell-Green, whose father was President (presumably of the Tasmanian UFO Group), were at Seven Mile Beach, at 9.30pm. Michelle went for a wash at about 9.30pm, when she heard:

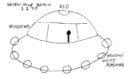

*"...a burring noise and looking out into the sky saw, to the east, an object, stationary, to begin with, before it moved behind trees.*

*It was dome-shaped, with what looked like windows around the middle. A wider area of light, disc-shaped, was spinning below.*

*There were flashing white and yellow lights on the edge of the 'disc' and a red light on top. The body of the object may have been white or just reflecting the bright lights. On one side of the centre window there looked to be a thin 'figure', with a bump or rounded head. It seemed to be moving back and forth in the window".*

**Another witness was Janine Horne:**

*"It was like two saucers, stuck together, spinning fast – then slowed down, a 'figure' being visible in what looked like a window, near the object's centre. The elliptical object had a row of windows across its top half. There was a red light on top with a green one below. A row of lights was visible across the centre. The 'figure' appeared to be thin, with a large rounded head, above what looked like a high collar. It had an arm visible to the right. The 'figure' moved its head and changed position. The object was last seen behind trees, east of the location."*

## 3rd February 1977 – UFO sighted by schoolchildren in South Wales

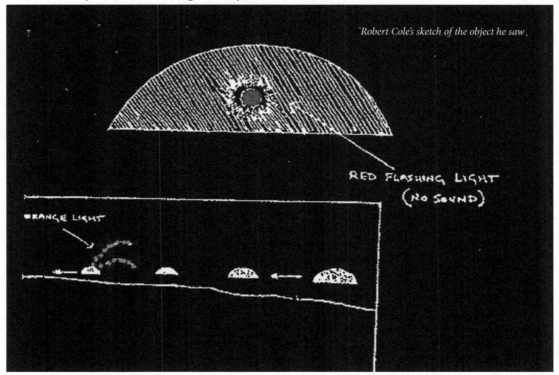

'Robert Cole's sketch of the object he saw'

RED FLASHING LIGHT
(NO SOUND)

ORANGE LIGHT

Schoolchildren and teachers from Hubberston School, Milford Haven, Dyfed, sighted *"a dark cigar-shaped object, motionless in the sky"*, during the lunchtime break.

James Saunders (now in his late 90s) was the headmaster, at the time. He had this to say, in an interview held with him in 2005:

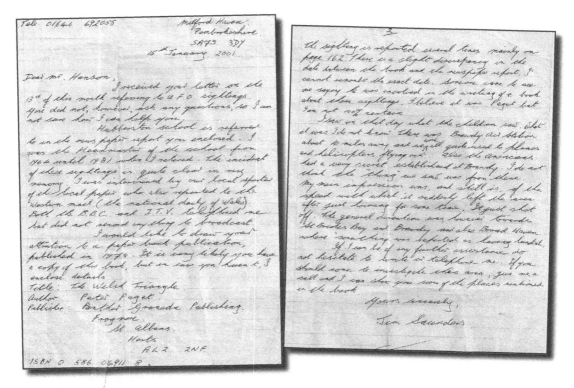

*"I remember the events very well. At least 20 of the pupils, and some teachers, saw this object. When they told me about it, I went outside and saw it about three-quarters of a mile away from the school, hovering over the town of Milford Haven, at 1.20 pm. Suddenly, to my great surprise, it shot off – like a bolt from out of the blue – towards St. Brides Bay. That was the last I saw of it."*

Robert Cole was on his way home at 6.42pm, the same day, and crossing Welland House, Maidstone, Kent, when he saw:

*"...a domed object with a dark mass and a red flashing light in its centre, travelling west to east. As it neared the western horizon, an orange light curved away from it – then I lost sight of it."*

**(Source: Personal interview/Mr J. Castle, BUFORA)**

## 4th February 1977 – UFO landing at school, Broad Haven, Dyfed

Many people will be aware of the extraordinary UFO events that took place in and around South Wales, during a 'wave' of activity, including the now immortalised sighting at Broad Haven Primary School, Broad Haven, Dyfed, when a silver 'craft', and its occupants, were seen by the children on the slope of the nearby hill – a matter subsequently brought to the attention of Randall Jones Pugh – a vet by occupation, and investigator for the British UFO Research Association.

Randall was to write a book, entitled *The Dyfed Enigma* (Randall Jones Pugh & F.W. Holiday, Faber & Faber, 1979) – still regarded as the 'benchmark' of a number of books of what became known as the Welsh UFO 'wave' of 1977.

We asked Mr Pugh, during a visit to his home address, what had triggered off his interests in the UFO subject some years ago.

DAILY EXPRESS Thursday October 11 1979

## NEW BOOKS Edited by Peter Grosvenor

# Now...close encounters of the Welsh kind

**Is Celtic insight looking into UFO-land?**

OF all the mysteries of our time, UFOs — the Unidentified Flying Objects reported periodically by people as diverse as airline pilots, merchant seamen, bird-nesting schoolboys and housewives hanging out the washing—are the most fiercely-discussed.

Self-hypnosis, mass hallucination, meteorological phenomena . . . the "rational" explanations are many.

By Douglas Orgill

But whether you believe in UFOs or not, it's a sobering thought that it needs only *one* UFO story to be true to prove UFOs exist.

So says Randall James Pugh, an experienced UFO case-historian who is co-author of a new book, THE DYFED ENIGMA (Faber, £5.95), a record of ufological and other worldly activities in West Wales between '74 and '77.

Not entirely between those dates, however, as evidenced by two of Mr Pugh's cases.

### Dwarfs

First, " On a fine summer day, my eldest sister and myself, with two of our next-door neighbour's children, were in a field near their house when one of us saw a company of—what shall I call them ?—*beings*, neither men, women nor children, dancing, more like dwarfs than children."

And second, " It was right up close to the window as if it was looking in. We couldn't see his face—or its face, whatever you like to call it—because it had a black visor round it. But there was actually a man in a silver suit standing there. Well, more of a monster, you could call it. It had a glow round the edge of the suit."

The first case was described by Doctor Edward Williams in his journal in the year 1757.

The second case was reported by Mrs Pauline Coombes, of Ripperston Farm, in Dyfed, on April 22, 1977.

Inquiries made by Mr Pugh and his co-author F. W. Holiday (who died early this year) have established that 1977 was a bumper year for "sightings."

Among them, a three-tier flying saucer seen on the ground by a university graduate farm manager near Ripperston on March 26, 1977. And a "silver human being," no eyes or nose, seen by two young children.

" What we are witnessing," Randall Jones Pugh told me " is a variation on an old, old, elemental theme.

" For centuries, sceptics have laughed at folklore—stories of mysterious beasts, goblins, the little people. Now we're going to discover the truth behind the myth.

" I believe certain people — it may be that Celts are peculiarly well-equipped in this respect — are able to trigger off what one can only describe as a mirrored reflection from another dimension."

Pugh has the last word. " Soon the question that will arise will not be so much 'Can such things be?' but rather ' Why are these things here ? '"

*"I was on holiday at the time, in Torrevieja, Spain, about 30 miles south of Alicante. One night I was unable to sleep, so I decided to go for a stroll just after midnight, on what was a clear night. As I walked along I noticed what looked like a wheel, with bits sticking out, moving north-west to south-west, so low I could make out 'portholes' on the flying object.*

*My first reaction was to wonder whether it was a satellite but I dismissed this idea when I saw a golden glow around the object, which had a dome on top.*

*I admit to being frightened by the passage of this object as it moved slowly over the landscape, at a height of between 500-1,000 feet, and ducked into a nearby building for five minutes, to recover my composure. When I ventured outside, it had gone."*

Randall urged us to take Holy Communion, believing that UFO sightings undoubtedly owed their origins to the occult rather than incursions onto our planet from any 'alien' visitors and that investigations into this subject should not be taken lightly, telling us,

*"We are dealing with manifestations of demonic forces interacting with our Dimension" – an attitude apparently shared by other UFO Researchers we were to meet, over the years.*

Following our visit to Mr Pugh, we made our way to Broad Haven Primary School and, after being given permission by the headmaster, examined a 'UFO scrapbook' still kept there – now very much the worse for wear, but offering an illuminating and sometimes entertaining glimpse into the events which took place all those years ago.

An example: a letter addressed to 'The UFO School at Broad Haven' and 'to where the UFO incident had taken place', sent out without any postal address ... but delivered, they were!

# THE GREAT UFO ENIGMA

**Some thoughts on interesting points made in a new book**

## *Charles Bowen*

IT is always an agreeable experience to read a new book on a side of the UFO phenomenon which has been carefully investigated and researched. Such a book is **The Dyfed Enigma**, by **Randall Jones Pugh** and **F. W. Holiday,*** which was inspired by the mass of UFO and humanoid incidents which were reported in the south western corner of Wales during 1977.

Very much in the book's favour is the fact that its authors each lived and worked in the area for a great part of their lives, Pugh as a veterinary surgeon, and Holiday as a writer and a regular columnist with *The Western Mail*. They knew the country and the people very well, and the idea of chonicling and commenting on the remarkable series of events, came to them early on in the wave. That much I gathered from correspondence with them, and the occasional telephone conversation; I knew too, thanks to the valuable contributions made by each of them to *Flying Saucer Review*, that with Holiday's skilful and fluent professionalism, and Pugh's easy style, we could expect a well-written book, which is just what it turned out to be. We are lucky that the arrival on the West Wales scene of paperback writers did not pressure them into trying to force the pace. Unhappily, however, poor Ted Holiday did not live to see the book published; he died on February 23, 1979.

Some of the book's recorded events have already been dealt with in FSR but now, in *The Dyfed Enigma*, they appear usually with enhanced detail, and often with new details. Furthermore they can now be appreciated in the true context as part of the on-going phenomenon in the region. Nevertheless there are also many cases which will be new to FSR readers, like the report of a "space ship" seen, at 3.00 a.m. one morning, hovering just above a window of a house in Milford Town, while a small humanoid figure stood on the window sill. There was also the unnerving double encounter of a lady driving home from Carmarthen to Ferryside on the River Towy, who was greeted in a most unaccustomed manner by her three dogs, one of which went on to suffer strange (psychological?) effects. Again, there was the case of a humanoid figure seen close to a sewage works at Herbrandston. There are many more besides these to whet the reader's appetite.

Study of, and speculation about the recorded phenomena is to be found in two chapters. The first of these, No. 6, is entitled "The ley correlation." To my way of thinking the leys shown in the example maps are largely unconvincing 2-point lines, and on that basis the locations of UFO sightings could be said to be correlated with almost any straight line ( = the shortest distance between two points) connecting ancient works, tumuli, knapps, standing stones and various antiquities, anywhere in the country.

The other chapter is No. 8, "Is there a 'Goblin Universe'?" After making a valid point — based on reported reactions to the phenomena — that there is "something apparently objective and external . . ." the authors state that there is no evidence that the extraordinary (*UFO*) activity comes from outer space "even though this is a view widely popular among cultists." Further on we find that "according to folklore such (*objective and external*) activity was not associated with space and the stars; but rather with supra-dimensions of being which are today conveniently categorised as 'the paranormal'." Again: "The notion that UFOs are 'visiting' the earth on some explorative venture strikes us as simplistic in the extreme. If such assumption is made, the evasive nature of UFO-human contacts seems entirely illogical."

The authors pursue their interesting argument through several pages and suggest eventually that there *is* a "Goblin Universe," and that all instances of the phenomenon could be a result of the tricks played by elemental beings on human observers, appearing throughout the decades, indeed throughout the centuries. And, as John Keel has written before, the frames of reference in which the manifestations are witnessed, have always kept just ahead of the state of knowledge and technology existing at the time of the manifestation.

Naturally there will be many — and not only "cultists" — who will challenge this argument. For instance, it could be said that it is equally hard to believe that there is any evidence that the extraordinary UFO activity is manipulated by elemental beings despite the fact that (*p.143*) "work over the last thirty years by parapsychologists in various countries into such phenomena as telepathy and precognition gives ground for supposing that . . . a supra-dimension, or dimensions, may indeed exist." Over the years contributors to FSR have pondered the existence of parallel universes and the possibility that they could be the source of the enigmatic UFO visitants. Nevertheless we have not lost sight of the fact that work over the last thirty years by astronomers in various countries gives ground for supposing that a plurality of star systems with life-bearing planets may indeed exist. Should but one of these have developed a civilisation of some sort, with a technology well in advance of ours (and therefore, in Arthur C. Clarke's words, like magic to us) it could, provided it had located us, monitor our earth's development either directly, or perhaps by long-distance orbiting probe, and use all manner of techniques, even illogical to us, should it be studying human reactions.

---

*Published by Faber & Faber, London, hardcover priced £5.95 net.

# THE THING!
## y the kids who saw it

It looked like this . . .

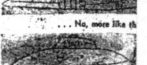

. . . No, more like th

. . . with a light on top.

**By IAN CAMERON**

IT came from outer space. At least, it looked unearthly. And it certainly proved a big draw.

Fourteen keen-eyed children, who say they saw an unidentified flying object, have produced sketches of The Thing.

It landed, they claim, in a field 200 yards from where they were playing.

The children, aged ten and eleven, told their headmaster, Mr. Richard Llewelin, at a school in Broad Haven, near Pembroke. He asked them to draw exactly what they had seen.

### Scared

One of the children, ten-year-old Michael Webb, said: "I watched it for between three and five minutes. It had a flashing red light and I'm sure it was a space ship. I believe in them, anyway."

He added: "We were all scared stiff, and ran away."

There was another ten-year-old boy, Philip Rees, had gained a vivid impression of The Thing. "It stuck in my mind like when the head-ached it when it," said Philip to draw it.

The headmaster said: "Each of them went away and did their drawings separately. There was no question of them putting their heads together.

"Having talked to each of them individually and seen their drawings—and allowing for any embellishment—I do not disbelieve that they saw something they had never seen before.

"I do not believe primary school children are capable of a sustained sophisticated hoax. The thread which appears to run through their stories is that the object was a silvery-yellow, cigar-shaped with a dome and possibly a light on top."

. . . There was a point to

. . . and a figure with !

ON THE SPOT: Some of the children who saw The Thing.

DAILY MIRROR, FEB 11, 1977.

*Bob Tibbitts and Steve Wills displaying copies of the pivitol book by Randall Jones Pugh and F. W. Holiday . . .*
The Dyfed Enigma

*Randall Jones Pugh and (right) with Dawn Holloway*

The scrapbook also contained a number of UFO sketches painted by other children who, while not having witnessed the event themselves, felt it necessary to draw *what they thought the object looked like* – no doubt after having seen the sketches supplied by the witnesses themselves, which should not be confused with the original drawings.

*Images taken of the UFO scrapbook from Broad Haven School*

*David Davies*

Over the years we were to speak to many of the 'boys' concerned, who were still as puzzled by what they saw all those years ago. One of them was David Davies, whom we spoke to in 2006 ...

Ms.Hanson & Holloway.

PO Box 6371.

Birmingham B48.7RW.

41.St.Brides View.

Roch.

Haverfordwest.

Dear Fellow Ufofologists,

In reply to your letter of Sept.21.for which I thank you,I shall of course be quite willing to discuss the implications of the UFO prodigy at any time convenient to yourselves,but it has to be either a Tuesday or a Friday.However,and on the basis of what information you give in your letter,I feel I should warn you that any delving into the realms of the occult-which is what the UFO phenomenon is all about-is fraught with many spiritual dangers-and such investigations are not to be undertaken lightly.This of course is confirmed in Isa.7;14.Da6;27.Mt.12;38. 1 Co.14;22.Ps.78;43.Da.6;27.Mt.24;24.Mk.16;17.Ac;2.19.2Cor.12;12.2.Th.2;9. On this basis therefore,and I'm sure my old friend Gordon Creghiton would agree,we are then in a position to discuss the signs and wonders which constitute the ufological battle for the soul of Mankind.

And the tempo of which is growing daily.

Yours Truely,

R.Jones Pugh.M.R.C.V.S.

# UFO in field, claim boys

**FOURTEEN SCHOOLCHILDREN** have claimed to UFO experts that a mystery craft landed near a village school in West Wales at the weekend.

They claim to have seen a large, silver-coloured machine in a field at Broad Haven, near Haverfordwest. They will be questioned about the sighting when they return to school today.

The South Wales co-ordinator for the British Unidentified Flying Objects Research Association, Mr. Randall Jones Pugh, of Roche, near Haverfordwest, spoke to some of the boys and then visited the field where they claimed to have seen the strange machine. Their reports are now being studied by the association.

"They obviously saw something and it is all very puzzling," said Mr. Pugh.

The big object with a dome on the top was apparently seen by 14 pupils of the lower school.

Michael Webb, aged 10, of Little Haven, said, "Everyone is convinced that they saw something. It seems cigar-shaped with a large dome on the top. I saw what appeared to be red or orangy red lights on it. It was on the ground and partly hidden behind some large bushes. I was frightened when I saw it. It was definitely not a helicopter."

David Davies, also aged 10, of Solbury, near Broad Haven, said that he heard some of the boys talking about the object, and went to see it for himself. It was a few hundred yards from the school and he claims that he saw part of it shoot up as though it was trying to get off the ground.

But it seemed to be stuck. "I was with another boy at the time and we just ran," he said.

Last night the headmaster, Mr. Ralph Llewhellin, said that he would talk to the boys thoroughly about the matter today. None of the adults at the school had seen the object.

*February 1977 The "Western Mail" (CARDIFF)*

*The view from the school and (below) the school playground*

"*Contrary to what a lot of books say, I was not the first person to sight the 'craft'. After I told my mother about it, she telephoned Randall Jones Pugh and he came to see me on the Saturday, when I took him to the school and showed him where I and the other boys had seen the UFO.*"

Although our journey to Broad Haven School and the surrounding areas was a well-trodden path taken by so many before us, *we had to see for ourselves* where this strange event had taken place, having the distinct advantage of being in possession of a number of *original* drawings, submitted by some of the children concerned, with their brief descriptions of what they saw contained overleaf, (obtained from the possession of Brenda Butler). The first one we looked at was drawn by David Davies.

**David Davies** (then aged 10 years nine months):

"*I sighted the UFO at about 3.40pm, after school. My friend, Philip, was trying to find a way over the stream, when this silver cigar-shaped object tried to take-off. It was about 300 metres away from the school.*"

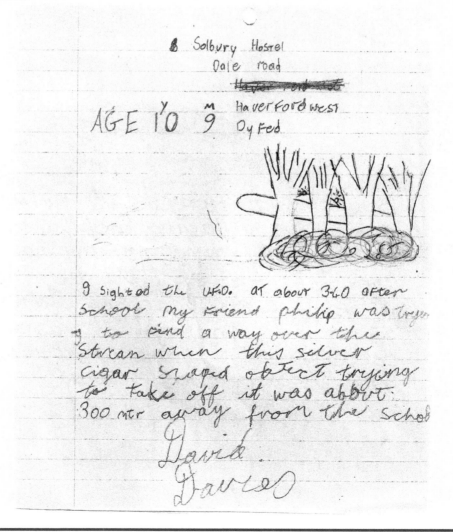

**Leslie Reohorn** (then aged 10):

*"One day, on Friday the 4th February, my friends and I was playing football, when some people came running down the field and they told me all about it, so I went up to see what it was. At first I thought it was a caravan – then I saw what it was. The distance was 300 yards."*

Leslie
Reohorn
age 10

Millemore Farm
Broad Haven
Haverfordwest
Dyfed

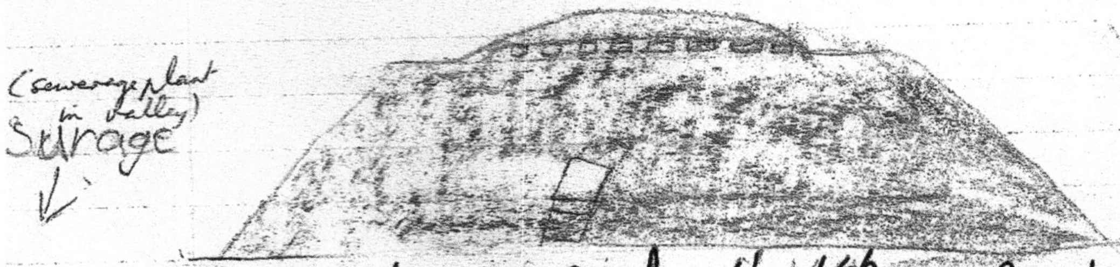

(sewerage plant in valley)
Surage

one day on friday the 4th my friends and I was playing footBall when some people came running down the field. And they told me all about it so I went up to see what it was at first. I thourght it was a caravan then I saw what it was. the distance was 300 yds

**Jane Hughes** (then aged 9 and a half):

*"The colour was sort of silvery, with a light on top. There were some trees covering it and a long ladder going up to a dome."*

name Jane. Hughes
Address Ellesmere
Broad Haven
Haverfordwest
age 1½

The colour was a sort of silvery with a the light on top there were some trees covering it and a long ladder going up to a dome. There were about six windows in the dome.

**Michael George** (then aged 9):

*"I saw a ship land in the bush, the third bush on the right. It had a red light on it, was grey, and I saw a grey man by it. The man had grey arms and he was grey all over him. He had big feet and long arms, and grey stomach, and a small stomach."*

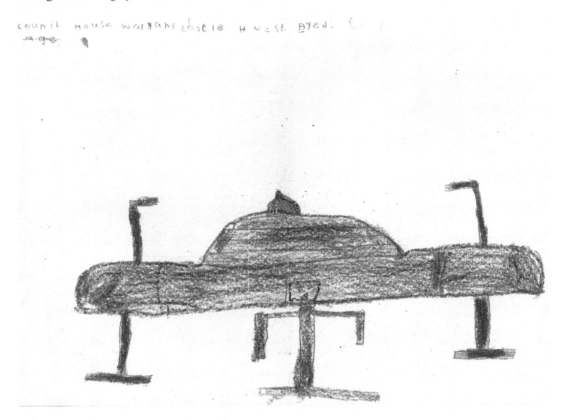

**David George** (then aged 9):

*"We were up on the playing field – then we saw a man. It had pointed ears and in a silver suit."*

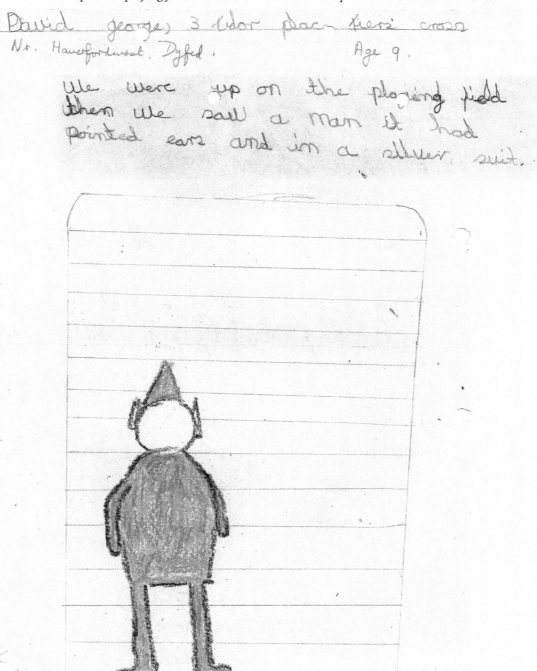

**Andrew Evans** (then aged 10 years nine months):

*"On Friday, 4th February, at half-past-three, just after school, I and my friend went to the top of the field, where people said to have seen a UFO. Some people were already there. Philip was trying to find a way to cross the stream – then I saw something try to take off behind a bush. It was a cigar-shaped object and was silver. It had a dome on top and on top of the dome was a light."*

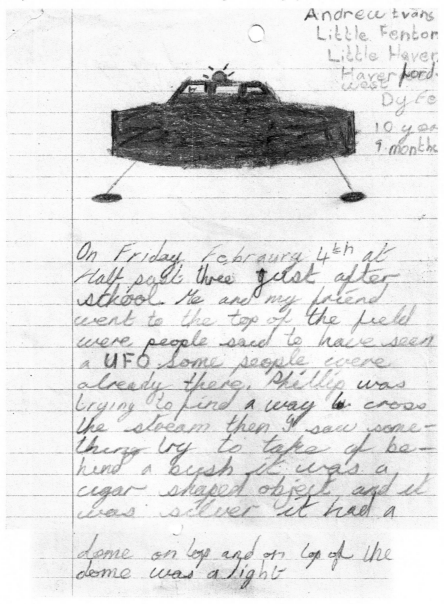

**Michael Webb** (then aged 11):

*"On Friday, the 4th February, I and some other boys saw what looked like a UFO. It was silver and looked like an orange light flashing on top. It was about 250 metres away and I would say 15-20 feet high."*

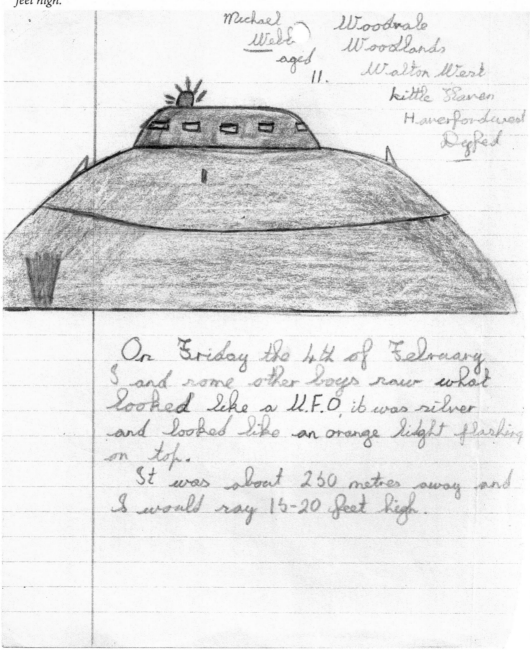

**Andrew Lewis** (then aged 9):

*This is what I saw. It had a red light on the top. The colour was grey. It had two windows on the top. A toddler was by the door. I saw no people there."*

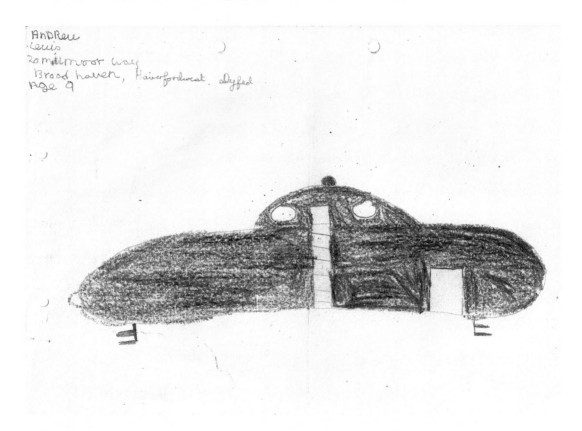

This is what I Saw. It had a red light on the top. the Colour was Grey. It had two windows on the top, a toddler was by the Door. I saw no people there.

**Jeremy Passmore:**

*"The object was about three hundred yards away, but I am sure it was there. It had a red light and it was silvery."*

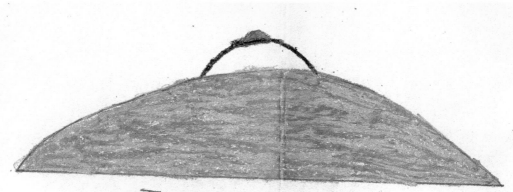

JEREMY. PASSMORE
35A ENField . Rd
BRoaD Haveh
HAVeRFORDWest. DYFED

The object was About
300 YarDs AWay but
I am sure it was
there. It had A
Red light and it
was Silvery.

**Martin Evans** (then aged 10):

*"It is silver colour and red light. I could not see it to well in the bushes. I also heard it to. It went bang and a circling noise."*

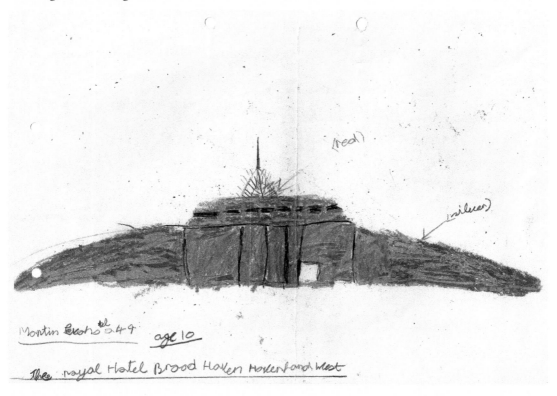

**Paul Williams:** (then aged 10):

*"We saw it in the field 300 yards away, and it was silver."*

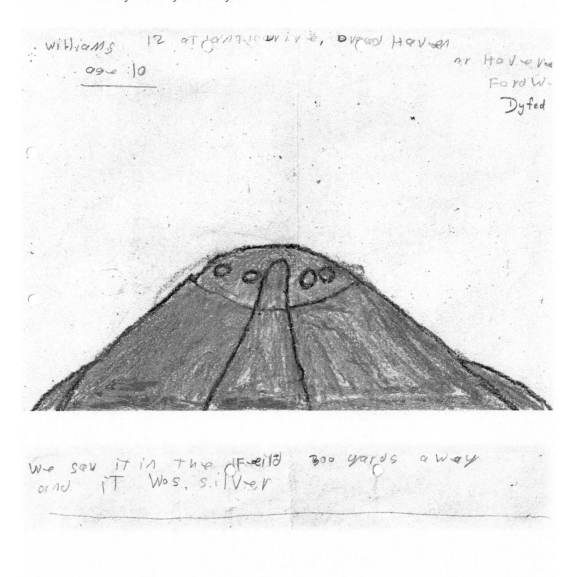

**David Ward** (then aged 10):

*"The man was silver. The ship was silver. The man had pointed ears."*

Research into the area, following a number of visits made to Webbs Hill, (which lies next to the church adjacent to Broad Haven School), revealed the path used to lead up the hill to the church, at the top (now blocked off). Was there any connection with the hill? Could it have been an ancient mound in by-gone days?

Much time has elapsed since this event was first brought to the public's attention. The children (as shown) have grown up and have their own children, but the mystery – now firmly instilled as part of the folklore of the village – still continues to create interest, despite ridiculous allegations that they may have seen a sewage wagon, or somebody wearing fancy dress.

*The church at the top of the hill opposite Broad Haven school*

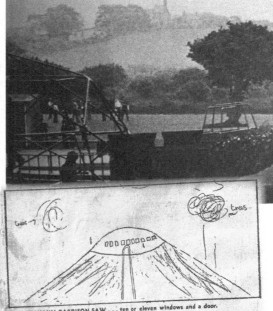

WHAT DAVID WARD SAW . . . the ship was silvery, the pepul wer green.

WHAT SHAUN GARRISON SAW . . . ten or eleven windows and a door.

# What our little earthlings saw...

### By MIKE SLATER

EARTH CALLING space ship, some schoolchildren have drawn a nicely detailed picture of your flying visit to their school in West Wales last week.

From the tip of your toes to your pointed ears they've got you down in black and white.

The score of children at Broad Haven, Dyfed, who saw a mysterious, disc-shaped, silver object in a field 300 yards from their school, have sketched and written about what they saw.

Their sightings corresponded with that of a woman in the same village who reported several bright objects in the sky and later, schoolchildren at Hubberston, Milford Haven, said they had seen a cigar-shaped object over the town.

The three sightings have convinced Mr. Randall Jones Pugh, South Wales co-ordinator for the

### 'THEY HAD POINTED EARS, THE SHIP WAS SILVERY'

British Unidentified Flying Objects Research Association, that the Broad Haven children really did see a UFO.

Two 10-year-olds, David Ward and Shaun Garrison, were among the first to spot it.

David wrote down for his headmaster, "The ship was silvery, the pepel wer green, the pepel had sort

of earners, (earers . . . cameras) the ship was smaller than the ships we have, they had pointed ears."

Paul Williams wasn't sure about the ears. "We saw something come out of it. It had a pointed [pointed] helmet.

"We ran and told Sir and when we went back it was not there."

Shaun says, "It was flattish and had about 10 or 11 windows and a door with a runway leading from the door and it was silver and it was in a clump of trees."

David and Shaun then told others.

Phillip Rees reported, "Shaun and David came running in and said that there was something there. So me and some other boys went up to the top of the playing field.

"We saw something silver disced shape. There seemed to be a door opening from the object. David Davies and Tudor Jones saw a figure they said it was silver. I did not see the figure.

The object had a dome on the top of it with a light. Tudor said he

WHAT PHILIP REES SAW . . . a dome on top of it and a light.

heard a noise like something trying to take off. It was a very dull day but I did see something."

Their headmaster, Mr. Ralph Llewhellin, who interviewed each child separately and suggested they drew what they saw, agreed they

had seen something unusual.

"I don't believe that children of junior school age are capable of playing such a sophisticated prank," he said. "I believe they did see something that they do not normally see."

*Malcolm Robinson with Randall Jones Pugh in 1980. Right: Ron Neville. Below: Matthew Williams*

## IMAGES FROM THE BROAD HAVEN SCHOOL UFO SCRAPBOOK

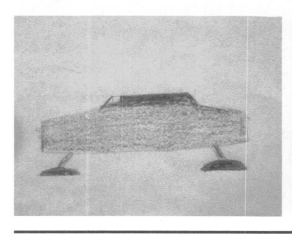 

# IMAGES FROM THE BROAD HAVEN SCHOOL UFO SCRAPBOOK

### On the 5th February 1977, Warminster

UFO enthusiasts – John and Maureen Rowston – accompanied by Barry and Judy Gooding, Brian Boyland, and his son from Wincanton, sighted an orange object descending through the sky at Upton Scudamore.

The group ran over to where they anticipated it would land, but it veered to the left and rose upwards into the sky. (**Source:** *UFO Magic in Motion*, **Arthur Shuttlewood**)

### 6th February 1977 – Staffordshire Police sight UFO

Four police officers from Staffordshire sighted a long, brilliant white, object crossing the sky, just before dawn – *"far too fast to have been an aircraft"*. (**Source: Margaret Westwood, UFOSIS**)

### 6th February 1977 – Motorist encounters UFO over Wales

Mrs Mary Louise Bassett was driving home from Carmarthen, at about 1am, where she and her husband run a restaurant. They live in the old manor house of Portiscliff, which is located in Ferryside. The road was deserted and the route familiar. The night was very dark.

As Mrs Bassett approached the village of Idole, she suddenly saw, on the right-hand side of the road, a blue flashing light and a rounded 'mass'. Her first thought was that there had been a bad accident and that the light was on an ambulance or police car. She slowed down at once. During her homeward drive she had had the radio switched on and tuned to *Radio Luxembourg*. Static had steadily increased as she came along the road, until – by the time she slowed near Idole – it was hardly possible to hear the programme.

As she slowed, she looked down the lanes of neighbouring farms but couldn't see any evidence of an accident, so carried on even slower, when the radio came back on. She carried on towards Llandyfaelog, and before reaching some pylons on top of a hill (on the left, this time), she saw the flashing blue light and the 'mass' again, and wondered what it could have been.

> *"The 'mass', was black and appeared to be a nebulous, rounded shape, with a flashing light protruding out of the top. I said to myself gosh! I think I've seen a UFO again. There was tremendous radio interference on my car radio. I stopped when I thought I saw a second light, because there is a little farm there and I wondered if it might be an ambulance after all. I got out of the car and had a very good look around, but couldn't see anything."*

Now feeling alarmed for the first time, she jumped back into the car and drove quickly down a side road for three miles to Ferryside, and then home to the old manor house of Portiscliff – which stands in its own grounds, surrounded by woods and shrubbery.

When she arrived home, her three Springer Spaniels did not greet her as they usually did, by making a fuss, but instead ran past her and outside – which was most uncharacteristic. Mrs Bassett made herself a hot drink and then went out to look for them. She called for them and the two bitches ran back in with their hackles up and shaking. The dog, Jasper, had disappeared. She went out to call for him and used a dog whistle. She looked around but there was no sign of him. She went part of the way down the long and winding drive but didn't go any further, due to feeling nervous in the dark. She went back in and phoned her husband at their restaurant in Carmarthen, to ask him to keep an eye out for the dog on his way home. She went back out to call for the dog again, and he rushed in again, like the bitches, with hackles raised and shaking. He had been frightened by something.

The next morning the dog was acting in a most peculiar way; he would not go out but just stayed under the kitchen table. This condition continued for two or three weeks, when his confidence slowly returned. The bitches, too, came round to normality after being off their food for a while. The behaviour of the three animals, the dog in particular, was totally out of character for them.

This case was investigated, at the time, by Randall Jones Pugh and F.W. Holiday, who speculated if Mrs

## Lights scared my dog

ANOTHER witness of the strange happenings in the Broad Haven Triangle was Louise Bassett.

But it was Jasper, her pet springer spaniel, who suffered the greatest after-effects.

The dog's character was totally changed the night Mrs Bassett, 31, saw flashing blue lights in the sky near her home at Ferryside, Carmarthen.

Mrs Bassett, mother of two, says: "I was driving home when I saw these lights. I thought there must have been a serious accident, so I took a detour.

"Two miles further up the road I saw the lights again. At the same time, my car radio cut out."

When she got home, Mrs Bassett, a caterer, let Jasper out for his nightly visit to the garden.

He returned half an hour later, and shot into the house, his hackles up, shaking and growling.

He did not leave his basket the next day.

Mrs Bassett says: "He behaved in the most peculiar way.

"For weeks he seemed completely terrified."

Bassett had been abducted on her way home – something which she could not recall, or whether she had been followed home – and the three spaniels had experienced something, to them, very frightening.

## 7th February 1977 – Berkshire Motorist followed by strange light

We spoke to Scientist – Peter Wroath, about his investigations into reports of UFO activity around the Berkshire area, one of which involved ex-Police woman – Jane Human from Lambourn, in Berkshire, who was driving home from Wallingford on the B4567, at 10.45pm on 7th February 1977, when she noticed what appeared to be the lights of a vehicle in the rear view mirror of the car, some way behind her, which then turned off right towards West Challow.

*Peter Wroath*

*Ex-police woman Jane Human*

A few minutes later, Jane noticed another 'light' behind her that she took to be a motorcycle, but realised from its position and its dimness that this was unlikely to be the answer, especially as it was showing different colours. Forcing herself not to panic, she slowed down the car to about five miles per hour, and turned around to have a close look at it, when she saw:

*"…something about eight inches in diameter, not an exact circle, jagged at the edge. It showed different shades of yellows and red, dim and hazy, and was darker red in the centre, filtering out towards the edges in paler red and yellow. It felt as if I was looking at it without my glasses on, which I have to wear for driving."*

Now frightened, Jane accelerated and drove as fast as the bends would allow, with the 'light' keeping pace with her vehicle.

*"I never felt so frightened in the whole of my life. It must have been behind me for another half-a-mile. As I went down a small dip in the road, it completely vanished. As I got to the top of the hill, just before you come to the crossroads where you turn either right to Childrey, or left to Lambourn, I saw it fleetingly once more, apparently hovering on top of the hill."*

Peter Wroath retraced the route taken by Jane – part of the ancient Icknield Way – (considered by the authors to play much prominence in sightings like this) and at the point where the lights were first seen, noticed a narrow road leading into an old quarry, roughly 100 yards in diameter, situated near Letcombe Bassett Field.

We also found a similar trait of background behaviour many years later at Wigmore, Herefordshire, when the 'light' which had paced the couple concerned, moved away diagonally across a field. Enquiries made revealed that the path of the original Roman road had gone across the field concerned, and that it matched up the direction as shown to us.

**(Source: Peter D. Wroath, Flying Saucer Review, Vol. 23, Number 3, 1977)**

### 8th February 1977

*Daily Mirror* – 'Kids flee a 'Flying Saucer' … brief outline of the Broad Haven sighting.

### 9th February 1977 – Schoolboy sights UFO

A pupil at Pembroke Comprehensive School, whose hobby is artwork, arrived at the school a little early … at 8.45am. He heard a buzzing noise and looked round to see:

**' Flashing egg-yolk '**

*Inv R Jones Pugh*

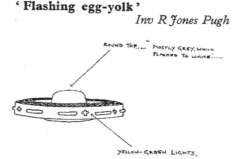

*"…a plate, or saucer-shaped UFO – mostly silver, with yellow/ green lights on the side, hovering in the sky".*

### 10th February 1977 – UFO sighted by police officers, Mississippi

Deputy Kenneth Creel was driving down the Smith School Road, four miles west of Flora, near the county line, with Constable James Luke, at the time.

**Deputy Kenneth Creel:**

*"We saw what looked like an evening star, or something, but it kept getting brighter and bigger.*

---

ary, 8, 1977  PAGE 5

# Kids flee a 'flying saucer'

### By IAN CAMERON

FOURTEEN children fled in terror when they saw an unidentified flying object in a field near their school.

Yesterday, the boys and girls, aged ten and eleven, drew the dome-topped, cigar-shaped object which they said was 45ft. long and silver coloured.

Michael Webb, ten, said: "It had flashing lights. It definitely wasn't a helicopter."

## Sightings

Richard Llewhelin, headmaster of the school at Broad Haven, near Pembroke, said: "I am convinced the children saw something extraordinary. What it was I haven't a clue."

The U F O Association said: "We have eliminated all natural or man-made explanations. It is one of the best sightings we have had."

*UFO, as described by Deputy Kenneth Creel*

*Then, when the shape of the object began to form, I contacted the Mississippi Highway Patrol with my car radio equipment. I kind of thought it was an airplane, flying low, or like it could have been. The strange object then came within about 200 yards of my car – out across the field. I stopped and cut my engine and my lights to listen. I heard a whirring noise – like a blender – like it was straining, when you first put ice in it, and then the UFO started coming closer. The thing came right over the car. It came right to us – like it was being piloted."*

Creel says he could not tell if anything or anyone was inside.

*"The thing just hovered over us, about 20 or 30 feet up, for more than a minute", said Creel, who at this time was looking straight up, from his patrol car window.*

*"I didn't get out; I wouldn't. There was light coming out from little windows, and the light apparently changed colours several times, from soft blue, to red, to green and other colours. The UFO was reportedly about 30 to 40 feet in diameter, and perfectly round.*

*It didn't spin or anything. It just hovered around there."*

After about a minute, Creel began backing up his patrol car, about 100 yards, to a place where he could turn around. By this time, however, Highway Patrolman Louis Younger drove up in his patrol car within a short distance of the UFO, and reported seeing the same object – with the same description Creel had given. The 'thing' then just picked up and took off, north-west, toward Satartia.

An unidentified object of the same general description was reported the same evening, by other Flora residents, and Deputy Charles Bowering and Highway Patrolman Joe Chandler and others said

*"They saw lights from an unidentified craft, from a distance".*

However, as far as Creel is concerned, he would rather not have the attention.

*"If I had known how much trouble it was going to cause, I wouldn't have reported the thing in the first place"*...

The deputy said from the Sheriff's office.

(**Source:** *Madison County Herald* (Canton, Mississippi), 17.2.1977 – 'UFO Spotting Focuses on Deputy')

## 10th February 1977 – Elliptical UFO in the sky over Essex

At 9.15pm, Mrs Whiting from Wingletye Lane, Hornchurch, in Essex, said goodnight to her children, but a few minutes later her son – Steven, came running downstairs and shouted:

*"Quick Mum, there's a 'thing' in the sky"*.

Mrs Whiting and her husband dashed outside with binoculars and saw an elliptical object, covered in lights, stationary in the sky. *"We watched it for a few minutes, before losing sight of it"*, she said.

(**Source: Dan Goring**)

## 12th February 1977 – UFO over Fulham, London

Two Hurlingham schoolgirls (then aged 12) from Fulham, London, contacted the *Fulham Chronicle* (18.2.1977) – 'We saw a Flying Saucer', after sighting a UFO from their bedroom window. Ester Bourlay was the first to see it, at 8.30pm, and called her friend – Toni Nielsen, who looked out and saw:

*"...a pale blue light in the sky moving from right to left, changing colour as it did so. It was mauve, yellow, red, green/blue, with a touch of white. We watched it for over ten minutes – then it backed away. It was a bit scary really, but my friend and I both believe in 'Flying Saucers'."*

Her mother, Mrs Stella Neilsen – who runs a health food shop in Fulham Road – confirmed the sighting but said by the time she got upstairs to have a look, it had gone. Enquiries made, revealed that a woman in the flat below had also seen the UFO.

## 12th February 1977 – 'Strange lights' over Geilston Bay, Tasmania

Mrs L. Dienaar – a resident of Geilston Bay, Tasmania – was sat on her front porch with her two children, seeking some relief from the heat during the evening, when:

*"...a flash of light was noticed in the north-west, over Mount Faulkner, and a white 'light' was seen heading southwards. A second later, two similar 'lights' were also noticed – one behind the other – following the same trail taken by the first. They moved south over the hills, towards Wellington. The leading 'light' paused and the following 'lights' merged with it. The single 'light' now changed brightness and moved up vertically, at great speed, before fading away about a minute later."*

## 13th February 1977 – UFO over Essex

Barking, Essex man – Mr Bessent (then aged 25) was looking out of his south facing window, when he noticed a deep yellow or gold star-like object in the sky, hovering above the high rise-flats in front of him. A few seconds later the object began to move slowly, eastwards, in a straight line.

After calling his wife the couple stood there watching, as the 'star' arced upwards 10-15 degrees, before flaring up to about twice its original size in a few seconds. It then turned red and was lost from view.

Ten seconds later, the sequence of actions was repeated. An aircraft flew past; immediately the object overtook the plane, at high speed, and was gone. (**Source: Barry King**)

## 13th February 1977 – UFO knocks youth off moped at Worcestershire

At 10.30pm Steven Hutton (16), Steven Clarke (17) from Thatchers Court, and another boy, were riding their mopeds along the Kidderminster Road into Droitwich, when they saw two 'bright lights' in the sky, about a mile and-a-half away.

After stopping to have a closer look, they continued on their journey – at which stage a gust of powerful wind hit them, knocking Steven Hutton off his moped. Steven was later treated at hospital for an arm injury and released.

(**Source: SkyScan/***Evening News***, Worcester (14.2.1977) – 'UFO scare unseats a teenager on moped'**)

## 16th February 1977 – UFO over Lancashire

At 8.45am, Bishops Lydeard residents – Anne Burnett and Julie Philips (15) – from Kingsmead, Wiveliscombe, were on their way to school at Preston Bowyer, Milverton, when they saw:

*"...a big, round, silver object, which seemed to be going around the woods before it went down under the hills."*

At 5.30pm Paul Almond (then 13) was in the playground at Chapel End Junior High School, Brookscroft Road, Walthamstow, on a bright, cold, day with eight other boys, when they saw something rushing across the sky.

**Paul:**

*"I saw a 'ball of light', some distance away, with a detached tail behind it. I lost sight of as it entered clouds."*

Ada Thornley of Hawthorne Street, Bolton, Lancashire, along with a dozen others, watched,

*"...a bright red circular object, hovering in the sky over Winter Hill. It seemed to make an odd turn and become banana-shaped. We watched it until 10pm – at which stage it was heading towards the Chorley direction, before disappearing from view."*

Mrs Thornley rushed home and tried to contact the police, but the telephone was out of operation for about ten minutes.[Nearby was the Winter Hill TV transmission mast.]

(**Source:** *West Somerset Free Press*, **25.2.1977 – 'UFO spotted'/***Evening News***, Bolton, 17.2.1977 – 'UFO buzzes Bolton again'**)

## 17th February 1977 – UFO over Llandudno Junction

*Maureen Williams*

Eight children at Maelgwn Primary School, Llandudno Junction, watched an orange and silver coloured 'Saucer' flying over the top of the school, at 10.40am. The first to see it was 11 year-old Stuart Roberts. He alerted the rest of the class and teacher – Maureen Williams, who were amazed how low it was flying.

The children – Gareth Steven Jenkins, Paul Richard Evans, Stewart Michael Roberts, Dylan Jones, Richard Evans, Bryn Tudor Owen, Nerys Roberts and Tracy Harrison – were later interviewed by a reporter from the *North Wales Conway News*, as a result of which an article showing the children together, with a drawing of the UFO, was published the following day – 17th February 1977.

**Teacher Maureen Williams:**

*"We looked up, just in time to see this metallic object disappearing over the roof. It was about two arms lengths in width and was far too small to carry a man. I can't think of a logical explanation for what we saw. It wasn't a life- boat flare. What amazed us was how low it was. I never thought of 'flying saucers' before and it's not a subject we've discussed in class."*

(**Source: Personal interview/Randall Jones Pugh**)

# Teacher and pupils see UFO

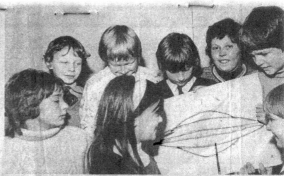

EIGHT children and a teacher at Maelgwn Primary School, Llandudno Junction, say they have seen an orange and silver flying saucer skim very low over the school roof.

"We were doing sums," said 11-year-old Stuart Roberts, 33 Pendyffryn, Llandudno Junction, and I looked out of the window and saw this thing shaped like a flying saucer just skimming the roof of the main school building. I shouted 'what's that'?"

Teacher Mrs. Maureen Williams said: "I and several children looked up in time to see the object disappearing over the roof.

"It was quite small, about two arms length in width — not big enough to carry a man. I don't think there can be any logical explanation for it. I have seen lifeboat flares, and it certainly wasn't that. It couldn't have been anything to do with a plane or we would have heard a noise.

"The sun was shining brightly, but I don't see how it can have been a reflection from anything. It looked metallic and what amazed us was how low it was flying.

"I've never thought about flying saucers before, and we haven't talked about them in class."

The sighting happened at about 10.40 a.m. yesterday. Stuart did a drawing of the object and gave it the headmaster. "It was silver on top and orange in the middle," he said.

"The children in this class are intelligent," said headmaster Mr. Hywel Jones. "I've no reason to think they are exaggerating. And the fact that a teacher has seen it makes me believe there was something there."

A spokesman at RAF Valley said they had nothing flying in that area at the time. The RNLI at Llandudno said they were not on a flare-firing exercise.

A drawing of the UFO with (back from left) Gareth Steven Jenkins 10, Paul Richard Evans 9, Stewart Michael Roberts 11, Dylan Jones 10, Richard Evans 10, Bryn Tudor Owen 10. Front: Nerys Roberts 9 and Tracy Harrison 10. (172-298)

## Close encounter, Anglesey

One hour later, at 11.40am, Nia Jones (then aged 11) was cycling to visit a friend living in Carreglefn, Anglesey.

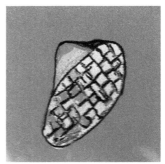

> *"All of a sudden a dark shadow fell over me. I wondered what was going on. I looked upwards and saw this silver coloured object, hovering silently, about six feet above me. I was scared, but managed to make a note of what I was seeing. I will never forget it as long as I live. It had a silver ringed dome on top, with a red glass-like under-dome that had less depth than the top one. The entire surface of the 'craft' was covered in 'squares'. They looked like patches, with a stud in each corner.*
>
> *I remember thinking how could a human being fit into it, because it was so narrow, even if they were lying down. My fears gave way to calm. It was most peculiar. I stood staring at it for what seemed like hours, but must have been minutes – then it slowly moved away, crossing a field, before shooting up into the sky at speed, and was gone. When I rushed home to tell my mother she told me not to be so silly, but we were both flabbergasted to hear on the news, later, that some girls from Rhosybol Primary School had seen it as well."* (**Source: Personal interview**)

*Rosybol School*

In the photo: Brynora Williams, Iona Jones, Nia Pritchard, Rhian Price, Gwawr Jones, Karen Williams, Catherine Griffiths, Nina Evans. Nicola Evans was also a witness to the U.F.O. sighting, but was away from school when the photographer called.

ilent, mysterious, glittering, flying craft are usually reserved for the futuristic comic strip, and science fiction films, but for ten Rhosybol primary school children, and their teacher, the imagined became reality last week.

Irs. Mair Williams, was teaching a class at Rhosybol primary school to play neball, when Gwawr Jones, 10, was the first to see the object. She shouted, drawing the attention of the other children, and Mrs. Williams.

The sky was an unblemished blue, only one cloud marring the scene. The UFO travelled, silently across the sky towards Porth Llechog, then vanishing behind the cloud. Mrs Williams immediately took the children back into the school, gave them pieces of paper, and asked to draw what each child thought she had seen, without consulting with each other.

The resulting sketches were very similar of a black-domed object, with a shiny, glittering base. Mrs. Williams said that it was so bright it left spots before your eyes after looking out — similar to the effect of looking at a bright electric light.

Mr. Richard Griffiths, headmaster, said that he did not see the object, but that the children seemed very enthusiastic.

A large painting, has been

hung up on the wall. The children are now busy making a papier-machie model of the UFO.

None of the children though there were 'little green men inside the object; they though it was probably a unmanned satelite sent to earth from another planet.

They all said, including Mrs Mair Williams, that they would like to see another UFO.

### 17th February 1977 – UFO sighted over Broad Haven School, South Wales

A daylight UFO sighting took place again over Broad Haven Primary School, involving teacher – Mrs Morgan, who sighted:

> "...a shiny oval UFO in the sky, with a small dome on top, with peculiar ridges around its base", at 10.30 am. (**Source: Tony Pace**)

### 18th February – Mystery lights and cigar-shaped UFO sighted over UK

*Nottingham Evening Post* – 'Mystery Light' ... Mr Jackson, of the Strange Phenomena Research Investigation and Notation Group, contacted them to report seeing, *"a 'bright light' in a north-west direction, over Radcliffe-on-Trent"*. [BBC Nationwide had recently showed a programme on UFOs]

It may be that there is a connection with what happened at Walthamstow, when Chapel End schoolboy – Daren Jones (13), of Wadham Road, was busy completing his homework when he heard a strange noise coming from the garden. He rushed to the window and saw a blue-green cigar shaped object fade away behind the houses. A short time later his friend – Stephen Wilkes, phoned him to say that he had also seen it.

(**Source:** *Waltham Forest Guardian and Independent*, 18.2.1977 – 'It's those UFOs again – claim schoolboys)

### 19th February 1977 – Large glowing object at Warminster, Wiltshire

Mr Howard Cook was driving home from holiday and nearing Warminster, in the early hours of Saturday morning, with two colleagues, when they were astonished to see:

> "...a large glowing object which appeared to be resting on a nearby hill. It had a curved surface, was giving off a greenish glow, and was the size of a large detached house."

The men kept it in sight for half-a-minute, before presumably loosing sight of it.

(Source: *Cheddar Valley Gazette*, Wells, 24.2.1977 – 'UFO with greenish glow')

At 4.30am, Stockport resident – Mrs Ann Howe from Hanover Towers, Lancashire Hill, who was finding it difficult to sleep, sighted *"a blinding, spinning 'light', travelling at fantastic speed, heading towards the Ashton under Lyne area"*, from her 19th floor flat. (Source: **Stockport Express**, 24.2.1977 -'UFO streaked past her sky flat window')

## 19th February 1977

The *Western Mail*, Cardiff (in their edition of the 19.2.1977), told of being contacted by Miss Ray Howard Jones – an artist of Martin's Haven, Marloes, who told them she had seen 'strange lights' out to sea, near the scene of the recent UFO sighting at Broad Haven School, three weeks previously.

## 21st February 1977 – Green 'star' over Boston, Lincolnshire

Lincolnshire woman – Mrs Lee Mosedale, of Sibsey, contacted the *Lincolnshire Echo*, after sighting *"a little green 'star', zigzagging across the sky, at 11pm."*

She telephoned RAF Coningsby to report the matter, but was advised that no aircraft were plotted in the area at that time. (**Source: *Lincolnshire Echo*, 22.2.1977**)

## 23rd February 1977 – Three 'lights' seen over London

At 9pm, Mr Gary Norfolk of Ealing Park Gardens, London, sighted a small 'red light' in the sky, flanked by two brilliant 'lights', moving slowly and silently across the sky. (**Source: *Ealing Gazette*, 25.2.1977**)

A strange silver *'star'* was seen in the sky over Great Barr (to the North of Birmingham), later the same day, by at least two separate residents living in the suburb, followed by a report of a *'perfect silver cone'* seen drifting across the sky (**Source: UFOSIS**)

## 24th February 1977 – Report of a UFO seen by motorists over Somerset

The *Salisbury Journal* published a report of a UFO sighting that took place a few days previously, involving a Bemerton, Salisbury man, who was on his way to Somerset. After having just climbed the hill beyond the A303, near Sparkford, Yeovil he noticed that a number of drivers had pulled-in and were pointing upwards into the sky. He stopped and was just in time to see:

*"...an amazing cigar-shaped object, shimmering in the clear night sky. It was brilliant orange with darker patches – like recesses – along its side. It was about 60 feet in length. We watched it hovering before it abruptly vanished from sight, about eight seconds later."*

## 24th February 1977 – UFO over Little Haven South Wales

*Pauline Coombes and family*

At 8pm, farmer's wife – Pauline Coombes from Ripperston Farm, St. Brides, in Pembrokeshire, was driving home from St. Ishmaels, with her three young children.

*"Near to Little Haven, we noticed a yellow 'ball of light' in front of the car. I tried to outrun it, and then it shot over the car.*

*My son – Kieron, shouted out it was now following us. As we approached the house, the lights failed and the engine cut out.*

*I bundled the kids into the house. When we looked through the window, a short time later, we saw it heading out towards the sea, projecting a beam of light from underneath it."*

(**Source: Randall Jones Pugh/Personal interview with Mrs Coombes**)

On the same day, a family travelling along the A31 noticed a 'bright light' in the sky, which was seen to *"merge into a cigar-shaped object"* before moving off towards London. Enquiries by BUFORA Researcher – Barry King, revealed a similar object was seen near Heathrow Airport that evening.

Barry was to provide the authors with a number of interesting cases over the years that had been investigated by him and his colleague – Andrew Collins. These included the Aveley Abduction case – Britain's first fully documented allegations of multiple abductions, involving members of the Day family, which took a full year to investigate.

A couple were driving home through the picturesque village of Earlswood, to the east of Birmingham, during the evening, when they noticed an intense 'flashing light', motionless in the sky, hovering over their car. They stopped and got out; it moved away towards the south.

**(Source: UFOSIS, Birmingham)**

During the same day, as twilight fell, Mr T. Rolfe, and his son – E. Rolfe, were outside in the garden of their house at Holtspur, Beaconsfield, in Buckinghamshire, when an object appeared over the rooftops of nearby houses, described as:

# How my car was chased by UFO

### By John Christopher

A MOTHER claimed last night that a U.F.O. chased her car.

She and her three children were driving home along a country road at night.

They saw a brilliant yellow flying orb with a silver tail skimming towards them on a collision course.

It whizzed silently overhead, turned around and chased the car at treetop height for three miles.

## Panic

Mrs. Pauline Coombes, 31, said : " We were terror-stricken. In a panic I drove at 80 miles an hour trying to get away from the thing but I could not shake it off."

Her children, twins Layann and Joann, aged eight, and son Keiron, 10, were screaming with fear as the U.F.O. flew along-side.

About 100 yards from their farmhouse home in Dale, West Wales, the lights and the engine of the car failed.

The family got out and ran for their lives to the house to call Mr. Coombes.

He saw the orb disappearing in the sky. When he tried the car it started immediately and the head-lights came back on.

Mrs. Coombes said : " Believe me, it was no illusion. We saw it clearly with a silver tail flashing downwards like a torch beam."

She and her children have been interviewed by the British U.F.O. Association.

Local investigator Mr. Randall Pugh, a veterinary surgeon, said : " Mrs. Coombes is a down-to-earth woman who was terrified by what she saw. We are looking into it as a serious U.F.O. sighting."

Two months ago 14 children at nearby Broad-haven School saw a 40ft. long cigar shape object with a dome and flashing lights taking off from a field.

There have been at least six U.F.O. sightings in the area in the last few months.

# SCARED!

THE Coombs family say they had a close encounter . . . twice.

And it was the most terrifying time of their lives.

FIRST, Mrs Pauline Coombs and her two children were driving back to their farm in Dyfed, South Wales.

A "glowing object" descended from the sky and began to "chase" them.

### Room

She accelerated and raced home . . . scared out of her life.

THEN, several days later, another frightening thing happened.

Mrs Coombs was sitting in her front room at the time.

Suddenly, she says, she was aware that someone or "something" was watching her.

## 'He was 7ft. tall . . . in our front room . . . he stared at us . . . we fled'

She saw a figure about seven feet tall, clothed in what appeared to be shimmering silver suit and surrounded by a halo of light.

"The head of the figure was covered by a large, square helmet," she says.

Her husband, seeing his wife's horrified expression, looked over his shoulder.

What he saw frightened him, too.

He leapt from his seat, grabbed his wife and the pair of them fled to make sure their children were safe.

Then Mrs Coombs telephoned the police.

The Coombs experience is told in the book, The Uninvited, by Clive Harold.

### Dog

According to the book, electricity was sucked from the Coombs' meter.

Five televisions and eight cars in the surrounding area had their wiring burnt out.

Billy Coombs says: "Our labrador, Blackie, went mad after the incident and we had to have him destroyed."

After the terrifying experience, the family decided to move.

● 1953 . . . an artist's impression of how Capt. Ulf Christiansson saw a mystery missile between Malmo and Stockholm.

### OVER TO YOU

★ *POLICEWOMAN* Louise Lee says she and a colleague saw a bright light in the sky over Sale, Greater Manchester, in 1978.

She says: "It was too bright and too low for a plane," she told Jodrell Bank Observatory.

"It moved across the sky completely noiselessly and at a speed that was way beyond the capabilites of any known aircraft.

"It was a frightening experience."

## Day 1

THE Welsh Triangle. Elevet Dwyer, a company director, did not believe in UFOs. Until February, 1978, that is Driving home in Carmarthen, he saw a mystery object.

"I have never seen anything like it before," he said, "Clearly it was not a plane. It was more like a cigar-shaped machine about 20ft. long. It made no sound and was flying

**NEXT WEEK: ARE STRANGE BEINGS ABDUCTING HUMANS FROM EARTH?**

*The lights and engine of Pauline Coombes' car failed the night she and three children were followed by a light like a football. Keiron Coombes (right)*

**DAILY MIRROR, Wednesday, April 13, 1977  PAGE 5**

# WIFE IS CHASED BY A UFF

**By IAN CAMERON**

FARMER'S wife Pauline Coombes didn't believe in flying saucers.

But she changed her mind after being chased by a UFF— an unidentified flying football.

The mysterious yellow sphere dropped from the sky as Mrs. Coombes was driving home with her three children.

It whizzed silently above the hedgerows, easily keeping pace with the terrified Mrs. Coombes as she accelerated to 80 m p h.

And it was still there

## (Unidentified Flying Football)

when Mrs. Coombes fled up the drive of her farmhouse with her son Keiron, 10, and twin daughters Layanne and Joanne, 8.

From the safety of her home, Mrs. Coombes watched with husband Bill and the children as the object, which had a silver torch-like beam shining from it, zoomed away.

The Coombes farm is

**SAUCER: One of the school sketches.**

at Dale, near Milford Haven, South Wales— just a few miles from the spot where a group of children saw a flying saucer two months ago.

Later, the children drew the object they had seen — and one of the drawings looked very much like a rugby ball.

Yesterday Mrs. Coombes, 31, said: "Keiron spotted the object dropping towards

us. I put my foot down. "We were scared stiff and the children were crying."

South Wales UFO Association investigator Randall Pugh said: "Mrs. Coombes is a down-to-earth person who is not easily deceived.

"There seems to have been increased UFO activity in this part of Wales in the past few months."

### ● DID YOU KNOW?

THE monks of Byland Abbey, Yorks., reported seeing a flying saucer in 1290.

*"...oval in shape with a central dome, showing a band around its body which flashed red green and blue, lights".*

Ten minutes later the UFO took off, heading in the north-east direction, and disappeared from view.

**(Source: Lennox Adams, Contact UK)**

## 25th February 1977 – Hampshire schoolgirls sight UFO

The *Basingstoke Gazette* published an article on the 25th February 1977 – 'Was it a flying saucer that Elizabeth saw?'

The story involves schoolgirl Elizabeth Olive of Malvern Close, Buckskin, and some twenty other children who were at Worting School, Old Kempshot Lane, Basingstoke, Hampshire, who saw a spinning orange 'disc' in the sky.

Although the date of the actual occurrence is not given (taken that Elizabeth wrote to the Newspaper) logically, it would have been a few days before – which suggests around the 20th February (possibly).

Elizabeth had this to say, at the time:

*"It couldn't have been a football or an aeroplane; it wasn't the right shape. There was no teacher with us at the time, as we had just been settling down to work, but when we talked to teachers*

# that Elizabeth saw?

ELIZABETH Olive and her friends are facing the double frustration of others who have seen strange lights in the sky – first of all the frustration of not being able to identify the cause and secondly the frustration of getting others to believe it.

What Olive and some twenty other children in her class at school saw in a cloudy sky out of a classroom window at Worting Junior School was a "spinning orange disc-shaped object".

"It couldn't have been a frisby because no one could throw one that high," explains Elizabeth. "And it was travelling too fast.

"If couldn't have been a football, or an aeroplane – it wasn't the right shape.

"There was no teacher with us at the time as we had just been settling down to work, but when we talked to teachers afterwards, I **don't** think they really believed us.

### Imagined

"They hadn't seen anything and they might have thought we had imagined it – but about 20 of us saw the same thing."

For Elizabeth, who wrote to the Gazette Page to tell of the sighting, it was a "first".

"I have never seen anything like it before and have never really had an interest in flying saucers or anything like that," she says.

"But I know I saw something and there is no other explanation that I know of. About the only one left is that it could have been some sort of UFO."

Footnote: Being a science fiction addict, there is nothing I would like more than to believe that one day there was going to be a meeting of men from Earth and space travellers.

Check

for the sighting is what we call a re-light.

"When one engine on a jet plane goes off – and this is no sort of emergency as they have three others – then the pilot will correct it by flooding the engine with fuel.

"This will allow the engine to re-light and gives a flash of flame.

### Reflection

"This can be seen from the ground and particularly in low cloud this can appear as a sort of thrown reflection.

"I was on a plane to Japan once and counted 108 re-lights on the journey - if any one person had been able to see those from the ground, they would have been forgiven for thinking we were about to have a space invasion."

**Three young UFO spotters from Worting County Junior School, left to right:** Olive, 11, Margaret Lee, 11 and Deborah Knight, 10, who watched an orange from their classroom window.

**The sight of a bright orange light in the sky remains clear in the mind of Elizabeth Olive, of Malvern – and this is her picture of what she and school friends saw from their classroom wind**

*afterwards I don't think they believed us. They hadn't seen anything and they might have thought we had imagined it, but about 20 of us saw the same thing. I have never seen anything like it before and have never really had an interest in 'flying saucers' or anything like that."*

One explanation given by an 'expert', at RAF Farnborough, as to what the girls saw, was a jet engine or an aircraft relighting in flight. He commented further by recanting his own experience of this while on a plane to Japan, when he counted 108 relights, quipping (as they nearly always do):

*"If any person on the ground had been able to see them, they would have been forgiven for thinking we were about to have a space invasion." [Authors: There's none so blind, as those that cannot or will not see!]*

2 5 FEB 1977

Peterborough Evening Telegraph
Planner No: 67-600
Daily – 29,802

# Sphere in sky gives city trio a night fright

By Paul Stratton

THREE frightened city people watched as a glowing sphere sped across the sky from horizon to horizon "in 30 seconds".

And as it passed over their heads there was a flash of light which lit up the whole area.

Mrs Rosemary Hopkins, her husband, Nicholas, and a friend, Mrs Pat Harris, were travelling on a lonely country road towards Corby one night this week when they saw the light in the sky.

"We were just coming to Lower Benefield, near Oundle, when we first saw the glow. It travelled right across the horizon so fast it was unbelievable," said Mrs Hopkins, of 64 Drayton, Bretton.

"From the time we first spotted it to the time it disappeared on the other horizon it could only have been 30 seconds.

"Then we saw it again coming towards us. We were frightened because there was no one else about and no houses nearby.

"It stopped at one point and we saw the silver coloured cigar shape object with what looked like a row of green lights in the middle.

"It was much bigger than a plane and lower than cloud level.

"It carried on our way and we did not see it again — it really was quite frightening," said Mrs Hopkins.

Wittering airbase could shed no light on the mystery.

"We had no activities in the area at that time. We finished flying at 5.30 pm," said a spokesman.

## 26th February 1977 – Brilliant 'red lights' seen in the sky over Croydon

Miss C. Fuller, of Long Lane, was with her mother when they saw two brilliant 'red lights' in the sky, which then gradually enlarged in size before becoming much fainter and then disappearing from view. Another 'red light' then appeared for a couple of seconds, and it too disappeared from view.

They contacted the *Croydon Advertiser*, who ran their story on the 11th March 1977 – 'Anyone see these UFOs?'

## 27th February 1977 – Strange object over London

Mr Frederick Edward Seddon, his wife and three children, living in Samantha Close, Walthamstow, East London, were watching TV, at 7.20pm, when one of the girls – Tracy, brought their attention to a strange object in the sky, about two miles away

**Mr Seddon:**

*"It certainly wasn't an aircraft. It was stationary and had a green tubular light which was pulsing brilliant green, and rotating like a lighthouse; to the right of it was a red 'ball'."*

Mr Seddon – who was familiar with aircraft recognition – said that the object was much lower than an aircraft. At 7.50pm, the object moved away northwards and was gone from view a couple of minutes later. (**Source: Essex UFO Study Group**)

## 28th February 1977 – Ex RAF man sights UFO over Worcester

At 5.15am, Ex RAF Serviceman Derek Craske from Suckley Road, Worcester, was awoken by the sound of cats, fighting.

Looking out he saw an object, hovering low down in the sky. After watching the object for ten minutes, Derek and his wife decided to go to bed. (**Source: Personal interview/*SKYSCAN***)

At 10.45pm, Margaret Catherine Chung (then aged 27) of Donald Way, Moulsham Lodge, Chelmsford, was driving home along Gloucester Avenue, with Glenda Collins (30) and Malcolm Collins (28) when their attention was caught by a strange object in the sky, which appeared to stop and move again. When head-on to the object, Margaret, saw:

> "...three gold lights and one green light below the others that was flashing vigorously; when we saw the object from the side, it was apparent that the lights (now five) fitted into a square shape, and they were flashing brilliantly. As we kept up our observations, we saw a sold grey form – again square in shape – around the silent lights. Whatever it was seemed to be not very high above the rooftops."

**Glenda Lesley Collins:**

> "We saw an object in the sky to our right. We stopped the car but couldn't hear any noise. At first we thought it was stationary, but then saw that it was moving slowly.

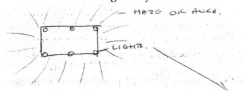

*We drove on to Donald Way, where we got out of the car and watched it. To me, it appeared rectangular – fairly large with a dark area around it. I could see six blue and white lights around the perimeter of the object. We then drove on towards Heath Drive and didn't see it again."*

**(Source: Douglas Canning, Essex UFO Study Group)**

### February 1977 – UFO sighting at Lancashire

A woman and her son (then aged 7) from Bickershaw Lane, Platt Bridge, Lancashire, were stood at the front door, after waving farewell to her husband, at 7pm, when she noticed a small bright 'star' in the sky.

> "As I'm stood at the door, the little 'dot' came towards me and my son. It must have been travelling at tremendous speed. I was frightened and thought it would come straight at us and crash. It stopped over the top of the shop on the other side of the road. It was a very bright, round object. It looked like the sun, but white shiny metal – very bright, and as wide as two cars. It then went back in the sky to being a little 'dot' across the sky. I could only follow it so far – then it disappeared out of sight. I really thought it was going to crash (into us). I was really frightened." **(Source: Bill Eatock)**

## February 1977 – Close Encounter – Huyton, Liverpool

In February 1977, Mrs Barbara Street was at her home address in St. Gabriel's Avenue, Huyton, Merseyside, one evening, and asked her son, Stephen (then aged 11), to empty the rubbish into the waste bin at the back of the house.

# Randall's the man behind UFOria . . .

● Mr. Randall Jones Pugh

RETIRED VET Mr. Randall Jones Pugh is building up the sort of dossier that will make it difficult for people not to believe in flying saucers.

Almost every mail has brought fresh reports of UFO sightings to his house at Roch, near Haverfordwest, where he spends a lot of his time investigating sightings.

His telephone rings constantly with people anxious to talk about mysterious sightings.

Since the recent spate of Uforia — sparked off by a strange sighting at Broad Haven, Dyfed, three weeks ago — Mr. Pugh has been inundated with letters and telephone calls.

As the co-ordinator for South Wales of the British Unidentified Flying Objects Research Association, he has the job of investigating and cataloguing sightings.

"Since the Broad Haven incident there has been a spate of reports. They are coming in fast and furious and most are unsolicited," he said.

One of the latest adds further mystery to what schoolboys claimed to have seen in a field near their school at Broad Haven. They talked of a large silver object with men dressed in silver.

Now three women, who want to remain anonymous, have seen something similar near the same spot.

Mr. Pugh said, "When they went to investigate there was nothing there, not even marks. They were mystified. I have been there since and there's absolutely no way that a lorry could have got there without leaving prints. The mystery deepens."

"He returned, a short time later, very agitated, and told me he had seen a large head looking at him. I naturally thought he must have been mistaken, and tried to calm him down – but he was insistent, so I decided to have a look for myself. I walked into the back garden and was shocked to see a pair of legs at the bottom of the garden, which belonged to a tall, well-built 'figure' (over nine feet tall), dressed in a white suit, with a kind of visor covering its face. I shouted, 'Get out of my garden'. It had no effect. It just stood there, looking at me.

I made my way back into the house, now feeling frightened, and told my son what I had seen. There was a knock on the door. It was Jenny – one of our neighbours. She asked me, 'What's the matter? You look like you've seen a ghost'. I explained what had happened. She went over to the window and looked out. After confirming she could also see it, she picked up a brush and opened the door, brandishing it at the 'figure' in a threatening motion. There was no effect … it just stood there. Jenny rushed back into the house, locked the door and stood with us, discussing what to do, when Don – a friend from up the road – called. We all told him what had happened. He suggested it must be someone playing a practical joke, and picked up a knife from the kitchen and went outside – but returned almost immediately, very frightened, exclaiming, 'It wasn't human'. I asked someone to telephone the police. While this was happening, I went upstairs with Don and looked out. The 'figure' seemed to be studying something on the ground. Don shouted, and it turned and pointed something at us. I felt calmness – as if tranquilised in some way. A short time later, two police officers arrived. We explained the situation to them. They went to the window and confirmed they could see the 'figure'. When they approached it, 'it just faded away in front of their eyes'. I asked them what they were going to do about the matter.

They told me, 'nothing, as nobody would believe us', but promised to return the following morning, in daylight – which they did – but found nothing of any significance and advised me, in a friendly manner, to forget about what happened.

**Brian Fishwicke:**

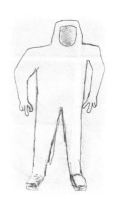

> *"I had no reason to disbelieve the version of events given to me by Mrs Street and her son, but wondered if it had been someone hoaxing, or something more sinister. Unfortunately, I was unable to trace the police officers who had allegedly seen it fade away. Their statements would have been most interesting. Mrs Street was later treated by her doctor for a rash that appeared on her body, which wasn't there before the sighting. I wasn't surprised to find out that she had a background of other strange sightings, going back many years, which included precognitions of future events. She did tell me about the time she and her sister were walking past Thingwall Lane, Huyton, when she sensed something bad was going to happen. A week later, the two girls found out a woman was stabbed to death at 10 Thingwall Lane."*

While we were unable to track down any of the participants involved in the incident, despite appeals made in the local newspaper, we confirmed a murder had taken place at the house.

*St. Gabriel's Avenue, Huyton*

**This was not the end of the story.**

On 15th March 1979, Mrs Street telephoned Brian Fishwicke about a visit made to the house on the 12th February 1979, when, just before 7.30pm, she received a visit from a couple – Mr Robert Dobson and his wife, Betty – who asked her about the 'giant figure' she had seen. After telling them what had happened, Mr Dobson told her he had been working with the 'Aliens', and had been taken inside a UFO, and that *"he had been brought back from the dead, five times, and 'they' had cured his wife"*. At this point, Mrs Street noticed the kitchen lights were flashing on and off, which attracted a comment made by Mr Dobson, who said:

> *"The Aliens are watching you, and if you continue telling people about your sighting, something would happen to you, or your son may be abducted."*

By now the lights in the lounge were also flickering, heightening the atmosphere in the house. Dobson then repeated his threats, including a verbal attack on the UFO researchers, stating something would happen to them as well. After they left, the lights went back to normal and a clock (which had stopped when the couple arrived) began to work once again.

Such outlandish claims made by the man, Mr Dobson, cannot be taken seriously. Unfortunately, we were unable to trace either him, his wife – Betty, or any knowledge of Tony Coffee – a man, they said, 'they had taken over from'. Whether the couple were Psychic investigators, members of a Church, or just interested members of the public, we don't know and will probably never know. **(Source: Brian Fishwicke)**

## CHAPTER 15 – MARCH 1977

### 1st March 1977 – Norfolk Schoolchildren sight UFOs

Teachers and pupils at Sandringham & West Newton Primary School spotted circular objects, surrounded by haloes, dropping diagonally from the moon. Teacher Elizabeth White thought they had been UFOs and reported it to RAF Marham. A spokesman at the Meteorological Office said they could have been parts of an exploded balloon, but thought it was unlikely; apart from that, he had no idea what they could have been. (**Source:** *Lynn News & Advertiser*, 1.3.1977 – 'Mystery in sky'/*Daily Mirror*, 1.3.1977)

[On the same date, *The Times* carried an advert in their business section: EXTRA TERRESTRIAL researchers want to meet with people from other planets or space/time continuums. Please write in first instance with details. Confidentiality guaranteed. Box 0618 J, *The Times*]

## 'Flying Saucer' seen over Gorleston, Norfolk

Later that day, Mrs Ivy Young of Sussex Road, Gorleston, was out walking in the town, at 8.30pm, when she saw:

> "…a 'flying saucer'-shaped object, or a 'soldier's tin hat', hovering in the sky above Lowestoft Road, between the Police Station and the Library. I showed it to my husband and I reported it to the police.

(**Source:** *Yarmouth Mercury*, 11.3.1977 – 'Did you see the UFO?')

## 2nd March 1977 – *Lancashire Evening Telegraph*, 'Hilda's flying saucer appeal'

Mrs Hilda Rogals of Helmshore, who was aerial phenomenon co-ordinator for Rossendale Amateur Astronomy Society, appealed to the public to report any unusual sightings.

Later that day, between 7.15pm and 7.30pm, Ivy Maynard (then aged 54) was walking along Baron Road to the phone box in Valence Avenue, near Mayfield Road, to speak to her son.

> "I spotted two orange flashing 'lights', racing across the bright moonlit sky in the direction of Goodmayes. I carried on and made the phone call. While walking back along Baron Road, I saw a third orange 'light' over Green Lane – also heading in the direction of Goodmayes. A larger in size white 'light' then appeared over Green Lane and dropped downwards in an arc across the sky, towards the Heathway direction." (**Source:** Barry King)

## 2nd March 1977 – Motorist reports 'strange light', while driving through Warwickshire

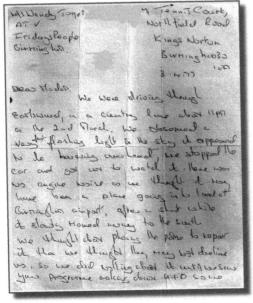

### 2nd March 1977 – UFO sighting over East Sussex

Just after 6pm, Mrs Margaret Hill from Hackhurst Lane, Lower Dicker, Hailsham, was called outside by her husband, who told her there was something strange in the sky. She went out and saw:

*"...an object motionless in the sky to the east, showing a red flashing light. This changed to green, then white. Five minutes later it disappeared from sight."*

The couple reported the incident to Hailsham Police. A few minutes later, they received a visit from a neighbour – US Colonel R. Buckley, who staying at a weekend cottage at Rushlake Green, Heathfield, in Brighton. He confirmed having seen the same object.

Just after 8.40pm, Trevor Geach of Torridge Avenue, Shiphay, Torquay, was called outside by his wife, who pointed out,

*"...four yellow iridescent orange objects, moving through the sky towards the north-east, over Brixham."*

(**Source:** *Evening Argus*, Brighton', 2.3.1977 – 'Colourful UFO pops up again'/*Herald Express,* 3.3.1977 – 'Flaming objects over Brixham')

### 2nd March 1977 – 'Double star' over Essex

Diane Elizabeth Briggs (then aged 12), of Mashiters Walk, Romford, Essex, was stood on the corner of Oaklands Avenue, at 8.25pm, with her father – Mr Leslie Arthur Briggs (44).

*"I looked into the cold but clear sky and saw what looked like a 'double star'. It then flared a brilliant white and sent down a beam of light, before shooting away towards the direction of our house. We walked home and watched it again from the back garden.*

*It went behind a house, reappeared again, and then vanished from view about twenty minutes later from when we had first seen it."*

### 2nd March 1977 – UFO display over Dagenham, Essex

At 7.15pm, Gary James from Dagenham, in Essex, sighted:

*"...a white light, accompanied by a smaller red flashing light, The two lights were soon joined by another two – each red light being close to the white light, at an angle of 75 degrees. Four such 'formations' were seen over the next half-hour.*

*The lights then broke formation. One of the red lights flew slowly over the top of me, allowing me to view the underside, which consisted of eight circular holes that glowed red to black. I started to walk down Parsloes Park, when one of the white lights flew overhead, showing me an eight sided, light-grey object, with a white light flashing on each 'wing' and a strip of red light at the back and front. After they had disappeared, I made my way to Becontree Station, situated on a hill, and saw ten white and red lights on the horizon. The only sound I heard was a jet-like whistling noise."*

(**Source: Barry King**)

### 2nd March 1977 – *Daily Mirror* – 'Lovers spot Peeping Tom from Space'

### 3rd March 1977 – UFO and 'aircraft' seen circling over Essex

Linda Williams (then 30) of Heron Walk, Cranham, in Essex, was on her way to pick up her daughter from the 'Brownies' at 7.25pm.

*"I saw what I took to be six aeroplanes, showing red and green lights, going around in a circle in the sky near to a huge fuzzy, stationary orange 'light'. I was puzzled that the 'aircraft' were silent and wondered what was going on. I picked my daughter up and pointed out the ongoing phenomena in the sky. She thought they might have been aircraft and then, because she was so frightened,*

*we made our way home and told my husband what we had seen. The next morning, we were astonished to see two helicopters circling the same locality."*

**(Source: Barry King)**

## Early March 1977 – UFO over Pendle Hill, Lancashire

4th March 1977 – The *Peterborough Evening Telegraph* told its readers, under the headline: 'Government lashed over the UFO 'hush up' – after being contacted by Robert Goodley, Chairman of the Norfolk and National UFO Investigation Society,

> *"As far as the MOD is concerned, the subject of UFOs is hushed up. I'm sure a lot more is known that the public is led to believe. I am sure some things are being held back."*

On the same day, Barry Cooper of Stanhope Road, Stockton-on-Tees, sighted:

> *"...a perfectly round 'disc', about five miles up in the sky, which vanished seconds later".*

At the time, he was accompanied by his friend – Bill Jordan, and travelling home from where they worked at British Chrome and Chemicals, at Urlay Nook. They contacted the *Middlesbrough Evening Gazette*, who published their account – 'Vanishing UFO gives Barry the Blues' on the 7.3.1977.

# Government lashed over the UFO 'hush-up'

**by Paul Stratton**

FACTS which would prove beyond doubt the existence of UFO's are being "hushed-up" by the Ministry of Defence, says the chairman of a local society.

Mr Robert Goodley, chairman of Norfolk and National UFO Investigation Society, feels that now is the time the public was made aware of just what is going on.

"As far as the Ministry of Defence is concerned the subject of UFOs is hushed up," he said.

"I'm sure a lot more is known than the public is led to believe. I am sure some things are held back."

"Ten countries now have admitted the existence of UFO's but I cannot see our government doing the same.

"I am sure p... in this country have seen UFOs but we get no co-operation from air bases. They are not allowed to tell us anything."

"If they admitted that pilots or trained navigators had spotted things in the sky it would prove beyond doubt their existence. I am convinced that pilots have seen UFOs."

He continued: "One case that did leak out concerned a visual and radar sighting of something in the sky. The sighting lasted for five hours and was picked up by the Lakenheath air base but all the reports are supposed to have been destroyed."

He said that the public have a right to know the full facts about any sightings.

"I cannot see why the Ministry of Defence is so secretive about UFOs."

**Peterborough Evening Telegraph**
Planner No: 67-600
Daily – 29,802

**4 MAR 1977**

## 7th March 1977 – Close Encounter, Winchester, Hampshire

Winchester housewife – Joyce Bowles, was to find herself the subject of a third and final confrontation with UFO entities, while driving home with a friend – Ann Stickland, (then aged 65). It began – as it had done on the previous occasion – with the Mini Clubman breaking down, followed by the sight of a glowing oval shape and the appearance of a 'man', who walked over to Joyce, and, after taking her hands in his, began to speak in a foreign language. He then switched to broken English, instructing her not to divulge the content of their conversation to anyone. Joyce later described the 'man' as being similar in description to the other 'spacemen' she had encountered, except...

> *"... he had long hair, like a woman's, and was wearing what looked like buckles on the bottom of his legs, and gaiters. After walking back into the 'thing', he took off up into the sky."*

Attempts made by Mr Harris and John Ledner to interview Joyce and Mrs Ann Stickland were unsuccess-ful, despite many calls to the house and letters left.

**Leslie Harris:**

> *"I believe her attitude was dictated by the influence of the Press. Having said that, I accept we have no proof Mrs Bowles didn't fabricate her 'Alien encounters', but she did have in her favour the support of another witness*

*to each of her encounters – not forgetting her psychic experiences were also well supported by other witnesses."*

Mrs Stickland, who was interviewed by newspaper reporters after the event, had this to say:

*"I was not privy to the conversation held between Edwin and the occupant of the craft. I've never experienced anything like that.*

*At my age, I am a bit too old to have shocks like that."*

As a result of this renewed publicity, Mrs Bowles alleged she was the victim of a nasty campaign, directed

# UFO MYSTERY COSTS JOYCE A JOB

MRS BOWLES: " A nasty campaign to get rid of me "

A WOMAN who claims she has been in a flying saucer has lost her job.

The woman, 42-year-old Joyce Bowles, has been told by her British Rail bosses that she is redundant.

Mrs Bowles had told the News of the World that she met spacemen three times in three months.

She said they wore shoulder - length hair, luminous silver suits and high jackboots with pointed toes.

## Insulting

Once, she said, she and a companion were in a car when they suddenly found themselves inside a UFO.

Now Mrs Bowles blames her sacking on the publicity given to her claims.

She has been given notice to quit her job as an attendant in the ladies' waiting-room at Winchester Station, Hants.

She said at her home in Quarry Road, Winchester: "The divisional manager says I'm redundant. But the whole thing's ridiculous.

"There are two vacancies at the station I could easily fill. One is in the parcels office and the other is on the platform. But they won't consider me for those.

"Besides, there's been a nasty campaign to get rid of me in other ways.

"I've had insulting quips about my meeting spacemen made to me over the telephone. I've had razor blades put under my car tyres at the station.

"My neighbour even took one phone call in my house warning that I shouldn't park my car at the station or I'd find a bomb under it. That frightened me."

Mrs Bowles's boss, Winchester stationmaster Donald Baker, said : "I'd be very disturbed if I thought anyone was taking it out on Mrs Bowles.

"I've simply been told she isn't needed at the station any more."

Mr Dennis William, a local National Union of Railwaymen official, said: "If they were removing Mrs Bowles because of her interest in spacemen I wouldn't stand by and let it happen.

"I'd do something about it—it would be too damn silly for words.

"We're conducting our own inquiry into the matter."

at her personally. This included razor blades placed under her car tyres while parked outside Winchester Railway Station, where she worked as a 'powder room attendant' before being made redundant.

We spoke to Don Tuersley, a noted researcher into the crop circles phenomena, who spoke about an occasion during a visit to Joyce at the family home in Quarry Road, with his wife, when the upstairs bedroom curtains inexplicably wrapped around him, seemingly of their own accord rather than being propelled by a breeze or some such other rational explanation.

*Don Tuersley*

Don told us there was a rumour exorcisms had been carried out at the house, which was later demolished by the Council after many complaints of ghostly manifestations were reported.

In an attempt to obtain details of these exorcisms we wrote to the Bishop of Winchester, in 2010, who replied, telling us he had no knowledge of any such incidents and suggested we check Hampshire Records on-line – which we did, but found nothing in the records. However, we were rewarded with some information from Carol, at Linton Archives, and Local Studies assistant, who remembered reading about the incidents involving Joyce Bowles at the time in the newspaper, although she never met her personally.

Further research revealed a priest – the Reverend Ramsdale Whalley, of Holy Trinity Church – had visited the house in Quarry Road, Winchester, where Mrs Bowles and her husband Ronald (who both worked at Winchester Railways Station) lived from 1967. Rumours suggested he had carried out an exorcism after reports of 'spirits' being seen.

One may think that the Catholic Churches and Church of England would maintain a list or file of exorcisms, carried out by them over the years – easier said than done. Our attempts to obtain sight of these files were unsuccessful, although common sense dictated that files of this nature would be recorded somewhere.

We contacted Mildred Whalley, (then aged 84 in 2006) – the wife of Reverend 'Dale' Whalley (who had passed away in 1984) and spoke to her, in March 2010, about her husband's involvement in exorcisms.

> *"He was a bit wary of it himself – but then he realised, just by touching people, somehow, they were getting better. He had a knack of helping people and that's why he applied to Bishop Faulkner Alison to be an exorcist, but he never told people about it as it was a very personal thing. 'I can't help everyone', he used to tell me. We retired in 1977 and went to Norfolk. 'Dale' died in 1983 and I came back seven years to live in Winchester."*

### Joyce Bowles makes contact

After placing an advert in the *Hampshire Chronicle*, in March 2010, seeking any additional information relating to what had happened to Joyce and Edwin Pratt, a telephone call was received at 9.15pm on the 8th April 2010, from Mrs Joyce Bowles, who wanted to put the record straight:

> *"You suggested that my house was pulled down following exorcisms; this it totally wrong. My house was one of a number of council houses that were redeveloped, at Quarry Road and Fairdown, because they were vey old. After the work was done, we went back up there to live. They gave us a four-bedroom house, because we had four children, and we were only there for a year because the children were then grown-up. Chris, my eldest, went into the Army, so I couldn't afford the house – even with the help of my husband, who was working on the Railway as well.*
>
> *I'm not being nasty, but I won't have any more to do with this. My boys have been ridiculed for years because of all of this, and we are still being ridiculed now. It's a dreadful place for something like that."*

Joyce told us at the time of interview that she was now aged 76, but still employed part-time, working for a firm of cleaning sub-contractors. Sadly, we learned from her that both Anne Stickland and Ted had passed away.

Unfortunately, the legacy of having the courage to report something inexplicable, as Joyce had done way back in the 1970s, was still attracting ridicule to this present day, not only towards Joyce but her sons – a matter for which we apologised to her.

**She said:**

> *"People are so horrible and nasty that it will all blow up again. The papers had a field day. All we ever saw was a man in a silver suit, while on our way to pick up my son from Chilcote, and reported it to the newspaper. They added so much more; some accounts even told lies about us. I never said we saw any aliens or spaceships, but I don't like talking about what we saw right up to this present day, because I am fearful that it might happen again. We still get ridiculed; worse, there are people that seem to believe we made money out of it. Well, we didn't! I bet you're surprised to hear from me. Did you think I was dead? To this present day I am still frightened about sleeping without the bedroom light on. I telephoned you to put you right with regard to the house being demolished. If people have said that, they are lying."*

It was clear from our conversation held with Joyce that we were talking to a confident, intelligent woman, who despite the level of ridicule directed at her, over the years, was still able to laugh and speak coherently about her experiences.

Unfortunately she refused to disclose her current address, feeling any further involvement would attract further bouts of ridicule to her and her sons. Whilst she confirmed having received a letter from us, many years ago, she reiterated, time and time again, that she wanted to forget about this episode in her life and move on.

We felt privileged to have spoken with Joyce, but saddened to think our actions may well possibly lead to further embarrassment and mocking from those sceptics. However, at the end of the day, these incidents should be recorded for posterity – if only to show others, in years to come, exactly what happened and not what they thought might have happened.

Somebody else who was curious enough to take in an interest in what Joyce and Ted had seen, rather than dismissing their claims straightaway (as many have done over the years as figments of an overwrought imagination) was Colin Andrews – a well-known researcher, author and expert on the Crop Circle phenomenon, and founder of Circles Phenomenon Research International – the first organisation established to investigate the crop circle phenomenon – after his curiosity was aroused, during 1983, when he saw an arrangement of five circles in a wheat field, near Winchester, England. Intrigued, he began investigations, accompanied by Pat Delgado – a retired NASA engineer, and Busty Taylor – a light aircraft pilot, (both of whom we had met over the years).

In 1989, Pat and Colin co-authored *Circular Evidence* – the first book written on the subject – which became an international best seller and was chosen by Queen Elizabeth for her prestigious 'Summer Reading List'. This was followed by *Crop Circles: The Latest Evidence*, in 1990, and *Crop Circles – Signs of Contact*, co-authored by Stephen Spignesi, and published in March 2003 by *New Page Books*.

**Colin:**

> "I visited Mrs Pratt [Bowles] on 21st January 1989, at her home in Church Road, Nether Wallop, in Hampshire. She described how they had arrived home very white and shaken, after having encountered what they described as tall 'ET's' with red eyes, wearing one-piece silver suits with a belt and large buckle, and having very long blond hair pulled in around their heads.

> She told me they went back to the locality where it happened, the following morning, and saw for herself the grass still flattened by tyre marks where the Mini Countryman had stopped. She said the paint pealed off the car roof after the encounter and the police took the car away – which she never saw again."

Mrs Pratt [Bowles] also told Colin that

> "Ted was instructed by the 'space people' that there would be a very loud bang over Nether Wallop on a certain date and time – which happened. On another occasion Ted was watching TV, when the picture broke up and a voice told him the date his daughter would give birth to her baby and the sex – both happened to be later correct."

**Colin:**

> "Mrs Pratt [Bowles] said she would look out more details for me, but I never heard from her again."

An appeal for further information in the *Hampshire Chronicle*, regarding this matter, attracted the attention of Julie Mawer (neé Mitchell), who told us that her grandmother 'Pansy' Bull, and her companion – Mrs Bessie Shears, were good friends of Mrs Bowles – Bessie being her neighbour for several years, following the demolition of her property in Colebrook Street, Winchester, and that they recalled several sightings or movements of the 'poltergeist' at Joyce's house, when items moved or fell for no reason, and of odd smells. Several times Bessie had been woken at night by Mrs Bowles' reports of activities that she couldn't explain.

**Julie:**

> "I also recall, on one particular day, Mrs Shears and Mrs Bowles were returning to the stables, after an eventful drive from Quarry Road to New Barton Farm via the A272, when the car stalled for no apparent reason and the ladies lost three hours of time. Mrs Shears was very white and talking of strange places and people. It is still reported that people travelling along this stretch of road experience the same problems and believe this was where the first crop circles where noted in Hampshire. Her sons – David and Stephen Bowles – still reside in Winchester, or they were. However, the house was not demolished because of reported poltergeist action but for a redevelopment by the then Winchester City Council Housing, to make more housing for Winchester. There were also neighbours on the attached side of Mrs Bowles' house, called Summerbell, with a daughter named Hazel, but I don't remember the other daughter's name."

(Sources: As above, 'Wife in UFO riddle is sacked', 'Space Gremlins are bugging my car', 'What did the man from the sky say to Joyce?' 'Can't tell anyone, I wouldn't dare', 'Scared Joyce can't escape a spaceman')

## 8th March 1977 – UFO over Hampshire

The *Herald*, in their edition of the 18th March 1977 – 'UFO sighting scare', told their readers about two Danish auxiliary workers – Mette Juul (then aged 19) and Anne Great Mortensen (then aged 20) – who were walking in the grounds of Le Court, Hampshire, at 9pm, when they saw a bright 'star' in the sky, which began to move towards them. Frightened, they ran for shelter under a tree and described the object as resembling a space capsule, showing a bright yellow light in front, a red flashing light and yellow lights underneath. It hovered above them momentarily, before moving away towards the Bordon area.

The next morning, the same – if not similar – UFO was sighted by Phyllis Young, who was in bed at the time, between 7.30-8pm, when she saw what looked like:

> "...*a white spinning top in the sky. It had a white light on top and looked as if it was about to land.*"

## 9th March 1977 – UFO over Lancashire

Brian Grimshaw and Jeffrey Farmer were driving through Nelson, in Lancashire, at 3.10 am, near the top of Railway Street, when they noticed some 'bright lights' in the sky over Pendle Hill.

### Mr Grimshaw:

> "*I stopped the car and the object slowly hovered over us. It had two bright lights, one at each side, and a mass of coloured light below it. The whole thing was surrounded by mist.*"

# UFO over Pendle shocks a driver ②

**MR GRIMSHAW**
Made a sketch

AN inexplicable object hovering over Pendle Hill brought Mr Brian Grimshaw's car to a standstill in the early hours.

As he watched the object drew nearer. "It had a shiny black body and was cigar shaped," said Mr Grimshaw, who lives in Lennox Road, Portsmouth, Todmorden.

"I was in my car with a friend, Mr Jeffery Farmer, of Chiltern Avenue, Burnley. We had taken a canteen assistant home from work at Carrington Menswear, Barrowford.

"At the top of Railway Street, Nelson, we saw bright lights in the sky over Pendle Hill. I stopped the car and the object slowly hovered towards us. It had two bright lights, one at each side, and a mass of coloured lights below it.

same Barrowford company, verified Mr Grimshaw's sighting. "I don't know what it was. It made a low humming noise as it came over the car.

"We watched for about 10 minutes and the whole

legs began to shake as it flew above us,' said Mr Farmer.

The sighting is one of many recently reported to East Lancashire astronomer Mrs Hilda Rogals, of Kenyon Clough, Helm-

This week she said tha during the past month sh had received 33 reports sightings in Blackbur Langho, Oswaldtwistl Padiham, Fence and Helm shore.

Coloured lights

Grey mist around

Shiny black body

Bright lights

Bright lights

Bottom view

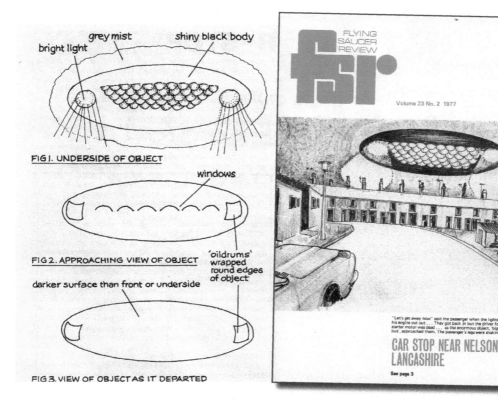

FIG I. UNDERSIDE OF OBJECT

FIG 2. APPROACHING VIEW OF OBJECT

FIG 3. VIEW OF OBJECT AS IT DEPARTED

**Mr Farmer:**

*"It made a low humming noise as it came over the car. We watched it for about ten minutes, and the whole thing was a bit eerie. My legs began to shake as it flew above us."*

(Source: **Jenny Randles/***Lancashire Evening Telegraph*, **11.3.1977 – 'UFO over Pendle Hill'/***Lancashire Evening Telegraph*, **11.3.1977 – 'UFO over Pendle shocks a driver')**

## 9th March 1977 – UFO over Harlow, Essex

Mrs Irene Gatrell of Collins Meadow, Harlow, went into her garden, at 6.30pm, and saw:

*"...a large white light, surrounded by four or five red lights, moving quite fast. Suddenly they stopped in mid-air, and the red lights seemed to disappear into the white light and then reappear again.*

*At times they were all absolutely stationary and there was no noise at all. I watched them for about twenty minutes and then went inside.*

*When I came out later, at 7.30pm, they had gone."*

It appears that the same phenomena was witnessed by Rene Draper, of Rushes Mead, at 7.30pm, who alleged she had seen the 'strange lights' on a number of occasions in the past.

*"I even tried to take photographs, but they didn't come out. I saw a bright triangular white light, which came closer and then seemed to break up into about nine red lights.*

*I phoned Stansted Airport and they told me they were aircraft going into land at Heathrow."*

(Source: *Harlow Gazette*, **11.3.1977 – 'Mystery lights in night sky – Were they UFOs?')**

# MYSTERY LIGHTS IN NIGHT SKY

## Were they UFOs?

THE UFOs were back over Harlow last Wednesday evening according to two people, who individually contacted the Gazette-Citizen to tell of the strange lights they saw in the sky.

Mrs Irene Gatrell saw the lights from her daughter's garden at Milwards, Harlow—and she claims they were in exactly the same formation as when she saw them three years ago in her own garden at Collins Meadow, Harlow.

She said: "The whole thing must have lasted about an hour. I went into the garden at about 6.30pm and saw a large white light surrounded by about four or five red lights. They were moving quite fast, then they suddenly stopped in mid-air and the red lights seemed to disappear into the white light and then reappear again.

"At times they were all absolutely stationary and there was no noise at all. I watched them for about 20 minutes, went indoors and went out again a little later. They were still there, but at about 7.30pm when I looked again, they had gone."

When Mrs Gatrell went to work the following day, other people said they had seen similar lights at about the same time.

"I have never really given UFOs much thought except when I saw the same thing three years ago, but I'm pretty convinced now that there must have been something up there, and it certainly wasn't an aeroplane," she said.

Mrs Rene Draper of Rushes Mead, Harlow, had a similar story to tell, but she saw the lights at about 7.30pm from her garden at Rushes Mead, Harlow.

She has seen the strange lights on a number of occasions in the past, and the last time tried to take some photographs, but they did not come out.

"I saw a bright triangular-shaped white light which, as it came closer, seemed to break up into about nine smaller red lights. I phoned Stansted Airport and they said they were aeroplanes waiting to land at Heathrow Airport, but I don't see how they could be," she said.

## 11th March 1977 – Strange blue 'light' over London

Edmonton resident – Julie Canning (then 19), was sat in a Ford transit van in Stanhope Gardens, Harringay, London, at 9.30pm.

*"I saw a dark blue 'light' move from left to right across the southern sky, which extinguished about eight seconds later."*

## 13th March 1977 – UFO landing and occupant seen

At 9pm, Stephen Taylor – a resident of Llethr, in the north east corner of St. Brides Bay – was walking home when he saw a glowing object, with a halo around, it hovering in the sky over Hendre Bridge. Puzzled he went to a friend's house and told them, but they laughed at him. After continuing his journey he saw a black dog, running away from the area, but thought no more of it at the time. Stephen decided to stop at a gateway at 9.30pm, which overlooks Brawdy NATO airbase, and have a cigarette, but was surprised to see no sign of the airfield lights. Suddenly he realised why! There was a large object blocking his view which he later described to Randall Jones Pugh as:

*"…like a dome. When I had seen it earlier in the sky, it was pear-shaped with a faint light around it. It took up a large piece of the field. I would say it was 20 feet high, by 30-40 feet wide. I then heard something coming across my extreme right and saw what looked like a tall man – about six feet tall – and I felt afraid. He had high cheek bones, and a suit that looked transparent. It had a zip thing down the front and he had what looked like a sort of breathing apparatus, like divers use. I took a swing at it and then ran home, which was about three miles. As soon as I got home I drew what I had seen on paper. One thing more, my dog kept barking and growling at me – as if I was a stranger."*

**(Sources: Randall Jones Pugh, *The Dyfed Enigma,*Faber and Faber, 1979/*The Western Telegraph*, 17.3.1977)**

## 14th March 1977 – Strange lights over London

Gillian Goring of Carlton Terrace, London, reported sighting:

> "...a huge 'star', visible in the sky over the car park near the house, at 7.50pm; half-an-hour later it dissolved from view.
>
> At 8.58pm an orange light – looking like an aircraft – appeared in the same place. A fuzzy red light attached to the edge of a yellow light was seen orbiting around the orange light. About 8 minutes later, the lights disappeared."

## 17th March 1977 – Heart-shaped UFO over Kent

At 5.54am, a resident of Birchington, Kent, was awoken by a loud rustling noise – as if water was rushing down the road.

On looking through the window, she saw a large, slightly '*heart*', or '*kidney-shaped*' object, with flashing red and white lights, travelling in an arc of movement across the sky, near the horizon. As it passed over the shoreline – now heading in a straight trajectory – the noise changed to a slight drone, then it was gone from view.

**(Source: *BUFORA Journal*, Volume 6, Number 4, November/December 1977/Valerie Martin)**

## 18th March 1977 – Five glowing 'discs' seen over South Wales Estuary

The archives of the Birmingham UFO Group – UFOSIS – tell of five glowing 'discs', seen travelling in formation over Birmingham, on 18th March 1977. Was it one of these, seen later by John Petts from Llanstephan, South Wales?

John – a local designer of stained glass – was looking out of his window, overlooking the *River Towy*, when he saw an object:

> "...sharp and clear, like the shape of a weaver's shuttle – sharply pointed, pale gold in colour, clearly visible in the night sky – until it suddenly disappeared."

**(Sources: Mrs Kusha Petts/*Western Mail*, 14.3.1977 – 'Golden object seen over Estuary')**

## 26th March 1977 – 'Flying Saucer' over Little Haven South Wales

Farmer's wife – Josephine Hewison from Broadmoor Farm, Little Haven, sighted a metallic silver coloured object, with three distinctive layers

**Littlehaven Landing**
*Inv W. G. Cale*

or edges around it, resembling an 'upside-down jelly mould', hovering just above the ground, obscuring the view of the greenhouse at their Pembrokeshire farm.

Further enquiries revealed that this had taken place at 7.50am and that the 'object' (and greenhouse) was situated about a hundred yards away. In front of the greenhouse were stacks of potato chitting trays, which are normally seen from the house quite clearly, but these were obstructed by the UFO. Randall asked her what shape it was. She replied:

> *"It was in three tiers; it seemed to be round, but when you see a thing in*

# Did boy see 'humanoid'?

PEOPLE in south-west Wales, where UFO activity has mysteriously intensified since January, should not feel alone with their phenomena. Randall Jones Pugh, retired vet and co-ordinator for South Wales of the British Unidentified Flying Objects Research Association, says there has also been a 'general flap' elsewhere.

In Wales, 14 pupils of a junior school at Broadhaven saw a silver-white, cigar-shaped object in a field about 100 yards from their school playground one lunch-hour in February. The headmaster made each child draw what he had seen. 'The similarity was remarkable,' said Mr Pugh.

Even more remarkable was the report Mr Pugh received a few weeks later when a boy of

**John Petts saw a UFO from his window and then painted it.**

17 saw one night in March 'a large dense object, with an orange-yellow glow round the edges' in a field, and also encountered a tall, thin figure 'with luminous eyes, high cheek-bones and a large mouth' approaching the gate where he stood. His mother told Mr Pugh next day that when he arrived home he had been 'very, very frightened'.

Whatever is to be made of the 'humanoid', as Mr Pugh termed it, even the most cynical observer could spot similarities between the object in the field and the 'luminous, pale gold, six-sided figure' seen by artist John Petts from the window of his house overlooking the Towy estuary another night in the same week.

Mr Petts immediately drew it. 'It was seen by a neighbour the same night and I was glad of corroboration.' What did he think it was? 'I just don't know.'

Mr Pugh said he had no idea what the objects were either, except that they seemed to be 'non-terrestrial'. But he thinks it's high time the British Government followed the French Government's example and set up an investigating committee.

*Ena Kendall*

As from Llansteffan                    4th Sept 00

Please excuse the delay in contacting you; I am briefly in Abergavenny.

Enclos. Many thanks for the original newsclipping please use the piece as you wish.

To my knowledge John had never seen a UFO before and I didn't witness it myself. We were always up late but I'd gone to bed that night.

Would you like this original back?

Good Wishes, Sincerely, Kusha Petts

cross-section I suppose you can never be sure. There was a definite dome, to start with, and then a central portion, but there seemed to be a rounded ridge (if you know what I mean) between the layers.

Randall asked her: *"...like a Rowntrees Jelly?*

**Josephine:**

*"Yes, rather like a jelly. When I described it to the children, I said it looked rather like a squashed jelly mould, which it really did. It was a smooth aluminium coloured, bulbous shape. It was pretty high – fifteen feet, maybe, and almost double the greenhouse in width, which would have made it 35-40 feet wide."*

The pony that is normally found standing at the gate was discovered at the perimeter of the nearby field, about 400 yards away, which was out of character. Had it been frightened away by the appearance of the UFO?

Mrs Hewison mentioned that she and her family have lived at Broadmoor Farm for a few years, but that no one seemed to have lived there longer than five or six years. What did she mean by this statement? Had other strange things happened there? We know she hasn't lived there for many years and our attempts to trace her failed, although we are sure she may well have received our letters sent to her last address.

## 27th/28th March 1977 – UFO over Glasgow Airport, Scotland

At 11.30pm, a triangular-shaped blue object, showing a turquoise glow, was seen over Rutherglen, Glasgow, by Mr Forsyth.

This was followed by an incident on the 28th March, involving John Wilson and his wife, who were driving from Headley to Sutton, in Surrey. As they approached the Tadworth roundabout on the A127, at 7.40pm, they noticed a 'white light' in the sky directly ahead.

*"It was stationary, and then it became very bright and started to pulsate rapidly, but was lost from sight as our vision became obstructed by a hedge. After passing the hedge we looked, but it had gone from sight."* (**Source: Bob Green**)

## 28th March 1977 – Mystery 'ball of light' in the sky over Tasmania

A Mount Stuart student was returning home, at 6.55pm, when he saw a moon sized 'ball of light', in a cloudy sky but with clear patches.

*"It was showing red, orange, and purple, colours, all merging together, heading southwards, and within 15 seconds had moved behind Knocklofty; seconds later it reappeared, going north at great speed. It made its third and final appearance moving back southwards, this time much lower and making a whistling noise. Once again, it was last seen heading behind Knocklofty."*

Mrs Carr, of New Town, was another witness to the passage of this strange object across the sky.

*"At 6.55pm, I heard a crackling noise and went to the front door and looked out. I saw a moon sized orange-apricot coloured 'light', darting away northwards – then it stopped and seemed to head towards me before pausing. I felt as if I was enveloped in an orange beam, or glow, for a few seconds. The 'light' shot off in a flash, towards the Mount Stuart direction, the incident over in 5-6 seconds."*

## Spring 1977 – 'Flying Saucer' over Hampshire

Barbara Aves living in Ringwood, in Hampshire, who described herself as *"a sceptic of such matters'* (UFOs), soon changed her mind when, during the same year, she and her son saw one of the strangest things she had ever seen.

*"It looked like an inverted saucer, all lit up, just hovering over the roof of my neighbour's bungalow. After about five minutes, it moved away towards Wimborne. We talked about what we had seen and decided not to report it. What was the point? Nobody would believe us.*

*When my son went to work, the following day, he was surprised to hear some of the workmates talking about a 'flying saucer' seen over Wimborne, by a man living in Grove Road, which was described as looking like 'a rocket, with flames coming from the rear, heading West to East."*

Enquiries with the police, at New Milton, revealed they had received a number of reports of a UFO sighted over Wimborne. (**Source: Personal interview**)

## 30th March 1977 – Landed UFO sighting, Birmingham

**See file 30.3.1977**

An unusual occurrence took place during the early hours of this day when, after being disturbed by the sounds of cats, fighting, a Kings Heath woman looked out of the window.

*"I saw what looked like a ghostly white plume of steam, or mist, rising over the next door neighbour's garden, funnelling away from a white dome lying on the ground at the bottom of my garden. I was so excited, I awoke my husband. He came rushing to the window, but after ten minutes we decided to go back to bed."*

The incident was later brought to the attention of the Birmingham UFO Group – UFOSIS – who discovered the woman's daughter was to complain of a mystery rash found on her face, after the incident – rather odd, understanding she was asleep at the time.

The investigators speculated the phenomenon may have been caused by a sharp ground frost, and lack of wind, but discounted this idea as time went on, particularly as the witness told them she had seen the same thing happening on the 12th April 1977.

Could there have been any connection with the discovery that the house had been rebuilt, after receiving a direct hit by a German bomb, during World War Two, which claimed the lives of the family living there? (**Source: UFOSIS**)

## Spring 1977 – Close Encounter, Worcestershire

We met up with Terry Ingram – then involved with the running of a hospital radio station at the Alexandra Hospital, Redditch, after being invited to talk about local UFOs.

Afterwards, Terry took us to one side and told us about a UFO he and other fellow workers had sighted, while working nights at the British Leyland car factory, Longbridge, in Birmingham, during the spring/summer of 1977.

> *"I was with another worker – 'Big John' – and just finishing a break before going back into the cylinder block section, adjacent to Cofton Church. 'Big John' suddenly stopped and pointed upwards, exclaiming 'What is that?' I looked up and was shocked to see this huge cigar-shaped object, motionless in the sky – no more than ten feet above the roof. It was so big, it blocked out the night sky. I would describe it as being thirty metres in length and forty metres in width. It had a curved underside, which was constructed of metal panels of varying sizes – small, square, large, and rectangular. It was just like standing under a Jumbo Jet.*
>
> *I tried to rationalise the situation. I hadn't had a drink, but didn't feel threatened. After what seemed like a considerable length of time, it began to vibrate slightly and then shot forwards into the sky and moved away.*
>
> *As soon as it had left I became aware of the sound of the pumping station and stumbled into work in such a state – taking some time to convince the foreman of what we had seen. About a fortnight later, after the encounter with the UFO, I was at home, in Martley Close, Redditch, when – during the early hours of the morning – there was a loud and persistent knocking noise on the front door.*
>
> *My wife urged me to go and see what was happening, thinking there was a family crisis. I looked at the clock. It was 3am.*
>
> *I shouted out, 'Whose there?' … No reply. The knocking went on, so I went downstairs and saw what appeared to be the outline of a small child, standing on the doorstep, through the glass panel set into the door.*
>
> *As I reached the front door, thinking it was a neighbour's child, seeking help, the letterbox lifted. Wary, I crouched down and peered through the letter box, feeling a 'wave' of fear rise over me with the hairs on the back of my neck standing up, after sighting a pair of slanted red eyes with jet black pupils. I found myself unable to move with fright. It was literally 'a creature from the depths of hell'. I watched, in horror, as the 'creature' slowly backed away, still keeping eye contact with me.*
>
> *It stood on top of a drain cover, a few feet away from the house. When I moved, so did it. I stood up. It did so and took a step towards the door, but stopped – as if realising my wife was walking down the stairs. It then turned around, crouched, and leapt up in the air over the tall fence and disappeared. I will never forget what I saw.*
>
> *It was really horrible. It was about 1.5 metres in height, with green scaly skin, pointed ears, and long filthy teeth. 'He' or 'she' had four fingers on its hand. The 'thing' was wearing what looked like ragged sackcloth, worn like a toga. It also had a tail, resembling a lizard's tail but with an arrowhead on the one end, quite substantive, and stood on its two back feet in a crouching mode."*

We accept there are those who will reject this fantastic event as being a flight of fancy, drawn from the very depths of imagination.

We disagree, and believe this is a genuine account. Whether we would, of course, have perceived the 'being' the same is a matter we will never (hopefully!) know. Mr Ingram has never sought publicity but now feels it is time to share his earth-shattering experience with others, hoping somebody else may have seen something similar.

## 1970s – Strange 'beings' seen, Farnham, Surrey

We spoke to Ray Dorset – British guitarist, songwriter and founder of 'Mungo Jerry' fame – now living in Germany – who described what happened in the early hours of the morning, while on his way home to Tilford Road, Frensham, Farnham, Surrey, during the late 1970s, accompanied by his then wife.

> *"We weren't far from the house when we both saw what appeared to be a group of small, grey, insubstantial people, with slightly oval heads and some kind of aerial – forming an impression, almost, as if someone had drawn them with a pencil, walking in a line, one behind each other, and at an angle from one side of the road to the other. We wondered if we could have been mistaken. Perhaps we had seen a group of deer, showing antlers.*
>
> *We made a search of the area but saw no sign of any deer, and eventually agreed we had seen something we were unable to explain even to this present day."*

Incidents like these seem, at first glance, almost too impossible to believe, except for the fact that Ray and his wife were not the only ones we were to come across, over the years, who had sighted similar described *'beings'* that may have resembled humans in their mannerisms, but certainly not in appearance.

**(Source: Personal interview)**

# CHAPTER 16 – APRIL 1977

## 7th April 1977 – Welsh children chased by 'green ball'

Jean Hubber – a Community Nursing Sister – was at home, at about 4.30pm, when her two young daughters came in from playing to tell her:

> *"Mummy, there's a 'green ball' chasing us."*

However, Mrs Hubber was busy with housework. She said:

> *"I did not take any notice of them. I told them to go back out to play, but ten minutes later the four-year-old came to me and asked me to come and see – 'it's out by the back door'."*

**Mrs Hubber:**

> *"Again I took no notice, although the girl became adamant about me going to see the 'green ball'. Half-an-hour later I noticed the children were playing indoors and when I asked them why they weren't playing outside, they replied, 'We're not going out – that 'green thing' keeps chasing us.'*
>
> *I then realised they were telling the truth. I went outside with the children to where they had seen the 'ball'; I could not see it but the four year-old claimed she could see it descending into swampland in a field. I can only say that, although I couldn't see it, I could sense that something was wrong. They described the 'ball' as 'dark on one side, shiny on the other' and that the object disappeared by 'going to ground'."*

Source: *The Dyfed Enigma*, **Randall Jones Pugh and F.W. Holiday, 1979)**

## 7th April 1977 – Close encounter with 'alien figure', Milford Haven, Wales

Mr Cyril John was staying with his daughter, at Milford Haven, when he was awoken by a pulsating orange light.

On looking through the window overlooking the rooftops, he saw:

> *"...two silver coloured objects, enclosed in an aura of orange light; the first resembling an Easter*

*egg, swinging to and fro behind the chimney, the other was a humanoid 'figure' wearing a silver one-piece suit, with its 'arms and legs' outstretched – like a freefall parachute jumper."*

**(Sources: *The Dyfed* Enigma, Randall Jones Pugh and F.W. Holiday/ Tony Pace, BUFORA)**

## 8th April 1977 – Police officer reports 'strange light' over West Yorkshire

Superintendent Cooper, of the West Yorkshire Police, was driving a patrol car, at Laisterdyke, when he noticed a 'bright light', low down in the sky, over the direction of Ferrand Avenue with the junction of Hambledon Avenue – which vanished from view.

The officer reported it to the police control room, who confirmed they had not received any other reports.

**(Source: Declassified MOD records)**

## 10th April 1977 – Strange 'being' seen on Cradle Hill

At 10pm, a group of UFO 'spotters' assembled on top of Cradle Hill, near to the now famous 'white gates', including Mrs Phyllis Palmer, her husband, and Arthur Shuttlewood.

**Phyllis:**

*"After a couple of hours, people began to drift away – as it was a very cold but clear night. A young man next to me set up his infrared camera on a tripod and stood waiting patiently with me, laughing and occasionally joking with us. All of sudden I saw a man, dressed in what looked like a spacesuit, walk up the hill towards us, from the direction of the Army barracks below us. He had a tight fitting helmet on his head – like a skin diver – and wearing a pair of brilliant white wellington style boots. He came up to the side of the gate and looked across at me (even though at least eight people were looking in that direction) and then bent down, straightened up, and walked into the field through the wire. I decided not to say anything but continued 'sky watching' with others, as some began to leave one by one.*

*Suddenly, I saw what looked like a large cloud, manifesting in the air, and brought it to the attention of Arthur and others, who looked over the gate. The 'cloud' then changed into what looked like a beehive shape, became clearer, and changed again into an oval 'disc', with six windows visible on the side. I was astounded and could hear my heart pounding. A 'man', dressed as before, came out of the 'craft' holding what appeared to look like a bathroom heater – oblong, with a row of grilles. He was joined by another, who pointed towards the area of the clubhouse on the opposite side of the hill. The two then set off along the path taken by the first 'man' across the fields.*

*A party of four teenagers, and Arthur, leapt over the gate and walked up towards where the 'craft' was, after I told them what I was seeing. They returned saying they couldn't see anything, but all remarked how hot the location was. One of them complained he had been tugged at by something, or someone, invisible. My husband, on the other side of the road, shouted that he could hear a high-pitched whistling noise – then the object disappeared from sight and I felt the cold creep over me, once again.*

*About fifteen minutes later, I felt myself grow hot again and saw the 'clouds' forming above the copse and the arrival of a similar 'craft' – as seen before. This one had a lovely azure blue colour around it and was higher up than the previous one seen.*

*It took on a sold appearance, followed by the entrance of two 'men'; one walking east, the other west. They had what appeared to be some sort of 'white line' with them – as though measuring something. One of them began to walk towards me and my heart began to pound again, although I was not afraid this time. He stopped halfway down the field, looked at us, and turned towards the direction taken by the others, then lifted his hand. A short, sharp, beam of light came from his hand, although I didn't see any torch. I went cold again and the 'craft' and its occupants disappeared from view. I had some sandwiches and tea and chattered away to the others.*

*Suddenly, I saw a 'man' on the other side of the road beckoning towards me. I walked over and followed him up the path. He had high cheekbones and rather oriental eyes, wearing a one-piece suit (as the others had done) with gauntlet type gloves. At this stage I panicked and ran back to my colleagues.*

*I appreciate this account may seem less credible to others but, in the pursuits of truth and research of UFOs, I feel it is my duty to place on record a faithful account of what I witnessed at the top of Cradle Hill on that eventful Easter morning."*

(Source: Letters to Peter Tate/Ian Mryzglod, *Probe*)

## 12th April 1977 – Close encounter near Milford Haven, Wales

On the 12th April 1977 (some accounts give the 16th), Mark Marston (12) of Herbrandston, near Milford Haven (a nephew of Billy and Pauline Coombs) reported having sighted a 'figure', dressed in a silver suit, about a hundred yards away, close to a local sewage farm at St. Margaret's Way.

*"It climbed easily over a big gate and when I started walking backwards it came towards me. I stopped under a street light and saw that it had a head, which was square-shaped with a black face.*

*It was wearing flat, black boots with no heels and looked to be well over six feet tall with an aerial sticking up from one shoulder."*

Mr Terry Marston confirmed, later, that his son had arrived home very frightened. He then accompanied his son back to the scene, where it was claimed they discovered a large footprint in slurry.

Mark also told of having seen a red glow in the field behind the 'figure' and the vague shape of an upside-down 'saucer'.

(Source: Randall Jones Pugh/*Western Mail*, 26.4.1977 – 'Huge figure in silver suit is seen in UFO area')

THE WESTERN MAIL

# 'Huge' figure in a silvery suit is seen in UFO area

A YOUNG West Wales couple are still recovering from the shock of having their late-night television viewing shattered by an unexpected visitor at the window — a huge figure dressed in a silvery suit.

Dairyman Mr. Billy Coombs and his wife Pauline, of Ripperston Farm, near Little Haven, claim the figure was so huge that they could not see its face.

Four miles away Mrs. Coombs's 12-year-old nephew claims that a figure dressed....

Both incidents are the latest in a spate of UFO sightings over the Broad Haven area which have baffled local people and have convinced a Ufologist that something mysterious is happening.

Less than two weeks ago Mrs. Coombs, aged 31, mother of five children, had her first contact with a UFO when a "fireball" shaped like a football followed her car.

### 'It was there'

Now, after the latest incident, she is aware that people will find it difficult to believe her story.

"Even my husband was a little hesitant about believing me when I saw the fireball, but after what happened outside our window he changed his mind," she said last night.

"And I'm beginning to think it seems more than just a coincidence that this huge figure was seen by two members of the same family."

Mr. and Mrs. Coombs were watching a television Western in the early hours of Saturday when the figure appeared outside their window.

"I saw something silvery through the window but I did not say anything about it to my husband in case he thought I was imagining things," said Mrs. Coombs.

"Then suddenly Billy looked out of the window and jumped up quickly from his chair. He said there was a figure outside in a silver suit and it was so big we could not see the face. It must have been well over seven feet tall. The window seemed to light up and we didn't know what to do. We called the local UFO investigator and then the police.

"I ran upstairs to my children and Billy put the outside lights on and went out through the front door, but when he got outside the figure had disappeared. I know it sounds stupid and hard to believe but it was there. It's not a hoax."

Mrs. Coombs's nephew, Mark

Marston, of St. Margaret's Way, Herbrandston, near Milford Haven, claims he saw a figure also dressed in a silver suit about 100 yards from his home.

It happened about 10 days ago and Mark, a pupil at Milford Haven central secondary school, later described the incident.

"It climbed easily over a big gate and when I started walking backwards it came towards me," he said. "It stopped underneath a street light and I could see that the head seemed to be square-shaped with a black face, an aerial sticking up, shoulders. It had flat, black boots with no heels. I ran home as fast as I could.... well over six feet tall."

His father, Mr. Terry Marston, said his son arrived home very frightened. He later went to where his son had claimed to have seen the figure and found a large footprint in some slurry.

Mark also claims to have seen a red glow in a field behind the figure and the vague shape of an upside-down saucer.

Other reports from Herbrandston are of red glows in the sky while some other children say they saw a silver-coloured football hovering in a hedge.

The latest sightings began when some children at Broad Haven school claimed they saw a UFO in a field in a silver suit.

The South Wales co-ordinator for the British Unidentified Flying Objects Research Association, Mr. Randall Jones-Pugh, of Roch, near Haverfordwest, believes that something mysterious is happening in Dyfed. The case of Mark was one of a "classical confrontation" in view of

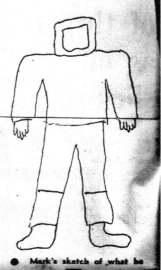

● Mark's sketch of what he

other happenings in the village.

Reports of sightings were coming in thick and fast, said Mr. Jones-Pugh. He has appealed for anyone who may have seen something mysterious to contact him at Camrose 246 so that a composite picture can be put together.

## 12th April 1977 – Landed UFO, Penrith, Cumbria

At 7.20 pm, farmer – Kenneth Moreton from Penrith, in Cumbria, was at home with his daughter, when they noticed what appeared to be *"a large aluminium van, close to a forest of pine trees"*, about a mile away from the family farm.

> *"My curiosity was aroused; I knew there was no road there. I stood watching, as this object (it was certainly no vehicle) began to rise up and down, before descending for good.*
>
> *The next day I walked over to have a look and noticed, straightaway, the tops of spruce trees had been broken off, consistent with a heavy object having landed on top of them – although there was no sign of anything that could have caused it.*
>
> *I decided to report the matter to the local newspaper but regretted this later, after being made the butt of ridicule by those who had not seen what I had."* (**Source: Personal interview**)

## 14th April 1977 – Silver gleaming sphere seen

Deborah Swan (then aged 13) accompanied by her brother, and five friends, were out playing in Herbrandston Park, Milford Haven, at 6.30pm. They decided to have a look around, after hearing of many reports of strange things seen in the South Wales area, and were stunned when, in the words of Deborah:

> *"There was something in the field opposite, out of the ordinary. I have never seen anything like it before in my life. I first thought my eyes were playing a trick on me, but they weren't. It was brilliant gleaming silver in colour and the shape of a round football.*
>
> *It moved at all angles – backwards and forwards, left to right; as we moved, so did it. For example – if you moved left, so did it; if you moved to the right, so did the object. We ran away as fast as we could. We didn't stop to look back, we were so frightened."* (**Source: Randall Jones Pugh**)

## 15th April 1977 – Three UFOs sighted over Staffordshire

Another bright silver object was sighted hovering over Alsager town centre, Staffordshire, at an estimated height of between 40-45,000 feet, at 6.50am, by Nigel Blagg( 13) and his ex-RAF Serviceman – John Blagg,

> *"It disappeared in a puff of cream coloured smoke, out of which emerged three smaller objects that shot off across the sky."*

At 7.30pm on the same date, *"a large orange/red coloured triangular-shaped object, with rounded edges"* was sighted over St. Paul's Cray, in Kent, by a housewife, who called her husband. At this point it shrank to the size of a star and disappeared, reappearing to their left, close to a block of flats, apparently near ground level – now covering about three or four storeys with white light, where it hovered for a few minutes.

> *"Through binoculars, the light was as bright as the sun and hurt the eyes to look at."*

(**Source: Wilfred Daniels/Larry Dale**)

## 17th April 1977 – Huge 'ball of light' with 'winged structure' seen at Lowestoft, Suffolk

At 8.30pm, Lowestoft resident – Mrs Norma Clarke, was settling down for the evening, when she noticed a 'bright light' in the sky that she took to be a flare. After a few minutes, she realised this could not be the case and pointed out the 'light' to her son and two of his friends. They stood watching, as the 'light' started to go

backwards, turned sideways, and began to move towards them, actually passing over the top of the house, looking like *"a huge 'ball of light' with two great big wing structures sticking out of the back. All around the 'light' you could see struts."* (**Source: Ivan W. Bunn, 'The Lantern' series, Lowestoft**)

## 19th April 1977 – UFO landing, Haven Fort Hotel, Little Haven, Pembrokeshire

At 2.30am, Rosa Granville – the owner of *Haven Fort Hotel*, Little Haven, overlooking St. Brides Bay (situated halfway between the villages of Broad Haven and Little Haven) was getting ready for bed, after a busy evening, when she heard a humming sound and thought she may have left the central heating on. She decided to check it out and made her way to the fire escape at the back of the property, close to the boiler room, but found this was not the case.

*Rosa Granville*

*"I looked outwards over the field, illuminated by a nearly full moon, and noticed an unusual blue coloured 'light', pulsating just above the ground. My first thoughts were... was it someone preparing to break in? I picked up a pair of binoculars and looked through them, when I was astonished to see an oval object (part of which was resting on the ground) with a slight dome on top, close to the gate at the rear of the field. Between the object and the gate were two tall 'figures' with pointed heads, I estimated to be six and-a-half to seven feet in height, dressed in what looked like boiler suits made up of a white plastic material, rather than silver. I watched, with disbelief, as the 'figures' appeared to be measuring the ground. At this point I became frightened, so I switched on the lights and awoke my husband. By the time we returned, there was nothing to be seen."*

### Photo of scene available

During conversation with Francine Granville about the incident, she confirmed an examination made of the field, the following morning, revealed a peculiar crescent-shaped patch of burnt grass – which was prominent for many years, as plants failed to grow inside it. Just as strange was the perplexing discovery of a burnt circle, about three feet in diameter, found on the inside of the blue slates of the roof, in the far uppermost corner of the north wing of the hotel – apparently caused by the application of tremendous heat. How and when this happened has never been determined, although this was only discovered by local builder, Mr Gibson, after the roof started leaking.

### Best not to alarm the general public!

Rosa wrote to her local Member of Parliament – Mr Nicholas Edwards, expressing concern about what she had

*Francine Granville*

*Rosa Granville (centre) with Hayden and Francine in 1980*

seen and the damage caused to her property. She received a visit from a Squadron Leader, based at RAF Brawdy, who interviewed her and then asked her not to say anything about the matter to anyone, suggesting, *'it was best not to alarm the general public'*. It appears this was, in fact, Flt. Lt. Cowan, who – in his report to MOD Chiefs – wrote:

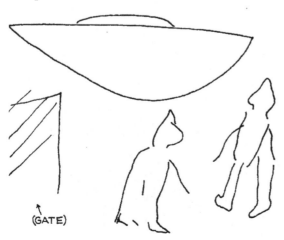

(GATE)

*"Mrs Granville told me that one night, in April of this year, she saw a round object, 'like the moon falling down', land in a field at the back of her property. Two very tall, faceless, 'humanoids' got out of this object (about the size of a mini bus) and appeared to 'take measurements, or gather things'."*

Flt. Lt. Cowan said he examined the landing site, but

*"could find no evidence of a landing",*

and could offer no further explanation, adding that,

*"should a UFO arrive at RAF Brawdy, we will charge normal landing fees and inform you immediately".*

*Burnt roof, Fort Haven*

*Dawn Holloway and Francine Granville*

We believe that humorous quips like these are borne from an underlying fear to accept the existence of someone, or something, whose presence was, and still is, being made known to us all these years later.

### Reply from Mr James Wellbeloved

In the fullness of time, Mr Edwards received a reply from Mr James Wellbeloved – the Parliamentary under-secretary of State for Defence for the Royal Air Force – containing the following:

*'Dear Nicholas,*

*My department have investigated the report about an unidentified flying object, which you referred to me on the 17th of May, on behalf of Mrs Rosa Granville, of the Haven Fort Hotel. I regret to say, however, that although a RAF Officer has visited Mrs Granville, we are unable to offer any further information. It is true that the Royal Observer Corps have a post in the adjoining field, but there is no evidence that their activities could have seemed unusual in any way and we have no record of any other unusual activity in the area. I am sorry I cannot be more helpful.*

*Yours sincerely,*

*Signed, James Wellbeloved'*

## Riddle of the silver-suited humanoids

BRITISH UFO watchers believe our defence chiefs have helped in an American cover-up about UFO activities.

So far, they say, the Defence Ministry have failed to explain an amazing sequence of sightings, some by RAF officers, in the Dyfed Triangle, around St Bride's Bay in West Wales.

Mrs Pauline Coombs claims she was chased by a UFO as she drove her children home to Ripplestone Farm. As she reached it the car wiring burned out.

That was in January, 1977. Before the year was out she, her husband Billy, and their children reported seeing UFOs at close quarters many times.

They also said they saw humanoids—7ft tall figures in glowing silver clothes and helmets.

### Weird

Across St Bride's Bay, Mrs Rosa Grenville, an honours graduate who runs the Haver Fort Hotel with her husband, Eddie, says she saw UFOs land twice.

Weird figures got out and prowled around.

At Broadhaven school, 14 children aged between 10 and 11 told their headmaster they had seen a UFO land 200 yards from where they were playing.

He separated them and told them to draw what they saw. Their drawings matched. So did their reports.

Headmaster Richard Llewhelin said: "Children of that age aren't capable of maintaining such an elaborate hoax."

It is an area bristling with defence establishments, some highly secret. The RAF con-

JAMES WELLBELOVED
" Nothing unusual "

firmed a flood of reports, and said the sightings did not match their operations.

But on June 15, 1977, the then Parliamentary Under-Secretary for Defence, Mr James Wellbeloved, told local Tory MP Nicholas Edwards— now Mrs Thatcher's Secretary for Wales—that, apart from Mrs Grenville, one report by the Ministry had no record of unusual activity in the area.

When pressed, a Ministry spokesman told me: " We accept that reports were made by sane, rational people. A hundred people do not imagine they saw something.

" But no physical evidence was found that anything had happened.

" We only investigate UFOs to find whether there is a threat to our defences.

" If there is no threat, that is the end of the matter. We do not investigate whether UFOs exist or what causes them."

Asked who decided there was no danger to this highly sensitive defence area, the spokesman added: " We are not prepared to discuss how we investigate."

### No record of any other unusual activity in the area!

There is something wrong here, if one takes into account the content of a letter written by MOD Minister – John Gilbert, M.P., who told officials in his department:

*"I am being inundated at the present time with representations about UFOs said to have been seen in Pembrokeshire."*

When asked whether investigations had been carried out, an MOD spokesman said,

*"We look into detailed reports of unexplained phenomena to see if they have a bearing on the National Defence. My department has carried out that type of investigation on the reports received from Wales, but there have been few in recent months.*

*No evidence has been revealed to suggest that the alleged sightings in Wales, or indeed those reported from other parts of Great Britain in the past, contain anything of significance from a defence point of view. All I can tell you on the basis of the department's past experience is that most reports of this nature can usually be referred to a common place object, which may have been observed from an unusual angle, or in somewhat unusual weather conditions."*

Unknown to the Minister, the RAF was asked to 'carry out a discreet investigation' in order to ascertain whether there was a readily discernible explanation – such as a practical joke, or whether there was prima facie evidence for a more serious enquiry.

### Courageous woman

Mrs Granville's courageous determination to discover for herself what lay behind these strange events, rather than meekly accepting the advice of those in authority, was to lead to unwarranted attention from 'something', or 'someone', who chose to pay a visit to the family residence, and is not so much speculation but fact.

### Francine Granville:

*"In 1977, I was studying abroad, in Spain, when my father wrote to me saying that my mother had spotted 'aliens' outside her window one night. The sighting left my mother very afraid and shaken up, but this was also no isolated event; other UFO landings had been spotted by other members of the community as well. Fourteen pupils from Broad Haven Primary School claimed to have seen the UFO landing in the area, with the head teacher seemingly backing their claim at the time. The children even produced drawings of what they saw. My mother was very afraid. She was too afraid to tell anyone, but she told my dad, and he wrote to me in Spain.*

*When I returned home, I heard that others had also sighted these aliens. A farmer had apparently seen 'strange figures' on his land and some school children said they had also seen bright lights and unusual 'figures'. Mum told me what happened.*

*It was early morning. Mum was woken by a buzzing noise and thought she'd left the gas boiler on. Once downstairs, she realised the noise was from outside. She looked out and saw, about 100 feet away, an oval object that she described as a 'spacecraft' with lights, slowly land and two 'figures' emerge from it wearing silver suits. She was terrified, because the 'figures', although reminiscent of men, had exceptionally long arms and legs. Their heads were covered by helmets. She called them 'creatures'. My hotel manager mum was not someone who subscribed to conspiracy theories; she was a no-nonsense sort of woman. This was very much out of character. She was not the type of person who would believe in aliens.*

*The object left a small crater in the ground, which had a ridge around the outside (still there today) – although now hidden beneath undergrowth."*

**Mysterious visitors to the hotel**

**Francine:**

> *"I was in the lounge at the hotel, with an unrestricted view of the driveway, when I noticed an incredible looking car outside the window. I thought … how on Earth had it arrived without me hearing it? It was silver in colour and enormous. I didn't know the make. It reminded me more like a boat than a car.*
>
> *I walked over to the reception area and found two men stood there. What I saw took me aback. They looked like identical twins, with high foreheads, piercing eyes, and black 'plastic' hair, brushed back. Their skin looked wax. One of them said, 'Where's your mother?' I told them I didn't know and they left. A couple of minutes later, my mother – Rosa, arrived home. I was shocked to find out she hadn't passed them on the way … perhaps it was as well. I later found out that a woman, living in the locality, had seen this 'weird car' approaching Haven Fort Hotel, moving over the fields. Unfortunately, she passed away some years ago."*

Was this a visit from the infamous 'Men in Black' – an organisation whose members have visited UFO witnesses over recent years, harassing and intimidating them? Are they humanoids, representing an alien species, or part of an orchestrated subterfuge, exercised by some sinister covert government department, knowing that any such report involving their presence to the media would not only divert attention from the original UFO incident but subject the witnesses to ridicule?

*The Western Telegraph* (12.5.1977) covered the sighting by Rosa Granville and included a photograph of the *'thing'* seen by her, which bore no resemblance to what she had observed.

We stood on the grassy knoll at the front of the hotel, trying to work out the connection between what had happened here and the multi-witness sighting at nearby Broad Haven Primary School, believing in the affinity between UFO sightings and ancient locations.

Our immediate suspicion that the *Haven Fort Hotel* had been a chapel was dashed when Francine explained it had been originally built as a Fort in the 14th Century. Was it an ancient Hill Fort? – Quite likely, in our opinion, bearing in mind its commanding position overlooking the nearby ocean. Was it right that a prehistoric

*The view over Broad Haven*

slab was found in the garden, some years ago, believed to be the capping stone of an ancient chieftain burial tomb, which lay partly buried in the turf facing the sea?

Over the years there has been considerable media interest in the events that took place around Wales, in 1977, involving all manner of strange sightings of what appear to be humanoids and saucer-shaped objects in the sky – matters that we have no particular thoughts on, despite speculation made by so many people who don't even know us but feel they should cast judgment based on often erroneous accounts of what we did or didn't see.

**Broad Haven County Primary School UFO Incident – 40th Anniversary**

While researching the background for this revised edition of *Haunted Skies*, in 2017 – taking into consideration that the information about this period of time (as previously published in *Haunted Skies*

Volume 6) was no longer available – [after our ex-publisher removed all six books from the Internet, following a dispute about royalties owing to us]- we learned that there was going to be a 40th Anniversary reunion, organised by the Swansea UFO Group. Accordingly, I (John) spoke to Emlyn Williams – who invited us to attend and speak about the books and our interest in the UFO subject.

We met up with Neil Spring, who spoke about the events that had taken place and wished him well. At that stage we had not read his book.

The following morning, accompanied by Amy Kerridge – a student from Cardiff University – we stopped off at the *Haven Fort Hotel*, in Little Haven, where we called in to see Francine Granville who's Mother Rosa of Spanish birth had ran the hotel along with her husband some years previously. When she eventually answered the door, she looked visibly upset.

We asked her what the problem was. She told us she felt quite aggrieved after having read a book, written by Neil Spring, about the mysterious events that had taken place around the Pembrokeshire area, in 1977, entitled: *The Watchers*.

### Satanic Rites

We obtained a copy of the book, which outlined some of the strange historic UFO events that had taken place in the Broad Haven area, around 1977, using pseudonyms for many of the people concerned, along with liberal doses of what appear to be fairly tales, folklore, and examination of MOD documents relating to reported fictional UFO events around the South Wales area, including Rosa's own sighting at the back of the hotel, when a mysterious figure was seen next to the 'craft'.

We were somewhat perturbed to see that Neil had written about a fictional hotel in Fort Haven, where the Spanish owner engaged in satanic activity (which included descriptions of dogs hanging, 'twitching' from the trees), referring the owner to this woman as 'Arecimo' – a Spanish name. While we do not suggest that Neil had intentionally inferred that 'Rosa' was involved in any such illegal practices, it is obvious that some people may feel – through word association alone – there is a connection to the hotel with the *Haven Fort Hotel*.

In short, we understood how Francine felt and sympathized with her – especially when, following the book being published, she had been the subject of verbal insinuations, calling into question her mother's character – this isn't right, and the least said about this the better. Francine said if she had known that Neil was appearing at the Broad Haven village hall, she would have taken him to task.

### Rosa and Hayden Granville

After the war, the family moved to Baghdad (Iraq), where Hayden Granville had business interests. Rosa had the opportunity to stay with friends in Jerusalem. She spent two years in Israel before moving to Haifa, where she met Hayden – a sergeant in the Palestine Police Force; after the War of Independence, the couple returned to Hayden's home, near Bridgend. He was a hairdresser, and Rosa opened her first fashion shop in 1953, followed by two other branches. She became a respected member of the business community in the town. After the devastating floods in Bridgend, in 1960, Rosa launched a fashion show to raise funds for floods victims, personally inviting the Lord and Lady Mayoress of Cardiff to open the show. In 1965, on a day out, Rosa and Hayden discovered the St. Brides Bay area – a part of Pembrokeshire they had not visited before. Shortly afterwards they purchased Glebe House, in Talbenny, and, in 1968, bought the property known as the ëHauensí, Little Haven, developing it into the *Haven Fort Hotel*, which opened in 1972. Rosa spent 40 years in the hotel business – a record in itself – notorious for her no-nonsense attitude, always telling it as it was. In 2005, Hayden passed away.

In 1993, Rosa was diagnosed with inoperable cancer of the larynx and given a 20% survival; she lived in remission for 19 years, but passed away (aged 83) on the 2nd February 2012. Rest in Peace, Rosa and Hayden.

### Francine, 2017:

> *"I have decided to put the property up for sale. My memories of this unique experience have left me feeling quite nostalgic. Yes, I will miss it here. I love the house and the position, and it's just that at my age it's only going to get harder. The older you get, the more you don't want to move. It is better that I do it now, as later on will be difficult. The last guests stayed here five years ago and it's a shame that the property isn't used for people to enjoy. It's a nice little investment for someone, and if they decide to use it as a hotel again, they will have a prize gem on their hands." Following a second visit to see Francine Granville at the Haven Fort Hotel, Little Haven, in February 2017, we stayed over at the Old Police House, in Spittal (just outside Haverfordwest). After a very comfortable night, we enjoyed toast and coffee and chatted to Swansea TV journalist, Gaynor Morgan – who seemed very interested in our work, after being shown a now defunct copy of Volume 6 of Haunted Skies, which catalogues the incidents that occurred around the South Wales area, in 1977.She suggested an interview with us but once again this never came to fruition. Gaynor is a very busy lady, has her own farm to run and another guesthouse! We thought we had a busy lifestyle!*

### Lloyd Davies and what he saw

This was followed by another scintillating conversation with Lloyd Davies, who is employed as an 'odd job man' at the establishment. Lloyd, who was then living in Haroldston, told us about an unusual incident that had happened to him at 10.30pm, one evening, in the 1970's , while a front seat passenger in a car being driven from Milford Haven to Broad Haven. He said:

> *"A bright orange 'light' appeared behind the car – then went out. I have no idea what it was; a*

*woman behind me in the car also saw the 'light'. It was a most unusual 'light', in the middle of which – even for that split second – I saw what looked like striations or a horizontal band of dark light – then it was gone, plunging the landscape into darkness."*

### Phil Hoyle

Another man who made a journey down to this beautiful part of the World to see for himself the location and more importantly speak to the witnesses to gain first hand knowledge rather than trusting other sources of information was our well respected Shropshire-based colleague the well respected Phil Hoyle who has been investigating reports of UFO sightings for many years now and is a credit to the UFO organisation.

Over the years Phil's expertise into the field of animal mutilation research along with David Clayton has often been the subject of media interest.

The two men are thorough and a pleasure to know.

In November 2017 I contacted Phil wishing to know more about his visits to the Pembroke area which took place in 1985.

### Phil:

*"Pembrokeshire is not only a beautiful national park but an unspoilt ancient land concealing secrets from the present and the past. Many stories over the years concerning encounters with strange lights, beings and paranormal experiences appear to culminate in the late 70's around St Brides Bay."*

### Interview with Francine Granville 11th April. 1985.

*"I interviewed Francine Granville who with her mother run the Haven Fort hotel situated between Broad Haven and Little Haven, the hotel is on small hill with beautiful view across the bay and opposite Stack Rocks which became a focal point of UFO sightings.*

*Francine related that in 1977 during the height of the UFO activity around the St Brides Bay area two men and a woman stayed at Haven Fort Hotel and the booking was arranged by RAF Brawdy.*

*One night they all returned from their nightly outing which became a routine during the weeklong stay. On this particular night the woman entered the hotel lobby crying and was virtually hysterical.*

*They all were wearing overalls and one was carrying a brown paper bag, Francine who was working near the hotel bar overheard the woman say, "They had just nearly blown up the world". The woman then proceeded to the public phone at the end of the hall to make a very long phone call apparently to the United States of America, in the morning the three mystery people left Haven Fort Hotel and were not seen again".*

### Oceanographic Research Facility

### Phil:

*"It is interesting that an Oceanographic Research Facility was based at RAF Brawdy and operated by the U.S Navy, this facility was still operational during 1985 while I was conducting investigations in the area. At night St Brides Bay looked like a giant aircraft runway with a corridor of lights running from just below RAF Brawdy out to sea, it was a spectacular sight and was clearly marked*

*as a restricted area on the maritime navigation maps. It is also interesting to note that it's the U.S Navy not the U.S Air Force who are conducting the really serious research in to UFO's on a global scale. The Oceanographic Research Facility at Brawdy was positioned there to apparently monitor the Cold War activities of Soviet submarines, but could it also serve as monitoring USO and UFO activity around the St Brides area as evidence for some kind of ET base?"*

### Stack Rocks – Underground cavern reports of abductions

**Phil:**

*"I have investigated a number of cases where witnesses have encountered UFO's or beings along the coastal path from St Brides Haven to Little Haven opposite to Stack Rocks, which was a 'hot spot' for the UFO sightings in the late 70's. Most of these cases have had to remain confidential by request of the witnesses but the pattern and content are very similar."*

*Witnesses who have been walking along the coastal path, mostly during the day, have reported sighting a UFO or craft and then suddenly finding their perception of time and reality changing. They have then found themselves in underground caverns with glass windows showing the sea on the other side. Small grey 'beings' and sometimes what are often referred to as the blond Nordic humanoids are encountered other instances dark bottle green or black skinned EBE beings are seen".*

### Frightening experiences

*"In some cases I have investigated at first sight the witnesses mistake these beings for seals in the sea as they look similar from a distance and then only to realise with shock and horror they are something quite different. Then the witnesses are returned sometimes many hours later to a different point on the coastal path confused and disorientated and later become aware of hours of missing time.*

*While investigating these cases I interviewed a group of divers from Cardiff in 1985 at Martin' Haven, they informed me that some of their friends had conducted dives off Stack Rocks and had discovered an underwater door and the water around Stack Rocks was abnormally warm".*

### Mike and his story

*"In 2004 I interviewed Mike a retired potato merchant who spent a lot of his time during the potato season buying large quantities of potatoes in Pembrokeshire for sale and distribution all over the country.*

*Mike used to drink at a very secluded hotel in the area called the* Druidstone Hotel, *which is just above Broad Haven. One night when he was having a quiet drink in the bar of the hotel an elderly man started up a conversation about the strange things that were happening around the coastline in St. Bride's Bay. The man said that people see strange things around here coming out of the caves by the sea. Mike was very intrigued by this and asked the old man what do you seen then. The man replied that many people see disks coming out of the caves at night, the man even described the many shapes of these disks. One night the old man was sitting looking over the bay and saw a disk come in very quickly and dive into the sea, it was travelling so quickly he thought it was going explode when it hit the sea as it was moving so fast. The year of this UFO activity was 1977 the same year as the Ripperstone Farm, contacts near St. Bride's Haven which centred on Mrs Coombes and her family."*

### UFO sightings and encounters still being reported!

Phil Hoyle points out that while the intensity of UFO activity subsided dramatically in the 1980's it did not stop completely, nor has it done to this day with sightings and encounters are still being reported. If as the evidence suggest there was a underwater base at ST Brides Bay it may now be dormant but not completely unused. He has visited Pembrokeshire over 30 times since 1985 sometimes for holidays others to continue his investigations in to encounters cases.

### Spring 2000

In the spring of 2000 Phil was staying with his wife at *Timber Hill Lodges* that overlook Broad Haven. He had been researching the early contact cases of Daniel Fry and Truman Bethurum, after having located the brother of a well-known but now deceased author from Shrewsbury who investigated UFO sightings in the 40's and 50's and have gained access to his research papers.

*"I had been reading with great interest the contact details of Daniel Fry's experiences on the Saturday and Sunday and had felt a sense of pending expectancy, I felt a presence, an understanding as if I was being led in a particular direction. On Sunday night after tea I was reading more of the Daniel Fry contacts when at 28 minutes past 7pm I had the sudden urge to go outside and stand on the log cabin balcony. The sky was crystal clear and the moon was full, I had my 10 x 50 binoculars with me so I could look at the stars and the moon.*

*It was very cold and I could see the star constellation Orion to the west, I just happened to look up suddenly and I could see a bright light about the same size and luminosity as Sirius moving slowly from west to east at about 45 degrees above the horizon."*

### Through Binoculars –bright white sphere seen

*"I looked at the object through my binoculars and I could see a bright white sphere, then suddenly a small red and white ball object shot out of the bottom left hand side of the white sphere. The sphere carried on slowly towards Haverfordwest and disappeared below the horizon, but the red and white small ball object seemed to stay in the same place as it was ejected from.*

*The small object darted horizontally over an approximate distance of 500 ft, it moved in a zig zag erratic manner from left to right. I called my wife out to also observe it but it just blinked out, the whole sighting lasted less than 2 minutes. The area has a busy commercial airline flight corridor and you could see passenger aircraft before and after the sighting, these aircraft were clearly distinguishable and you could easily see their vapour trails and navigation lights."*

## 22nd April 1977 – Giant 'figure' seen at Ripperston Farm, South Wales

Pauline and Billie Coombes from Lower Ripperston Farm, near Little Haven, were watching a late night film, when Pauline glimpsed what she took to be 'a giant figure' out of the corner of her eye …

*" . . . but I ignored it, thinking it was my imagination – until Billie jumped to his feet, shouting and pointing towards the window, through which he saw a silver-grey 'figure' with a black face (or something like that, covering the face) stood outside the window – far too broad to have been a human being".*

Pauline telephoned Mr Randall Jones Pugh, from Roch – a BUFORA Investigator – and told him what had happened. He advised her to ring the police – which she did.

A short time later, two officers arrived. One of them was PC John Lynch – to whom we spoke about the incident, many years later.

*"They reported having seen this silver suited man, with a blacked out face, peering in through the window. We had a look around, but couldn't find anything. The couple were really terrified."*

The couple confirmed that an inspection of the wall and surrounding window revealed scorch marks.

 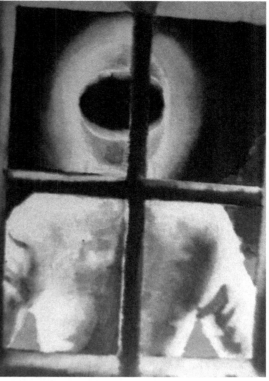

*Pauline Coombes with her two daughters at the window where they saw the visiter*

Subsequent attempts made to repaint over the marks were not successful, and later brought the matter to the attention of Clive Harold – who wrote their story in his book, *The Uninvited*. Having examined the windows where this took place, during a visit by us to the farm, we felt it unlikely a person could have stood outside and looked in through the windows, because the only way to have done this would have been to stand on something to reach the desired height of the windows to look in.

We certainly dismissed as nonsense the suggestion made, by some people, that the offender had been a hoaxer, dressed in a fireman's suit, and felt documentaries televised in 2009, depicting the same, were misleading. In 2017, there was no trace of any window having ever been there – presumably, this was done to deter people from visiting the location.

In early May 1977, pupils and children arriving at Broad Haven County Primary School (the scene of a remarkable encounter in February of that year) discovered a long rocket, lying in the school playground – later identified as a fuel pod, or tank from an aircraft, (as shown in many contemporary newspaper photographs) – a matter which was brought to the attention of the police, who said they had no objection to it remaining there as long as it was safe

It seems very suspicious, to say the least, why anyone would covertly deposit a substantial object of this size onto the school playground. Was it done to divert attention away from the incident that had taken place there on the 4th February 1977, and create the impression that the UFO story was nothing but the product of children's vivid imaginations? On whose instructions was the tank deposited at the school, and who eventually took it away?

**14** DAILY STAR, Monday, July 30, 1979

# The night a space creature called at the farm

## By PAT CODD

IT LOOKED as if it would be a normal evening as Pauline and Billy Coombs watched television in their isolated farmhouse.

Their five children were sleeping upstairs. The dog dozed in front of the fire.

It was 34-year-old Pauline who noticed a bright light, shimmering like a chandelier, at the window.

First it fascinated her. Then she recalled the strange, silver ball of light which had seemed to follow her car along the country lanes some weeks earlier.

Billy, who was sitting with his back to the window, had been amused by his wife's story.

"He had pulled my leg about it so much that I didn't like to say anything to him," says Pauline.

The light at the window came and went during the next two hours. Billy sat unaware as Pauline watched in horror.

Casually, Billy turned round at last. Pauline says:

### Towering figure

"He jumped to his feet, with his arms across his face as if to ward something off, and shouted: "What the hell is that?"

"He pulled me to my feet, clung to me, and then I saw what had frightened him—a towering figure, at least eight feet tall, glowing in a silver suit.

"It was so big we couldn't even see the top of its head as it looked in. It was wearing a helmet with some sort of black, shiny visor.

"A pipe went from the mouth to the back of its head. I was petrified. We were rooted to the spot with terror.

And that night in April 1977 was only the beginning of what they believe was their contact with creatures from space.

The experience of the down-to-earth farming family was so out of this world that their story has been told in a book, published last week.

All sorts of strange things began to happen around their home, Ripperstone Farm.

The children said that silver-suited creatures emerged from saucer-shaped machines which left charred circles in the fields.

They also found huge footprints nearby.

One day, Pauline and two of her daughters saw a small plate-like object fly into rocks on the coast.

### Most bizarre

Pauline says: "We went down to the cliff edge for a closer look and saw two figures in silver suits. One seemed to be walking up and down stairs inside the rocks while the other was walking almost on the water. Then they disappeared inside the rocks."

But the most bizarre incidents involved the Coombs' cattle. "That was a queer thing, and it still takes some believing," says Billy.

Quite simply, Billy's herd kept disappearing!

Billy says: "One day it happened five or six times. The herd kept disappearing, although I padlocked them in, and turning up on someone else's farm.

"Every time I brought them back to my farm they would vanish again. I thought I was going round the bend."

For a year the family's life was misery. Five TVs and eight cars were burned out. Two of the children

"It radiated a sort of luminous light and when it touched the window, the pane started to rattle like all hell had broken loose—yet there was no wind.

"Slowly, I got my wits together and raced upstairs to see if the children were all right while Billy kept watch.

"Billy put the dog out, but he went mad with fear. Eventually, six months later, he had to be destroyed."

### Ordeal ended

Pauline rang some neighbours and the police. "All the time the thing was looking in.

"I don't think it had any ill feeling towards us. If it meant to harm us it had plenty of time."

Fifteen minutes later the ordeal ended for Pauline and Billy.

As the police car's lights swept the lane of the Coombs' farm—near St Brides Bay, Haverfordwest, South Wales—the strange figure disappeared.

But there were two reminders of their close encounter. The TV set was burned out and a rose bush near the window was scorched.

### Strange sightings

Then the mysterious incidents stopped as suddenly as they started.

By that time, more than 100 reports of strange sightings had been made by other people in the area.

And a local police inspector admitted: "After what I've seen around here nothing would surprise me now."

*So what is the answer?*

Certainly the Coombs' farm lies in a sensitive military area with a nearby rocket range.

But Squadron-Leader Tim Webb, from the Brawdy air base, believes his son and most of his school have seen a UFO.

He said: "I've yet to see a UFO, but I think there has been something supernatural or paranormal going on here."

The Coombs are now leaving the farm.

But Billy denies that the aliens have driven them away.

*The Uninvited, by Clive Harold. Published by Star Paperbacks (W H Allen), 95p.*

SKY-WATCHERS : Billy, Pauline and three of their children

## OF DIVORCE BY CHARLOTTE FOR

# Advice wit

## 30th April 1977 – Oval-shaped UFO sighted over Essex

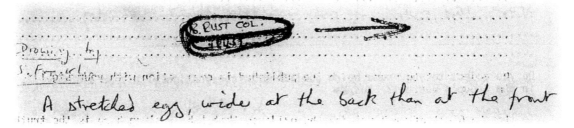

Mr Steve Franklin (then aged 19) of Queen's Drive, Waltham Cross, Essex, was out in his back garden, smoking, just after 9.30pm, when he heard:

> "...*a high-pitched whining noise – like a worn wheel bearing, or noisy back axle. I thought, at first, it might have been coming from the nearby main A12 road. I looked up and saw a red egg or oval object in the sky, showing a dark patch in the middle of its side.It came overhead and suddenly accelerated out of sight, in a few seconds. I told my father to phone Jodrell Bank, but couldn't find the number.*" (**Source: Letter to Essex UFO study Group**)

# CHAPTER 17 – MAY 1977

## 1st May 1977 – UFO over York Hill, Loughton Essex

Mrs Griffiths was driving home, at 2.30am, up York Hill – a steep, narrow incline, a quarter-of-a-mile from her house in Baldwin's Hill, Loughton, in Essex. She stopped the car to adjust a tape cassette she was playing, when she noticed a very bright white and orange rounded 'light', motionless in the sky, through her offside window. Frightened, she just sat there – deciding not to get out and have a closer look, even though she estimated the object to be a long way off.

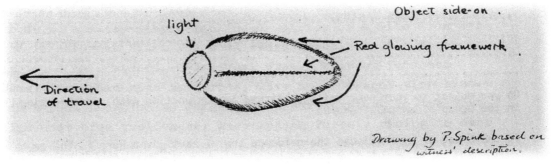

About five or ten minutes later it then moved, accelerating away to her left, allowing her to see "*a glowing red framework, attached to the light*". It then increased its speed and was then lost from sight, heading towards the Epping area. (**Source: BUFORA**)

## 3rd May 1977 – Police officers sight landed UFO, Essex

Another UFO incident which caught our attention took place following a 999 call made to the police, by a Mr Samuels, at 3.55am, who told of having seen something strange hovering over the lake in Hainault Recreation Ground, at Chigwell, in Essex – as a result of which Police Constable C 369J Bill Hefferman, from Barkingside, along with another Officer, attended.

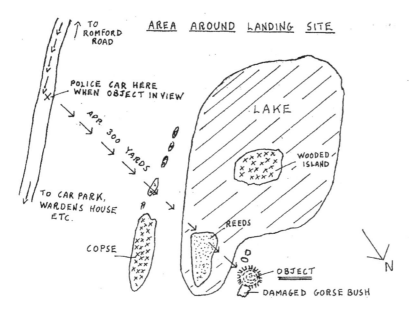

After interviewing Mr Samuels about what had been seen, the officers unlocked the gate that led into the grounds of the park, at 4.12am, and proceeded along the small road, when they noticed

> "... a large, bright red light near ground level, over the eastern part of the lake, about 300 yards away".

They then stopped the police car and made their way on foot, when they were astonished to come across an object they later described as:

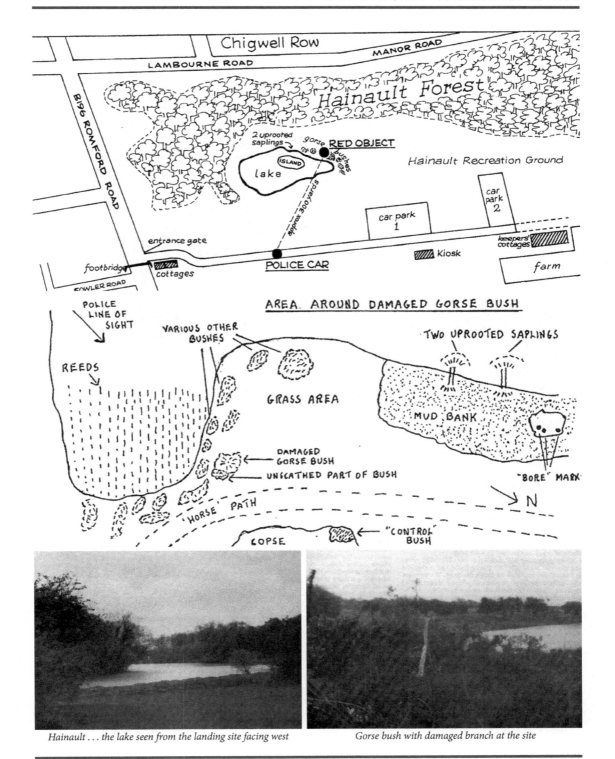

Chigwell Row

MANOR ROAD

LAMBOURNE ROAD

B196 ROMFORD ROAD

Hainault Forest

2 uprooted saplings    gorse bushes    RED OBJECT

ISLAND

lake

approx 300 yards

Hainault Recreation Ground

car park 1

car park 2

entrance gate

footbridge

cottages

FOWLER ROAD

POLICE CAR

Kiosk

keepers' cottages

farm

## AREA AROUND DAMAGED GORSE BUSH

POLICE LINE OF SIGHT

REEDS

VARIOUS OTHER BUSHES

GRASS AREA

TWO UPROOTED SAPLINGS

MUD BANK

DAMAGED GORSE BUSH

UNSCATHED PART OF BUSH

"BORE" MARK

HORSE PATH

N

COPSE

"CONTROL" BUSH

*Hainault . . . the lake seen from the landing site facing west*

*Gorse bush with damaged branch at the site*

*"...red in colour; its shape was like that of a bell tent – the size of a thumbnail, at arm's length. It continuously pulsated from dull to bright red, hovering silently off the ground. Suddenly, it seemed to dissolve on the spot."*

*Barry King examines the damaged branch*

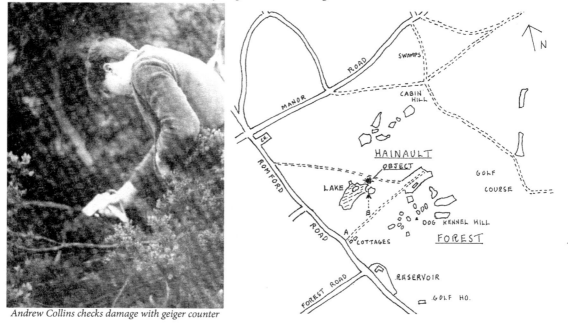

*Andrew Collins checks damage with geiger counter*

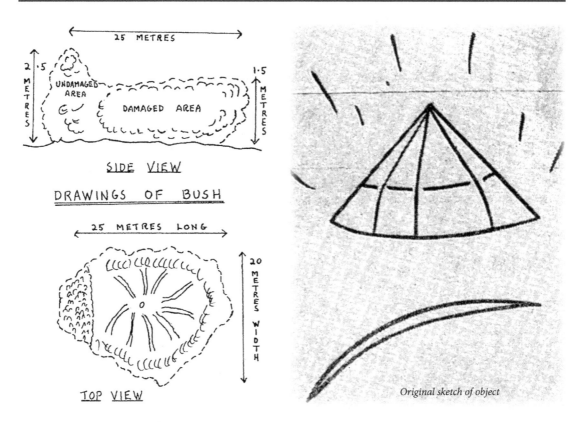

← 25 METRES →

2·5 METRES / 1·5 METRES

UNDAMAGED AREA

DAMAGED AREA

SIDE VIEW

DRAWINGS OF BUSH

← 25 METRES LONG →

20 METRES WIDTH

TOP VIEW

*Original sketch of object*

With some understandable reluctance, the officers split up and made a search of the area. Almost immedi-ately, Bill Hefferman's colleague noticed a large, white coloured, inverted crescent-shaped object directly above him, which 'dissolved' from sight, followed by a smell of burning. They made their way back to the car and radioed in a report of what had happened.

After dropping off his colleague, PC Hefferman went back to Barkingside Police Station, and later contacted the Essex UFO hotline number – as a result of which he was later interviewed about the matter by Barry King, the following morning.

*Barry King*

### 3rd May 1977 – Motorist sights 'strange light'

Frederick George Bateman (then 20) of Plaistow, London, was travelling along the Barking Road, (Greengate to *The Abbey Arms* Public House) at 10.35pm, accompanied by Chris Fisher. They saw a large 'light', motionless in the sky – far too big to be any aircraft or helicopter, in their opinion, although they considered the possibility of navigation lights.

About two minutes later, they reached *The Abbey Arms* Public House, but could not see it anymore. The reason why they brought it to the attention of the Essex UFO Study Group was after reading a report in the *Newham Recorder* – 'UFOs over Newham'.

Of course there may be a simple explanation, but one should take into account the previous report.

On the 4th May, Barry drove over to Hainault to examine the scene, and found recent damage to a large bush at the location given by the officer.

**Barry:**

> *"It was flattened in the centre and damaged in several places; one part in particular was broken cleanly almost in half, at a height of about five feet. I took 35-40 photos of the scene. I then drove home and telephoned Andy Collins, asking him to bring his equipment over to the site to make a further examination of the area."*

## 8th May 1977 – 'Strange figure' reported in the Hainault area

At 7pm on 8th May 1977, Barry's brother – Steven – was driving home from Stapleford airfield, near Abridge, along the B196 road, (which ran alongside Hainault Forest) when he noticed a blue and white Austin A60 Cambridge car emerging from the entrance leading into the park, and move up behind him. The driver then began to flash his headlights behind him.

Steven stopped near the foot of Hog Hill and two men got out of the car and walked up to him, explaining they had seen the UFO sticker on his car windscreen, and wanted to tell him about a strange experience. They told him they had parked their car over the other side of the forest, near the public house, about half-a-mile from the lake, near the area known as 'the Swamps', close to Taylor's plain and Cabin Hill, and were exercising their dog, when:

> *"Suddenly, we heard a rustling close to us and saw this large 'figure' loom into sight and disappear into the bushes and shrubs.*
>
> *It was dark blue in colour, brighter than the surroundings, resembling a large person in outline with no discernible arms or legs.*
>
> *It was about eight feet in height, four feet wide, and was some 25 feet away when we saw it."*

Steven contacted his brother – Barry, who made arrangements to meet the two men, who never showed up, which left their version of the events to be only taken at face value, although Barry significantly points out that the men could not have known of the earlier incident involving the police.

**(Sources: Barry M. King/Steven King/Andrew Collins, UFOIN report published by *Flying Saucer Review*, Volume l, 23, Number 2, 1977/*The Recorder* (Ilford) 8.10.1977/*BUFORA Journal*, Volume 6, Number 3, September/October 1977)**

## 11th May 1977 – UFO, Leicestershire

At 8.45pm, a bright 'ball of light' was seen moving across the sky over Spencer Avenue, Thurmaston, in Leicestershire. Half-a-mile away, schoolboy – Andrew Draycott, was playing cricket in the field at the back of his house, in Colby Drive, with his friend – Lance 'Compo' Crouch, at 8.45pm, when they noticed a light aircraft passing overhead, surrounded by a peculiar glow, but decided to continue the game.

> *"As 'Compo' bowled the cricket ball at me, it bounced and we both saw sparks flying from it. Frightened, we dropped the cricket gear and 'legged it' back home. When we arrived there, my parents and grandparents were outside; they told us they had seen this peculiar 'ball of light' fly over the house. I later discovered a man,*

Dear Mr Hanson

Sorry I've been late in replying, yes I was one of the people who witnessed the sighting of a UFO that day. My friends and I were playing cricket in the field at the back of our home in Colby Dr Thurmaston when we noticed a light aircraft flying above us, a light then surrounded the plane but we carried on playing cricket, my friend bowled a ball (Compo) to me and when it bounced up to me it had sparks around it, I don't know whether this was to do with the UFO, I don't know, but it scared us enough to run home leaving the cricket kit behind. When we walked into our garden my parents and grandparents were out on the patio they to had seen the light fly over the house and apparently someone had witnessed it hovering over a nearby train line.

I have saw you a magazine that we were in at the time, the drawing on the front of the mag was what we drew and being kids I think we exaggerated a bit by putting lights and a devil on the saucer as kids do, but it was definitely a UFO or a ball of light reported from the mag at the time rang local airports asking if any pilots had witnessed anything they said no.

If you need anymore information ring

with Thanks
A. Draycott

*living locally, had also seen it hovering over the railway line. I don't know what it was when the investigators came to see us. We did embellish it a bit, saying it was a 'flying saucer', but we were only kids and got excited. It was just a weird 'ball of light'."*

**(Source: Personal interview/BUFORA)**

## 15th May 1977 – Silver suited 'figure' seen at Ripperston Farm South Wales

*Left: Ripperston Farm and (right) Stack Rocks seen from the farm*

*A silver suited 'figure' with a 'square black face'* was seen walking across the fields, by Pauline Coombes' twin daughters, who told their mother:

> *"A 'plate' came out of the sky and hovered in front of us. A door then opened and what looked like stairs came out, followed by a red box – which dropped down in the field. The 'plate' then flew off over nearby cliffs and entered the sea, between Stack Rocks and the coast."*

Despite a thorough search of the field, nothing was ever found.

**(Sources: Phil Hoyle/Personal interview with Pauline Coombes/Tony Pace, BUFORA)**

## 15th May 1977 – Crop Circles discovered at Bristol, after UFO sighting

At midnight on this date, Sharon Robbins, from Bristol, was driving home when she noticed a very 'bright light' in the sky – *"like a spotlight"* shining down onto a neighbouring bungalow. As she continued on her journey, she saw that the 'light' was coming from the brow of a hill and moving slowly across the sky. She said:

> *"It was like a large 'ball of bright fire', deep orange in colour, showing a smaller 'light' at its tail. This orange light only lasted for a few seconds and then vanished. The larger 'ball of bright' light hovered over the ground and then rose and came back down again. I thought it was going to land."*

This large 'bright light' – about the size of the moon in visual image – floated across the width of the field and vanished when it reached the other side; the sighting had taken about five minutes.

On the 16th May 1977, Sharon returned to the locality (which frustratingly wasn't identified) and discovered two flattened circles in the grass, one 8 feet in diameter – larger than the other. Interestingly, she described seeing a number of stones around the outskirts of the circles that were all scratched in the same direction. **(Source: *Fountain Journal*, Number 11, 1977)**

## 17th May 1977 – UFO crash-lands, West Yorkshire

Mrs June Cadman (then aged 31) was returning home at Emley, West Yorkshire, along the M1, approaching junction 39, where she would turn off for the village of Crigglestone and then turn along the A636 for the final few miles drive home.

When about two miles from the junction, she noticed what she first thought was a bright star, behind her in the north-west direction, but then realised it was following the car.

A few minutes later, a 'white ball' passed directly overhead – its glow now blinding in its intensity.

*"I thought it was going to crash into the car. It then changed shape, looking like an oblong with a tapered top portion. It changed shape constantly as the brilliance increased, lighting up the roadway in front of me."*

The object struck the grass, yards from her. She heard it thud as it bounced, once, and then totally disintegrated. This was the only time she had heard any sound. The glow then disappeared. Very frightened she stopped the car and turned the engine off, her eyes blinded by the light. She felt a strange, mild, tingling sensation – not unlike a gentle burning – noticeable on her lips, but also on her face and arms. Within seconds she had recovered.

Glancing upwards at the source of this terrifying 'missile', she saw (through slowly improving eyesight):

*"...a dark rectangular shape, with a mass of red and yellow lights on it – at least half-a-dozen. I was positive it wasn't an aircraft – then in a flash it was gone, like a 'rocket', straight upwards into the night sky.*

Trevor Whitaker, from the Halifax Branch of BUFORA, carried out an investigation for UFOIN, as a result of which Jenny Randles published an excellent, well-written up account in *Flying Saucer Review*, Volume 25, Number 1, January/February, 1979.

The *Huddersfield Examiner* carried the story on the 19th May 1977, as a result of which Mr Jack Roberts from that town told of seeing a 'bright white light' from his bedroom, for a few seconds – presumably on the same evening.

## 17th May 1977 – UFOs sighted over East Lothian, Scotland

On what was a clear and sunny day, with very little cloud cover, a spate of UFO sightings occurred around the Firth of Forth area of East Lothian, in Scotland. Thanks to David Sydserff – a local resident of Tranent, East Lothian, and member of the UFOIN group, who was assisted by Dr. A.J. Rostron – science teacher at the local school, we are able to examine for ourselves their investigation into a total of 27 separate sightings of unidentified flying objects that were seen just before 9.20pm, and onwards.

### Object shaped like a Sombrero sighted

At 9.05pm, Tranent schoolboy – Stewart McKenzie (then aged13) was watching boys playing football behind his home, when he noticed what looked like:

*"...an object moving across the sky, about ten miles away, towards the Firth of Forth, some 2,000 feet off the ground, smaller than a civil aircraft and shaped like a Sombrero hat, discoid with a dome on top. It had a belt of white 'kitchen' lights on the base and a flashing light on top."*

### Saucer-shaped object sighted

At about the same time, Frankie Kraviec (then aged13) was in his garden at Tranent, looking southwards, when he saw an object hovering in the sky over West Windygoul Farm.

*"It was white, saucer-shaped with a dome on top, but reflecting the setting sun. I watched it for two minutes and then got fed-up looking."*

### Object with flashing red light on top sighted

In another part of the town, Frank McLoughlan (also then aged 14) sighted an object, moving at about 20 mile per hour through the sky, heading towards the coast in a south to north direction.

*"It was about half the size of the sun, silvery coloured with a round, flat, base and a flashing red light on the top. It hovered over the top of Tranent for about fifteen seconds."*

### Two UFOs sighted

Just before 9.20pm, Mrs J.E. Foley, from Joppa, sighted two objects in the north-west direction, over Granton.

Stage 1: Mrs. Folley, Joppa

> *"They were hovering at about a thousand feet and were roughly round in shape, although one was slightly larger than the other. Both were pink in colour and apparently joined by a horizontal cable. By the time I had gone to fetch a camera, one had disappeared from view; the other then faded away."*

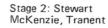

Stage 2: Stewart McKenzie, Tranent

Stage 3: Frankie Kraviec, Tranent

### UFO trailing smoke sighted

Just after 9.20pm, Stuart Logan (then aged 13), from Macmerry, was standing by some stall at a travelling fayre, accompanied by five other people (including members of the showground), when a dull yellow, flattish, oval object – estimated to be about the size of a lorry, with white smoke or vapour trailing from its rear – was seen stationary in the west-north-west direction of the sky. It was then seen to move slowly northwards and descend out of view over the County of Fife, before being lost from sight at 9.50pm.

Stage 4: Frank McLoughlan, Tranent

Stage 5: Stuart Logan, MacMerry

Stage 6: Sandy Cunningham, Pencaitland

Stage 7: William Ritchie, Ormston

### 'Silver cigar' sighted

At 9.40pm, Mr and Mrs McCulloch, of Dirleton, sighted an object, resembling a *'silver cigar'* in the sky, over the Firth of Forth area.

> *"We saw it move rapidly away, towards Dunfermline, where it pulsated six times before heading northwards. By now it was glowing bright red, but we lost sight of it at 10.30pm."*

### UFO over the colliery

Adam Young (then aged 15) and a keen bird watcher from Ormiston, looked out of his house, as dusk fell at 9.40pm, after hearing what he thought was a partridge in the fields nearby. He looked out and saw, in the west direction:

> *"...a small, thin, white/silver oval object; there was a small red light on its underside and the whole thing sparkled. It was over a disused coal tip. It then moved northwards, at about the height of an electricity pylon, approximately half-a-mile away. I called my parents and we watched it for about ten minutes."*

### Saucer-shaped object sighted

At 9.45pm, a 'reddish' saucer-shaped object was sighted moving through the sky, heading towards the Ochil Hills, by Mrs A. Hutton. This was followed by a report of a golden-yellow, flattened, oval object, seen at 10pm, by Tranent resident – John Quinn (then aged 17).

### 'Gramophone disc' shaped object sighted

Between 9.30pm and 10pm, an object resembling a 'gramophone disc' was sighted moving slowly across the sky, from Macmerry towards Tranent, by John Anderson (then aged 13).

> *"It followed several tight spirals over Tranent and then moved away to the south-west; it was seen for fifteen minutes."*

Another witness was Colin Scott (then aged 12) and Heather Smith (then aged14), who appear to have seen the same object at the same time, *"which had a glowing small dome, and performed three or four tight spirals over the town"*, as witnessed by John Anderson previously.

### UFO over Pencaitland

At 10pm, staff members – Thomas Kemperer and Jane Player, from Dr. Barnados, Tyneholm House, and seven others, including Sandy Cunningham (then aged 13) – sighted an oval object:

> "...yellow-white in colour surrounded by an aura of some kind, moving towards the south-east direction. At 10.10pm it stopped for a few seconds, before disappearing from view behind trees."

### Domed UFO sighted

At 10pm, south-west of Ormiston, William Ritchie (then aged 16), and his companions, sighted a stationary object close to the summit, described as 30-40 feet long, oval in shape with a dome on top. Ten seconds later it was seen to fly away northwards, towards Elphinstone.

Enquiries carried out by the RAF, revealed that according to them, no aircraft were logged as flying in that locality at the time given. Mr Allan Pickup, of the Royal Observatory, Edinburgh, confirmed they had received a number of calls, but had disregarded them, because he thought it was *"barium vapour, released from rockets, to study airflow and the Earth's magnetic field in the upper atmosphere"*. Clearly, they were not that! In addition to this, the Weapons Research Establishment, at Aldermaston, and the rocket range at Benbecula, in the Outer Hebrides, was contacted. Likewise, they denied that they were responsible.

(**Source:** As above/*Scottish Daily Record*, 31.5.1977/*East Lothian Courier*, 20.5.1977/*Flying Saucer Review*, **Volume 24, Number 3, November 1978; 'Multi-witness sightings over the Firth of Forth', David Sydserff**)

## 18th May 1977 – UFO over Surrey

At 12.30am on the 18th May 1977, Mr Stuart Gurney and his wife were travelling southwards in their car, along the A29 Dorking to Bognor road, on a dull, overcast, misty night. Stuart was the first to sight a bright 'point of light' ahead of them in the darkness and brought it to his wife's attention, wondering if it was the lights of an approaching aircraft. However, the 'lights' seemed to be moving very slowly. At this point, the road began to drop towards a junction – their view of the object being lost, due to trees at the side of the road. A few hundred yards later the trees thinned out, enabling them to see that the object was now on their right, which consisted of a group of lights.

> "It reminded me of the lights in a marshalling yard – those placed on high towers, sending down beams of light onto the ground below. I was surprised and mystified but thought, logically, they must be coming from a low flying aircraft, because they were so low and I could hear no sound."

Ian stopped the car and sat there, looking through the windscreen, watching the strange moving 'lights'. He lowered the window and heard a faint 'swishing noise' coming from the object – now heading away towards the north-east, at an estimated height of 500 feet above the road. He said:

> "There were three main beams and two smaller lights in the centre. We were unable to determine any shape". (**Source:** *UFOs: Guardians of the Planet Earth*, **Omar Fowler**)

### Tall 'being' seen in Scotland

Later that day, two girls were to find themselves in a frightening situation at New Elgin, Morayshire, when 'a metallic, cylindrical object, surmounted by a small dome with a red light on top, about 300 feet long, with a red band around its lower section, was seen hovering two feet off the ground. The girls told of hearing a humming noise, then the discovery of the UFO, next to which stood:

> "...a tall, thin man, partially hidden by bushes, at least six feet tall, with short arms and dressed in a silver suit".

To their horror, the 'man' began to move towards them. Frightened, the girls ran away. When they summoned the courage to glance back, they saw a UFO taking off in three jerky steps, before accelerating out of view. Was there any connection with the events that had taken place over the Firth of Forth, the previous day? (**Source:** **Jenny Randles,** *Flying Saucer Review*, **Volume 23**)

## 18th May 1977 – The Sun – 'Spacemen mystery of The Terror Triangle')

THE SUN, Wednesday, May 18, 1977   9

### SUN EXCLUSIVE ON THE SIGHTINGS THAT PUZZLE THE EXPERTS

- **EITHER** you believe in them, or you don't. Thousands have seen them and have been labelled as cranks.

But now intelligent, famous and sensible people have entered the great UFO (Unidentified Flying Object) controversy.

- **President** Jimmy Carter says that he saw a flying saucer.

- **But down** in sleepy West Wales, there have been a record number of sightings in the last three months.

Thirty mysterious objects—ranging from silver spacemen and their spaceships to flashing lights—have been seen in what is now being called The Broad Haven Triangle.

- **They** have all been seen in an area of intense defence activity. There are missile ranges, an ocean research station and a huge RAF base.

Can these phenomena be put down to defence operations? To imagination or did the strange visitations really occur?

### By FRANKLYN WOOD

IT WAS almost one o'clock on a Saturday morning when a seven-foot giant wearing a silver suit blocked the window of Billy and Pauline Coombs' lonely farm cottage.

A luminous glow hung around the figure. The head on the massive shoulders had no discernible features.

A box-shaped helmet framed a dark square area like a blank watch-face.

Pauline, 32, who saw it first, said nothing to Billy, who was sitting with his back to the window. She was too frightened.

A few days earlier, she and two of her five children had been terrified when a glowing orb followed their car along the track leading to their home — Ripperton Farm, in Dyfed, South-West Wales.

Billy, 38, had discussed the incident with Pauline. Now, sitting in their front room, he glanced over his shoulder — and yelled: "Good God! What the hell is that?"

#### Fright

Pauline says: "We stood trembling, sweating and crying with fright." phoned the police and Mr Hewison, our boss.

"Then we rushed upstairs to fetch the children from their beds.

"The dog, which usually barks at the slightest noise, walked round and round very agitated but without a whimper. Later it would not go out of the house."

Farmer Richard Hewison drove the half-mile to the farmhouse.

He says: "They were genuinely terrified when I arrived. They were frightened out of their wits."

- **Josephine**, Richard Hewison's 33-year-old wife, had an equally terrifying experience shortly before the Coombs saw their spaceman.

#### Bright

- **Josephine**, 33, who has a BSc degree in agriculture and an honours degree in agricultural botany, says: "Richard was up and about the farm. It was ten to eight on a bright, sunny morning.

"I went to the bedroom window and saw this thing parked alongside the greenhouse.

"I wasn't in the least frightened. I just couldn't believe my eyes. I thought, 'What on earth is it doing by my greenhouse?'

"It was a silver colour, about 50-foot across the base and shaped like a jelly mould.

"It was as high as a double-decker bus. The greenhouse is 13-foot to

the eaves but it towered above it.

"There was no movement, it had no visible windows or openings. I waited for something to emerge. It went after ten minutes.

"It left no mark. Not even a broken twig".

Within a 20-mile radius of the Hewisons' home, there are: the Royal Aircraft Establishment Missile Range; RAF Brawdy, an operational station; the Army's Pendine Ranges; a missile testing ground; supersonic low - flying air corridors; and an American submarine tracking station.

- **Louise** and David Bassett, both 31, live in Ferryside, Carmarthen. Their house is set in six wooded acres.

They are young, wealthy, and run a gourmet's restaurant in Carmarthen.

He is a crack shot, a first-class fisherman and an international powerboat racer.

Louise says: "I was driving home from the

restaurant about 1 am. David had stayed behind to clear up. I'd had enough for one night.

"Coming through the village of Iddole, my radio started to play up.

"I saw flashing blue lights and took a detour. Two miles further on the flashing lights appeared again.

"I thought it must have been a major accident. But the police told me no police cars, fire appliances or ambulances had been anywhere near that spot."

#### Night

Carmarthen police confirm that no exceptional police activity took place in the area that night. Nor were RAF or private helicopters operating.

When Louise's radio blew, so did a lot of other people's television receivers.

Radio dealers and repairmen complained to the BBC and ITA that signal strength throughout the area was falling off. So badly that colour

could not be received in some districts.

"The BBC said that there had been no drop in transmitted signals.

- **John** Petts, 62, an artist, lives across the estuary from the Bassetts.

He says: "I was working at night in my studio. I switched off the light, and looking across the estuary above, the hills I saw a shaft of brilliant light.

"It was a brightly-lit, cigar-shaped object. I goggled and told myself. 'For heaven's sake, be objective, have a hard stare.

"The object had no sense of movement or change. Then it vanished. One minute it was there, the next gone."

Mrs Margaret Lowndes, who is in her 50s, wife of an agricultural engineer, confirms the story.

She says: "I walked from my sitting room, looked through my window and stopped in my tracks.

"Above the level of the land was an extraordinary bright light.

where there was no reason for a light to be.

"I am not the 'sort of person who would believe in UFOs. My inclination is to say, 'Rubbish.' But this I did see.

- **Teenager Stephen** Taylor, of Pen-y-gwn, Haverfordwest, may have come nearer than anybody to one of the figures.

#### Funny

Stephen, 18, who works women's clothing shop in Haverfordwest was walking along a lane bordering RAF Brawdy.

He says: "I'd taken my girlfriend home and said goodnight about nine o'clock. I was walking home when I saw something funny in the sky.

"A dog came tearing out of the darkness towards me. I called at a friend's house and we joked about me seeing a UFO. Then I walked on.

"Then I made out a black shape. It looked about 40 to 50 feet across. At its widest point I noticed a dim glow around what seemed to be the underside.

"Suddenly this figure popped up, right next to me. I was terrified. It was dressed in silver. It seemed to have high cheek-bones. Its eyes were like fish eyes—completely round.

#### Swing

"I took a swing at it and fled. I don't know whether I hit it. I ran the three miles home."

- **Mr** David Edward Smith, a solicitor, is chief legal officer to Gwynedd County Council.

He says: "I saw and clearly identified a phenomenon in the sky.

"It was a golden-yellow pencil lying in the sky, accompanied by a yellow, pulsating light."

He was holidaying at St David's when the object appeared.

It was, he says, no trick of light or conventional flying machine and, like John Petts' object, it was sharply and clearly defined.

He says: "Something like this cannot be just a figment of the imagination. It is worthy of thorough investigation."

PAULINE COOMBS: Crying with fright.   JOSEPHINE HEWISON: Terrifying experience.   STEPHEN TAYLOR: Shape in silver.   JOHN PETTS: Cigar-shaped object.   LOUISE BASSETT: Flashing blue lights.

### 'There may be life in outer space'

REPORTS of the sightings in The Broad Haven Triangle have reached Whitehall.

A Ministry of Defence spokesman in London said: "We have heard the reports of sightings of unexplained objects in the West Wales area.

"The people who report these sightings are not nutcases. They are genuinely sincere people, genuinely concerned.

"We investigate every report on this assumption. We do not discount the possibility of intelligent life in outer space."

Flight-Lieutenant Cowan, community relations officer at RAF Brawdy said: "There have been a flood of these reports.

"The ground sightings do not, in time or place, fit in with our operations."

"Neither do the descriptions of spacemen fit with the protective clothing used by oil refineries in the area.

#### TARGET

"We accept the possibility of life in outer space. But none of our radar units can explain these sightings."

A spokesman for the top secret Royal Aircraft Establishment station said that their aircraft sometimes towed a target three and a half miles behind the planes.

"The target may appear to be dissociated from the towing aircraft."

It could, therefore, seem like a flying saucer.

### 'THIS WAS NO HOAX'

FOURTEEN keen-eyed children at Broad Haven primary school spotted a strange object in a field 200 yards from where they were playing.

This sparked the biggest UFO hunt since 1896. Reports of sightings and even meetings with spacemen poured into the UFO research association.

Their headmaster, Ralph Llewellyn, persuaded the children to draw the object they had seen.

He kept them separate and compared their finished results. They showed a remarkable similarity.

Mr Llewellyn says: "I do not believe that children this age could sustain a hoax of this nature."

## 18th May 1977 – UFO sighed over Cheshire

At 1.10pm, ex-World War Two Serviceman – Jack Allen, was carrying out maintenance work on the railway line near Rookery Bridge, Sandbach, in Cheshire, when he noticed:

> *"...an aircraft, moving slowly across the clear blue sky, above which was a second, much transparent, smaller object showing grey patches covering its body, reminding me of an X ray photo, with small stubby wings sliced off at the ends*
>
> *Shortly after the sighting I developed an itchy rash over my forehead, arms and fingers, which lasted for three days, which went away, reappeared, and completely cleared up for good."*

**(Source: MAPIT & CUFOR)**

At 9.30pm that evening, Darren Hawkes (then aged 14), David Gillitt (then aged 19), and Richard Huggins (then aged14), were walking along Wycombe Lane, Woodburn Green, High Wycombe, when they noticed a yellow 'light', shimmering in the sky towards their right, over the direction of Wooburn Green.

> *"After a minute or two it stopped, and suddenly grew to about three times its size, before returning to its original size – then turned left, showing a metallic structure with a red light on its front – eventually disappearing towards the north-west."*

### UFO over Barking, Essex

At approximately 10pm the same day, North Street, Barking, Essex resident – Mrs Steel – sighted a large yellow sphere moving through the air, before loosing sight of it as it went behind a chimney. She shouted for her husband and the couple watched with the next door neighbours on their flat balcony, as the object rose up from behind the rooftops, showing:

> *"...a large yellow sphere, whose underside seemed to have an inward travelling spiral and spinning rim around its centre.*
>
> *A small plane appeared from the south and headed towards the object, which shot straight at the aircraft and 'leapfrogged' over it. The plane and UFO continued northwards, for a few seconds, before the UFO moved away – now heading east – and was lost from view."*

**(Source: Andrew Collins/Barry King/***BUFORA Journal***/Volume 6, Number 3, September/October 1977)**

## 20th May 1977 – UFO display over Bournemouth

A married couple were driving along the South Molton Road, in Devon, at 9pm, when they saw:

> *"...three cigar-shaped objects, the colour of 'congealed snowflakes', metallic looking in appearance, moving across the sky in line, but wide apart. The one on the right suddenly turned tail and emitted a pale coloured flare, before immediately vanishing from view."*

Just after 10pm, Bournemouth-based UFO investigator, Leslie Harris, began to receive a number of telephone calls from the public, reporting UFOs seen over the town. They included a sighting at 10.05pm, by Brian Haylett from Poole – approximately two miles away from Canford Heath – who sighted a bright round object appear from behind clouds, which began to circle the area, illuminating the cloud above. Others also reported having seen strange objects in the sky, beaming 'cones of light' downwards.

**Clifford Rowe** and his girlfriend were parked near Hurn Airport. They said:

> *"We noticed a very pale green 'cigar' – somewhat larger than the sun in size – travelling fast across the sky, from east to west, before passing behind distant trees, making a right angle turn and dropping like a stone out of the sky. Feeling rather nervous, we decided to leave. As we approached a set of traffic lights along the main road, near the Airport, we spotted the 'cigar' again. We watched as it overtook us, before stopping in the sky ahead of us. A patchy beam of light – darker green in*

**EXCLUSIVE**

**WATCH OUT! THERE'S A UFO ABOUT**

A WEIRD TRAIL OF FEAR

# MYSTERY OF THE SILVER SPACE BEAM

Day Two of a Sun series

## There were two moons that night

RICHARD MORSE "I was shocked"

● IN one night, a strange beam of "solid" silver light shining from a saucer-shaped craft was seen in three different places in Dorset.

● Similar sightings have been reported around the world, adding to the huge international dossier on Unidentified Flying Objects.

● Next month, the Queen will watch some of the weirdest of these experiences in the blockbusting sci-fi film Close Encounters Of The Third Kind at its premiere in London.

THE BEAM fell across the bonnet of Mrs Pauline Fall's car as she and a woman friend drove down a dark country lane.

Pauline, 31, said: "It came down four or five times, always in exactly the same place on the bonnet. It was as if the light was tracking us."

At first she couldn't make out where the beam was coming from.

"One minute there was nothing in the sky, the next, there it was," she said. "It looked like the underside of a dinner plate, and out of the centre came a silvery white light.

"The light was narrow at the top, widening into a cone shape as it touched the ground.

"It was solid light, as if a line had been drawn around it.

"I'm not normally one to panic, but the pit of my stomach went ice cold. My friend was unnerved, too."

The two women were near the Dorset village of Longham when the beam appeared.

Pauline noticed the beam getting shorter as the object started to come down.

"Then it disappeared, as if it had been swallowed up by the ground," Pauline said.

"Even talking about it now, I start to tremble. I couldn't take the car out on my own at night for four months afterwards."

Odd things happened to Pauline's car after the sighting.

Its petrol consumption shot up. And the engine cut out while she was driving, although the power returned when her husband took the wheel.

Pauline said: "I've done a lot of soul-searching, and I haven't a logical explanation for what I saw. It must have been a UFO.

"I just wish someone could tell me where it came from and what it wants from us."

● On the same night—

*PAULINE FALL Cone-shaped beam*

**By SUE FREEMAN**

'*It was like nothing I'd ever seen in my life*'

*KAREN IVESON traces the path of the silvery disc she saw*

RICHARD MORSE was taking a short cut home from the bus stop when he saw a light flickering from the sky.

"I thought it was the moon behind the clouds," says 27-year-old Morse, of Poole, Dorset. "Then I saw the moon in another part of the sky.

"Just looking at it gave me a weird feeling. It was a typical flying-saucer shape with another shape on top of it and a white light shone from its centre to the ground.

"Time seemed to stand still as I watched it. Then it started to move off, banking very fast before it disappeared.

### Fast

"Friends have come up with normal explanations of what it might have been, but none have convinced me.

"I felt so emotional after I'd seen it. When I got home, I was shocked and upset.

"It wasn't like anything from this planet."

Morse, who had a temporary job as a deck chair attendant at the time, said: "Frankly, this caused me some embarrassment. I've had to take some ribbing from my friends over it.

"I was really glad to hear others had had similar experiences that night."

### Power

"I was desperate to get home and shut the front door on the outside world."

When her husband, John, saw her terrified face, he thought she must have had an accident.

"Don't laugh," she told him, "but I think I've seen a UFO."

Pauline, a builder's wife, of Wimborne, Dorset, said: "My hands were ice cold, but the skin beyond the wristbands of my blouse was a normal temperature. It took nearly an hour afterwards to get my hands warm.

Saturday, May 21, 1977—pretty Karen Iveson and her 19-year-old boyfriend, Cliff Rowe, had parked their car to do some courting when the beam fell on them.

Cliff, an apprentice technician, said: "It shone across the back of the car."

Karen and Cliff were parked off a road near Parley Cross, Dorset.

"It was a lonely spot," Cliff said. "And not being able to see what caused the beam scared us a bit. We moved on."

They found out exactly where the beam came from as they drove along the road.

### Panic

Karen, an 18-year-old tax officer, of Guernsey Road, Poole, Dorset, said: "A large, silvery disc-shaped object hovered over a field, and a silver-green, cone-shaped beam shone down from the centre of it. We stopped to watch. It seemed to stay there for ages.

"Then suddenly, it veered off fast, and dropped behind some trees, much lower than any plane could go.

"We both panicked a bit afterwards. It was scaring, not knowing what on earth it was. It was like nothing I'd ever seen in my life.

"I believe in UFOs. Now I know there must be something up there."

## THE STRANGE ONES

WHAT do these aliens who fly UFOs look like?

Some face-to-face encounters have revealed them as figures between 6ft and 8ft tall, wearing shimmering silver spacesuits similar to those worn by human astronauts.

Their heads, set on massive shoulders, have no discernible features. A box-shaped silver space helmet frames a dark area, like a blank watch face.

Other close encounters have been with small creatures, between 2½ft and 3ft tall, with bald, egg-shaped heads and hawk-like talons for hands.

In Kentucky, America, a group of farmworkers shot at these strange creatures. Whenever one was hit, it would float or fall over and then scurry for cover.

The shots sounded as though they were hitting a bucket — but the creatures themselves, whether jumping or walking, made no sound.

**TOMORROW:** *UFOs that haunt the Broadhaven Triangle*

*colour than the 'object' – extended from its centre and projected to the ground, but switched off a few seconds later. It then shot off towards Canford Heath. I don't know if there is any connection but, a few minutes prior to the sighting, we saw a number of light flashes in the sky, accompanied by a loud bang and a noise like a heavy board being dragged along the ground."*

Another witness was **Mr Richard Morse:**

*"I was walking home, at 11 pm, through nearby woodland. It was a windy night when I saw four 'dancing discs' projecting beams of light upwards, rather than downwards in the sky, as one might have imagined – that's the only way I can explain it. Another silver-grey luminous 'disc' then appeared from behind a cloud, to the left of the others. It had what looked like two short 'protrusions of light' sticking out of its top. Suddenly, a 'cone of white light' projected from underneath the centre of this 'disc' and slowly extended downwards to the ground. By this time I was feeling frightened, but noticed the wind had dropped. Everything was still – like a vacuum. To my relief, the 'beam' extinguished itself, leaving night to close in again – then the 'disc' banked over and sped away to the west, leaving me so frightened that I could hardly summon the courage to walk home."*

**Mrs Pauline Fall** was driving along Ham Lane, when she saw:

*"...a 'light' that went downwards – narrow at the top and wide at the bottom – not only that, but the whole circle came down at the same time as the beam".*

She later rejected an explanation put to her that the 'lights' were actually searchlight beams, with a candle power of two and-a-half million, projected into the sky for 150 former members of the Royal Artillery Second Regiment Searchlight, who were attending a Royal British Legion 22nd Annual Reunion, at Wimborne. The organiser – Mr Lesley Scott, explained away the colours in the sky as being caused by red and green screens, placed over the searchlights.

**(Source: As above/Personal interview/*Bournemouth Echo*, 26.5.1977)**

## 21st May 1977 – Three UFOs seen by motorist on the M1 Motorway

During the early hours of this morning, three peculiar lights were seen in the sky, over Birmingham.

At 9.30pm, Coal Board Press Officer – Peter Heron, was travelling north along the M1, towards his home in Gateshead, when he saw:

*"...a cigar-shaped object, with what looked like a nozzle at one end, which eventually moved away and out of sight."*

Ten minutes later, Chartered Surveyor – Mr Leslie Chadwick, was driving towards his West Rainton home, from Durham, when some pedestrians flagged him down, pointing upwards at an object in the sky.

*"It was about 10,000 feet up in the sky and over the direction of the Lumley Castle area. I thought, at first, it was an airship. Ten minutes later, it moved away and out of sight."*

At 9.45pm, three 'lights' were seen motionless in the sky over Rochester Airport. This was no doubt connected with a sighting, a few minutes later – this time over the A2, between Bapchild and Sittingbourne, in Kent – when a 'white light' was seen hovering in the sky over Sittingbourne, by ex-RAF Technician – Neville Goldsmith, who got out of his car to have a closer look.

*"It was, in fact, one large light, with three or four smaller ones pulsing around it. A short time later, it faded away."*

At 9.57pm, 'three lights' were seen in the sky over Bexley, in Kent. Several seconds later, they disappeared from view.

At 10pm a UFO, showing 'three lights', was seen over Rochester but, once again, within a minute, they

## Mystery lights explained

**THE** mystery of the strange lights seen in the sky over East Dorset on Saturday night was solved today—without any contact with another world.

The lights were actually searchlight beams sent out as a treat for 150 former members of the Royal Artillery's Second Searchlight Regiment.

The men were attending their 22nd annual reunion at Wimborne's Royal British Legion Hall.

Organiser Mr. Les Scott, of Victoria Road, Wimborne, said: "I had to laugh when I read of people's reactions. Members of the searchlight unit are not allowed to shine the lights straight into the sky in case aircraft home in on them — and three miles away it would look as though the lights were disappearing and reappearing.

"The different colours people described were caused by red and green screens put over the searchlights. There would also have been a certain amount of reflection from the normal atmosphere."

The searchlights used on Saturday were ones used to pinpoint enemy aircraft during the war.

Each light has a candle power of two and a half million.

### NOT CONVINCED

Mrs. Pauline Fall, of Heron Drive, Colehill, who saw the lights as she was driving home along Ham Lane, said today she was still not convinced by the searchlight explanation.

"I don't know an awful lot about searchlights, admittedly, but my impression was of a light that went downwards, narrow at the top and wide at the bottom.

"And what would explain

A drawing by Mrs. Fall of what she saw.

such a big circle in the sky if the light was diminishing and there were no clouds at the time? Not only that, the whole circle came down at the same time as the beam."

Mrs. Fall said she would accept the explanation if her points could be answered logically. She added that she was frightened by what she saw and felt, and if searchlight activity was the explanation some advance notice should have been given to the public, to avoid alarm or confusion.

---

disappeared from view. Housewife – Elaine Hazeldine, from Warrington, was at her home address when she and her husband saw a bright object heading across the sky, high up. The couple picked-up binoculars and rushed out into the garden. By this time the object – looking like a star – had dropped down in the sky and was passing overhead.

Mrs Hazeldine alerted the next door neighbours, who came running out to have a look at the object, which remained stationary for a few minutes before dropping down even further – far too large to have been any aircraft, according to the family.

**(Sources: Peter Paget/UFOSIS/*Newcastle Journal*, 31.5.1977 – 'Riddle of flying object in sky')**

### 22nd May 1977 – *Basildon Standard* tells of youth being terrified by UFO

The newspaper told of a teenager who was walking along the Langdon Hills, Laindon, Basildon, in Essex, when he saw a yellow spherical shaped object heading towards him; when some 200 feet away, it vanished from view. It then reappeared as a red cigar-shaped object, showing flashing lights on top with a black outline around it, before moving away. The youth ran home and a doctor was called to sedate him – such was his condition.

## May 1977 – UFO over Swansea

Mrs Vivienne Gammon of Ely Gardens, Townhill, Swansea, glanced out of the window of her aunt's home in Gwynedd Gardens, Townhill, at about 9pm, and saw two unidentified flying objects, hovering in and out of a cloud.

> "One of them was flat, like a plate, and the other was long and oval. They gave off a glow, like a lighthouse, and kept bobbing up and down."

To reassure herself that she wasn't imaging it she called her Aunt Gladys, who confirmed she could also see it.

*"We then called her neighbour, Mr Graham Noel, and the three of us went outside and watched the objects – until they disappeared, ten minutes later." Swansea coastguards came up with a theory to explain the sighting: two Boeing 747s passing each other and reflecting the setting sun's light, but the objects were hovering for over ten minutes."* (**Source:** *South Wales Evening Post,* **Saturday 21st May 1977**)

## 22nd May 1977 – Strange object over London and Top Secret file

At 9.30pm, Mr and Mrs Steel from North Street, Barking, Essex, began their observations of the sky from their balcony, hoping to catch sight of a strange object seen a couple of days previously, once again accompanied by their neighbours.

*"At 10.16pm, a similar object was seen slowly drifting towards the East End of London. Suddenly, it stopped and hovered at an angle of 75 degrees, for 34 minutes, before reappearing much closer. We thought we could hear a noise, like a whistling kettle. At 10.50pm, it shot away, eastwards, and out of sight."* (**Source: Barry King,** *BUFORA Journal,* **Volume 6, No. 3, Sept/Oct. 1977**)

A declassified Top Secret report, released by the MOD, in 2006, outlined a sighting by three unnamed airmen at RAF Patrington, (where 'Vulcan' Bombers, armed with atomic bombs, were kept), on 21st/22nd May 1977, of:

*"...a triangular-shaped 'white light' moving erratically overhead, at 10.20 pm, followed by a report from the station's radar, confirming an unidentified contact moving in a zigzag manner in a similar direction".*

Apparently, the same UFO was also tracked by radar operators, at RAF Waddington, who observed the UFO for four minutes before their screens were partially obliterated by high-powered interference, which subsided when the UFO disappeared.

## 24th May 1977 – 'Flying Saucer' over Yorkshire

At 9pm, motorist – Roger Crowther (then aged 22), was approaching the village of Cattal, heading towards Whixley, near York, accompanied by his girlfriend – Margaret Hornby.

*"As we drove over the steeply inclined bridge into Cattal, we caught sight of a strange pink glow in the sky at a slight angle from vertical, before losing sight of it as we drove past some houses. We saw it again as we left the village and stopped the car, by which time it was closer and metallic looking in appearance, with what looked like a jet of pink vapour dropping downwards from it.*

*By now, others had stopped their cars; quite a few people were stood watching it. I estimated it was at a height of a few thousand feet. I tried to rationalise what it could be. The nearest comparison would be a 'Harrier' Jump Jet – except this object was saucer-shaped, with a low dome. We watched in amazement as it silently passed overhead, heading towards Tockwith, at about 200 miles per hour – then, in a blur of speed, it had gone."*

Roger contacted the police, the next day, to report the incident. During an interview with two officers, who came to his house, they divulged having received other similar sightings but nothing for the Cattal/Whixley areas. (**Source: Personal interview**)

## 26th May 1977 – UFO over South Humberside

At around 3.35am, Mr Roy Thompson, living in Burringham – a small village, located a few miles from west of Scunthorpe – was awoken from his sleep by a tremendous noise –

*"...like a whirlwind or pressure building up – as if an object was on the ground and about to take off."*

The noise lasted for several seconds and then began to fade. It was intense. He got out of bed and looked out of the window.

(People adjacent to his caravan also heard a strange noise, at the same time. One woman described it as sounding like the rumble of heavy Lorries).

He saw:

> "*...a silvery-white or grey, inflated, elliptical object in the sky, at an elevation of about 70 degrees; it was 20 feet wide, 15 feet high, and at a height of between 3,000-4,000 feet. I couldn't see any lights on it. It was spinning slowly – like a globe of the world – and moved at a tremendous speed across the sky, vanishing a few seconds later.*"

Seconds later Roy glanced to his right and saw a very similar object, surrounded by a greyish black cloud of amorphous shape over a row of houses further away, in the direction of Keadby. He looked over to where he had seen the first object – there was still nothing there. When he glanced back at where the second object had been, again nothing was seen.

The next morning he contacted the police and they released the story to the Press, because of a possible connection with a sighting seen the evening before (25th May 1977) at Bransholme, Hull, on the other side of the estuary.

Nigel Watson, of Northern UFO Network, investigated this incident, accompanied by Roger Hebb and Keith Beacroft – members of the Scunthorpe UFO Research Society. According to Nigel, a major Air Force exercise took place between 2am and 4.45am, involving aircraft from the Humberside and Lincolnshire area.

Mr Thompson, while not claiming that he saw a UFO, was adamant that what he did see was no Jet because:

> "*Jets do not spin horizontally, and a jet needs at least a mile before it can turn over and come back.*"

(Apparently, most of the exercise took place over the sea.)

**(Source: Nigel Watson – 'Encounter at Burringham', *Flying Saucer Review*, Volume 23, Number 3, 1977)**

## 28th May 1977 – Saucer-shaped object sighted over Clacton-on-Sea

Kathleen Irene Green (then aged 59) was in Alton Park, Clacton-on-Sea, Essex, at 8pm, when she was amazed to see:

> "*...an object at an angle of about 30 degrees in the sky, glittering at the top, resembling two inverted soup plates; it was completely silent and just hung there.*" **(Source: Ron West)**

## 28th May 1977 – Pulsing red light seen over Birmingham

A luminous 'globe', pulsing with red light, was seen over Great Barr, Birmingham, at 8.15pm.

At 11.15pm on the same day, David Glover – a schoolboy from Lincoln, was preparing to get ready for bed, when the bedroom was illuminated by a bright flash of light. Rushing to the window, he saw:

> "*...three or four illuminated objects crossing the sky – unlike any clouds I had ever seen before in my life*".

**(Source: Richard Thompson/UFOSIS)**

---

## Riddle of 'flying object' in sky

MYSTERY last night surrounded an unidentified flying object spotted in the sky.

Police on Tyneside are investigating one report. And several other people saw what was believed to have been the same object in County Durham.

But at Newcastle Airport, where UFO sightings are logged, a spokesman said they had no record of the "happening." One suggestion put forward by airport director Jim Denyer is that it was a hot air balloon which is flying in the area.

But two people who saw the object discount the theory. One is Coal Board Press Officer Peter Heron. He was travelling north on the A1 motorway towards his Low Fell, Gateshead, home, at about 9.30 p.m. on Thursday when he saw it.

Mr. Heron said yesterday: "It was about 200ft. long cigar-shaped and with what looked like a nozzle at one end. It eventually moved away."

Chartered surveyor Les Chadwick, a partner in a Sunderland-based firm, was travelling towards his West Rainton home from Durham at about 9.40 the same night when he was stopped by pedestrians who had spotted an object in the sky.

He got out of his car to take a look. He said: "It was about 10,000 feet up and above the Lumley Castle area.

"It remained in the one place for about 10 minutes and I thought at first it was an airship.

A police spokesman said they had been informed by Mr. Heron of his sighting and were investigating.

● There were several reports of UFO sightings in the North Humberside area on Thursday and Friday night.

### 30th May 1977 – Nottinghamshire schoolchildren sight UFOs

At 11.30am, two silver cigar-shaped objects were seen travelling across the sky – one behind the other – by teachers and pupils at Ashfield School, Kirkby-in-Ashfield, Nottinghamshire, moving south-westwards, towards the village of Huthwaite, at an estimated speed of between 500-1,000 miles per hour.
**(Source: BUFORA)**

## CHAPTER 18 – JUNE 1977

### 1st June 1977 – UFO over Wales

Mrs Rosemary Lewis and her husband, who live at Simpson Cross on the St. David's road, had a local power blackout at 8.45pm.

The evening was still fairly light about 10 o'clock, when Mr Lewis wandered into the kitchen to get a snack. The view from the window, at a range of about two miles, is of a ridge of low hills known as Cuffern Mountain.

Mr Lewis was studying these hills to see if the electricity supply had been restored to nearby farms, and then he saw something which amazed him. He said:

> *"I was eating a biscuit, when this terrific red glow came out of nowhere. It had a larger base, as it were, pear-shaped – then it moved up towards the horizon for, perhaps, twenty yards. Finally it moved in its entirety towards the horizon and disappeared. It moved quickly over this twenty yards; it looked like a fire moving – then went to the horizon and disappeared. It was something that I've never seen in the whole of my life. I just don't know what it was."*

Alerted by her husband, Rosemary Lewis also went to see the phenomenon. At first, she thought it was a big gorse fire on the mountain. **(Source: Randall Jones Pugh)**

### 3rd June 1977 – Diamond-shaped UFO seen over Essex

Carol Anne Finch (then aged 33) of Severn Road, Clacton-on-Sea, was returning home with a friend, at 10.45pm, after having been to the pictures. As they got out of the car,

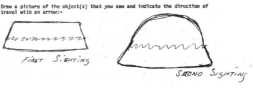

> *"We saw a bright orange diamond-shaped object in the sky. We stood watching it for a few minutes – then went indoors. We came back out, a short time later, and saw that it was now oblong in shape but still shining bright orange. Several seconds later it disappeared from sight."*

**(Source: Essex UFO Study Group)**

### 5th June 1977 – 'Bulbous light' over Essex

Christine Pratt (then aged 40) of Sunset Avenue, Chingford, Essex, was preparing supper, at 10pm, when she happened to look out of the kitchen window.

> *"I saw a 'bright light' in the sky, which was bulbous at the top, over the Edmonton and Enfield areas. It appeared to be motionless in the sky. I watched it for several minutes, until it just disappeared from view – now just a tiny speck of light in the distance. I have never seen anything move so fast in my life. The sky was clear at the time."* **(Source: Essex UFO Study Group)**

At 10.10pm, Pauline Billotte of Parkhill Road, Chingford, was called by her daughter – who told her she could see something strange in the sky.

> *"We looked and I saw what resembled a lightbulb, motionless in the sky. We watched it for five minutes, during which time we fetched some high-powered binoculars. When I looked through*

*them, all I could see was a vivid light – so bright I couldn't make anything else out. An aircraft approached in the sky; the light then dimmed and shot away at fantastic speed."*

Pauline's son, who also saw it, said that it looked like *"a dark disc-shaped object".*

**(Source: Essex UFO Study Group)**

## 6th June 1977 – Close encounter by Durham motorcyclist

Mark Henshall (then aged 16) was riding his motorcycle along the B6278, close to the North Yorkshire border, near Barnard Castle, County Durham, when he noticed the brief appearance of:

*"...two purple objects in the sky – looking like car headlight beams – apparently keeping pace with him, for some distance, before disappearing 30 seconds later".*

A glimpse through the rear mirror on the bike showed a car about to overtake him. As it did so, a brilliant pink/purple light seemed to shine over them, with a solid outline, resembling 'a meat dish in shape'.

*"At this point, I noticed the power beginning to drain from the machine. I could not understand what was happening, at first. I moved the throttle – there was no response. I felt my legs and back becoming hot and noticed the jacket beginning to steam. I took off my gloves and felt my arm and petrol tank; they were both very hot. After travelling about a hundred yards, the object just disappeared."* Mark then pulled onto the side of the road, being joined by the car driver – who was very shaken and unable to explain why his car had suddenly begun to lose power. Unfortunately, because of his position inside the car, he had only seen a glow surrounding the car rather than any object.

Mr Henshall was later interviewed by UFOIN investigators – Edwin Ollis, Malcolm Leech and Brian Straight, who discovered that the back of his leather jacket was rougher than the rest of the garment, and an examination of the motorcycle revealed the brakes were so worn that they needed replacing.

**(Source: Cleveland UFO Group [CHRYSIS])**

## 6th June 1977 – A frightening visit by the 'Men in Blue' to Welsh UFO witnesses

Following on from the very odd incident that befell Rosa Granville, involving a visit from 'two black suited men in a silver car', at *Haven Fort Hotel*, in Little Haven, history was to be repeated when 'they' paid a visit to Ripperston Farm – the residence of Pauline and Billie Coombes – who were not at home, but spoke to their son, Clinton (then aged 16), the only one in the house at the time – whom we spoke to during a visit to see him, in 2006. He said:

*"A huge silver car turned up at the house, stopped, and two men got out. Straightaway, I felt frightened because, as they approached the house, I knew there was something wrong about them. They were both unusually tall in height and wearing blue one-piece suits.*

*I saw them go over to my neighbour's house, next door – Carole Klass, and ask her where Pauline was. From the look on her face, I could see she was frightened. I heard her say, 'I don't know', and shut the door. I made sure the doors were all locked and hid until they left. The strange thing was that after they left, my mum turned up. I was amazed she hadn't seen them as she drove in."*

Our efforts to trace Carole were doomed to failure. We did find out where we believed she was living, but letters sent to her remained unanswered – disappointing, but who can blame her?

In September 2006, we made our way to South Wales, determined to find Pauline and Billie Coombes, and see for ourselves Lower Ripperston Farm, St. Brides, Haverfordwest, which lay at the end of a single lane track, bordered by bushes and trees on either side, approximately half-a-mile long – an eerie drive in the half light. We spoke to the current residents of the house, who were tenant farmers – Alan and Sue Davis – who made us very welcome, after explaining the reason for our visit. Imagine our surprise when

the couple, with three young children, admitted they had experienced for themselves various examples of strange phenomenon occurring at the house, including ghostly black shadows seen.

We eventually met up with Pauline and Billie, at Milford Haven, in 2006, who also treated us as friends, welcoming us into their house, Billie even asking if we had any objection if he smoked a cigarette!

During conversations held with them, we felt they never made any attempt to embellish – just tell things how they saw them at the time.

Pauline described the enormous media interest which besieged them, following the events being brought to the attention of the local newspapers, especially after the book – *The Uninvited* – written by Clive Harold, was released. Sadly, she told us that Clive Harold had sold the rights of the book to *The People* Newspaper, 20 years ago, and that while royalties were paid on 75,000 copies. . .

> *"...Neither I, or Billie, ever received any monies from the sale of these books.*
>
> *Representatives from RAF Brawdy came to see us. We received interest from the* National Enquirer, *in America. The BBC came around to see us and suggested we had imagined everything. The Star Newspaper offered us ten thousand pounds to admit the whole thing was a hoax. We refused."*

In an interview, tape-recorded by Phil Hoyle, during a visit he made to the couple, in 1985, Pauline told of one occasion:

> *"I remember going to bed. The next thing I became aware of was an impression of a needle in my arm and seeing two people stood next to me. They were beautiful in appearance and had black roll-neck jumpers, with neat hair – page-boy style. I was sat on this bench. This one was stood right opposite, watching me, so I leaned forward to look down the corridor. When a door opened at the side of me, loads of women came into the room.*

*The next thing I was aware of was being back in the bedroom; it was 4.30am. I shouted 'Time to get up, Billie', and wondered where the time had gone, as it was 1.30am when we went to bed. I thought I must have dreamt it – until I saw a programme on the TV, a few weeks later, about some women in America who spoke of having been abducted into a UFO, and wondered if the same thing had happened to me, especially as I was left a star-shaped mark on my left arm, which hadn't been there before – although it has faded with the passing of years."*

## 7th June 1977 – Three lights seen over Middlesex

At 10.20pm, three stationary lights were seen in the sky over Stoneleigh Avenue, Enfield, in Middlesex.

## 8th June1977 – UFO over Hertfordshire

Mr and Mrs Lloyd were sat in their car at Flaunden, in Hertfordshire, at 6.30pm, when they noticed a strange object in the sky above them, which came to a halt. Mr Lloyd – who had studied aircraft recognition for fifteen years – happened to have a telescopic gun sight with him. He looked through it and saw a greyish pewter coloured object, from which an illustration was later obtained.

Was there any connection with Bill Dillon's sighting, in May 1957, at Ramridge School, in Bedfordshire, or the strange object seen over the Rogue River, Oregon, in 1964?

**(Source: Jenny Randles, *Flying Saucer Review*, Volume 28, Number 4, 1983)**

## 9th June 1977 – UFOs over County Durham

During the early hours, retired WRAF Radar operator – Bessie Thomas from Consett, County Durham (aged 85 in 2009) – spoke of what she saw:

*"My husband was having problems sleeping, because of a cough. He went to the window facing north-east, overlooking the Sunderland area, and peered out, when he observed a strange shape in the sky. He awoke me and I went to have a look. I saw what appeared to be a large mushroom-shaped object in the sky. I checked my watch; it was 2.30am.*

*Four other smaller objects then appeared in the sky and flew straight into the larger one, before they went off at speed.*

*I was quite shaken by what we saw and made a note straightaway in my diary. I've never seen anything like that before, even while working on Radar in Suffolk, plotting the V1 and V2 'Doodlebugs' during the Second World War."* **(Source: Personal interview)**

## 11th June 1977 – Misty UFO at Stone, Staffordshire

Two teenagers were walking home, at 4am, across the 'common plot' pen land when they saw a strange area of light, about two to three feet off the ground, about 250 feet away from them. Further observation revealed a misty white dome with sharp edges; it looked like it had been cut precisely from a square. It was estimated to be two feet thick and 60 feet wide and was a milky colour. There was no wobbling or swirling. A faint light was caste onto the ground. Some bulls in a nearby field were running about in frenzy.

Thirty seconds later, as they approached closer, it faded away. **(Source: Martin Keatman)**

### 12th June 1977 – UFO over Brecon Wales

At 3.15am, Mrs Glenys Price was driving her friends – Mrs Mable Jones and Mr Steven Williams – home, on a cloudy night along the main A40 road, near Brecon, Powys, in Wales.

Mrs Price sighted an object – about the size of a small car in the sky. She slowed the car down and told the other passengers, who described it as:

*"...being golden in colour, roughly sausage-shaped with a hazy glow around it, with a lump or darker protuberance sticking up from the top" (although Mrs Price felt this was in the middle). Behind the object was a cloud of vapour-like substance. This moved with the object and was darker in colour and irregular in shape – roughly oval. A couple of minutes later, it disappeared from view instantly.* (**Source: Derek James, NUFON**)

### 16th June 1977 – Close Encounter, Worcestershire

In the same month, Mrs Mary Hill – then caretaker of the Baptist Church at Bewdley, Worcestershire (who lived next door) – was in her bedroom, at 11.30pm, getting ready for bed, when she noticed a silvery-white object in the sky, transparent in appearance, and at eye level with the window.

*"The light in the middle of the object became hazy. I was astonished to see two 'figures' standing inside. They were looking out – one was taller than the other and I thought he might be male; the other, a female. After a few minutes, the 'light' began to glow very bright and it swept away at an angle, upwards, very quickly."*

Details of the incident were brought to the attention of the 'Sky Scan' Group, Worcester, who carried out an investigation into the matter. Unfortunately, the results of any documents pertaining to this investigation, carried out by this highly respected professionally run group, whom we contacted over the years, were mislaid many years ago. Their spokesman – Derek Lawrence, told us he had no reason to disbelieve the account given by Mrs Hill, whom he found very genuine, after being initially contacted by Mrs Hill's nephew – Lee Hatton.

(**Source: Sky Scan/***Magic Saucer,* **Crystal Hogben**)

### 21st June 1977 – Motorcycle paced by UFO over Lancashire

John Bracewell (then aged 31) from Nelson, in Lancashire, was a pillion passenger on a motorcycle being ridden by his wife, along the A56 trunk road out of Salford, on the evening, when his attention was caught by a 'light' in the sky – which he took to be reflection off his motorcycle visor of an aircraft. It was still there as they rode through Bury, travelling at the same speed as they were, about 35 miles per hour. About a quarter-of-a-mile out of the town, John noticed the 'aircraft' was definitely keeping pace with them, almost emulating their movements – slowing down while negotiating corners, and then speeding up, parallel with the bike at all times.

*"It was as if it was locked to us by some invisible beam. I lifted my visor and had a look, when I saw a bright silver, cigar-shaped object, between 20-40 feet in length, with a darker patch in the middle. I shook my wife's shoulder and she pulled up onto the side of the road. At the same instant I saw it stop, then hover for a few seconds before reversing back along its original route, and disappeared behind some trees and a house. I ran to obtain a closer look, but it had gone."*

John was absolutely astonished by what he and his wife had witnessed and couldn't understand why a UFO would want to escort an ordinary couple, like themselves, part of the way from Manchester to Nelson.

At 10pm (21.6.77), laboratory worker – Mr John Harnforth, and his wife from Marton, Cleveland, reported having sighted an object, which they described as:

> "...grey coloured, cone-shaped with the top cut off, making a whirring noise, with a flashing light on top. It was bigger than a helicopter and stayed in the area for about five minutes. It left an orange vapour trail behind it as it moved out of sight." (**Source: Cleveland UFO Association**)

### UFOs sighted over Birmingham by Bob Bierd

Later, the same evening, UFO researcher and custodian of a small archive of UFO material for the North Birmingham area – Bob Bierd from Castle Vale, Birmingham [who was to provide valuable help to the authors] was walking home with some other youths, just before midnight, when:

> "...a formation of UFOs swept across the sky, high up in the atmosphere. I was stunned when, about 30 minutes later, I saw another four UFOs – this time in a diamond formation crossing the sky, seemingly oblivious to the presence of man. They glowed incandescently – like a gas fire left on – and imparted a sense of grandeur."

*Bob Bierd*

Bob told us he saw a parked police car and raced over to tell the officer what was happening. By the time he directed his attention skywards, there was nothing to be seen.

## 26th June 1977 – Essex motorist sights 'ball of light'

At 11.40pm, Mrs Kilby and her family were returning from a day out, travelling along Mossford Lane – a minor road situated in Barkingside,

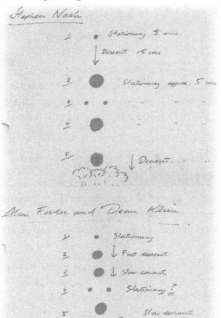

Ilford, Essex – when a large pink-red 'ball of light' was seen in the sky above the rooftops of houses on their left-hand side, before being seen to pass silently across the road and drop down behind nearby houses. They were not the only witnesses. Four teenage boys – Chris Hodges, Chris May, Steve David Nash, (then 15) and Alan David Fowler (then 15) walking along Manford Way, Chigwell, in Essex (about one-and-three-quarters of a mile away) when they sighted a 'reddish' star, low down in the sky, close to a local school and its grounds.

The boys continued to watch the object, which increased in size and descended rapidly through the sky – now pink-red in colour.

Their curiously aroused, the boys walked along Bearing Way and up to the entrance of Hainault Forest Country Park, arriving five minutes later, and were surprised to see:

> "...a flat grey 'mist', several feet thick, lying about ten feet off the ground, accompanied by a burning or scorched smell."

The 'mist' – apparently holding its form – moved away along

Bearing Way, covering the width of the road for 20-50 yards. At this point the boys decided against entering the forest, feeling rather scared of what they might find.

An intensive search was made of the locality, by members of the Essex Unidentified Flying Object Study Group – run by Dan Goring. Unfortunately, nothing of any interest was found.

(**Source: As above/***Volume 1* **– EUFOSG, September 1977, Number 5/***Ilford Recorder*)

### 28th June 1977 – Large sphere in the sky

Shopkeeper John Hopkins of Long Riding, Basildon, in Essex, was travelling on the A127 road to Southend, accompanied by his brother and wife, and passing *The Halfway House*, at 10.30pm, when:

> *"I saw a large sphere in the sky, which appeared stationary. About 30 seconds later, it vanished from sight – then it reappeared and started to move in the same direction as I was driving. About half-a-minute later, it vanished again and for good."* (**Source: Ron West**)

### 29th June 1977 – Strange object seen in the sky

Debra O'Brien of Cranborne Road, Barking, in Essex (then aged 14) had been playing tennis at her local school, situated behind Barking Bus Garage, in Barking. She happened to look upwards into the sky, at 10.25am, when she sighted:

> *"...a strange white 'thing' – like a friend egg, with silver on top of what appeared to be squares".*

She brought it to the attention of her friends, but they didn't seem to be interested. Debra and friend – Katherine Oakley (then aged 14) [daughter of a Police Officer] waved at the luminous object, which was as big as a football in the sky.

> *"It seemed to follow us as we walked along. The strange thing was that when an aircraft appeared, the object would move into a cloud. After a while the cloud broke up and that was the last time we saw it."* **Source: Essex UFO Study Group**)

### 30th June 1977 – UFOs over Nottinghamshire

At 11.30am, *"two white or silver coloured cigar-shaped objects – flying in tandem, one behind the other – estimated to be travelling at a speed of between 500-1,000 miles per hour"* were sighted by a PE teacher and fifteen children at Ashfield School, Kirkby-in-Ashfield. The objects were seen heading in an approximate direction, from north-east to south-west, over the village of Huthwaite (about two miles from the school).

According to the librarian at the school, a 'Goodyear' airship had been sighted earlier in the day by the same teacher, who was adamant that the UFOs in no way resembled airships. (**Source: BUFORA**)

### June 1977 – Cylindrical UFO over Holyhead, Anglesey, North Wales

Mr Dennis Waters wrote to us from Anglesey, with regard to what he saw while recovering from a major operation at the now demolished Stanley Hospital, in Holyhead. After returning from a visit to the bathroom, in the middle of the night, he happened to glance out of a ward window, overlooking the town and nearby coast of Holyhead, when he was staggered to see:

> *"...a cylindrical object, dull yellow in colour – more of a solid light than a solid object – crossing the skyline, very low, on what appeared to be a collision course with the town. I braced myself, expecting an explosion as it raced downwards, but nothing happened. I looked out again – nothing, just darkness. It couldn't have been an aircraft as there would have been an explosion, although I don't believe what I saw was any Alien spacecraft. I am still curious as to what it was I saw. If it was a meteorite, or space debris, why was it cylindrical in shape?"*

## CHAPTER 19 – JULY 1977

### July 1977 – Randall Jones Pugh (interview)

Randall Jones Pugh – BUFORA Investigator – who was to be inundated with UFO reports during the 1977 'wave', described to us what he saw during July, 1977.

*"I was getting ready for bed, at 10.30pm, when I happened to look through the bedroom window, noting a thick sea mist moving over St. Brides Bay. I was taken aback to see a crescent shaped object, with a pipe-like stem sticking upwards, with the outline of an upper dome, stationary above a field directly opposite the house. As soon as I pulled the curtain, allowing the bedroom light to show, whatever it was took off, upwards, at a fast rate. The pipe-like stem, or tube, appeared to be made of glass, or plastic, and flashed bright, three times – so bright I could see what looked like filaments in the tube, like those of a domestic light bulb."* (**Source: Personal interview**)

1 3 JAN 1977 media information group mig

# More Welsh UFOs

A PREDICTED increase in UFO sightings over South Wales has proved correct and there have been more sightings during the first fortnight of the New Year.

Reports from as far apart as Haverfordwest and Pontypool refer to bright lights and mysterious objects being seen in the sky. All the sightings will be fully reported to the British Unidentified Flying Objects Research Association.

The man who predicted a cycle of increased UFO activity, retired veterinary surgeon Mr. Randall Jones Pugh, of Roch, near Haverfordwest, has received five reports of sightings within the last seven to 10 days.

As well as fresh sightings he has also heard from people who spotted mysterious objects in the sky as far back as 1948.

"It shows that people are now beginning to realise that they won't be ridiculed or laughed at by revealing what they have seen," he said.

Mr. Jones Pugh, the regional co-ordinator in South Wales for BUFORA, has been told of such sightings as a bright light apparently landing in a field near Haverfordwest, of cigar-shaped objects near Burry Port and of a machine seen in the air over Milford Haven harbour.

He has also had letters claiming mysterious sightings over a small village near Haverfordwest and over Pontypool.

There was a substantial increase in sightings during 1976 and he then predicted that this trend would continue.

"For some reason there has been a spate of activity and it could well carry on," he said.

# NOW IT'S ALL QUIET IN THE BRO.

# UFO spotter's guide to the vanishing spacemen

*Weston Telegraph 7/7/1977*

The great Pembrokeshire flying saucer scare is over, says the man who predicted it, Ufologist Randall Pugh.

**A SPECIAL REPORT**

**By Hugh Turnbull**

With no major sightings reported in the past few weeks, he now believes that we've seen the last of the faceless spacemen and their assorted craft.

"It's certainly waning appreciably," said Mr. Pugh, the West Wales co-ordinator for the British UFO Research Association, who has investigated more than 40 sightings in Pembrokeshire this year.

"We'll still get the occasional report, but I think it's more or less at an end now."

The sightings started coming thick and fast after the *Telegraph* carried Mr. Pugh's prediction of a UFO invasion in December.

People all over the county reported strange lights and objects in the sky, but nobody took them too seriously.

Then - in February - came a sighting that was harder to ignore. Fifteen children saw a 50-foot spacecraft which had landed within yards of Broad Haven Primary School.

Some of the children claimed to have seen a silver-suited spaceman - and even their sceptical headmaster, Ralph Llewhellin, was convinced it wasn't a hoax.

The story made national news, film crews dashed to Broad Haven and the children travelled to Leeds to make a film for Yorkshire Television. Mr. Llewhellin even has a cutting from a New Zealand paper which reported the sighting.

A couple of weeks later came confirmation of the children's claims from three women who had made two separate sightings at the same spot.

Soon, more spacemen were popping up all over the place. One terrified 17-year-old Stephen Taylor at Penycwm, another scared 11-year-old

Mr. Randall Pugh: He has investigated 40 sightings this year.

Mark Marston while he was out looking for birds' nests near Herbrandston.

Farmer's wife Pauline Coombs - whose car had earlier been chased by a "flying football" - came face-to-something with a faceless invader at the window of her isolated farmhouse near Little Haven.

Another faceless spaceman hung suspended in mid-air outside a Milford pensioner's home, but hotelier Mrs. Rosa Granville outdid all the other witnesses. She saw two of the silver-suited visitors apparently measuring something outside her Little Haven hotel.

Meanwhile, reports of UFOs and mysterious nocturnal lights continued unabated all over West Wales.

They came in all shapes and sizes, from tiny craft a few feet across to full-blown spaceships the size of a Jumbo jet.

Another farmer's wife, Mrs. Josephine Hewison, saw a 50-foot flying saucer parked right next to her greenhouse at Little Haven. Sightings in the area were now so common that the national papers christened it the "Broad Haven Triangle."

There was talk of Pembrokeshire becoming another Warminster, where UFO activity has been going on for years. But then - as suddenly as it began - the saucer invasion stopped.

Mr. Pugh, a retired vet who has been working virtually full-time to keep up with the flood of reports, said the Pembrokeshire scare had

followed the classic pattern seen in many parts of the world.

He is grateful that the unearthly visitors have decided to give him a rest after three months of intense activity in the West Wales skies.

"It will give me time to get my second wind and let me get on with the book I'm writing," he said.

Unlike the people who have contributed various outlandish theories to the

*Telegraph*, Mr. Pugh has no ready explanation for the UFO phenomenon.

And none of the sightings he has investigated this year has provided him with any new clues.

"Either they're happy with what they've seen here, or they've written us off," he said. "I honestly don't know."

Since one theory is as good as another, perhaps the spacemen were on holiday from Warminster and have gone back now that the tourists have left them with nowhere to park their saucers.

Whatever the truth behind the UFO mystery, one thing is certain. A good many Pembrokeshire people who scoffed at flying saucers a few months ago are now totally convinced that they really do exist.

28 FEB 1977

## Randall's the man behind UFOria ... .

RETIRED VET Mr. Randall Jones Pugh is building up the sort of dossier that will make it difficult for people not to believe in flying saucers.

Almost every mail has brought fresh reports of UFO sightings to his house at Roch, near Haverfordwest, where he spends a lot of his time investigating sightings.

His telephone rings constantly with people anxious to talk about mysterious sightings.

Since the recent spate of Uforia — sparked off by a strange sighting at Broad Haven, Dyfed, three weeks ago — Mr. Pugh has been inundated with letters and telephone calls.

As the co-ordinator for South Wales of the British Unidentified Flying Objects Research Association, he has the job of investigating and cataloguing sightings.

"Since the Broad Haven incident there has been a spate of reports. They are coming in fast and furious and most are unsolicited," he said.

One of the latest adds further mystery to what schoolboys claimed to have seen in a field near their school at Broad Haven. They talked of a large silver object with men dressed in silver.

Now three women, who want to remain anonymous, have seen something similar near the same spot.

Mr. Pugh said, "When they went to investigate there was nothing there, not even marks. They were mystified. I have been there since and there's absolutely no way that a lorry could have got there without leaving prints. The mystery deepens."

● Mr. Randall Jones Pugh

## 3rd July 1977 – Strange Phenomena Northumberland

At 2.15am, a 'grey half-moon shaped object, with a rectangular base', was sighted over Hamstead, Birmingham, heading towards the north-east.

At 3pm, members of the Hall family from Apperley Dene, situated between Hexham and Newcastle-upon-Tyne (south of the *River Tyne*, Northumberland) were at their home address when Mr John Hall told his wife and son – Barry, that he had seen a *"black oval shaped object"* a few feet in diameter, above low trees at the bottom of their property. The family then watched what appeared to be a mass of material swirling around inside a 'vortex', which rose slowly in the air to about the height of the pine trees (40-50 feet in the air). Barry walked towards the phenomena; as he did so it began to move slowly towards him and the house. Strangely, none of the 'material' was falling to the ground as one would have expected if it had been grass or wheat, but seemed to be dissolving and continuous in motion as it floated through the air, allowing Barry the opportunity to obtain a closer look.

> *"I could see a black hairline substance within – unlike anything I had ever seen before – completely different from grass or straw. It covered an area of about twenty square feet and was like a swarm of insects, although this was not the explanation. As it moved away it seemed to be thinning out, but none of the 'material' was falling to the ground."*

Jenny Randles, who conducted an investigation into the matter, ascertained that a gust of wind of very strong proportions was felt during the sighting by the family. This unusual gust of wind was also experienced by the next door neighbour, although they didn't see anything unusual at the time. This was a highly usual incident and something we had never come across before. We, like Jenny, wondered if it could have been an example of 'Angel Hair'.

**(Source: Jenny Randles/Flying Saucer Review, Volume 25, No. 2, 1978 – 'Cloudlike object with 'Angel Hair' effect)**

**4th July 1977 – *Daily Mirror* – 'My Hat … here's a saucer!'**

DAILY MIRROR, Monday, July 4, 1977

# My hat .. here's a saucer!

YOUNG Martin Tominey wants the world to know that flying saucers really DO exist.

And if you won't take his word for it, he has pictures to persuade you!

Armed with his "evidence," 21-year-old Martin said last night: "I have never believed in Space craft. But what else could it have been?"

Martin's conversion came on the road to the Wicked Lady pub at Wheathampstead, Herts. With Martin in his Mini car was his pal Steve Bletch, 25.

Steve said: "The thing was like a great Mexican hat—but it didn't seem to take any firm shape."

Martin, of Sandridge Road, St. Albans, grabbed his brother's Polaroid camera from the back of the car.

Both lads work at Polaroid's St. Albans factory. But they insist the photos are genuine.

Mirror cameraman Alisdair Macdonald has his doubts, though. He said: "I reckon it could be a practical joke.

"Yet again the 'flying saucers' are fuzzy images — yet everything else is in focus."

MYSTERY: Martin's own picture.

BELIEVERS: Martin, left, and Steve.

### 5th/6th/7th July 1977 – UFO over Cheshire

At 10.20pm, Mrs Helen Simpson – in charge of a children's home, at Marple, Cheshire – was approached by some of the children, who told of having sighted a UFO hovering just above the tree line near to a lake and electricity power lines.

Her curiously aroused, she made her way to an upstairs window with some of the children, and looked out seeing:

> *"...a yellowy object, with sides that shimmered or trembled, seeming to alter shape on a number of occasions from 'cigar' to something resembling the edge of a saucer. It was hovering over the lake and had a number of beams of light, slanting outwards, illuminating the area beneath it."*

At 10 40pm, Mr Alfred Simpson arrived at the home. After being told what was going on, he and his younger brother then kept observations on the stationary UFO, which was *"at least three times as bright as the brightest star in the sky"* for a further twenty minutes. Mr Simpson managed to obtain some binoculars and, through these, saw:

> *"...an elongated silver shape, with what seemed to be lumps on its side".*

The object then slowly moved across to the south-east and stopped in a clearing behind the trees. It then faded from orange to red and eventually disappeared from view.

At 12.10am on 6th July 1977, Mrs Simpson telephoned Jenny Randles, a member of 'UFOIN' (then living at Warrington, some 14 miles away), who had just returned home, and informed her of what had taken place. Jenny advised them to take a long duration exposure of the UFO if it returned, and then made her way to a high vantage position, but saw nothing untoward.

At 12.25am, the UFO was reported to have returned but, as it was only visible for a few seconds, no photos were taken. Ironically, Jenny was to discover that a UFO had been seen in Irlam on the same evening, by two teenage boys, who claimed they were looking south-eastwards, in the direction of Marple, when they saw:

> *"...a dark cigar-shaped object, showing a beam of light from one end, sweeping backwards and forwards in a slow arc, hovering over the Manchester Ship Canal, before moving away"* – apparently following the course of the canal, southwards.

### As seen over Meadow School on the 7th of July 1977

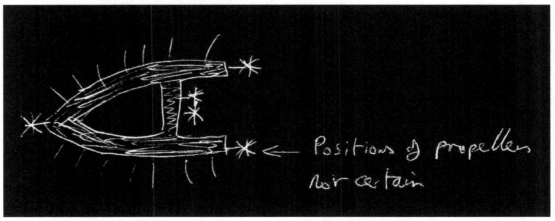

(Source: *Flying Saucer Review*, Volume 23, No. 4, 1977, Jenny Randles – 'Strange object near children's home)

At 4.33am, Constable Trueman and his colleague – PC Kirkbright, sighted a UFO crossing the sky over Bradley, near Skipton, North Yorkshire.

(**Source:** *North-East Evening Gazette,* **6.7.1977 – 'Police report UFO sighting'**)

At 5am, Thomas Allen – a retired painter, living in Bournemouth – was getting ready to go to work, when he happened to glance through the window and see:

> *"...a white cigar shaped object, moving over the sky. I shouted my wife and picked up a camera, which was nearby, and took a photo.*
>
> *When later processed, it showed what looked like a light bulb in shape, rather than a 'cigar'. I sent the photo off to a UFO organisation, but never heard anymore. I've no idea what happened to the photograph, although the memory of what I saw will never leave me."*

(**Source: Leslie Harris/John Ledner/Ron Sergeant, DIGAP/Arthur Tomlinson, MUFORA & Jenny Randles/** *Flying Saucer Review publication/***Personal interviews**)

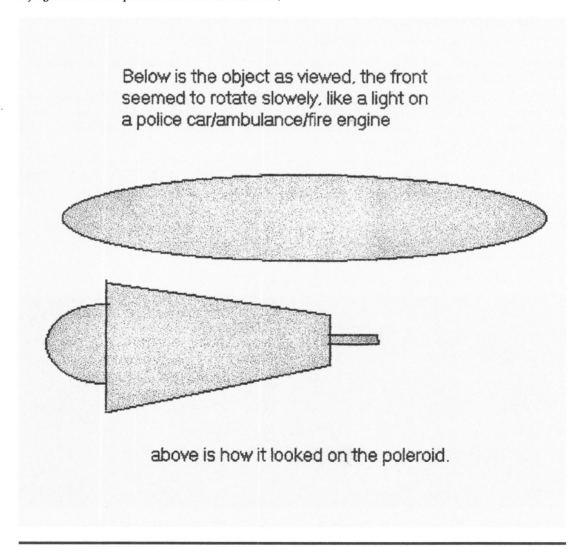

Below is the object as viewed, the front seemed to rotate slowly, like a light on a police car/ambulance/fire engine

above is how it looked on the poleroid.

9th November 2000

Dear John,

Since your phone call and the long lapse of time, I have forgot or put it in the back of my mind. I did see something in a fread paper quite recently, and wandered if it was you, the ad was looking for Mr Harriss? the local UFO bloke in the 70s from Bournemouth.
I did cut this out but I have mislaid it, was it you?

What I am about to write is the story, it is still very vivid in my mind!
I will start by telling you that it was possible to trespass on the local rubbish dump and find resalable items. Scrap metals were what most of us were after, but now and again one could find items of greater value, I have personally found many antiques discarded by a stupid public (thank God) and are now in circulation rather than being buried in landfill sights. We were ripped off by dealers but that is another story.

I would get up early in the morning and head for this sight, and as the summer was light enough it made sense to get there at first light or just after, and leave before the workers arrived.
The morning in question 7th July 1977 was a morning that would see me having a wash at the kitchen sink (to wake myself up) and looking out of the window. It was 4am and the sun was shining, I did notice that there was a small cloud in the sky, this was the only one evident, and it was from behind this cloud that the object appeared. Imagine the most beautiful blue sky, feeling great in yourself, and seeing a mystery object. This also giving me time to find the Polaroid and photograph this object, and still give me time to wake the wife so she can witness same. The postman on his way to work did not see this object, what he saw was my wife's breasts peering out the front bedroom window facing the main road, I did point toward the object and told him to look but he put his head down and headed away, obviously embarrassed. The object then just switched off.

I took the photo to the Echo office that same morning and left it with them, I returned that afternoon and was told it would not magnify so it was no good to them (I can still feel them laughing at me) but somewhere along the line I was contacted by Mr Harriss? he kept the photo for a long time, I don't think it impressed him. a magnifying glass was essential to view it and imagination aside it was there for all to see as illustrated. Eventually I sent the photo to the UFO Bureau Belsize Square, in writing to them many times I have had no acknowledgement.

This did happen and I do not give a monkeys whether I am believed or not, I want no reward, so take it as read.

A funny spin off happened when I watched an episode of Invaders starring Roy Thiness, it was mentioned by an invader in the control room, that a ship would be on its way to Bournemouth on the 7th July (the mind boggles weird or what)?

*Jonny*

### 7th July 1977 – Spinning cloud obver Cumbria

At 7.20pm, what looked like a large cloud spinning in an anticlockwise direction was seen in the sky over Stainton, Cumbria, by a local resident, who dashed in to get a camera and was lucky enough to take a photo. Unfortunately, it was the last frame on the film. The object was then seen to spin slightly faster, its diameter grew smaller, and it disappeared in a flash of light twenty seconds later.

(**Source: Mr R. Hall, BUFORA**)

### 9th July 1977– UFO over junction of A128 and A13 Middlesex

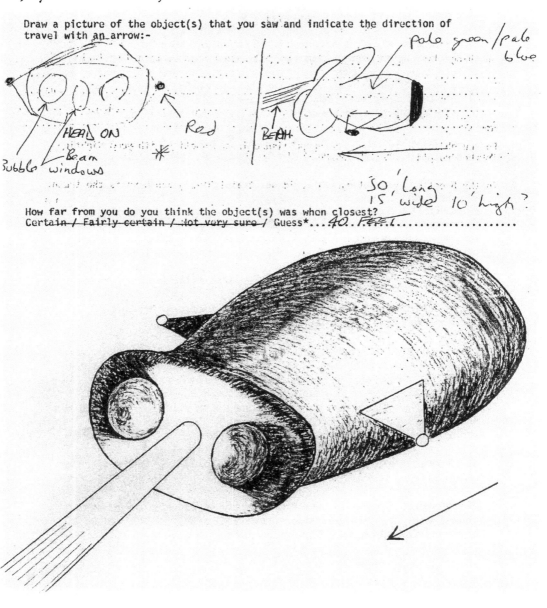

## 14th July 1977 – Mysterious deaths of ponies, Devon …UFOs blamed!

The discovery of fifteen mutilated ponies, found in a remote Dartmoor valley, and the manner of their death, sparked off a wave of publicity, fuelling speculation by one Devon based UFO Group, who suggested they had been crushed in the anti-gravitation field of a 'flying saucer', as it took off! – A conclusion brought about after examination of the bodies revealed the corpses had decomposed to virtual skeletons, within a time period of 48 hours. Additionally, no footprints or tyre marks were found. One of the first people to come across the bodies was Alan Hicks, from the Taunton area.

> *"I was out, walking, and came across a clump of four bullocks and eleven ponies, strewn about on the ground, completely unmarked but stone dead, with no obvious sign as to how their deaths had occurred. I telephoned the RSPCA and thought they would be removed, but on a visit to the area, a week later, was astounded to discover the bodies were still there – now badly decomposed, with much damage done by predatory animals. I believe they were struck by lightning, which would explain the lack of injuries to their bodies."*

DAILY MIRROR, Friday, July 15, 1977     PAGE 13

# UFO HUNT IN PONY DEATH HORROR

By BARRY WIGMORE

A BIZARRE probe began yesterday into the mystery deaths of fifteen Dartmoor ponies.

A four-man investigation team scoured the moor for signs of . . . invaders from outer space.

For the hunters — armed with geiger counter, metal detectors and face masks to protect themselves from alien forces—believe the animals were killed by a flying saucer.

The deaths have certainly baffled animal experts.

The ponies' mutilated carcases were found close together in a little valley on the heart of the moor, miles f r o m the nearest road.

M a n y had crushed bones and cracked ribs. One had a broken neck.

And their bodies decomposed to skeletons within 48 hours — far faster than normal.

Yesterday's hunt was launched by the Devon Unidentified Flying Objects Centre, which believes the deaths are linked to similar strange incidents in America.

## Gravity

And though they found nothing, they're sticking to their theory.

Centre leader J o h n Wyse, an Army bandsman, said: "I think the ponies were crushed by the anti-gravity field of a flying saucer as it took off."

### DID PONIES DIE IN STAMPEDE?

A NEW theory was put forward yesterday about the mystery deaths of 15 wild ponies on Dartmoor.

The riddle began after their bodies were found on marshy grassland in a remote valley. All apparently died at the same time and many had shattered bones.

Bizarre suggestions about the cause have been circulating in the West Country including one that a flying saucer was responsible.

But now, after carrying out post mortem examinations on the ponies, Mrs Ruth Murray, president of the Animal Defence Society, believes they were probably stampeded down a hill by vehicles.

Mrs. Murray, who breeds ponies, said at her Devon home: "I have carried out a detailed examination of the area.

"Vehicles could easily have reached the plateau where the ponies would have been grazing before they were killed.

"I even found a skidmark on the ground which I believed was connected with the incident.

"I think the most likely explanation is that a group of people were fooling around out there and playing cowboys with the ponies.

"Some of the injuries could have been caused by a vehicle such as a Land-Rover crashing into the sides of the ponies."

*daily express sept? 77*

We wrote to Chief Inspector A. Booth, of the RSPCA, after discovering this was a case he had been involved in, and received a letter back, in 2001.

*"Dear Mr Hanson,*

*I am in receipt of your letter, dated the 22/2/01, and the request that you have made; I remember the incident well. I was new to the area, at the time, having been down on Dartmoor for 11 months. I think, now, I am much wiser and more aware of what some of the persons around the moor are capable of. In this particular incident there had been a falling out between farmers, who had grazing rights on the moor. Long after the event, and certainly not within the six months time scale, I found out that one farmer had taken another farmer's ponies from the Low Moor to the High Moor, out of spite, and released them into the area, which they did not know, and certainly not able to stand the rigors of the weather conditions.*

*All forms of identity were removed and, eventually, they succumbed to the weather. At the time, all sorts of rumours were being put forward – that of UFOs. Obviously, once the matter had died down and no factual evidence found of the UFOs, the matter was forgotten – until now."*

THE DEVON AND CORNWALL
CONSTABULARY MUSEUM

POLICE HEADQUARTERS
MIDDLEMOOR EXETER EX2 7HQ

Tel: 01392 203025
Fax: 01392 426496

March 2, 2001

John Hanson
P.O. Box 6371
Birmingham
B48 7RW

Dear Mr Hanson

Thank you for your letter with regard to the death of ponies on Dartmoor. I am sorry that I am unable to help as no record of this incident remains in our files. I wish you luck with your enterprise.

Sincerely,

*Trevor Finbow*

Sgt 2577 T. A .FINBOW
Temporary Curator

## SEARCHERS SEEK 'FLYING SAUCER LINK'

DAILY MAIL 15 JULY 1977.

# Dartmoor death riddle of 15 mangled ponies

**By CHRISTOPHER WHITE**

MEN in face masks, using metal detectors and a geiger counter, yesterday scoured a remote Dartmoor valley in a bid to solve a m a c a b r e mystery.

Their search centred on marshy grassland where 15 wild ponies were found dead, their bodies mangled and torn.

All appeared to have died at about the same time, and many of the bones had been inexplicably shattered.

### Skeletons

To add to the riddle, their bodies decomposed to virtual skeletons within only 48 hours.

Animal experts confess they are baffled by the deaths at Cherry Brook Valley, near Postbridge.

Yesterday's search was carried out by members of the Devon Unidentified Flying Objects centre, at Torquay, who are trying to prove a link with outer space.

They believe that flying saucers may have flown low over the area and created a vortex which hurled the ponies to their deaths.

Mr John Wyse, head of the four-man team, said : 'If a spacecraft has been in the vicinity, there may still be detectable evidence.

'We wanted to see if there was any sign that the ponies had been shot, but we have found nothing. This incident bears an uncanny resemblance to similar events reported in America.

'There have been strange cases of animals found dead with bones smashed, or their bodies drained of blood.'

The ponies were found by pet shop owner Mr Alan Hicks, of Tavistock, while he was walking in the wild beauty spot with his wife and two children.

He said : "They were all grouped together within a hundred yard section of the valley. There are no cliffs or anything at that spot where the animals could have fallen.'

The RSPCA investigated the deaths within 48 hours but reported that the speed of decomposition meant it was impossible to determine the cause of death.

'Decomposition was unusually fast —that in itself is a mystery,' said the Society's Chief Inspector Tony Booth.

### Violent

The Dartmoor Livestock Protection Society and the Animal Defence Society made a joint investigation.

Secretary Mrs Joanna Vinson said : 'We have spent many hours dissecting and examining what was left of the carcases. The ponies had broken bones and torn arteries.

'Whatever happened was fairly violent. We are keeping an open mind. I am fascinated by the UFO theory. There is no reason to reject t h a t possibility, since there is no other rational explanation.'

## 17th July 1977 – Essex police officer sights UFO

Chelmsford police dog handler – Police Constable Peter Frost (35), of the Essex Constabulary, based at Sandon dog training school, was on duty at 2.50am, when he saw:

> "...a cigar-shaped object hanging vertically in the sky, about 30 degrees off the horizon, over the village of Arkesden, near Saffron Waldon, Essex".

The officer watched it for fifteen minutes, during which time it commenced a series of manoeuvres across the early morning sky – unlike anything he had ever seen before – and then reported the incident, by radio, to his police controller, at Chelmsford Police HQ, who then contacted Stansted Airport Traffic Control; they in turn confirmed that no aircraft were plotted over the locality.

**Peter:**

> "I've always had an open mind about 'Flying Saucers', but I m not a great believer. I expect my mates will really jibe me about this story."

A similar – if not the same – UFO was sighted over Great Yeldham.

(**Source:** *Newsman Herald*, **19.7.1977 – UFO over Essex**)

### PC spots a flying cigar

A POLICE dog-handler put in a special report to his station yesterday—he said he had seen a UFO.

PC Peter Frost, 35, stationed at the Essex police head-quarters in Chelmsford, spotted a white cigar-shaped object in the sky hovering over the village of Arkesden, near Saffron Walden.

'It stayed for about 25 minutes in all,' he said last night. 'It must have been about 13,000 feet high and was very big.

'I m pretty sure it was a UFO'

A similar object was spotted in the sky at about the same time by a woman in a village 20 miles from Arkesden.

She also reported it to Essex police, who notified the Ministry of Defence and UFO experts.

EAST LONDON · WALTHAMSTOW GUARDIAN, JULY 22, 1977

# Strange object spotted in the sky at night

A WEIRD and wonderful flying machine is scudding about the skies—and there have been independent sightings in Waltham Forest and Redbridge.

The latest person to spot the Unidentified Flying Object is a woman in Leyton, and luckily her 27-year-old son was on hand to confirm the sighting.

What Mrs Olive Fitzgerald and her son Alan saw in the early hours of Sunday morning bears a remarkable resemblance to "something" seen by three South Woodford school girls just a week before.

It was only when Mrs Fitzgerald of St Joseph's Court, Leyton, spoke to her daughter-in-law—who lives in the circulation area of the Redbridge Guardian—that she realised that she was not the only one to spot a UFO.

She explained: " It definitely wasn't a star. I was waiting up for my son and it was about 3.30. I just looked out of the window and saw what looked like three billiard balls grouped on a table.

" They seemed to be making a pyramid. At first I thought it was my eyes but then I realised that it wasn't—it was very very bright."

What Mrs Fitzgerald didn't know then is that the three schoolgirls had seen something like " a capital A in shape "—in other words a pyramid.

Mrs Fitzgerald went on: " I called to one of my sons and he said that this must be one of those UFOs."

To make matters more intriguing, Mrs Fitzgerald's bedroom faces roughly towards Whipps Cross and beyond that the South Woodford area where the UFO was first seen.

She went on: " It wasn't frightening—it was rather fascinating. I wasn't looking for it."

Said Mr Alan Fitzgerald: " First of all I thought it must be a big star but the more I looked at it I realised that it was a triangle.

" I'm not really that much of a believer in this sort of thing."

Was this the same object seen at 3.30am, by Olive Fitzgerald?

### 18th July 1977 – UFO over Essex

At 4am, local resident Mrs B. Waller of Great Yeldham, let the dog outside. As she did so, she saw a bright object stationary in the sky, showing a circular cross section. Protruding from the centre of each side was a 'wing' – quite thin, with slight dihedral; these appeared to be wider than an aircraft's wings. Pointed towards the ground were two 'legs' – also slightly angled outwards. The whole object was silvery, shiny, and self-luminous.

*"It remained stationary for about eight minutes, at an angle of 20-30 degrees, before being lost from view behind clouds. It was then seen to reappear towards the south-east, still face-on, before disappearing behind cloud. Finally it was seen briefly in a patch of clear sky, towards the north-east."*

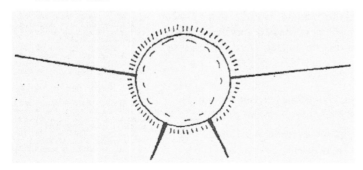

(Authors: The illustration reminds us of the object seen by Jessie Cleghorn, not forgetting the famous Bob Taylor case, in Scotland, when an object was seen to land.)

It was also claimed that earlier in the week, at Southend, the electrical equipment in a police car was disabled by a UFO – although we were unable to confirm this account, as published in the following newspaper.

**(Sources: *Newsman Herald*, 19.7.1977 – Mystery UFO over Essex/Andrew Collins, BUFORA – 'Legs and wings over Great Yeldham')**

At 3pm, a shiny, gunmetal grey coloured object, showing a red band around the top, was seen moving across the clear blue sky over the Woodcock Road Caravan Park, Warminster, by a number of people, including Jonathon Marsden from Stone, in Staffordshire.

> *"It seemed to be rotating slowly, clockwise, and wobbling slightly when viewed through binoculars. However, to the naked eye it looked like a globe, with one side glowing red occasionally; the other a permanent silver colour."*

As darkness closed-in on Broom Square, Milton, Portsmouth, on the same day (18.7.1977), Mrs Hilda Kebble (then aged 76), noticed what she took to be an aircraft on fire in the sky. She alerted neighbour, Rose Prior. The two women then stood watching, as:

> *"...a glowing orange object moved directly above us, now visible as a half 'disc', with the flat edge downwards, showing what appeared to be portholes, or shadowy circles on the body of the object, with a distinctive cross in each circle."*

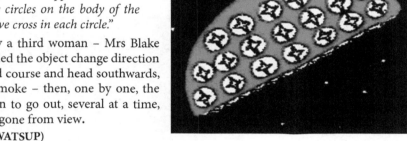

They were then joined by a third woman – Mrs Blake (then aged 75), who watched the object change direction from its original westward course and head southwards, emitting a trail of grey smoke – then, one by one, the *'lights'* on the object began to go out, several at a time, until, seconds later, it had gone from view.

**(Source: Nicholas Maloret, WATSUP)**

## 20th July 1977 – Disc-shaped UFO seen, Wiltshire

A large pearly-white coloured disc-shaped flying object, about one and a half times the size of a Jumbo Jet, looking like 'a soup plate in appearance', was seen over Whitley, near Melksham, Wiltshire, at 4.15pm, followed by the 'scream' of jet engines as six RAF Jets appeared – which were then seen to head along the same course taken by the UFO. **(Source: letter to Peter Tate)**

## 23rd July 1977 – Hampshire couple disturbed by two UFOs

Mr Andrew Mills – a former RAF Maintenance fitter – and his wife, Jean, from Fair Oak, Eastleigh, Hampshire, were awoken by the sound of agitated farmyard animals and domestic dogs, 'making a terrible noise', as early morning light flooded the sky.

The couple rushed to the window and saw two spherical 'star-like objects', which grew brighter – as if moving closer – before they moved away and out of sight. **(Source: *Southampton Echo*, 23.7.1977)**

## 25th July 1977 – UFOs over Somerset

At 10.30pm, an object was seen moving at speed across the sky over Litton, near Radstock, in Somerset, by a family on their way home. They stopped the car and, being fortunate to have a pair of high powered binoculars on board, focused them on the object.

*"It was glowing brilliantly and was 'disc-like' in shape, travelling at a steady speed, at a height I estimated to be 1,500-2,000 feet.*

*To my amazement, another of these objects came into view. Both of them seemed to be hovering above us. While we were watching, a car pulled up; two young girls got out and, after seeing the objects, one of them dashed into the nearby* King's Arms *Public House to ask the landlord to telephone the police. In the meantime, the objects disappeared at tremendous speed in different directions – one towards Bath, the other towards Midsomer Norton."*

The next day the witnesses were interviewed by the police, details of the sighting being taken down on a MOD report.

The MOD later contacted the people involved and advised them that they could give no indication as to what was seen that night, but would record the details. (**Source: UFO-INFO Exchange Library**)

## 26th July 1977 – RAF chase UFO over Warminster

This sighting was too important not to include. At 9.42pm, about a dozen 'sky watchers', including Chris Hardwick, Soteris Georgio, Anne Reynolds and Martin Keatman, were stood on Cradle Hill (near the 'white gate'), Warminster, when they sighted the bright flashing navigation lights of a RAF jet fighter crossing the sky, at full speed, in front of which was seen a solitary point of red light .

*"At this stage another jet fighter arrived, going 'flat out', both jets converging on the 'red light'. All three disappeared into a cloud, followed by the jets reappearing on the other side. There was no sign of the 'red light' UFO".* (**Source: Peter Tate**)

## July 1977 – Schoolchildren sight UFO over Hartlepool

Carmel Guy emailed us, in 2006, about an incident which took place in July 1977, when a pupil at St. Bega's Primary School, Hartlepool, at the end of term.

> *"There were a few children filing out of school, at 3.30pm, when someone pointed upwards into the sky. I looked and saw a round saucer-shaped object, flying towards the docks – then it seemed to just disappear. There was a girl, called Sharon Cooper (now Porter). I can't say if she saw it, but I remember her being there at the time."*

## July 1977 – 'Flying Saucer' over Northumbria

Towards the end of July, Ernest Longstaff – a builder by trade, living in the small coastal town of Newbiggin-upon-Sea (16 miles from Newcastle-upon-Tyne) – was out walking his dog along Lyne Sands (a mile to the north of the town), at 9pm, as the sun began to set. As he turned around, wondering where the dog had gone, he was literally 'stopped in his tracks' by the awe inspiring sight of:

> *"...a grey, saucer-shaped, object 'like two plates, stuck together', with a slight dome on top. Around the middle was a band of square portholes revolving around the rim, from left to right, emitting red smokeless flames. Curiously, the 'portholes' didn't revolve around the object but appeared to pass into the 'saucer' at the right-hand edge. I estimated it was 25 feet wide and 15 feet high, about a hundred yards away, 60-70 feet above the shore."*

Mr Longstaff found himself trembling with fear, rooted to the spot (as was the dog) and sat there, motionless, as the 'saucer' began to move and slowly approached their position, descending at about 10 miles per hour, until just off the ground, some 30 yards away.

It remained stationary for a few seconds, before moving slowly to the right and back to the shore and descending even lower, skimming over the tops of sand dunes, creating an impression it was going to land – at which point, Mr Longstaff decided

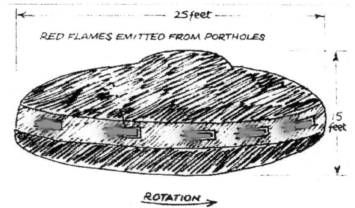

*The object, based on Mr Longstaff's sketch*

to make his way home. Mr Longstaff's wife confirmed her husband had arrived in a very agitated state and kept looking out of the window. He also had great difficulty in sleeping that night.

**(Source: Alan & Trisha Price, UFOIN [UFO Investigators Network]/Jenny Randles)**

## 30th July 1977 – UFOs over RAF Boulmer

One is bound to wonder if there was a connection between what Mr Longstaff saw and a sighting over the North Sea, by Military personnel, during the early hours of the 30th July 1977, involving RAF Flt. Lt. A.M. Wood and two NCO's – Corporal Torrington and Sgt. Graham from RAF Boulmer, in Northumberland, who saw:

> *"...two bright objects, hanging over the sea. The closest object was luminous, round, and four to five times larger than a 'Whirlwind' helicopter, estimated to be three miles out to sea, at a height of about 5,000 feet. The objects separated – one went west of the other. As it manoeuvred, it changed shape to become body-shaped with projection-like arms and legs."*

The men, who were positioned at the picket post at the RAF Station, were able to observe the strange objects for one hour and 40 minutes. At the same time, a radar station detected the objects in exactly the same position as the men had observed them, between 30 to 35 degrees, before they disappeared from the screen. The report describes Flt. Lt. Wood as 'reliable and sober'. It adds:

> *'Two contacts were noted on radar – both T84 and T85, at RAF Boulmer. They were also seen on the Staxton Wold radar picture, which is relayed to West Drayton. On seeing the objects on radar, the duty controller checked with the SRO at RAF West Drayton as to whether he could see the objects on radar supplied from RAF Staxton Wold.'* (**Source: Declassified MOD file, January 2005**)

## July 1977 – 'Flying Saucer' landing near Bradford

Another incident involving a landed UFO took place during July 1977, adjacent to Cliff Hollins Lane, East Brierley, Bradford, in Yorkshire, which was brought to the attention of Nigel Mortimer, of the West Yorkshire UFO group.

It involved a local woman – Mrs Frater – who was walking thorough a field beside Copley Spring Wood, at 7pm, one evening in July 1977, taking a short cut to visit her stabled horse on what was described as a beautiful evening and bright after a hot day.

While casually glancing across to the north, she was stunned and *"frozen to the spot with fear"* at the sight of a strange object, *"which should not have been there"*, hovering silently about a foot off the ground.

> *"It was circular in shape, about 30 feet in diameter, and appeared to be made out of dark grey gunmetal. There was a dome on top and a row of portholes lined the junction between the two places. From the underneath came a short burst of red flame, directed downwards.*

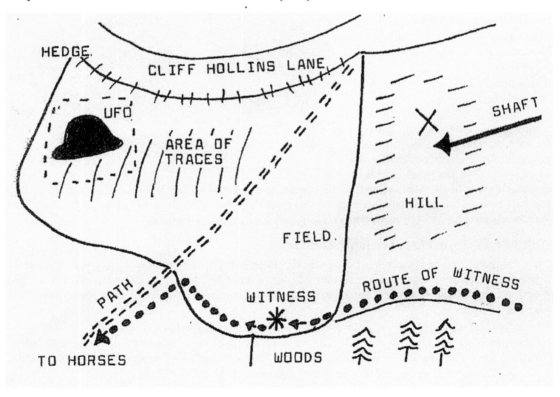

*After about five seconds of stable motion, the craft wobbled slightly and then began a swift clockwise motion – then in a very brief instant of time, it rose upwards and accelerated dramatically into the sky until out of sight."*

Nigel visited the locality and noticed that a small hummock (Hunsworth Hill) was very close to the 'landing spot' and that it contained an old pit shaft. At a spot about a hundred feet away from the postulated location of the object was found a bare patch of land. In this were found two small holes about an inch in diameter, separated by two feet, which were thought had been postholes used previously in tethering horses. However, enquiries with the farmer ruled this out.

In 1983, following another visit to the location by Walter Reid, a strange circle of grass measuring 16.666 feet in diameter, with a band of grass about a foot wide forming the outer edge which was much greener was discovered. Examination revealed that it appeared about six inches of grass had been removed, leaving the ground darker in appearance. Whether there was any connection with the 'circle' of grass and the UFO landing that occurred six years previously is something we are unable to comment on, although we would not be surprised if there was.

**(Source: Jenny Randles/Nigel Mortimer/BUFORA/West Yorkshire Research Group)**

# CHAPTER 20 – AUGUST 1977

### 1st August 1977

An illuminated oblong object was seen floating silently across the sky, by at least nine people, over Rodney Stoke, Cheddar.

SOUTH WALES EVENING POST
SWANSEA, GLAMORGANSHIRE
ISSUE DATED 2 AUG 1977

## Another UFO is sighted

WAS it a bird? No. Was it a plane? No. It was another in the epidemic of West Wales unidentified flying object sightings.

This one — a large, silver football - like object — was spotted hovering above Betws Mountain, near Ammanford yesterday by two people on their way to work at the Morriston DVLC. Mrs. Janet Box, of Maes Grenig, Glanamman, spotted

It first: "We were coming across the mountain at about twenty to eight when I caught sight of something silver flashing in the sun.

"It hovered like a helicopter in one place, and was a brilliant silver.

"Further on, after the road had changed direction, I saw it again—it must have travelled at a terrific speed to have got there. It looked flat but rounded."

Mrs. Box pointed it out to the driver, Mr. David

Gravette.

"It seemed cylindrical," said Mr. Gravette, of Llwyn Celyn, Salem, Llandeilo. "It wasn't a plane, and it definitely wasn't a bird.

"This thing was virtually stationary, but it had disappeared by the time we had got up the hill. It was peculiar, like a big silver football."

One possible explanation is that the object was a meteorological balloon recording upper-air conditions. These balloons carry instru-

ments which descend by parachute when the balloon bursts—which could explain the rapid way it disappeared."

But local weatherman Mr. John Powell, of Gower, said he knew of no balloons in the area yesterday.

And the Flight Lieutenant duty officer with RAF Brawdy's operations wing yesterday said: "It sounds as if it was too low to be a weather balloon. I can't offer any explanation."

### 1st August 1977 – Schoolboys encounter UFO

Bishopston schoolboys – Andrew Evason and Michael Jenkins – were spending the last day of the summer holidays quietly picking blackberries, when suddenly from behind a hedge soared:

*"...something from outer space. It was definitely a UFO. We were so frightened we dropped everything and ran home like mad", said Andrew, (then aged 12), of The Rectory, Bishopston, and Michael, (then also aged 12), of Ship Cottage, Pwlldu Bay.*

The boys – pupils at Bishopston Comprehensive School – described the 'craft' as being about the size of a bus and whitish-silver in colour with a dome on the top. It was so clear in their minds that they drew a rough sketch of the 'craft' to show disbelievers. There was no noise or disturbance. It just rose up from behind the hedge and soared off into the sky, said the boys – still excited by their sighting.

> *"We were picking blackberries along a hedge in a field, when we both looked up and saw the UFO a little further down. We only saw it for a few seconds, because we were frightened. We are convinced we saw it and that it was a UFO",* they added. *The boys returned to the field with Andrew's father – Reverend Evason.*

> *"I went down to the field with them and there was some kind of mark on the grass. It was as if the grass was a yellowish colour."* (**Source:** *South Wales Evening Post,* 1.9.1977)

### 3rd August 1977 – UFO over Derbyshire

The wife of a licensee of a public house was looking out of the bedroom window, at 2.45am, overlooking the north-west, when she saw a brilliant 'light' in the sky in the direction of Gleadless, towards Woodhouse. She called her husband and they saw it dim and become much brighter, showing tiny flecks of blue and red. Through binoculars the 'flecks' could be see as blue and red flashing lights. The object faded away but then came back, twice, before fading to a tiny speck fifteen minutes later. The witnesses declined to be identified, fearing they would be the subject of ridicule from their patrons.

(**Source: Linda and Derek Thompson –UFORUM**)

### Motorist encounters UFOs over Essex

Andrew Collins, author of a number of books, with an interest in the UFO/Paranormal subjects, whose excellent investigation into the now famous 'Aveley Abduction' case of 1974, with colleague Barry King – (members of 'UFOIN') – were contacted by the police at Chelmsford, on the 3rd August 1977, at 5.50am, and told of an incident involving Mr Mike Stevens, a 24 year-old musician and postman, from Chelmsford, who was travelling home on the A130 road, through the village of Thaxted. When some three quarters of a mile outside the village, heading towards Great Dunmow, he noticed *"a red/orange, or peachy, coloured glow through an opening in some bushes to the right"* – apparently close by, but thinking it to be a light from a building, continued on his journey. As he passed another gap at the side of the road, he noticed there were, in fact, two separate glows with much more detail. Realising this to be something unusual, he pulled off the road and saw:

> *"...two orange/red stationary objects, some 50 feet off the ground, 3-400 yards away from where he was stood, hovering above and beyond a small clump of trees over open fields – almost parallel with the horizon; the one on the left seemed to be further away than the other and was seen as a diffuse oval light. The one on the right, being nearer, consisted of a circular centre in which the light emitted was concentrated. On each side of the circular centre was a diffuse glow; the left-hand side shaped like a Christmas cracker, its right-hand side tapering to a point between the glows and the circular light. There was a definite division, as though the sections were not attached."*

Thinking they may have been giant lights, attached to the tops of poles, he continued his observations. However, within a few seconds, the right-hand object began to glide towards him at a slow pace – apparently travelling in an upward arc of a few degrees as it did so. Beginning to feel a little worried, he decided to leave and moved off, changing down in gear so as to drive up the hill.

When he reached the top, he drove down the other side but realised, although he had his foot hard down on the accelerator pedal, the vehicle would only reach a speed of 35 miles per hour. This strange effect lasted for, perhaps, 400 yards, when suddenly the car surged forward in full power, rising up to 50 miles per hour. When he reached Chelmsford, Mike went to the police station and reported the matter. The police sent a patrol car to investigate, but by the time they arrived there was nothing to be seen.

Andrew visited the site of the occurrence on 6th August, with Barry King, and later arranged for the hire car being driven by Mike to be thoroughly examined at the premises of Tricentral, when it was discovered nothing untoward was found, other than minor faults with the size of the distributor points and slight play in the accelerator cable at the carburettor, from which he formed the following conclusion:

> *"Having found no real faults with the vehicle, and after visiting the sighting location, it would seem that the details given by Mr Stevens seem consistent with our own findings. Although I cannot rule out 100% a normal malfunction of the vehicle, I feel it is not impossible that an outside energy, or force, could have been responsible for temporarily preventing Mr Stevens from leaving the area by way of limiting his car's speed."*

**(Source: As above/*Flying Saucer Review*, Volume 23, No. 4 – 'CE11 at Thaxted … Vehicle interference reported')**

## 4th August 1977 – UFO over Truro

We spoke to Sydney Thorne – a retired headmaster of a school in Truro, Cornwall, with regard to his detailed knowledge of a number of local UFO sightings brought to his attention. He told us about a silver object seen crossing the sky, heading towards the direction of St Austell, at 11.45pm.

During the early evening of the same day, an object resembling *"a torpedo, showing five large portholes or windows, set into its body, with mist or vapour, circulating inside"*, was seen hovering over the *River Thames*, at Teddington.

## 6th August 1977 – UFO over Chester

Graham Drake spoke to us about what he saw hovering over the *Dee Estuary*, Chester, at 9.20pm, when accompanied by his friend – David, of Glan Aber Park. The two men were out driving when they saw a bright object in the sky and stopped the car. They got out and continued to watch, until it disappeared behind a cloud bank. After arriving home, Graham was astounded to discover his wife had also seen it from a downstairs window. Enquiries made by the couple revealed others had also seen the UFO on that day.

## 6th August 1977 – Close encounter with aliens in Georgia, USA

The *Georgia Journal*, of 11th August 1977, headlined – 'Did he or didn't he?' – told of a very unusual occurrence brought to their attention, by a Tom Dawson (then aged 63) – a retired automobile dealer, living near Pelham on a Georgia caravan park, with his wife and seven year-old daughter.

At 10.30am he went outside with his two dogs, as he used to do on days off. He stopped at the home of Jimmy and Linda Kolbie, played some time with their baby, then walked towards a fishing pond located behind some pines. To get there, he had to cross a pasture where approximately 20 or 30 or 40 cows grazed quietly. He wanted to see whether it would have been pleasant to fish later in the course of the day.

### Circular object lands in front of him

He stepped inside a gate leading to a field. Before he could close it, a strange circular-shaped object set down in front of him, hovering a few feet off the ground, described as being 40 to 50 feet in diameter, 12 to 14 feet high, and a dome at the top with a row of portholes around. It did not make any noise and changed colours quickly.

*Tom Dawson*

*"I felt unable to move a muscle – as did the dogs and cattle; we seemed to freeze in the same position prior to the 'ship' landing. A hatch opened and five strange looking 'humans' marched out – two women and three men – their skin as white as flour sacks."*

### 'Beings' emerge from craft

*"One of the men and his female partner were completely nude and hairless. The first out tested the ground, then motioned the others to join him. Two more emerged from the craft, seemingly there to guard the hatch. The clothing worn was extremely beautiful; shoes were made of a silky material and were turned up with the toes pointed."*

### Device placed on top of Tom's head

Without saying a word, the 'chief' of the strange men placed a sort of skullcap-like device on Dawson's head. This device had several circular dials and lights, and wires connected to a device similar to a hula hoop with a dial. They made his trousers fall and lifted his shirt for the examination, passing the hoop above his body and around his waist, attaching small devices – like suction cups of a luminous orange colour – on various parts of his body, touching and poking him, and reading the dials.

Towards the end of this examination, a loud human voice came from the inside of the 'saucer', shouting three or four times,

*"I am 'Jimmy Hoffa!"*

('Jimmy Hoffa was the famous and controversial trade unionist leader who had disappeared in unresolved and possibly criminal circumstances, two years before.)

A fourth repetition was interrupted – as if somebody had muted the shouting with a hand, and the voice was not heard any more.

After the 'examination' was finished, the 'entities' moved approximately 10 feet away from him, close together – as if conferring secretly – speaking with high-pitched and shrieking voices. Tom did not understand their language, but thinks he heard that one of them said *"Jupiter"*. He noticed two of the men watched him occasionally, and suspected that they talked about him and were perhaps discussing whether they should take him, but they did not and Dawson later speculated that if he had been a younger man, they may have abducted him. The 'chief' then passed his palm through his chest, as if to make a goodbye sign. They gathered leaves and 'stuff' and half-jumped, half-floated, into the trapdoor of the 'saucer', closed it, and the object took off and disappeared instantly.

### Taken to Mitchell County Hospital

Once free, pulling his trousers up, Dawson ran some 300 yards to his trailer (according to one version), or to the house of his friend Jolie, or Linda Kolbie, who was working on her lawn, and who thought that Dawson had been confronted with a toxic snake in the field. Breathless, waving the arms, with insane eyes, Dawson could barely speak and could only say *"spaceship"*. Mrs Kolbie made him sit down and wiped his face with a wet rag – then he was taken to the Mitchell County Hospital, where the doctor said that he had been shaken mentally and physically by his UFO encounter. He was given a pill to calm him down and later released. Linda Kolbie told the Press that Dawson was respected in the community, hard working, nice – a gentleman who adored his daughter and who wasn't known as a prankster, in spite of the bad reputation which characterized his profession.

### Small group of men visit scene and take measurements

The couple also reported that a small group of ufologists visited and examined the place, saying they were MUFOC members. One of them claimed that he was from Mason County, in Georgia. They took ground samples and made radiation measurements. There appears to be some wild speculation from Linda that as these men didn't look like natives of Georgia, having olive coloured skin and a foreign glance, they must have been 'Men in Black'.

Tom Dawson admitted he did not expect people to believe his story, saying that he would not believe it if it did not happen to him, but that he didn't care not to be believed. He insisted that he was not crazy, had not been drinking, and had no such experience previously.

[Authors: Over the years, we have interviewed many others, who have fallen victim to what is after all, to most, the strangest thing that has ever happened to them. One man who interviewed him was Jim Miles – a history teacher that retired after 31 years. He has written a book about all the weird and strange things he has read about and seen in Georgia – (one of many other books).

Jim Miles

According to Jim Miles – who teaches US History at Peach County High School, in Fort Valley – there are lots of weird and unusual people and places throughout the State of Georgia. He thinks it is not unusual for people to experience the unusual.

*"Everybody has either experienced something strange themselves, or someone they trust has – it's that widespread"*, he said.

*Jim Miles*

### The Pelham UFO case

During an interview in the United States, Miles said his favourite UFO story is one that stems from the small South Georgia town of Pelham (as shown above). A man named Tom Dawson (then aged 63), was walking his two dogs on 6th August 1977, when a spacecraft landed. Somehow, he was paralyzed. Five aliens walked out of the craft. *"They started doing a medical examination, taking his clothes off and prodding and touching him",* Miles said, adding, *"The really strange part is that from inside the UFO, Dawson heard a human voice saying, 'My name is Jimmy Hoffa. My name is Jimmy Hoffa'."*

### Miles actually visited Dawson to discuss the encounter

*"I believe he experienced something that he truly believes was real".*

Today, Dawson's story is rarely talked about. Contacted about the case, Pelham Police Chief – Nealie McCormick – remembered the UFO incident and said it made national news, at the time.

*"It's sort of all died off and nobody talks about it anymore now",* he said.

### Ghostly encounter at a church

**Jim:**

*"They all have the same characteristics; they're all physical, people can see them, feel them, but then they're gone.*

*You can never actually prove they were there. I believe there is some unknown force out there that has manifested itself to humans for thousands of years, and generally it changes as we do through time."*

In 1972, Jim and his wife were driving around in Middle Georgia when they came upon a country church. They stopped, looked around and walked into the cemetery, where they saw some freshly laid cement on a grave. They walked over to see who was buried.

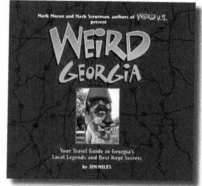

*"On one corner of the grave, this white vaporous cloud came out. We watched as it grew bigger and bigger. Eventually, it began taking the shape of a person. At that point, I took my wife under my arm and ran back to the car and we got out of there."*

(**Source:** *BUFORA Journal*, **Volume 6, Number 5, Jan/February 1978**)

# 7th August 1977 – Triangular object over Enfield, Middlesex

Joan Wilson (then aged 49) of 55, Durrants Road, Ponders End, Enfield, was fetching the washing in at 1.55pm.

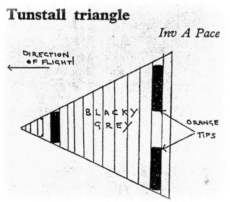

*"I heard this piercing, whistling noise, and looked up to see a white-grey triangular-shaped object moving up and down in the sky, before if moved into a cloud and I lost sight of it, 20 seconds later."*

(**Source: BUFORA**)

# 9th August 1977 – Triangular UFO over Stoke-on-Trent

*"A dark mass, with a green and red light set into each edge, forming a triangle",* was reported over Stoke-on-Trent, by local resident – Paul Mottram, who contacted

(**Source: Tony Pace, BUFORA**)

## 10th August 1977 – Domed object near chemical plant

In the early hours, four youths aged between 15 and 17 in Port Talbot saw a dome-shaped object with flashing lights on it, creeping over the mountain above the town. After hovering over the town for a while, it shot along the seafront at high speed and then *"acted in a highly suspicious manner"* in the vicinity of the BP chemical plant, at Baglan Bay, before disappearing.

The youths were terrified by what they saw. They said the object was definitely not a plane and it was capable of travelling at very high speed and then apparently hovering on the spot.

(**Source:** *South Wales Evening Post*, **12.8.1977**)

## 14th August 1977 – 'Flying Saucer' reported over Wales

At 11pm, Mr C. Powis of Neath in Glamorgan, sighted a 'Flying Saucer' heading across the sky, over McHowell mountainside, while preparing for bed. (**Source: Personal interview**)

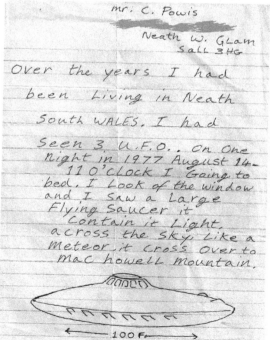

mr. C. Powis

Neath W. Glam
SA11 3HG

Over the years I had
been Living in Neath
South WALES. I had
Seen 3 U.F.O. On One
night in 1977 August 14.
11 O'Clock I Going to
bed, I Look of the window
and I saw a Large
Flying Saucer it
Contain it Light
across the sky, Like a
Meteor it cross over to
Mac howell mountain.

← 100 F →

### 14th August 1977 – UFO over Warminster

On the 14th of August 1977, a woman resident living in Boreham Road, near the Sutton Veny turn off behind the Yew Tree Public House at Warminster was awoken at 4am by thenoise of stampeding cattle. Looking out of the window she saw a light hovering above a field which was causing the livestock to run in panic. She picked up a pair of binoculars and looked through to see *"a bright white beam of light reaching up into the early morning sky, then there was nothing"* The incident was later reported to Ken Rogers by the witness, who was very frightened. Ken examined the field but found nothing untoward.

### 18th August 1966 – Strange objects seen over California

An interesting report was published in the *Aerial Phenomena Research Association Inc.* bulletin of August 1977, Volume 26, No. 2, *'Ghost Riders through the Gates of Hercules'*, by field investigator Dennis Leatart.

Dennis, living in Crestline, California, using a field telescope – (focal length 17inches and a 12.5mm orthoscopic eyepiece) – tells of having seen something crossing below M13, at 9.35pm, located in the constellation of Hercules, some 27,000 light years away.

*"It was moving rapidly in a straight line, covering the full width of my eyepiece in approximately two to three seconds. I continued to track its path as it headed in a south to north direction, blinking on and off every one second. I lost the object over a hill after following it through 60 degrees of arc. The object was in an apparent orbit and a magnitude of about 7-8 and appeared pointed or tapered at the front. It was not visible with the naked eye. My impression was that it could have been a satellite of some kind; however, its speed seemed too rapid and I have never seen them blink – unless it was spinning and catching the sunlight."*

Dennis was able to confirm a number of other instances of what appear to be similar objects seen on the 24th and 25th August 1977, while observing M13, which he refers to as satellite objects, but clearly this doesn't appear to be the case.

### 21st August 1977 – Police officer sights UFO

Further UFO sightings took place over Cumbria. One of the witnesses was Police Constable Bill White, (who sadly passed away, some years ago).

*"I've had my leg pulled but I know what I saw. There were two white lights, with a bluish hue – rather like two TV screens, hanging above a tree. I drove down the road to look from another direction and I could still see them about 150 feet up in the air. There was no noise, so it wasn't an aircraft. It was visible for about four minutes."*

**(Source: Unknown Cumbrian newspaper – UFOs galore alarm the Law)**

SUNDAY MIRROR REPORTER

**P OLICE reports in the Lake District have an unearthly similarity these days.**

"As I was proceeding along the lane I perceived a strange object in the sky . . ."

Five dazzled bobbies have made this same claim in the past two weeks.

Their observations have been backed up by dozens of public sightings of Unidentified Flying Objects — known as U F Os—in the area near Kendal, Cumbria.

P c Bill White, 31, made one of the reports.

He said: "It wasn't a plane—it was a UFO.

*P.c Bill White*

**Hovering**

"I've had my leg pulled but I know what I saw. There were two white lights with a bluish hue, rather like two TV screens, hanging above a tree.

"I drove down the road to look from another direction and I could still see them hovering about 150ft in the air.

"There was no noise so it wasn't an aircraft. It remained visible for about four minutes.

"I'm not saying it was a spacecraft but whatever it was seemed to be keeping observation."

Two other policemen also reported the same lights.

It was a week later that 25-year-old P c David Wild was on patrol at Windermere with two officers and saw "a silver object in the sky."

He said: "It travelled at fantastic speed. It was too high and too fast to be an aircraft.

"We were all impressed by what we saw."

But the sightings have not impressed Kendal police Superintendent Leslie Thompson.

He said: "These are experienced, sensible and level-headed officers and I respect what they say.

'But I take UFOs with a pinch of salt."

## UFO landing at Cumbria

A number of years ago Carl Dixon (13) from Barbon Cumbria three miles north from Kirby Lonsdale and two miles north of Casterton was walking through a local wood when he saw luminous blue object estimated to be 6ft in length and four ft in height hovering at various heights above the ground. It then moved towards him but stopped about 6ft away, and remained motionless for several minutes until something resembling a mechanical arm came out from underneath the object Frightened Carl ran away but returned later with a companion who confirmed the 'craft' was still in the wood. During conversation with Mr R Hall ( BUFORA) who interviewed him about the matter he told of seeing triangular shape above and below with a small dome underneath As seen from the side

[Authors] Objects like this seen exercising what appears to be some form of mechanical apparatus for an unspecified purpose, will always be of great interest to researchers of the UFO subject. At first glance they

seem too incredible to believe, especially when the details surrounding the incident are so sketchy. But we should at least entertain the possibility that this may well have been a genuine sighting, and without being to trace Carl in order to speak to him personally cannot take it any further.

## 24th August 1977 – UFO over Cheshire

A dull silver object was seen hovering in the sky, a few hundred feet above bungalows, at Willaston, near Nantwich, Cheshire. Seconds later, it vanished from view. (**Source: Steve Cleaver, FUFOR**)

## 24th August 1977 – UFO over Bournemouth

Later the same day, Terry Broadbank – a member of the British Astronomical Association, and Vice Chairman of the Wessex Astronomical Society – was completing a fine adjustment to the finder scope of a four and-a-half inch reflecting telescope on the bright star Vega, in the constellation of Lyra, at 9.20pm, when:

*"I noticed a large stationary light in the south-west of the sky, so I swung the telescope towards the direction of the object, and was surprised to see that it filled the field of the telescope. My impression of the object was that it had been travelling very fast and had slowed down with our atmosphere drifting around it.*

*It then moved off, towards the direction of Bournemouth, where I lost sight of it on the scope, although you could still see it with the naked eye. Suddenly, it increased its speed and was lost from view. What I saw wasn't Venus, or Jupiter, as these planets weren't visible at the time. It couldn't have been a satellite, or aircraft, as it was stationary in the sky long enough for me to line it up with*

*the telescope, that had a field so narrow the Pleiades, or 'Seven Sisters', constellations couldn't all be seen in the same field of view."*

Sadly, we were unable to speak personally to Terry, as he had died some years ago, but we spoke to Janet, his wife at the time, who forwarded an illustration to us of what she and her husband had seen.

**Janet:**

*"I remember the sighting very well. I was with Terry, at the time. When I looked through the telescope, I saw a smaller object break away from the larger body. Terry later made some enquiries (locally) and traced, through publicity, a couple living in Corfe Mullen, who spoke of having seen three objects in the sky at the same time as our sighting."*

We traced the elderly couple – still living in Corfe Mullen – who confirmed the sighting.

About an hour later, a group of people were leaving the *King's Arms* Public House, Litton, Somerset, when they saw what at first they took to be star moving at speed across the sky. Through binoculars, a glowing disc-shaped object was seen passing overhead, at a height of between 15-20,000 feet. To the assembled party's amazement, another similar object appeared in the sky. This joined up with the first before both of them split up; one heading towards Bath, the other toward Midsomer Norton.

## 25th August 1977 – Strange sighting over Middlesbrough

Mrs Mary Stott of Kinross Avenue, Park End Estate, Middlesbrough, was putting out the milk bottles for collection at the end of the evening, when she noticed:

*"...a bright 'star' over Ormesby Road, and another one (this time bright red), moving slowly over Park End School. I couldn't believe my eyes, for following at a distance was another and then further back, another – the strangest thing I had ever seen in my life."*

## 27th August 1977 – Close encounter, Dyfed

Lorry driver – Francis Lloyd, from Broad Haven, Dyfed, was proceeding towards Nantycaws Hill, on the A48, (south-east of Carmarthen), accompanied by Francis Dwyer – the son of the haulage company he worked for.

*"As we neared a junction, halfway up the hill, we both saw, caught in the glare of the lorry's headlights, the weird sight of two 'figures', standing at the side of the road, approximately seven feet in height. They reminded me of guardsman, at attention. They were dressed all over in what looked like red Perspex. I've never seen anything like them before. They weren't human beings. They were far too tall. I just carried on and didn't look back."*

In conversation with Francis, in 2010, he brought our attention to the fact that, following the event, the diesel engine on the lorry cut out while driving past the same location during subsequent trips along the same stretch of road – something which was the cause of much frustration to the mechanics who laboured unsuccessfully to fix the fault. We thought there were strong similarities with what Mr Lloyd had seen and the sighting at Torva, Cumbria, in 1980. Were such entities part of some 'Alien' regiment, or was there a more logical explanation?

(**Sources:** *The Dyfed Enigma*, **Randall Jones Pugh/Personal interview**)

*Nantycaws Hill, Carmarthen*

*Francis Lloyd*

## 28th August 1977 – UFOs over the Lake District

Just after midnight, on the 28th August 1977, Mr and Mrs Currie were travelling home to Silverdale, in the Lake District, when they sighted *two* 'lights' passing overhead,

> "…*like a 'flying catamaran' sailing through the sky. When viewed through a pair of binoculars, no distinguishing features could be seen, apart from a matt black underneath. As it moved over, we realised it could only be seen from head on. From the side, you wouldn't have seen anything at all … most strange*".

At 12.22am, Police Constable Alexander Laurie Inglis was with three other police officers – Simon Woodrow, David Miller, and Archibald Beattie – driving home to Carlisle from Keswick, along the A591 Keswick to Bothel Road, near the Kiln Hill and Grisedale junction.

> "*We noticed two extremely bright white lights in the sky over the hills, at a height of about 1,500-2,000 feet.*
>
> *We stopped the car and watched them move slowly through the sky, towards the direction of Skiddaw, noticing the distance between the two lights didn't change. We couldn't make out any fuselage between the lights, even when it was overhead, but we all heard a faint purring noise – unlike any helicopter or aircraft – then two more lights appeared slightly fainter than the first two, but apparently forming part of the same object.*
>
> *As the lights passed into the moonlight to the face of the moon, they disappeared from sight. When we got back to the police car we received a radio message, informing us that the object had been sighted in the direction of Ullswater and Keswick, by other officers*".

### Police Sergeant Irvin Trohear:

> "*I was talking to another officer, at 12.27am, when I noticed what I first took to be a pair of car headlamps travelling above Loughrigg Fell, which I knew was 1,101 feet in height, some five miles north of our position. It didn't register, to begin with, but the other officer interrupted the conversation to point out the two lights were now gliding along the top of the lake, towards us.*

*Irvin Trohear*

▆▆▆▆▆▆▆,
Kents Bank,
Grange over Sands,
Cumbria,
▆▆▆▆▆▆▆

9 January, 2001

Dear John,

Thank you for your communication which I received a couple of days ago.

The only thing I can do to help you is to confirm that I did, on August Bank Holiday Saturday in 1977, actually see what I would term as a UFO in the night sky over Lake Windermere. I was with another officer, (now deceased) on the shore of the lake when at first I saw what appeared to be two car headlights in the sky coming over the top of Loughrigg Fell, about 5 miles north of where we were. Loughrigg incidentally is 1101 feet high and they would seem to have been a couple of hundred feet above that.

As I was involved in a conversation with another person, at the time, (just after midnight,) I did not think anything about it but a couple of minutes later the officer with me drew my attention to the lights. I looked up and there, seemingly gliding down the lake towards us were two horizontal, large, circular white lights.

We stood rooted to the spot as they went past us over the centre of the lake, in a southerly direction. The lack of clouds made it impossible to judge how high it was. There was no noise and whatever it was could not have been

towed by another aircraft as we would have heard it and it was a very still night. There may have been other, dimmer lights on the Object but time has erased the finer points from my memory. It did not have any flashing lights like most aircraft. I completed a BUFORA form a few days later.

I feel that it was only one object although I could not see any framework. It went out of our line of vision behind the trees where we were standing and that was the last I saw of it. It did not seem to be moving very fast, and I don't think it was at a high altitude due to the large size of the lights. If it had been very high the lights would have to have been massive.

The lights had been seen previously at Bassenthwaite, about 20 miles to the north by other police officers, and about a dozen of us who were on duty in Windermere that night. None of us knew what it was but I think the general agreement was that it was not a conventional aircraft, and if it had been a secret, why show such bright lights?

That is about all I can remember about the incident, and I hope it may be useful in your research into solving the causes of these weird apparitions. May I take this opportunity to wish you a success in the publication of your book, which I will look out for in due course.

Yours Sincerely,

Irvin Troned

*We stood, rooted to the spot, as these two globes – one opposite each other, in horizontal line – flew silently above our heads.*

*I believe that it was only one object, although I could not see any framework. It went out of our line of vision behind the trees, where we were standing, and that was the last I saw of it. We weren't the only ones to see them. I later heard that at least a dozen other police officers, as far away as Bassenthwaite, twenty miles away from us, had also seen these go over."*

Irvin sent us an OS map, illustrating the line of 'flight' of the UFO, from Castlerigg Stone Circle, near Keswick (Grid Reference 293236), to his position on the shore of the lake (Grid reference 3733034).

### Police Sergeant Joseph Roger Maw:

*"Although I still retain an open mind on UFOs in general, I am unable to explain what it was that I saw all those years ago – still sharp in my mind, as it was so unusual. Shortly after midnight, on Bank Holiday, 28th August 1977, I was with another PC and Police Sergeant Clifton, driving a Police Ford Transit van, when we received a radio call, directing us to the Priory Hotel, Haverigg, to deal with a group of disorderly youths.*

Joseph Roger Maw

WESTMORLAND GAZETTE 16/9/77

# Bright lights start new UFO mystery

More lights in the sky believed by some to be UFO's have been spotted by at least 10 Windermere policemen.

Last week the Gazette reported two sightings by people in Cartmel and Silverdale and on the same night the glowing lights were seen in five different parts of Windermere.

A fortnight ago in the early hours of Sunday morning a police spokesman said he saw "two extremely bright lights going down Lake Windermere

from the direction of Loughrigg.

"It was a very cold night and the lake was like a millpond, but the lights passed overhead with no sound at all. It was impossible to determine the height because there was nothing to relate it to."

As the lights were seen in five different parts of Windermere they were the subject of quite a lot of discussion, the spokesman told the Gazette.

On the same night 12-year-old Peter Simpson, of Helmside Road, Oxenholme, also saw strange-looking lights and decided to investigate further

by looking through his refractor telescope.

Although the telescope multiplies 100 times the lights still looked just the same, but Peter is not convinced it was UFO as it was flying along a regular air route.

"At first I thought it might be a UFO because it appeared to be coming very slowly over Kendal, but then it quickened up as it came towards us," said Peter, a pupil of Heversham Grammar School, who is keen on astronomy.

### Surprised

"I was a bit surprised by the lights, but not frightened."

This week in the early hours of Monday morning a Sedgwick man looked out of his window to see a "very bright light in the sky."

"It seemed to be a very bright object longer than a full moon and on the west side of Kendal," said Mr M. W. G. Overton, of The Spinney, Sedgwick.

During the summer there has been a spate of sightings of what many believe are unidentified flying objects throughout South Lakeland.

## Help solve the South Lakeland UFO mystery

The British UFO Research Association is trying to get to the bottom of the mysterious sightings reported throughout South Lakeland on the night of September 8.

Hundreds of people saw the objects—bright lights moving slowly and silently across the sky—and this week BUFORA appealed for witnesses to write to its regional investigations co-ordinator, Mr B. M. Hartley, of Westdene, 23 Hastings Road, Thornton-le-Fylde, Lancs.

"We would like to establish what was seen that night and the only way we are going to do this is by getting all the facts together concerning the sighting," said Mr Hartley.

## ANOTHER UFO SPOTTED

A mysterious flying object has been seen by a 19-year-old Gazette reader within two weeks of the paper reporting two more UFO sightings in South Lakeland

She was driving from her home at Crosthwaite to Underbarrow on Monday evening when she saw three large lights in the sky over Mount Joy Hill. They were in a line and coloured blue, red and amber. At first, she thought

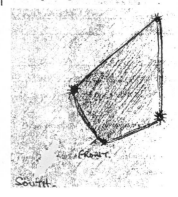

*After arriving and dealing with the incident, somebody mentioned about something in the sky. I looked up and gazed over the moonlit lake below us, to the west, on a clear and still night. You could hear a pin drop, despite the noise of the disco in the background.*

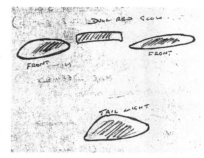

*As more of the assembled group behind me realised something was happening, stillness fell upon us. We saw a large object heading across the sky, over the direction of Keswick, to the west, about 1,500 feet up, displaying three lights. It came to a halt over a nearby hill, allowing us to see it closer. I felt the hairs on the back of my neck start to rise. Sergeant Clifton decided to contact the Police Control room, at Penrith, and report the incident, who confirmed they had received a number of calls from the public about the UFO, and that enquiries with the RAF and Air Traffic Control as to the identity of this object were negative."*

WESTMORLAND GAZETTE. SEPT. 2. 1977.

## In the sky at midnight

TWO separate sightings of UFOs seen at about midnight on Saturday have been reported to the Gazette.

A large, silent object in the sky, displaying two lights, baffled Mr J. R. Currie as he was returning home to New Redbridge Farm, Silverdale, just after midnight.

He told the Gazette that as he was approaching his house in the car he noticed this object in the sky, and after stopping the car outside the house he dashed indoors to get his binoculars. By the time he got outside it had passed overhead and he could no longer see the lights.

"There was absolutely no sound", he said, "and the two lights must have been facing front as they could not be seen from the rear. It came overland and went across Morecambe Bay in the direction of Heysham. It was difficult to estimate the height at which it was travelling, but I should say about 400 or 500ft".

Mr and Mrs Jack Platt, of "Fairmile", Haggs Lane, Cartmel, were entertaining visitors at their home on Saturday.

At about midnight Mrs Platt walked into the garden with her guests to see the full moon shining overhead when suddenly they became aware of four strange lights in the sky.

They thought the lights must be attached to some object which they could not distinguish. For a time the lights hovered over Hampsfell but there was no sound of any engine.

Eventually they moved slowly away towards the Cartmel Fell area and then returned headed towards Grange, and disappeared.

Mrs Platt said: "I have watched TV programmes about such objects but have never actually seen anything like this before myself.

"I couldn't sleep during the night for thinking about it. I wonder if anyone else in the area saw these lights".

The Officer agreed that a photograph sent to him (relating to a sighting by Colin Saunders, of a UFO over the Fosse Way, in Leicestershire, many years later) bore uncanny similarities with what he and the others saw.

### Police Constable David Wild:

*"I was on foot patrol, walking along the A592 Haverigg Road, at 12.27am. I noticed two very bright lights, hovering over the Fells. They then started to move over and I became aware of a third bright light, positioned to the rear, forming a triangle – resembling something like a kite, or skate fish in the sky, with a very odd horizontal section. As it moved away, it left a dull red glow behind in the sky."*

### Police Constable Brian Guy Nicholson also confirmed having seen:

*"...two bright white lights, apparently hovering over Lake Windermere, at 12.27am, with PC Wild. They remained stationary for some time and then began moving along the lake towards us. The*

| | BUFORA REF. | YEAR | NUMBER | INVESTIGATOR | CASE SUMMARY | |
|---|---|---|---|---|---|---|
| | | | | | *DATE | |
| | | | | EVALUATOR | TIME | |
| | | | | | LOCATION | |
| RN FORM TO:– R. HALL | | | | | EVAL'N | |
| . 26, FRENCHFIELD GARDENS | | | | | UFO CLASS | |
| CARLETON, PENRITH, CUMBRIA | | | | | CLOSED | |

# UFO SIGHTING ACCOUNT FORM

## SECTION A

Please write an account of your sighting, make a drawing of what you saw and then answer the questions in section B overleaf as fully as possible. Write in BLOCK CAPITALS using a ball point pen.

At 12.27am on Sunday 28 Aug. 1977 in company with
other Police officers at Hayrigg Rd Bowness my attention
was drawn to two bright white lights ① that
appeared to be hovering over Lake windermere near
Ambleside. They remained stationary for quite a
time and then began moving along the lake
towards us. The two lights went out and as
they came closer I saw several white lights
forming a shape as at ② & passed overhead
but I could not detect any engine sound.

Please continue on a separate sheet if necessary.

DRAWING*

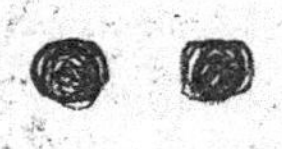

Your full name (Mr/~~Mrs/Miss~~)
Brian Guy Nicholson  Age 24 yrs.

Address 72, Sandgate,
Kendal, CUMBRIA

Telephone No. 21665 (STD. 0539 )

Occupation during last two years
Police Constable

Any professional, technical or academic qualifications or special interests

Do you object to the publication of your name?
*Yes/~~No~~. *Delete as applicable.

Today's Date 18.9.77.

Signature B. G. Nicholson

* If preferred, use a separate sheet of paper.

Published by the British UFO Research Association (BUFORA LTD.) for the use of investigators throughout Great Britain. Further copies may be obtained from BUFORA Research Headquarters., Newchapel Observatory., Newchapel, Stoke-on-Trent, Staffs., England

Form B1

| GROUP /INVEST REF. | | BUFORA REF. | YEAR | NUMBER |
|---|---|---|---|---|
| | | | | |

**SECTION B**

1. Where were you when you saw the object(s)? Exact location...... Rayrigg Rd, Bowness.
   Nearest ~~town~~/village...... Bowness ...... County/District...... Windermere / Cumbria.

2. What was the date of your sighting?...... ~~Thursday~~ day 28 of August 1977

3. At what time did you see the object(s)? 12.27 *am/pm/midday/midnight. *Delete which ever does not apply. How did you know the time? Pc 703 who had checked his watch.

4. For how long did you observe the object(s)? 5-10 Mins If not certain please state — for not less than 3 MINS and for not more than 10 MINS.

5. If each of the following objects were held at arm's length which one would just cover the object(s) you saw, i.e. have the same apparent size? (underline) ~~Pinhead/pea~~/halfpenny/~~penny/~~ ~~twopence/golf ball~~/tennis ball/other—

(i) 90° 75° 60° 45° 30° A 15° 0°

(ii) N, NW, NE, W, A, E, SW, S, SE

Place an 'A' on the curved line in diagram (i) to show the altitude of the object(s) above the horizon when you **first** noticed it/them and a 'B' when you **last** noticed it/them. Also place an 'A' on the outside edge of the compass in diagram (ii) to indicate the direction in which you **first** observed the object(s) and a 'B' when you **last** saw it/them.

Did you see the object(s) at or near ground level? NO

How did the object(s) disappear from view? Gradually into distance.

If you took a photograph or made any measurements, give details NO

0. If you noticed any unusual effects on people, animals, plants, objects or equipment nearby: Describe these NO

1. What was the main feature of the sighting which made you feel that the object(s) was/were not natural or man-made? As it passed over head there was no engine sound.

2. How many other people at the same time saw the object(s)? 4 Give the names, addresses, age and relationship to you of other witnesses Pc's 703 Wild, 202 Mark 300 Maw 917 Lawston (All of Kendal Task Force)

3. Give a brief description of the object(s) under the following headings:-
   (a) Number of objects 1 (b) Colour white light (c) Sound NONE
   (d) Shape As Diagram was this sharply defined or hazy?
   (e) Brightness DIM (compared to star, venus, moon, sun etc.)

4. What were the local conditions? Please tick in box where applicable.

| Clouds | | Temperature | | Wind | | Precipitation | | Astronomical | |
|---|---|---|---|---|---|---|---|---|---|
| Clear Sky | ☑ | Cold | ☐ | None | ☑ | Dry | ☑ | Stars | ☑ |
| Scattered cloud | ☐ | Cool | ☑ | Breeze | ☑ | Fog or mist | ☐ | Moon | ☐ |
| Much cloud | ☐ | Warm | ☐ | Moderate | ☐ | Rain | ☐ | Planet | ☐ |
| Overcast | ☐ | Hot | ☐ | Strong | ☐ | Snow | ☐ | Sun | ☐ |

Other conditions if any ......

*two lights went out and, as they came closer, I saw several white lights forming a shape in the sky, which passed silently overhead". (The illustration provided shows four lights forming a diamond shape with a white light underneath the top one.)*

### Police Constable Ronald Jones:

*"I remember seeing what looked like a diamond kite-shaped object passing across the clear night sky, while I was driving past Skelwith Bridge on the A59. It had a light at the front, a bright light at each side, and a reddish/pink light at the rear – totally unlike anything I had ever seen before in my life."*

### Police Sergeant Geoffrey Merckel:

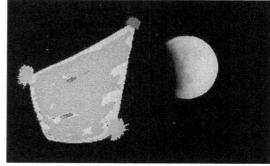

*"I saw bright lights travelling over the lake directly above my position. I got out of the police car and gazed upwards at this greyish diamond-shaped object, flying silently southwards towards Morecambe Bay, sharply silhouetted against the left-hand side of the moon. Within two and-a-half minutes, it had disappeared from sight."*

### David Wild:

*"Shortly after the incident, a group of us was interviewed for a* Border TV *broadcast on the side of Lake Windermere. Geoff Merckel set up a group to meet once a month in a pub at Arnside, to discuss similar incidents and to try and arrange 'sky watches' in the local area. This didn't last too long, but is an indication of how seriously he took the sighting. I can tell you that the local Chief Inspector was also on duty that night, and witnessed the UFO, but refused to speak to anyone about the incident or speak to the Press."*

(**Source: Personal interviews/Mr Richard Hall, BUFORA/***Westmorland Gazette***, 2.9.1977 – 'In the sky at** midnight')

1977

COUNTY POLICE STATION
BARROW IN FURNESS
CUMBRIA.
LA14 2LE.

Dear John,

Thank you for your letter of the 13th August 2001. Sorry for the delay in replying as I have just returned from A.L.. I refer to your letter, copy articles and Nicholas Redfern " A COVERT AGENDA".

Can I state that I have an open mind on reports on UFO's and on the night in question, I merely reported the occurance as I would report any other!. It was my first such sighting and it made such an impression on me that I can still see it in my mind today.

I have read page 131 and 132 on sighting and it is _not_ quite correct in detail. If I can explain my version to you. =

Just after midnight on Sunday August 28th 1977. I was on uniform patrol in a Police Transit carrier, In company with. Sgt Myles CLIFTON, Pc David WILD, Pc Brian NICHOLSON. We were located on the top layby of Rayrigg Road, Windermere near the Priory Hotel (Disco) now flats. We were dealing with some disorderly youths and I think we later arrested them for theft.

As we were dealing, one of the combined group saw something in the sky and attracted our attention. If I can paint the picture to you. We on duty on a mild, quiet moonlit night. Other than the distant noise of the disco and the youths arguing you could hear a pin drop. The lake to our front (Facing West) looking down was clear and still, like a mirror. The weather being clear, you could see for many miles and In fact you could see out to the West coast and the Mountains.

2

I know this part sounds silly but as more of us became aware of the object, everyone including the disorderly youth became still and quiet as we just looked over the lake to see the object in the sky. It came over from the West Coast and in a direction from the Keswick area. It was about 1500 feet up and had 3 big lights in the shape of Aircraft designer A.Colin Saunders. That model bears an uncanny resemblance to this object, it seemed to float along noiselessly. It stayed over a hill just before the lake, so we had time to get a good look. The moon did not reflect from the object and although in text by Nicholas Redfern it states "I said it was slightly buzzing." I do not recall this or having made that comment. What I can say it was large and was not in a hurry to move away. One thing I remember was the hair on the back of my head standing up.

Sgt Clifton decided that as it was, such an odd sighting he would contact our main control "M2BB" at Penrith H.Q. They replied that, they had several sightings from members of the public and other officers on duty. A short time later they contacted us (Z·54) to say the control had been in touch touch with the R.A.F. and Air Traffic Control, who were not aware of any air traffic in our area at becoming like this. We were witness to other patrol shouting in about the sighting. I heard Sgt Merckel and PC Jones of the T.S.G. because as the shape left us it travelled down the lake and out over the coast past the Mealbryn/Grange over South area.

To clarify, this object was low enough to be seen and heard with ease. It was not a weather balloon at an air ship of any sort. Had it had an engine or flame jets, we were very close and could easily of heard it.

3.

All the Police with me were T.S.G. and very experienced, we were officers who were highly trained at not easily scared or gone to imagination. This was something none of us including the disorderly youth had ever seen before and I have never seen since. On the instruction of the Sergeant we all recorded what we saw in our pocket books. This was a U.F.O. in the sense that I cannot explain it and noone with me that night could explain it. None of us at the time or since have rubbished the matter nor did anyone ough at us or rubbish what we saw! then or since. I am aware that weeks later Pc David WILD was approached by a T.V. company to be interviewed by them over what he saw, but I cannot remember if he was interviewed?.

As I stated earlier I keep an open mind on other Space People and I do not see that we are the only live beings in the galaxy, nor do I believe the educated people with the "BIG BANG" idea. What I do know is people like you do a good job and one day you will be proved right.

Yours faithfully

J.R. MAW (retired Sergeant, Cumbria)

C/O ... 70'S. KENDAL TASK FORCE

| | | YEAR | NUMBER | INVESTIGATOR | CASE SUMMARY | ⑪ |
|---|---|---|---|---|---|---|
| ROUP | BUFORA REF. | | | | *DATE | |
| INVEST EF. | | | | EVALUATOR | TIME | |
| | | | | | LOCATION | |

RETURN FORM TO: R. HALL
26, FRENCHFIELD GARDENS,
CARLETON, PENRITH, CUMBRIA

| | |
|---|---|
| EVAL'N | |
| UFO CLASS | |
| CLOSED | |

# UFO SIGHTING ACCOUNT FORM

## SECTION A

Please write an account of your sighting, make a drawing of what you saw and then answer the questions in section B overleaf as fully as possible. Write in **BLOCK CAPITALS** using a ball point pen.

APPROX 12·35 AM ON SUNDAY 28th AUGUST 1977
ON POLICE PATROL DUTY IN THE LAKE DISTRICT.
RECEIVED INFORMATION OVER THE FORCE RADIO THAT
2 BRIGHT LIGHS HAD BEEN SEEN IN THE SKY OVER
WINDERMERE LAKE. AT THAT TIME I WAS DRIVING
SLOWLY ALONG THE A 593 FROM SKELWITH TOWARDS
AMBLESIDE (MAP REF 369.036) AT A POINT OVERLOOKING
THE LAKE. SAW BRIGHT LIGHTS NEARLY DIRECTLY
ABOVE. STOPPED VEHICLE GOT OUT AND WATCHED
OBJECT — WHICH HAD VERY BRIGHT/LARGE STILL LIGHTS
(WHITE) ON EITHER SIDE (MUCH BRIGHTER THAN AVIATION LIGHTS)
ALSO WHITE LIGHT ON FRONT AND LIGHT ON REAR
APPEARED REDDISH. OBJECT FLYING SILENTLY SOUTH
SLOW SPEED — 800 - 1000 FEET UP. (FLEW OVERHEAD
ON LEFT HAND SIDE OF MOON FROM WHERE WE WERE
WHICH OUTLINED IT AGAINST SKY CARRIED ON FLYING
SOUTH. TOWARDS M/CAMBE BAY.

Please continue on a separate sheet if necessary.

**DRAWING**

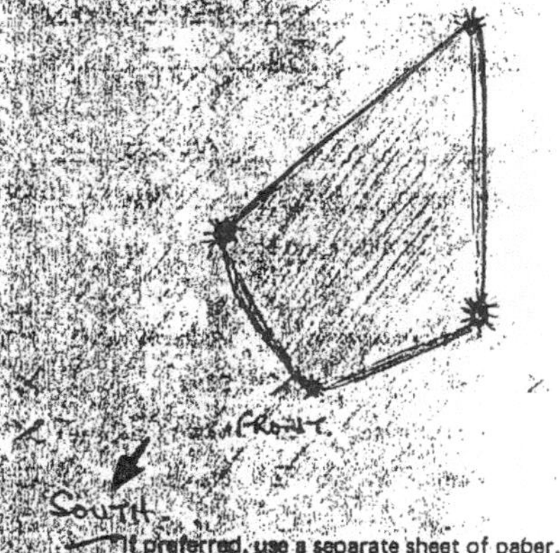

SOUTH

*If preferred, use a separate sheet of paper.

Your full name (Mr/Mrs/Miss/Ms) GEOFFREY ANTHONY MARTIN MERCKEL Age 39 yrs

Address 2 APPLETREE ROAD
ULVERSTON. CUMBRIA

Telephone No. 54686 (STD 0229 )

Occupation during last two years POLICE SERGEANT.

Any professional, technical or academic qualifications or special interests

Do you object to the publication of your name?
Yes/No. *Delete as applicable.

Today's Date 11th September '77

Signature

28. AUGUST 77

| GROUP /INVEST REF: | | BUFORA REF. | | INVESTIGATOR | | CASE SUMMARY | |
|---|---|---|---|---|---|---|---|
| | | | | | | DATE | |
| | | | | EVALUATOR | | TIME | |
| | | | | | | LOCATION | |
| RETURN FORM TO:— | R. HALL. 26, FRENCHFIELD GARDENS CARLETON PENRITH, CUMBRIA | | | | 528 | EVAL'N | |
| | | | | | | UFO CLASS | |
| | | | | | | CLOSED | |

C/O  WILD  KENDAL  TASK FORCE

# UFO SIGHTING ACCOUNT FORM

## SECTION A

Please write an account of your sighting, make a drawing of what you saw and then answer the questions in section B overleaf as fully as possible. Write in **BLOCK CAPITALS** using a ball point pen.

*[handwritten account]* At approximately 00.25 hrs on Sunday 28th August 1977 myself and PC Clayton were on duty, standing on the A592 road at Miller Ground, Bowness on Windermere. At this time the weather was good, clear, which was well lit by strong moonlight. On looking North West in the direction of Buttermere we saw two extremely bright lights side by side, low over the fells at about 1500—2000 ft the lights were coming towards us slowly. As it approached us the lights stayed at a constant position in relation to each other. As it came ahead we saw a third bright light to the rear of the object. A fourth light appeared in the centre and four from the first two lights, this was not as bright in the other light. All lights appeared to belong to the same object. As it came directly in line with the moon no fuselage could be seen, but a slight noise was heard. We reported this to our H.Q. who confirmed other report of the same sightings.

Please continue on a separate sheet if necessary.

DRAWING*

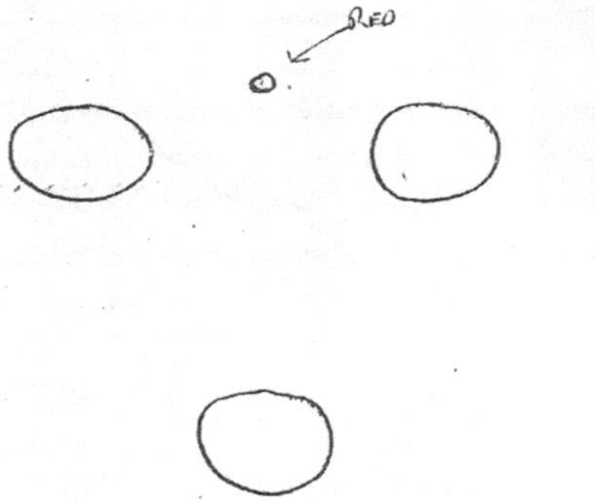

RED

Your full name (Mr/Mrs/Miss/Ms)
Joseph Roger MAW ........ Age 28.
Address 76 Appleby Road.
Kendal

Telephone No. .................... (STD ............. )
Occupation during last two years. Police Constable

Any professional, technical or academic qualifications or special interests

Do you object to the publication of your name?
*Yes/No. *Delete as applicable.
Today's Date. 19 – 9 – 77
Signature. *[signature]*

*If preferred, use a separate sheet of paper.

Published by the British UFO Research Association (BUFORA LTD.) for the use of investigators throughout Great Britain. Further copies may be obtained from BUFORA Research Headquarters., Newchapel Observatory

| GROUP | | BUFORA REF. | YEAR | NUMBER | INVESTIGATOR | CASE SUMMARY | |
|---|---|---|---|---|---|---|---|
| /INVEST REF: | | | | | EVALUATOR | *DATE | |
| | | | | | | TIME | |
| RETURN FORM TO:- | R. HALL 26, FRENCHFIELD GARDENS, CARLETON, PENRITH, CUMBRIA. | | | | | LOCATION | |
| | | | | | | EVAL'N | |
| | | | | | | UFO CLASS | |
| | | | | | | CLOSED | |

# UFO SIGHTING ACCOUNT FORM

## SECTION A

Please write an account of your sighting, make a drawing of what you saw and then answer the questions in section B overleaf as fully as possible. Write in BLOCK CAPITALS using a ball point pen.

AT 12:22 AM ON SUNDAY 28.8.77, 2 POLICE OFFICERS AND MYSELF WERE DRIVING HOME TO CARLISLE FROM KESWICK ALONG THE A591 KESWICK TO BOTHEL ROAD NEAR KILNHILLS / MANGRISEDALE JUNCTION. THE NIGHT WAS CLEAR WITH BRIGHT MOONLIGHT. ON LOOKING NORTH WEST TOWARDS THE SOLWAY BEYOND THE HILLS WE ALL NOTICED TWO EXTREMELY BRIGHT WHITE LIGHTS IN THE SKY OVER THE HILLS AT APPROX 1500 - 2000 FEET. WE ALL LEFT THE CAR IT WAS THEN APPARENT THAT THE OBJECT WAS TRAVELLING SLOWLY (IN COMPARISON TO AN AIRCRAFT) IN OUR DIRECTION) ie IN THE DIRECTION OF SKIDDAW. IT WAS REMARKED AT THE TIME BECAUSE OF THE HEIGHT OF THE OBJECT THAT THE LIGHTS MUST HAVE BEEN HUGE. IT ALSO APPEARED THAT THE TWO LIGHTS WERE PART OF THE SAME OBJECT IN OTHER WORDS THE DISTANCE BETWEEN THE LIGHTS DID NOT ALTER. NO ONE OF US COULD MAKE OUT ANY FUSELAGE BETWEEN THE LIGHTS. WHEN THE OBJECT WAS DIRECTLY ABOVE I COULD HEAR A VERY FAINT PURRING NOISE (NOT LIKE HELICOPTER OR NORMAL AIRCRAFT). TWO FURTHER LIGHTS APPEARED SLIGHTLY FAINTER THAN FIRST TWO BUT STILL APPARENTLY BELONGING TO THE SAME OBJECT. IN OTHER WORDS IT SEEMED TO BE AN OBJECT WITH TWO FRONT LIGHTS AND TWO LIGHTS BENEATH AT FRONT AND REAR. NO FUSELAGE WAS VISIBLE. THE MOON WAS DIRECTLY OVER SKIDDAW, AS THE

Please continue on a separate sheet if necessary.
LIGHTS PASSED INTO THE MOON LIGHT TO THE FACE OF THE MOON THEY DISAPPEARED

DRAWING* See separate sheet.

FROM SIGHT, WE FULLY EXPECTED TO SEE THE OUTLINE OF AN AIRCRAFT. BUT DID NOT. ON RETURNING TO THE CAR, A RADIO MESSAGE CONFIRMED THAT THE OBJECT HAD BEEN SIGHTED IN THE DIRECTION OF ULLSWATER AND KESWICK. BY OTHER OFFICERS.

*If preferred, use a separate sheet of paper.

Your full name (Mr/Mrs/Miss/Ms)
ALEXANDER, LAURIE INGLIS., Age 36 yrs.

Address 25 HILLCREST AVENUE. CARLISLE.

Telephone No. 35677. (STD 0228 )

Occupation during last two years POLICE OFFICER.

Any professional, technical or academic qualifications or special interests

Do you object to the publication of your name?
*Yes/No *Delete as applicable.

Today's Date 16th September 1977.

Signature Alexander L Inglis

Published by the British UFO Research Association (BUFORA LTD.) for the use of investigators throughout Great Britain. Further copies may be obtained from BUFORA Research Headquarters., Newchapel Observatory, Newchapel, Stoke-on-Trent, Staffs., England

1
Form R1

| GROUP /INVEST REF: | BUFORA REF. | YEAR | NUMBER | INVESTIGATOR | CASE SUMMARY |
|---|---|---|---|---|---|
| | | | | | ·DATE |
| | | | | EVALUATOR | TIME |
| | | | | | LOCATION |
| RETURN FORM TO:— | R. HALL 26, FRENCHFIELD GARDENS CARLETON, PENRITH, CUMBRIA | | | | EVAL'N |
| | | | | | UFO CLASS |
| | | | | | CLOSED |

# UFO SIGHTING ACCOUNT FORM

## SECTION A

Please write an account of your sighting, make a drawing of what you saw and then answer the questions in section B overleaf as fully as possible. Write in **BLOCK CAPITALS** using a ball point pen.

Report over car radio of unusual object in sky at 0030 28-8-77 — just past Skelwith Bridge A591. On Ambleside side of Skelwith Bridge when he saw above us a diamond kite shaped object with 4 lights — one white light at front — one bright light at each side and a reddish pink light at rear. Object about 2000 feet high no noise no other visable signs ie. slip stream a vapour trail — flew in straight line away from us.

Direction from Skelwith Bridge straight line for GRANGE over Morecambe Bay area.

No definite shape except area inside of lights appeared darker than sky lighting.
GOOD CLEAR SKY.

Please continue on a separate sheet if necessary.

DRAWING* View as he saw it from underside.

REDDY/PINKISH LIGHT.

UNDERSIDE    BRIGHT LIGHT

BRIGHT LIGHT.    FRONT. LIGHT.

*If preferred, use a separate sheet of paper.

Your full name (Mr/Mrs/Miss/Ms)
RONALD JONES ...... Age 24 YRS.
Address 10 CLOVELLY TERRACE,
BARROW-IN-FURNESS.

Telephone No .......... (STD ...... )

Occupation during last two years ...........
POLICE CONSTABLE.

Any professional, technical or academic qualifications or special interests
9 'O' LEVELS — 2 C.SE.

Do you object to the publication of your name?
*Yes/No. *Delete as applicable.

Today's Date ...........
Signature R.Jones

Published by the British UFO Research Association (BUFORA LTD.) for the use of investigators throughout Great Britain. Further copies may be obtained from BUFORA Research Headquarters., Newchapel Observatory, Newchapel, Stoke-on-Trent, Staffs., England                          Form R1

WESTERN DAILY ESS, Wednesday, August 31, 1977—PAGE 7

## SKYWATCH GIRL TAKES MYSTERY SNAP

# Is this a Thing from Outer Space?

### By Colin Bateman

TO THE cynical this odd object could be just about anything from a boiled egg to a street lamp.

But for factory worker Miss Bridget Chivers there are no doubts.

She is convinced it is a flying saucer.

And it is being used by UFO Info, the Wiltshire skywatch group, to boost their claims of visitors from outer space.

Bridget, aged 25, of Eden Grove, Whitley, near Melksham took the misty orange-and-blue picture in a week-end skywatch on Cradle Hill, Warminster.

She says it shows a circular craft fringed with pink lights which touched down towards the end of the watch.

### SHUTTER

The shutter on her infrared camera jammed but quick thinking Bridget swooped to her standby Instamatic in time to snap the mystery object.

The UFO then disappeared leaving only a yellow mist, said Bridget.

The film was developed yesterday at the UFO group's data headquarters in Trowbridge.

"We use our own developers because it's safer, the films don't get tampered with or lost," said group member Mr Barry Gooding.

To add weight to Bridget's report another sighting, this time an orange light, was logged at UFO Info headquarters last night.

It was seen over Imber, the ghost village now in the centre of the Army training area on Salisbury Plain.

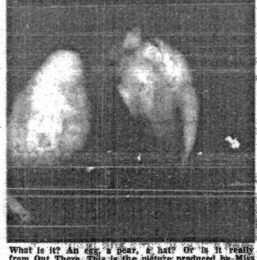

What is it? An egg, a pear, a hat? Or is it really from Out There. This is the picture produced by Miss Bridget Chivers.

## UFO's over Warminster

The Officers weren't the only ones to sight something unusual that morning. At 10.30 pm. a party of nine people, including Bob Strong, Arthur Shuttlewood, and John and Maureen Rowston were on Cley Hill when an object was seen rising above the horizon, described as being two or three times the size of a star, which rapidly decreased in size when approximately 45 degrees off the horizon. Other witnesses included Andy Lee, Soteris Georgiou, Steve from Worcester, George Woods of Liverpool, Chris and Pauline Trubridge and Richard Gardner. (**Source: Peter Tate /Ian Mryzglod, Probe**)

At 11.30pm 28th August 1977 Miss Bridget Chivers a regular sky watcher to Cradle Hill Warminster was driving back to her home at Whitley near Melksham along the A36 when she noticed a bluish oval object ahead of her and to the right

> *"I slowed the car right down and then wound down the car window. The object was now a dark silhouette rather than the bluish light I had seen first. As I drew level with the object now standing in the field I stopped my car and grabbed my camera (Halina 2000-35mm but it wouldn't work The shutter release had jammed. I changed to my Kodak Instamatic and managed to take three shots of the object which looked like an inverted cone standing in a shallow dish. There was a string of green and pink lights about halfway down the cone and a large searchlight type at the top. The blue light was no longer visible. I had just taken the third shot when the object disappeared leaving a yellow musky type smoke. I went back to Cradle Hill to fetch the others but they had all left"*

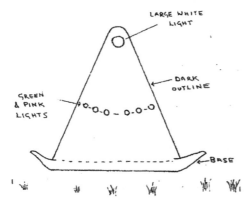

LARGE WHITE LIGHT

DARK OUTLINE

GREEN & PINK LIGHTS

BASE

The next day reporters from the *Wiltshire Times* called on Bridget asking for further details of the landing, and promised to process the photos and get them back to her by Tuesday .The photos didn't arrive but *Report West and HTV local News programme* showed a print from one of the shots.

On the 31st of August the *Western Daily Press* printed the same photo and it was again shown on HTV accompanied by analysis from Bristol University that it was a fake.

The next day one of the UFO INFO members from Trowbridge made a visit to Bristol University, but drew a blank trying to obtain the whereabouts of the photos

A phone call was then made to HTV, who advised him that the negatives/photographs were now in the possession of the *Sunday Mirror*. It was then established the photos were on their way to London. Eventually all of the negatives were returned to Bridget on the 9th of September.

Somebody else who took an interest in the matter was BUFORA Regional Investigation Co-ordinator Mr Ken Philips. He published a brief article about the matter in the *BUFORA Journal* Vol 6 No 5 January/February 1978 'Warminster Cone' and concluded:

> "*The Warminster group UFO INFO carried out an analysis on the photos which do not show what Bridget saw but had suffered through being passed around amongst various people. He (Ken) though the report open to considerable doubt but though not happy with the photos UFO INFO believes Bridget to be a reliable witness.*"

Which appears somewhat ambiguous in our opinion. Ken also included an illustration that we presume Bridget sketched from what she saw as opposed to what was captured on film 21A. Not that their is anything strange about this at all – many photos taken of UFOs are often found to be completely different to what was seen with the naked eye.

Although we never met Bridget Chivers we spoke to her sisters some years ago, and together with what we gleaned about her character over the years talking too many that knew her, have no reason to believe they were faked.

As far as we are concerned this young lady's integrity was not and never will be in question.

We initially thought that Bridget had misidentified a hoaxed device, details of which can be found in the 1st of October sighting report. But it appears this is unlikely to be the case taking into consideration the distance involved, unless they knew that Bridget was going to be passing that field, which appears unlikely.

*Bridget Chivers*

Between 11.45 pm. and midnight 28th August, John Rowston was walking past Parsonage Farm, on the way to Cradle Hill, when he saw . . .

> "*. . . what appeared to be a thick black cloud hanging over the hill, with a 'bump' at each end. Suddenly, the cloud started disappearing, then the two 'bumps' split as it did so. Two hours late, a similar object was seen in the sky by three others, which split into two before disappearing.*"

**(Source: Peter Tate)**

### 30th August 1977-mystery light seen over Warminster

Warminster resident – Chris Curtis – was returning home, along the Westbury to Warminster road at 10.45pm, when he sighted an orange coloured light over the area of Colloway Clump, on the outskirts of Warminster, before it shot away towards Cley Hill, Corsley.

### 31st August 1977 – Illustration of UFO?

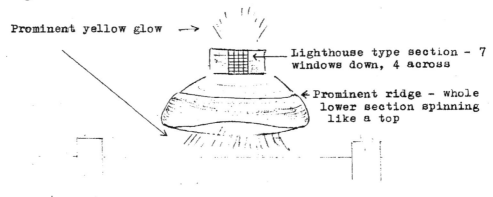

Prominent yellow glow ⟶

Lighthouse type section - 7 windows down, 4 across

← Prominent ridge - whole lower section spinning like a top

Object appeared between ~~time~~ chimmney pots – exact size could be gauged by reference to width of windows in house.

## CHAPTER 21 – SEPTEMBER 1977

### 1st September 1977 – Bell-shaped UFO frightens couple over Essex

Donna and Terry were on their way home to Charlton Crescent, Barking, Essex, at around teatime, when they saw an object in the sky showing a red flashing light, projecting a white beam downwards. The light was then seen to move slowly to another position and began to move towards them, allowing view of a bell-shaped object showing a white rotating light underneath, a white light on the front and red one on top. The couple, now frightened, ran inside the house. When they plucked up courage to have a look, a short time later, it was seen heading away before rapidly accelerating – and then lost from sight.

**(Source: Ron West)**

Here are some other examples of bell-shaped UFOs, as reported to Ron West and other researchers from around the 1970s.

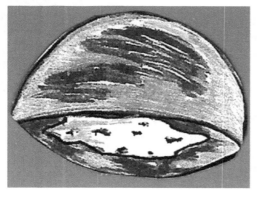
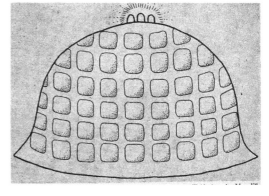

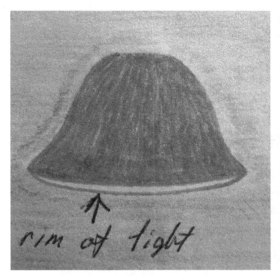

rim of light

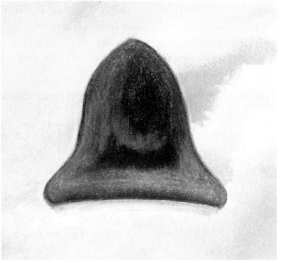

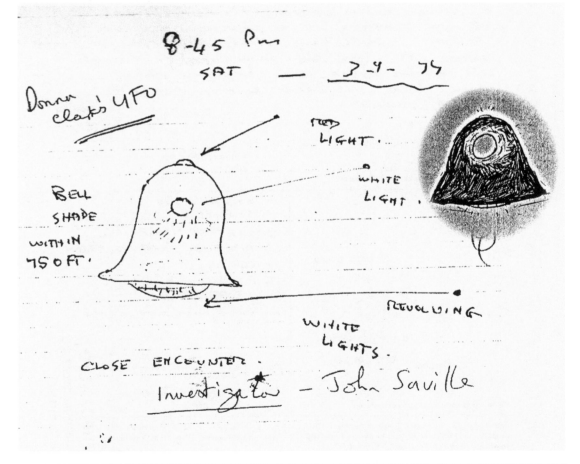

8-45 Pm
SAT — 3-4-74

Donna clark's UFO

RED LIGHT.

WHITE LIGHT.

BELL SHADE

WITHIN 750 FT.

REVOLVING

WHITE LIGHTS.

CLOSE ENCOUNTER.

Investigator — John Saville

## 2nd September 1977 – Three UFOs sighted over Peterborough

At 10.25pm, Peterborough resident – Chris Shuell – was disturbed by dogs barking frenziedly outside.

*"I opened the door, wondering what on earth was going on, and saw three orange coloured 'cigars' moving across the misty sky. One of them shot outwards, to form a triangle.*

(Source: Personal interview)

## 3rd September 1977 – UFO seen over Barking, Essex by Tony Steel UFO investigator

# UFO SIGHTING ACCOUNT FORM

**SECTION A**

Please write an account of your sighting, make a drawing of what you saw and then answer the questions in section B overleaf as fully as possible. Write in **BLOCK CAPITALS** using a ball point pen.

*It appeared in South West as a light, the time was 8.55pm, it came nearly above me a stopped, two military aircraft came over and the light went out at 9.15 it came back on and started to descend towards me, the light turned into a saucer shaped object with red (7) lights it was rotating in a clockwise direction, it was a dull grey colour, there was no noise, the object then moved slowly towards the electric pylons and disappeared behind some flats. The whole sighting was for fourly minutes*

Please continue on a separate sheet if necessary.

**DRAWING\***

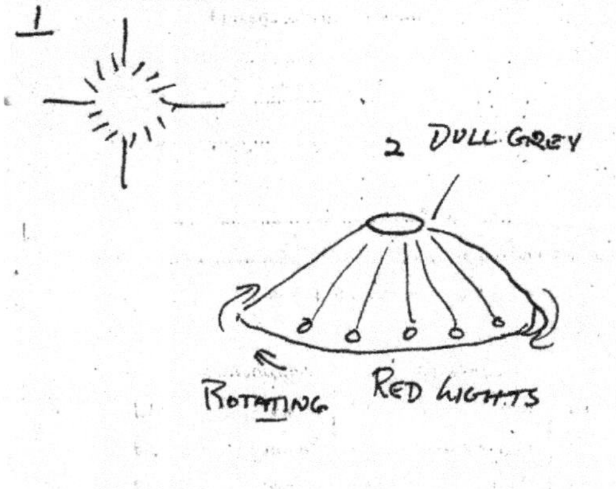

1

2 DULL GREY

ROTATING   RED LIGHTS

\*If preferred, use a separate sheet of paper.

Your full name (Mr/Mrs/Miss/Ms)
TONY STEEL    Age 36
Address WEBBER HOUSE
NORTH STREET, BARKING ESSEX
Telephone No................(STD........)

Occupation during last two years.....
POSTMAN

Any professional, technical or academic qualifications or special interests

Do you object to the publication of your name?
\*Yes/No. \*Delete as applicable.

Today's Date.....6-14-78
Signature...Tony Steel

**UFORA LTD**
16 SOUTHWAY BURGESS HILL
SUSSEX RH15 9ST

Published by the British UFO Research Association (BUFORA LTD.) for the use of investigators throughout Great Britain. Further copies may be obtained from BUFORA Research Headquarters.; Newchapel Observatory; Newchapel; Stoke-on-Trent, Staffs:, England

Form R1

## 4th September 1977 – UFO seen over Surrey

What Doris saw!

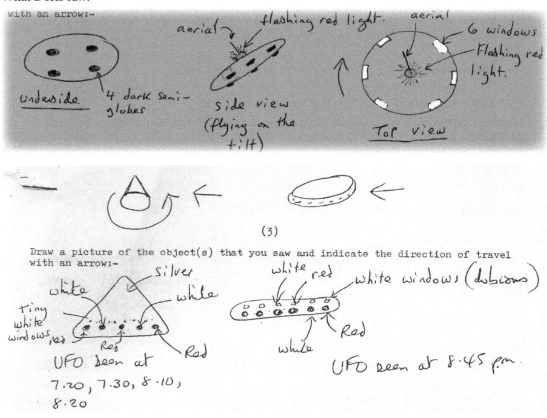

Draw a picture of the object(s) that you saw and indicate the direction of travel with an arrow:-

## 7th September 1977 – **Flashing light over Motorway Yorkshire**

Mr David Wayne, of Rochdale, was driving along the M627 towards the M62, at 9.15pm, when he noticed a solitary white flashing light in the sky. He pulled over and got out on the hard shoulder. On closer observation, the object seemed to flash white then down to dull red, as it moved slowly across the sky. He watched it for five minutes and then left. It was a dry night and cloudless.

**(Source: Rochdale and District UFO Research Group)**

In the same month, a bright 'star' with a cigar-shaped outline was seen over Alsager, Staffordshire, under 2,000 feet, flashing in a sequence of red, green, blue and white lights, *"looking like cellophane on a child's toy"*, at 9.20pm, before heading towards Crewe at high speed.

At 9.35pm, four pinheads of white light were seen over Crewe, changing formation as they headed across the sky. **(Source: Steven Cleaver, FUFOR)**

## 8th September 1977 – **Three lights UFO over Lancashire**

Hundreds of people living in the Lancashire area sighted bright lights moving across the sky. One of the witnesses was Mrs Lillian Hudson from Bolton-upon-Dearne, near Mexborough.

*"My son ran into the house, at 10pm, in a very excited state, shouting about a 'Flying Saucer' in the*

*sky. I thought he was joking and ignored him, but decided to humour him as he was so insistent and very agitated. I was stunned to see one of the most beautiful things I have ever seen in the world – a circular object, hovering low in the sky, with a large bright flashing light on it. There were loads of people in the street, some of whom were shining torches up into the sky and shouting. About twenty minutes later it moved away, leaving me bewildered and saddened by its departure.*

*When I read the newspapers, the next day, I discovered there had been many sightings from all over the country, but none from our locality." (Source: Personal interview)*

A number of mysterious lights were seen moving slowly and silently across the sky over South Lakeland, Cumbria, on the 8th September 1977, by hundreds of people.

Four pulsating 'lights', with red centres, were seen over Devon and Cornwall, heading north, at 8.45pm on the 10th September 1977, followed by a sighting of *"a blue, pulsating, pear-shaped object"* on the 12th, by a retired RAF pilot, who reported that:

*"It stopped and hovered, for a few seconds, before reversing along its original path and then shot upwards into the sky."*

## 9th September 1977 – Black oval UFO sighted over Cleethorpes

At 5.35am Mr Bruce, of Cleethorpes, was on his way to work at the bakery, when he noticed a strange object in the sky heading from the direction of the fish docks, towards the local swimming pool.

*"It was round, but as it travelled across the sky its shape changed to oval; its colour was black and its height about 1,000 feet.*

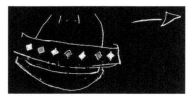

*It kept on a steady course and at the same altitude, until it disappeared from view over the housetops. There was no wind, the sky was clear and dawn was breaking."* (**Source: Peter Tate**)

## 10th September 1977 – Strange 'lights' over Devon

At 8.45pm, a bright blue and white flashing 'light' was seen in the sky over Teignmouth, by resident – Mr Eastbrook.

The sighting was followed by other reports of strange 'lights' in the sky. They included a bright blue flashing 'light', accompanied by two very bright 'lights', one smaller red one in the middle (*forming a triangle?*), at 8.50pm, seen heading in the same direction as before.

At 9.20pm, a large orange-yellow glow was seen in the sky to the south-east, which appeared to halt at one stage. It then passed overhead and changed to red, before changing direction towards the North. At 9.25pm, a similar object was seen in the eastern sky. This was also seen to change to red in colour. (Source: UFO-Info Exchange Library)

Judy Longhurst from Maidstone, Kent, was sat in her car near her home, on the same evening.

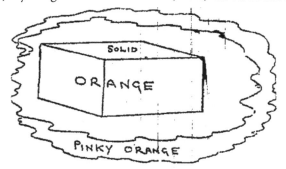

*"I saw a large bright orange coloured rectangular-shaped object, hovering silently, about twenty feet above the rooftops in Long Rede Lane, Barming, surrounded by a bright pink glow, which spread over two houses in size. After about a minute, it dropped down behind the house. A short time later, the pink glow suddenly vanished from sight."*

(**Source: Mr J. Castle, BUFORA/Personal interview**)

### 11th September 1977 – Motorist frightened

Schoolteacher – Mrs Waterman – was driving along Halshanger Lane, Ashburton, Devon, at 3am, when she was confronted by a 'bright light' hovering 3 feet above a cattle grid. Mrs Waterman felt frightened and, after making a three point turn, went home by another route.

### 12th September 1977 – Seven 'Flying Saucers' over Cleveland

Keen Astronomer – Malcolm Leech, and his wife – Marjorie from Dormanstown, Cleveland, were in their back garden on the evening, when they saw seven 'Flying Saucers' – five of which just disappeared as they headed out to sea.

In a later interview, conducted with local UFO Researcher – Brian Straight, the couple pointed out:

> *"The objects were too slow for shooting stars, and too fast or close to each other to be aircraft. They had no wings, or vapour trails."*

**(Source: Brian Straight, 'CHRYSIS'/Unknown newspaper – 'Riddle of the seven lights, star gazer Malcolm spots pack of UFOs')**

They weren't the only ones to sight something unusual that evening. Ex-RAF Pilot – Frank Chapman, living in the Torbay area of Devon, who has flown RAF 'Mosquitoes' and 'Lightning' jets, was at home with a friend – John Henley, on the same evening, when they sighted:

**Mr Chapman:**

> *"...a blue pulsating 'light' moving from the direction of Orestone, heading south-south-east to north-north-west; it stopped and hovered for a few seconds, before reversing along its original path towards Torbay. It then picked up speed to about 250 miles per hour and shot upwards into the sky at a 55 degree angle. I estimated that the object was at a height of about 5,000 feet and three times the size of a 'Lightning' Fighter Jet. It was tear-shaped and brilliant as twelve street lamps,"*

**(Source: UFO-Info Exchange Library, Christmas 1977, Volume 1, No. 4)**

**14th September 1977 – UFO reported over USA**

**·By WILLIAM DICK**

# UFO Tracked on Radar Screens in Florida
## ... It Causes Air Force to Scramble Jet Fighters

A mysterious unidentified flying object (UFO), tracked on three radar screens, recently caused the Air Force to scramble two F106 fighter jets into the early morning sky over Florida and nearby coastal waters.

The supersonic interceptors, part of the Air Defense Command and each armed with four air-to-air missiles, were sent aloft from Homestead Air Force Base, south of Miami, at 6 a.m. on September 14.

Earlier, Palm Beach County Sheriff William Heidtman took a department helicopter 10 miles out to sea in an attempt to investigate the intensely bright light.

In addition, visual sightings were made by expert witnesses, including an Eastern Airlines pilot, a Federal Aviation Authority (FAA) official, and the FAA flight controller on duty at the Palm Beach International Airport.

The flight controller, Bill Brown, was first alerted to the presence of the UFO at 4 a.m. by calls from several local police departments. They told him a mysterious, very bright light could be seen, northeast of Palm Beach, over the Atlantic Ocean.

"At first, I couldn't see anything.

. FLIGHT CONTROLLER Bill Brown was alerted to presence of UFO by calls from police.

Then, suddenly, there was this very bright light – as if someone had turned a switch on." Brown explained to The ENQUIRER.

"I looked on the radar screen and there was a definite contact. It was slightly hazy, not the sharply defined contact we get from an aircraft. Besides, I knew there were no planes in that sector of the sky.

"The contact was about 10 miles over the ocean and between 7,000 and 11,000 feet high. It was moving slower than an aircraft but seemed to be six to eight times larger.

"The radar screen showed it to be moving west (toward land) at about 5 miles an hour. Then it turned to the northwest, where it remained more or less stationary," said Brown, who has been a flight controller for seven years.

"I didn't believe what I saw, so I called Miami International Airport. They said they also had it on their screens.

"In the meantime, Sheriff Heidtman had contacted Air Defense Command at Homestead and they also reported contact.

"Homestead asked me to contact an Eastern Airlines DC9 due in at Palm Beach from Miami and ask the pilot to look out for the object. The captain of the DC9 – Capt. B.F. Ferguson – radioed back that he'd seen a very bright light and that it was not a star. The whole business began to take on an eerie quality.

"When I reported to Homestead what the DC9 pilot had told me, they scrambled the jets." Brown said.

By that time, it was 6 a.m. The jets, traveling at altitudes ranging from 500 to 15,000 feet, crisscrossed the search area but could find nothing.

"By the time the jets arrived overhead, radar contact with the object had been lost on our screen," Brown said.

The 20th Air Division headquarters at Fort Lee, Va., from where the Homestead interceptors are controlled, said "the radar contact was caused by weather phenomena."

However, a spokesman for the

weather bureau at Palm Beach International disagreed, saying: "There was absolutely no unusual weather that morning that could have caused such a radar contact."

After his helicopter flight, Sheriff Heidtman told The ENQUIRER: "I could see the light quite clearly.

"It was very bright with occasional flashes of red and green. In my opinion what I was looking at was the planet Venus."

But flight controller Brown said: "It's impossible that Venus, millions of miles away, could have been picked up on three different radar screens."

James Moon Jr., senior FAA official in charge of air traffic at the Palm Beach International Airport, told The ENQUIRER that he also saw a light in the sky. He added: "Taking into account the radar contacts, I believe there were two different objects in the sky and that Venus was only one of them.

"I'm not saying the second object

**EXPERT WITNESS:** James Moon Jr., in charge of air traffic at Palm Beach International Airport, says there was definite radar contact.

**SHERIFF** William Heidtman flew in helicopter to investigate UFO.

was something from space, but there was a definite radar contact no one seems able to explain."

## 15th September 1977 – UFOS sighted over West Midlands

Seven blue and white UFOs were seen moving across the sky over Pensnett, Wolverhampton – apparently moving in formation. **Source: UFOSIS)**

## 18th September 1977 – UFO over Essex

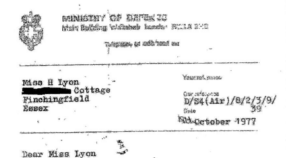

MINISTRY OF DEFENCE
Main Building Whitehall London SW1A 2HB

Telephone: 01 218 7941 ext

Miss H Lyon
Cottage
Finchingfield
Essex

Your reference

Our reference
D/S4(Air)/8/2/3/9/
39

Date
3rd October 1977

Dear Miss Lyon

I am writing to thank you for your report of an unidentified flying object seen on the 18th September 1977.

We are grateful to you for advising the Department of this incident and your report will be examined in the Ministry of Defence to see if there are any defence implications. We cannot however undertake to pursue our research, other than for defence implications, to a point where positive correlation with a known object is established, nor to advise you of the probable identity of the object seen.

Yours faithfully

MISS J McBLAIN

SIGHTING

I saw the object from a landing window on the night of Sunday, September 18th, 1977. The time was exactly 8.55.p.m. I always check my watch before taking the dog out at 9.p.m.

The night was very brighh and clear with many stars, satellites,etc.

This object appeared very low down much closer and bigger than anything else in the sky. It resembled a very large 10p piece.

I thought it was an extra large satellite and was turning away when it moved to the right. It stopped, appeared to explode into a red glow, then moved to the left towards Gt. Bardfield direction. It had charnged shape and looked like a large cigar with a glowing end.

I think it was quiet but the windows were shut. Time, probably about7 minutes.

*Hazel Lyon. 28·9·1977*

*shape changes*

## 19th September 1977 – UFO over Essex

According to the *Ilford recorder* newspaper, 'There's a blue bird on my shoulder' Mrs Hilda Hacker(then aged 70) of Arundel Gardens, Hainault Essex and her husband watched an object moving from side to side during the early hours. *"It had a light on each side, it's the third time we've seen it."* One wonders why people bother to report incidents taking into consideration the unwillingness of the majority of journalists to even want to investigate –its easier to write it off with a silly headline!

## 21st September – Shining UFO over Winchester

At 6.20am, Mr P. Justice from Stoney Lane, Winchester, was walking his dog 'Lucky' along Stoney Lane, towards the direction of Bereweeke Avenue.

*"On looking up into the sky I saw a plane pass overhead, flying parallel to Stoney Lane. It entered the thin cloud and disappeared towards the east direction. I turned around and saw another Jet airliner heading towards the cloud from the north-west direction, but behind, following at the same speed, was a circular shining object with a diameter near to half the length of the plane. On*

entering the cloud, the bright shining object tuned dark red and vanished. I watched the cloud for a few minutes, but the object did not reappear or continue to follow the aircraft."

**(Source: UFO-Info Exchange Library)**

## 21st September 1977 – UFOs sighted over Phoenix, Arizona

At 8.40pm, Phoenix resident – Jim Ray (junior), (then aged 17), was lying on his back in the front yard of a friend's house, when a flash lit up the sky which they took to be a meteor, although no trail was seen. Ten seconds later, another flash was seen in the same part of the sky – (60 degrees elevation, northwards) – then, ten seconds later, a third flash. Jim called his friend to come and have a look. The two of them watched as a further five flashes happened at 10 second intervals. By this time it was 8.45pm. At 8.47pm, Ray sighted a line of objects flying overhead.

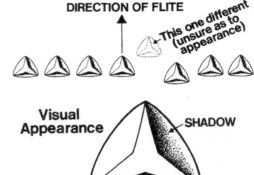

*"There were eight of them in formation; they displayed no lights or glow but were clearly visible as they reflected the street lights. Three of* the objects passed in front of the moon, allowing a clear view of their outline – then they disappeared while in flight. The sky was clear; no cloud, light wind."

## 22nd September – Hexagonal object sighted over Cleveland

A hexagonal object, *"with lines along its side, accompanied by a loud whirring noise"*, was seen performing a 'figure of eight' across the sky" over Redcar, Cleveland, by Mrs Margaret Plant and her then 12 year-old son – Adrian, and at least three other people in the neighbourhood.

**(Source: CHRYSIS [Cleveland Study of UFOs and Associated Phenomenon])**

## Winter 1977 – UFO over Norfolk

Mr John Child – an Environmental controller by occupation, was driving along the country lanes, south-west of Gorleston, near Great Yarmouth, at around 11pm, on a clear but moonless night. As he turned west onto a narrow lane that passes between the reservoirs of Lound Waterworks, he saw a 'bright light' in the sky, some distance ahead of him, roughly in the direction of an expanse of spring fed open water.

*"It was an odd looking 'light' – opaque in colour. It reminded me of a stream of milk being poured from a bottle – unlike anything I had ever seen before. The outpouring of this 'brilliant light' appeared to flow from a fairly low altitude – maybe 500 feet, disappearing below the treetops,* and lasted for several seconds. I then became aware of a roaring noise, so I turned off the car radio and wound down the window. The noise increased in volume, so I parked the car at the side of the road, next to a small reservoir, and got out. I saw, through the trees, a dark and roughly cylindrical or cigar shaped object, moving slowly eastwards, at low altitude, above the shore of the lake.

*The object had a ring of predominately fixed red and white lights towards it rear, rather than something flashing. I watched it for about 30 seconds, until the noise (like a low frequency rumble) stopped. The object then disappeared completely in front of my eyes.*

*I felt cold and alone and drove home."* **(Source: Personal interview)**

## As seen on the 28th of September 1977 over Essex

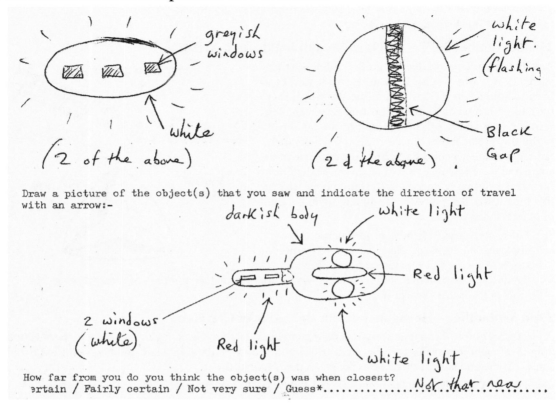

Draw a picture of the object(s) that you saw and indicate the direction of travel with an arrow:-

How far from you do you think the object(s) was when closest? *Not that near*

ertain / Fairly certain / Not very sure / Guess*..............

## 1977 – Diamond-shaped UFO over Cheltenham

Allan Tipthorpe was to sight something unusual in the later part of 1977, while delivering car parts from Swindon to the Longbridge car factory, at Birmingham – a regular route of his, at the time.

> "I was ascending the hill at Charlton Kings, just outside Cheltenham, on the A40, at 3am. I saw this giant blue diamond-shaped object hovering in the sky above the hill. I thought it might have been some sort of reflection, to start with, then knew this wasn't the case. Whatever it was moved away towards the Oxford Road, where I lost sight of it. A few nights later, while on another delivery, I stopped the lorry at the same place and discovered it had been hovering over a reservoir."

(Source: Personal interview)

## September 1977 – 'Flying Cigar' over Bournemouth

Thanks to Bournemouth-based UFO Researcher Leslie Harris, we traced Terry – then living in Ferndown, Bournemouth – who had a most interesting story to tell about what he had witnessed, one evening.

> "I was parked in Boundary Lane, close to Hurn Airport, with my girlfriend. The airport was closed.
>
> At 11.30pm, I saw what I took to be the landing lights of an aircraft approaching the runway, accompanied by an odd whirring noise, which appeared to cause interference with the car radio. I looked through the window and was staggered to see a 'Flying Cigar', with cabins of light dotted along its side, slowly descending to the ground. It had no wings and was neither an aircraft nor airship."

*My girlfriend began to panic and told me to get away, so I dropped her off but decided to go and have a another look – curiosity getting the better of me.*

*When I arrived back at the airfield, all was quiet – just a red glow over the sky. I parked up at the side of the road and switched off the lights; a Range Rover pulled up and parked in the lane. It was one of those vehicles which had been specially lengthened. Inside were three men, dressed in dark boiler suits, sitting next to loads of electronic equipment; one of the men got out of the vehicle and started walking along the lane carrying a device, with an aerial on top, pointing it towards the direction where I had seen the UFO. Their arrival worried me so I decided to leave very quietly and with no lights, rather than risk any confrontation with them."*

Terry was to find himself the target of unwarranted attention, after being plagued with strangers knocking his door at all times of the night, eager to hear what he had seen – not that this worried him. He was, of course, far more concerned with drawing attention from those mysterious strangers, whose appearance instilled much unease, despite the passing of the years. (**Source: Personal interview/Leslie Harris**)

## September 1977 – UFO over Anglesey

Mair Jeffrey – a resident of Penysarn, near Amlwch, Anglesey, was exercising her family dog, just outside the village, a few years before 1980 (although the exact year eludes her).

*"I saw this cigar-shaped object in the sky. It reminded me of a submarine, stationary over the Parys Mountain. It had this huge spotlight constantly flashing on and off – almost as if it was signalling to someone, or something. I then noticed a second similar object appear over Dulas Bay. What I found interesting was that when one object stopped flashing, the other responded – as if communicating with each other. When I told my family, they laughed at me!"* (**Source: Personal interview**)

### September 1977 – Harrowing close encounter, Somerset

Elizabeth, her husband, and two young sons – Jeff and Tony (then aged seven and six years) – were returning home to Chard, along the A30, approaching Windwhistle Hill (a couple of miles outside the town), just before 10pm, when they noticed a huge orange 'light', diffused by cloud, to their left-hand side, at the far end of the hill. As they approached closer, they were able to clearly see a massive cigar-shaped object, 2-300 feet in length, hovering between 8-10,000 feet above their heads. Elizabeth checked her watch. The time was 10.10pm. Feeling uneasy, she instructed her husband to put his foot down and get them away from the area.

The next thing she became aware of was seeing what looked like a cyclist's headlamp approaching from the opposite direction.

#### Missing time

After arriving home, Elizabeth discovered the time was 10.50pm, which meant (bearing in mind a journey that normally only took 10-15 minutes) she was unable to account for approximately 25-35 minutes.

A few days after this incident, Elizabeth was to experience something out of the normal again, while returning home along the same stretch of road – this time 2-300 yards away from the scene of the previous night's encounter.

> "We saw two 'people', who appeared to be lying down on the verge, with a third 'person' standing. I thought there may have been an accident and went to slow down. I was astonished when the 'person' (who was standing up) put a foot out, which stretched out into the centre of the road, making him an abnormally tall figure with horrendously long, thin legs. My husband swerved to go around the 'figure' and we didn't look back."

Despite a search of the local newspapers over the following days, there were no reports of anybody being injured or of an accident having occurred on the hill were found, which may have cast some light on what had taken place.

Eighteen years later, Elizabeth (now remarried) happened to mention during conversation with her sons, aged 25 and 26, if they remembered seeing the strange orange 'light' at Windwhistle Hill, and was astounded to hear of Jeff's recollection of the event – which she was totally unaware of. He confirmed hearing her tell his father to put his foot down.

> "The engine cut out and the car lights failed. My father tried to restart the car, without success. Everything seemed to happen in slow motion. I recall my father lunging across to the passenger seat and of hearing this deep, slow and rhythmic humming vibration.
>
> The passenger door was open but I couldn't understand why my dad lunged across the seat, as I had no recollection of my mother being there at all. He then punched the dashboard repeatedly. My brother, Tony, was watching out of the side window in the back.
>
> He seemed excited but I didn't know why. My father was shouting and pointing, although I couldn't hear him, but he had this terrified expression on his face and was staring, as Tony was, out of the back window, saying, 'Look Jeff, look Jeff'. At this point I realised there was something behind the car and felt almost paralysed with terror. I glanced up and saw the car bathed in white light – 'like being inside lightning'. The last memory I had was of seeing a dark shape outside the car, beside the window – very tall and bending towards the window, peering in, and of realising that whatever it was, it wasn't human. When I looked back at the orange 'light', it had gone."

Jeff pointed out to BUFORA Investigator John Heponstall, that initially he only remembered seeing the orange 'light' and 'cigar' shape, and of hearing the strange hum and vibration, but over the years other fragments of memory of the event were to slowly return. He now believes the four of them were 'taken' in some way, and remembers *a total of five 'black figures' seen*.

**(Sources: John Heponstall, BUFORA/Robert Moor/Jason Eastwood/Gloria Heather Dixon Investigations Diary, BUFORA Bulletin 24)**

## 1977 – British 'Coronation Street' TV star sights UFO

Actress Freda Driver – (the sister of Betty Driver, more familiar for her role as evergreen barmaid Betty Turpin, of *Coronation Street* fame) – spoke to us about a strange incident she and her sister witnessed, during the 1970s.

*Actresses Freda (left) and Betty Driver*

**Freda:**

*"I was sitting in the lounge at the Cheshire farmhouse where we lived at the time, one stormy evening, and happened to glance through the window, when I saw this large circular yellow 'ball of light' hovering above some trees – apparently unaffected by the gale force wind blowing outside. I watched it, noting it had a slightly misty halo around it, and thought to myself it's watching me as well! After about 15 minutes, I decided to summon up the courage and venture outside, asking my sister, Betty, to come with me.*

*When we opened the door, accompanied by the three boxer dogs, the wind was so strong that we had trouble standing. As soon as the dogs saw the UFO they ran back inside and hid under the table, at which stage we began to feel frightened and went back inside the house. After 5 minutes or so, it shot up into the sky and disappeared, followed by the wind dropping dramatically.*

*We found out that others had also seen this UFO, which was explained away as a weather balloon!"*

Freda described another incident which took place, while home with her sister, Betty one evening, approximately ten miles from Ellesmere Port, when they noticed a curious 'ball of light' travelling in tandem with their vehicle, about a hundred yards away.

**Freda:**

> "I stopped the car to have a closer look at this object and was surprised to see it had also stopped, motionless in the air – as if somehow watching us. Unsure of what to do, we got back into the car and continued on our journey, noting, with fright, that it was still following us – always at the same distance away from us, irrespective of whatever speed we were doing. It stayed with us for about 20 miles and was clearly seen by other motorists, some of whom stopped their cars. To our relief, when we entered a built-up area, it shot off upwards into the sky and disappeared."

A few days after the incident Freda was not surprised to learn, from reading a local newspaper, that the UFO had been seen by other drivers on the road – one of whom launched an appeal, asking for any other witnesses to contact him. Needless to say, Freda and Betty decided to keep quiet, fearing ridicule.

**(Source: Personal interview)**

## Autumn 1977 – UFO display over West Midlands

Kenneth Wintle, from West Bromwich, was stood outside the *Junction Inn* public house, at Hill Top, looking out over a jet

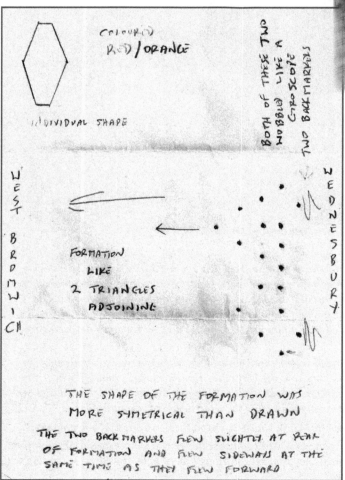

black clear night sky, in autumn 1977, with the constellation of the 'Plough' etched sharply across the sky.

> "I looked downwards from my high vantage point and was surprised to see a symmetrical forma-tion of between18-20 UFOs moving towards my position from the Wednesbury direction. I shouted out to Dennis – one of the 'regulars' (who was stood in the passage) – and pointed upwards. He looked up and blanched with fear.
>
> I later contacted the Express and Star Newspaper. They published my story, with the headlines: 'I saw a UFO Squadron – Ken', which I felt made very little impact, and personally wondered why I had bothered."

**Source: Personal interview)**

```
J Hanson,                              K.E. Wintle,
P.O. Box 6371,                         ██, Berkshire Close,
Birmingham.                            West Bromwich,
B48 7RW.                               West Midlands.
                                       ██ 2SJ.

                                       0121 ██████

                                       22nd April 02.
```

Dear Mr Hanson,

    Thank you for your letter of the 20th inst, and the information contained therein.  I'm not connected to any website or know how to send e mail.  Basically I'm too busy helping people to find their ex service pals.  It's a full time undertaking to feed information into my computer, and to type and send off letters to numerous people.  I do this as an 'Act of Charity towards my fellowman' in accordance with my religious beliefs.  It's very interesting to chat to people of all ages, ranks, and services, obviously also including women.

    In reply to your questions about the other observer 'Dennis' I'm afraid that I cannot offer much more information.  I believe his surname was Causer or Carver and he lived in a one bedromm flat on the nearby Hateley Heath housing estate in West Bromwich.  I don't know if he was married or had any other relatives living nearby.  I suppose you could check the Electoral Roll for 1977, and get his full address, and this would then reveal if he was living alone.  He was very frightened by what he saw; his nature was innoffensive and quiet, the sort of person to whom most of us take a liking.

    I would like to make it perfectly clear that I myself didn't recognise or describe the UFO's as 'coffins.'  To me they definitely appeared to be an elongated diamond shape with their tops and bottoms snipped off, or blunted.  I've never been very good at drawing pictures, so perhaps my clumsy sketch may have mislead you.  They were also not 'triangular' shaped; though the main formation and the smaller one adjoining it could be described in that manner.

    As I watched and observed the formation my attention was drawn to its entire perfect symmetry with the exception of the two flying slightly at the rear.  The penultimate UFO's at each end bf the rear rank also flew sideways at the same time as the kept their station. They flew from side to side within a short area and wobbled like gyroscope's. I pondered this and came to the conclusion that it must be a training session.  Such a wonderful display.

    With regard to incorporating my sighting in your chronological journal.  As long as it's recorded as I stated I have no objections.

                                       Yours Sincerely

                                       *Kenneth Wintle*

# CHAPTER 22 – OCTOBER 1977

## 1st October 1977 – Triangle of red lights over Cambridgeshire

At 11.30pm, Norwich resident – David Brown, noticed a small red light in the sky moving slowly eastwards.

> *"When it arrived in the north-east part of the sky, it was joined by two similar objects which had approached from different directions. The three lights then formed an upside-down triangle. After a few seconds two of them shot away, leaving the third one to carry on its course.*

**(Sources: Brenda Butler/Ron West)**

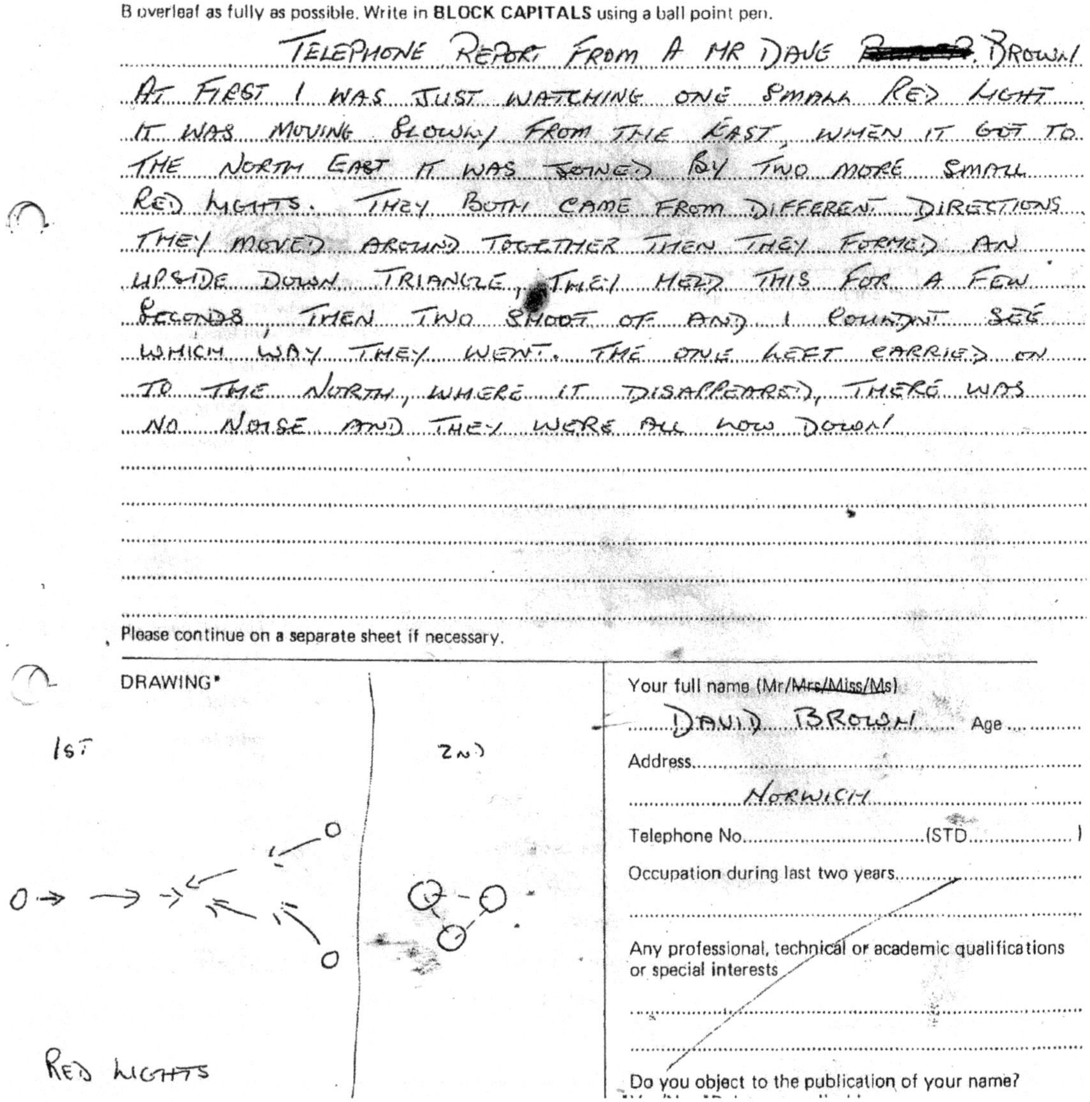

B overleaf as fully as possible. Write in **BLOCK CAPITALS** using a ball point pen.

TELEPHONE REPORT FROM A MR DAVE ~~BROWN~~ BROWN
AT FIRST I WAS JUST WATCHING ONE SMALL RED LIGHT
IT WAS MOVING SLOWLY FROM THE EAST. WHEN IT GOT TO
THE NORTH EAST IT WAS JOINED BY TWO MORE SMALL
RED LIGHTS. THEY BOTH CAME FROM DIFFERENT DIRECTIONS
THEY MOVED AROUND TOGETHER THEN THEY FORMED AN
UPSIDE DOWN TRIANGLE, THEY HELD THIS FOR A FEW
SECONDS, THEN TWO SHOOT OFF AND I COULDNT SEE
WHICH WAY THEY WENT. THE ONE LEFT CARRIED ON
TO THE NORTH, WHERE IT DISAPPEARED, THERE WAS
NO NOISE AND THEY WERE ALL LOW DOWN

Please continue on a separate sheet if necessary.

DRAWING*

1ST                    2ND

O →  →  →

RED LIGHTS

Your full name (Mr/Mrs/Miss/Ms)

DAVID BROWN    Age ...........

Address...........................
.................. NORWICH ...............

Telephone No..................(STD...........)

Occupation during last two years...........

Any professional, technical or academic qualifications or special interests.........

Do you object to the publication of your name?

## 2nd October 1977 – UFO over Dudley

A resident of Dudley was walking along Grange Road, in the evening, when he heard a *"humming, roaring, noise"*. Looking upwards, he saw a circular object, hovering approximately 250 feet to 350 feet in the sky above him.

> *"It had a dirty silver coloured flat bottom, in the centre of which were seen a number of bright multicoloured lights rotating around its perimeter, clockwise. The lights were not flashing but blending into each other as they (the lights) moved around, rather than the lights flashing on and off separately. I estimated it was about 150 feet in length and watched for about 25 seconds, as it continued to make a high-pitched turbine noise. Suddenly, all the lights went out and it shot away at high speed, towards the Malvern Hills, leaving two trails of green/white colour, which soon disappeared."*

(**Source: UFOSIS, Birmingham**)

## 4th October 1977 – Three UFOs sighted over West Midlands

At 8.30pm, three mysterious 'silver globes' were seen crossing the sky over the West Midlands. At or about the same time, British Rail engine driver – Mr Prince – was driving his car towards Crewe, through Balterley Heath, accompanied by Mr German, when they suddenly saw *"an orange rugby ball shaped light"* rising up from a field to their left, about six feet off the ground and some 25 yards from the road. Mr Prince stopped the car to obtain a closer look at the object, which was accelerating at high speed towards the south. Oddly, Mr German sighted nothing at all. An intensive search was made of the field, but nothing was found.

This was followed by a report from a postman, at Skipton, in Yorkshire, who told of sighting *"two long yellow lines"* in the sky, hovering over a nearby moor. On the same date, Mr P. Beddoes of Stoney Cross, in Hampshire, reported having sighted:

> *"...a white triangular object, which changed to luminous green. As it did so, three smaller triangles were seen above some nearby trees."*

(**Sources: Stephen Cleaver, FUFOR/UFOSIS, Birmingham**)

## 5th October 1977 – Cone shaped UFO sighted over Hertfordshire

Patricia Castel of Potters Bar, in Hertfordshire, was approaching Hildenborough, in Kent, when she saw an object hovering over the town *"resembling an ice-cream cone – as big as a double-decker bus"*.

Another witness was Mr Reginald Cranton of Barcombe Cross, East Sussex, who saw:

> *"...a huge cigar-shaped object in the sky, ten miles to the south of Hildenborough."*

Other sightings around the general area included reports of unusual whirring noises, strange lights, and a silver and orange object sighted over Tonbridge, as dusk fell, by Mrs Judith Wells.

(**Source: UFO-Info Exchange Library**)

## 6th October 1977 –Skywatch

*Members of the Essex UFO Study Group*

# THE SAUCER RIDGE STAKE OUT

IN twos and threes they came, like members of a secret society, torches winking in the darkness as they trudged uphill to the rendezvous.

It was a cold Saturday night. Other people were out dancing, at parties, or just relaxing at home. But these weren't ordinary people. They preferred to spend their evening on top of a Hainault hill and scanning the night sky.

The event was a "skywatch" by the Essex UFO Study Group because of the spate of unusual sightings in the area.

### Taking part

And the 30 enthusiasts taking part desperately wanted to see evidence that Hainault was the subject of extra-terrestrial attentions.

Stargazers like Mrs. Barbara Ireland who had come all the way from Harlow.

"Of course I believe in UFOs," she said indignantly. "It's pretentious to think we are the only intelligent life in the Universe."

Just then, Dan Goring, editor of the group's journal, called everyone around him. News of the Hainault "landing" had just been released, and like the Sermon on the Mount, Dan told the story as the gathered flock stood in awed silence.

The account of the eight-foot-tall humanoid caused some mirth, but Dan explained that similar creatures had been seen worldwide — going under such divers names as Bigfoot and Abominable Swamp Slob.

The suggestion that such things could exist didn't sound so fantastic in the dark, with the reported UFO landing spot only a few hundred yards away.

And the situation wasn't helped by a gang of yobbos who persisted in bursting out of trees trying to scare the wits out of everyone.

Like everyone else, Chris Minall, 15, had turned up hoping to spot a UFC. But he had an advantage, having alrea<sup>..</sup>y seen one.

Chris was with friends near his home in Stainforth Road, Newbury Park, when he saw "two white lights with a massive beam of white light coming out!"

Though no UFOs obliged anyone by allowing themselves to be seen, Dan wasn't too disappointed.

"Essex is an excellent area for UFOs — we get around three reports a week," he said.

"Activity seems to be linked with the cycle of sunspots, and we are expecting a big wave of sightings around October and November.

"We will just have to keep our eyes open."

## 7th October 1977 – Silent orange lights sighted over Norwich

Two small orange lights were reported in the sky over Unthank Road, Norwich, at 7.30pm, by Mr David Brown. According to the witness, initially an orange light was seen heading from the east direction, towards another moving from the north – as if on a collision course.

*"They then made a sharp turn, heading north-eastwards, side by side, until splitting away from each other, and I lost sight of them a short time later." (Source: Ron West)*

## 9th October 1977 – UFO over Manchester

Mr L. Goldstone of Crumpsall, Manchester, was with his wife, casually looking through the window of their house, at 3.45pm, overlooking the Yorkshire moors, when they were stunned to see a stationary object in the blue sky with an accumulation of billowy clouds underneath it.

*"We watched it for at least half an hour, as it hovered in the same spot for most of the time, at a height I estimated to be 500 feet, although it did fractionally shift its position on four occasions, when it seemed to tilt slightly upwards and its colour changed from a black silhouette to luminous pale yellow – then it went behind a small greyish cloud and disappeared."*

**(Source UFO-Info Exchange Library)**

## 10th October 1977 – Strange 'lights' over Lancashire

At 8.29pm, Mrs M. Robinson of Rossendale, Lancashire, her husband and two daughters, were stood outside on a clear, fine, cloudless night, when they noticed an orange/red object travelling slowly through the air, low down in the sky.

The object, which had been heading from the Burnley direction towards Rochdale, was then seen to halt and reverse along the course taken, before gradually disappearing out of sight four minutes and thirty seconds later.

At 8.50pm, a large white 'light' was sighted heading across the sky.

At 9pm, a Stockton couple – William and Emma Thompson – were with their sons (Kevin and Stuart), when they saw two objects hovering over Bishopston Road West, Stockton-on-Tees, at 9pm, accompanied by *"weird noises"* for about 20 minutes.

(READING) **EVENING POST** Saturday, October 8, 1977

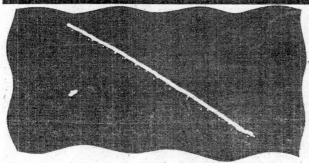

■ FLASHBACK . . . to September 1968. This "UFO", however, was later identified as an aircraft from the Radio and Space Research Station at Slough.

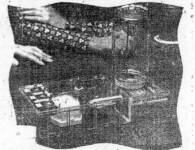

■ FLASHBACK . . . to August 1971. A fiendish-looking "UFO detector" built by Rodney Lloyds of the South West Aerial Phenomena Society.

# Suddenly, UFOs pop up everywhere

THE skies over the Thames Valley have been alive with Unidentified Flying Objects lately, according to one of Britain's top Ufologists.

In fact, there were more sightings in the triangle bordered by Reading, Basingstoke and Yateley than anywhere else in the country.

Mr Omar Fowler, chairman of the Surrey Investigatioin Group on Aerial Phenomena, called the sighting a "UFO flap."

Now, two more Basingstoke housewives have testified that unknown objects have been whizzing over the town.

Mrs Hilda Downes, of Wilmott Way, saw a mystery object "like a flying dustbin lid" hurtle over Winklebury and vanish in the direction of the Lansing Bagnall factory.

And her near-neighbour, Mrs Peggie Nevill, said that earlier this year, she saw a light hovering over the town, getting alternately dim and bright for five minutes before suddenly disappearing. She said she was certain it was not a helicopter, as it made no noise.

Mrs Downes' "dustbin lid" was spotted at 11pm on Saturday August 27 as she was putting out her milk bottles. She glanced up at the sky and saw what appeared to be two stars, one larger than the other.

"The larger one seemed to split into two," she said. "As it did so, I thought it was a shooting star, but it

## Couple sight 'sky object'

A WOKINGHAM couple have reported an unidentified flying object — and the description matches an earlier, unconnected sighting

## Schoolboys admit UFO was hoax

BRACKNELL schoolboy Simon Carson has confessed hoaxing most of Berkshire's Press and UFO experts. Last week, Simon, of Hubbenholme, Wildridings, faced pictures and a description of a flying saucer

■ A UFO that was not disproved — and one that was.

### EVENING POST SPECIAL REPORT

formed what looked like a ball of condensed smoke. The other half disappeared.

"The ball dropped until it seemed like the size of a football, then it veered off towards Lansing Bagnall, by which time it was like a dustbin lid.

"As it was moving, the moon broke through and I saw that the object was dull, grey and metallic — rather like the colour of wartime barrage balloons."

Mrs Downes said that when she first spotted the star-like object, it

was stationary. It was "much bigger and brighter than any star." The forming of the "football" and its disappearance happened in seconds, she said.

"I went to bed at 1.30am on August 28 and, shining over Basingstoke Industrial Estate was a star similar to the one I'd seen earlier."

These were not Mrs Downes' first "sightings".

She said that in April this year a searchlight stabbed down from the sky over Winklebury.

Said Mrs Downes: "It was a

Thursday night at 7.30, and lots of other people must have seen it, as there were many people about, including children playing.

"A few stars were shining, then I noticed a very, very large star which seemed to have six or seven points. Suddenly a big beam, like a blueish-green searchlight, came on from just below this star right down to just above the trees at Winklebury. It was the same colour the sea sometimes goes.

"After a second or two it went out, although the star remained for half an hour before disappearing."

Just along the road, Mrs Peggie Nevill recalled the spring morning she was in her bedroom when she saw a "very bright light" over Sainsburys.

It was 10am, but she saw no shape or aircraft — just the light.

Said Mrs Nevill: "It go very bright, then went very dim. This happened about four times before the light vanished. There was no noise and no aircraft to be seen.

"This happened on a Thursday. The following Sunday at 6.30am I saw the same thing over the Crooks premises. Both lights remained stationary for five minutes before going."

**Mr Thompson:** *"One had red, green, and white lights. I never believed in UFOs before – until now."*

A police spokesman for Cleveland Police said there had been no reports in Fairfield, or anywhere else.

**(Source: Tyneside UFO Society/Unknown newspaper, 11.10.1977 – 'Mystery over UFO sighting')**

At 9.30pm, Mrs M. Robinson and her family sighted two 'lights'; one was orange/red, the other a bright white one. (The orange 'light' appeared to be apparently manoeuvring around the other). They remained in the same position in the sky until 9.55pm – at which point the orange 'light' disappeared leaving the other, which was still visible in the sky at 10.50pm when the family then decided to go to bed.

**(Source: UFO-Info Exchange Library)**

On this date (October 10th), the *Daily Mirror* published details of the claims made by Travis Walton.

## 11th/12th October 1977 – UFO projects 'beam of light' downwards

Melanie Howes, of Purton, was on her way home, at 9.40pm, when a 'brilliant light' lit up the sky above her head, followed by a 'beam of light' projected down from a UFO, accompanied by a buzzing noise. Frightened, she ran home. Within seconds, whatever it was had gone. Another witness was Barbara Kitchen, from Lechlade, who thought it was a fireball – until it turned green.

**(Source: The *Swindon Evening Advertiser,* 14.10.1977 – 'Help! Flying Saucer puts them all in a spin')**

On the 12th October 1977, at 3.30am, a newspaper delivery driver stopped his car while approaching the centre of Middleton, after seeing a police officer standing on the pavement staring up into the empty sky. When he asked the officer if he was all right, the man said to him *"I've just had the fright of my bloody life"* and went on to describe having seen a large 'ball of white light' drop down out of sight, behind buildings opposite. Despite enquiries made later with the police, at Middleton, no comment was forthcoming.

What lay behind the appearance of a red and green glowing object, seen by residents over Calderdale, at 8.20pm? One of the main witnesses was company director Kenneth Campbell, who was at home when his son – Craig, and three friends, rushed into the house telling him of a UFO hovering in the sky, over Ogden. Mr Campbell fetched a pair of binoculars and, after viewing the object himself, suggested they jump into the car to try and get closer.

*"We drove towards it, about five miles away. When we got to Upper Brockholes, it appeared to be over Mixenden Reservoir.*

*After parking the car, it suddenly changed to a bright rectangular object, flashed and disappeared, reappearing a few seconds later in the sky over the direction of Booth and Wainstalls – red and green again. We followed it to Mixenden, as far as Stocks Lane, where we stopped to watch it – now over the Cragg Vale district. After about 45 minutes it began to turn brilliant white, split into two parts, rejoined itself and disappeared."*

There were a number of explanations put forward to explain this. They included misidentification of a planet, or space debris (part of the ill-fated Russian Soyuz satellite, burning up) – which can hardly be said to fit, in our opinion, accepting the duration and nature of this sighting.

**(Source: Trevor Whittaker, BUFORA/*Halifax Evening Courier,* 14.10.1977 – 'Five chase UFO for two hours)**

## 13th October 1977 – Silver pulsating 'light' seen over Lancashire

Mrs Maureen Kagadis of Darnhill, Heywood, Lancashire, sighted a large silver 'pulsating light' moving across the sky in the direction of Bury.

*"It stopped over the Darnhill area for about 5-6 seconds – then moved off slowly in a zigzag movement towards Heywood and Middleton."*

Another witness was Mr Donald Woods.

At 8.35pm, Susan Williams, of Heywood, saw what appears to have been the same UFO moving in the sky, towards Manchester.

*"It had a glowing orange bottom and had a fin on either side of the object."* **(Source: UFOSIS)**

## 14th October 1977 – Finned UFO over Sheffield

Schoolboy Timothy Cox was playing football outside his house in North Leverton, near Sheffield, when he saw what looked like *"a bomb"* in flight, showing a blue light, with pieces falling from its fin at the rear, as it descended through the sky. Although the police and RAF were informed, they were unable to offer any explanation. **(Source: Dr. David Clarke)**

## 16th October 1977 – UFO over Lancashire

At 2.50pm an object was seen in the sky from Cambridge Airport, heading from the south-west direction, and was initially thought to be an aircraft. A radar control officer (who happened to be on the runway, at the time) thought that this was not the case, as the object was too fast and not on its approach flight path.

*"It then passed overhead, returned along its path taken, made a half-circle and started to rotate, before leaving at high speed.*

*I estimated it was at a height of 15,000 feet."* **(Source: Ken Rogers)**

Later the same day, Deborah Hale was looking out of her bedroom window at Warton, Lancashire, at 8pm, when she noticed:

> "...an oval grey object, flashing with lights, hovering over a nearby crag; it had a slight bump on the top."

It then moved away slowly westwards, making a droning noise, and was lost from view five minutes later. **(Source: Ian Creswell)**

### 21st October 1977 – UFO over Anglesey

Police Constable John P. Owen from Bodorgan, Anglesey, North Wales (then aged 37, with 19 years service) arrived home.

As he did so, his wife came running into the garage telling him excitedly about what she had seen in the sky.

> "My wife told me she had seen a long, thin, red coloured flame in the sky, apparently vibrating over Aberffraw Common, Anglesey, at 12.50am on 21st October 1977. At first, she took it to be an aircraft on fire. Within seconds, the flame appeared to form a circle and a domed 'figure' appeared going backwards and forwards; there was no mistaking the shape and such things as portholes could be seen quite easily."

John rushed into the kitchen and saw for himself the object in the sky, which was the colour of the setting sun and about double the size.

He then ran into the garden and called his wife to fetch his binoculars. Unfortunately, by then, the object appeared to be going backwards and then faded away.

> "I telephoned RAF Valley and spoke to the air traffic controller and explained what we had seen – then I also telephoned Police HQ, at Colwyn Bay, and my subdivision at Llangefni, reporting what we had seen. The sketch was drawn by my wife on the kitchen window in lipstick during the time she was watching it."

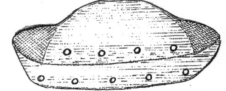

©John Owen **(Sources: Personal interview/***BUFORA Magazine***, Jan/February 1978, Volume 6, Number 5)**

### 24th October 1977 – Luminous triangular object seen over West Midlands

A number of UFO sightings took place over the Midlands, during the evening. They included *"a luminous triangle, made up of five glowing lights"*, sighted over Woden Road, Wolverhampton, *"a golden 'cigar, with a sphere balanced on top"*, seen standing upwards, just off the horizon, over Erdington, Birmingham, at 5pm, and a number of other reports, involving the appearance of clusters of red and white lights, seen moving across the sky over Northfield, Birmingham, at 7.55pm. **(Source: UFOSIS)**

### 25th October 1977 – As seen on this date by Mr Brown

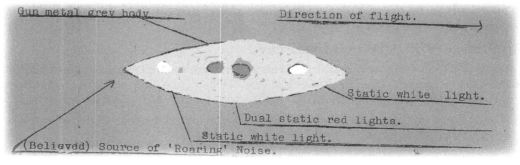

## 27th October 1977 – 'Flying Saucer' over Salisbury, Wiltshire

At 6.18am, policewoman Vivienne Crisp, from the Wiltshire Constabulary, was with another officer, travelling in a 'Panda' car along Churchfields Road, Salisbury, when they noticed an object in the sky to the east, at an estimated height of 5-700 feet.

*"It looked like a mushroom without its stalk, mottled orange in colour with dark blotches or shapes on its surface. After a short time, it began to decrease in size before vanishing from view, as if wiped out from right to left, leaving a very odd yellow cloud in the sky that slowly faded away from top to bottom, rather than the other way around.*

*After reporting it the Press, who 'got wind of the sighting', I had to laugh because when they published the illustration, it showed what appeared to be windows when, of course, it didn't look like that at all. After the event I was approached by many people, who suggested all manner of explanations, but I know what I saw could not be explained rationally."*
(**Source: Personal interview**)

## Cops sight a UFO

### By ALAN GORDON

TWO police officers yesterday put in a startling report to their station: We've seen a UFO

The claim was made by P C Chris Bazire, 20, and policewoman Vivienne White, 22, who were on panda patrol duty at dawn in Salisbury, Wilts.

They spotted "what appeared to be a flying saucer" at a height of 500-700 feet over Salisbury Plain, scene of several reported UFO sightings.

Chris said: "It was oblong with a domed top and flat bottom. It was travelling very slowly at first. Suddenly it shot off at tremendous speed, leaving a vapour trail."

A spokesman at the Boscombe Down secret experimental station on the Plain said that it was none of their apparatus. And the Army could shed no light on the mystery.

groups put together
28/10/77

## Panda patrol spots a UFO

### By David Humphrey

TWO WHITE faced young constables returned to Salisbury police station yesterday and told their inspector: "This may be a bit of a sauce, sir, but we have just seen a UFO."

P-c Christopher Bazier and W P-c Vivienne White were in a Panda car patrolling Churchfields trading estate when they saw the mystery object.

It was just after 6 am and the two officers were nearing the end of an eight-hour shift.

Through the windscreen they saw a saucer-shaped object with a dome on top hovering between 500 and 700 feet up.

They stopped the car and got out for a better view of the flat-bottomed object, which was a mottled orange-yellow colour marked by several oblong shaped dark objects.

It made no sound, there were no lights and after about 45 seconds it vanished.

### No mistake

"The object appeared to shrink in size and finally disappear leaving a short vapour trail which dispersed in about 15 seconds" said a senior police officer. "It did not reappear."

P-c Bazier, aged 20, and WPC White, 22, both single officers with two years in the force, were off duty yesterday and not available for comment, but left a pencil sketch of the UFO for their superiors to scrutinise.

"They are sure they did not mistake the object for street lamps, the moon or any reflection in the windscreen of their car," said the spokesman.

The police are taking no further action on the siting nor reporting it to the Ministry of Defence. "Their report will simply be placed in the files," added the spokesman.

## 30th October 1977 – UFO sighting … Stack Rocks, Dyfed

At 3pm on 30th October 1977, Pauline Coombes, her stepmother – Mrs Grycz (of Polish descent), and their four children, were on their way back to Ripperston Farm. Mrs Grycz suddenly pointed upwards and shouted, *"What on earth is that?"*

Pauline stopped the car and they got out and watched *"a round flat 'disc', whitish in colour"*, moving slowly across the sky, heading towards the coast, which lay at the back of the farm – some two fields away.

After watching the object drop down over the nearby Stack Rocks, Pauline and her mother made their way to the edge the field, which affords an excellent view of them.

> *"I saw two silver clad men moving about on the rock. At first, I though they were skin divers but then realised their heads were elongated and far larger than a human head – definitely*

Artist's impression of the climax of a bizarre incident reported from Dyfed, West Wales

**STACK ROCKS HUMANOIDS**

See page 7

FLYING SAUCER REVIEW
Volume 23, No. 6          70p

> *rectangular in shape, with the corners rounded off. We watched them move about on the uneven surface of the rocks, and then noticed what looked like a door opening and shutting on the right-hand side of the rock facing Broad Haven, exposing a black interior. Inside this opening could be seen a silvery clad 'figure' – apparently, from his actions, walking up and down steps. First his head would appear – then the shoulders and chest, then he would go back down again. The other 'figure' walked about with a normal gait, as though walking on a flat surface, appearing to literally walk on the water, before, like its companion, it abruptly vanished from view."*

(Source: Personal interview with Pauline Coombes/Tony Pace, BUFORA/Randall Jones Pugh – FSR *'Stack Rocks Humanoid Display'*, Volume 23, No. 6, April 1978)

## UFO display filmed over Stonehenge

A UFO over Stonehenge, captured on cine camera by a family, camping, was shown to television viewers on 21st April 1978, by '*News at Ten*'- but later explained away as being a fireball, despite a number of lengthy manoeuvres across the sky!

The actual incident took place in October 1977 and involved two Cheshire families a total of six people who were on holiday near Stonehenge when they captured on Super 8 colour movie film three and a half minutes of footage showing numerous manoeuvring balls of light in the sky. One object is said to have hovered for fifty minutes.

According to Dan Goring of the Essex UFO study Group, he learnt that a portable TV and compasses were affected, and that more worryingly one of the two men present was taken to hospital needing treatment to a skin disease, caused by one suspects getting to close to one of the objects. (We learnt from Peter's article below that his body was completely covered with this rash and that the skin appeared as if scalded).

The incident was also investigated by Peter Warrington then Chairman of Manchester UFO Research Association and founder member of UFOIN wrote an article in *FSR* Volume 23 No 6 April 1978 'Remarkable Encounter at Stonehenge'. In an interview conducted by Peter and Jenny Randles with three of the witnesses, and a researcher from Granada TV the family outlined what had taken place.

Our efforts to track down the whereabouts of this intriguing piece of film which shows objects resembling brilliant lights appearing in the sky, clearly visible on the film shown by Granada TV's 'Reports Extra' on 22 April 1978. When an astrophysicist on the programme admitted the behaviour of the lights could not be that of ball-lightning and suggested Army flares instead.

This was refuted by the Army who had been consulted, they stated that none of their activities on the date could have accounted for the lights, and that the witnesses had in any case seen the UFOs travel upwards before disappearing.

Having regard to the nature of the evidence presented so far it seems highly unlikely this could have been '*flares fired in the sky during an Army Exercise on Salisbury Plain,*' or '*fireballs,*' as suggested in the Press, or whatever inane other explanations that had been proffered as the explanation

Details of the incident were published by the *Daily Express* on the 21st of April 1978 and *Granada TV* screened a half hour programme on UFOS *which included interviews with all of the witnesses* and of course a sceptical Doctor (*unnamed*) who debunked the whole affair, despite Kodak pronouncing the film as genuine and that the film recorded in their opinion a natural phenomenon such as ball-lightning.

(**Source: as above/Volume 23 No 6 *FSR* April 1978**)

# CHAPTER 23 – NOVEMBER 1977

## 3rd November 1977 – UFO seen over Cheshire

A vivid round 'light' with rainbow colouring, lighting up the immediate area, was seen by four elderly people returning home at 12.30am, two and a half miles south-east of Crewe – last seen heading over the direction of Nantwich, in Cheshire.

(**Source: FUFOR, M.A. Tyrrell and P. Clarke**)

## 4th November 1977 – UFOs reported over Leicestershire

This was followed by reports of "*strange flashing lights and humming sounds*" seen over South Wigston, Braunstone, Hinckley, and Leicester, during the day and early evening.

### 4th November 1977 – Triangular object seen over dwelling house, Essex

Mr Roy George of Anders Fall, Whitehouse Meadows, Eastwood, Leigh-on-sea, Essex, was driving towards Billericay, at 8.30pm.

> *"I noticed two white lights in the south-eastern sky, which appeared to be about 15 feet apart from each other. In the middle was a red light, creating a triangular shape – not a defined triangle but more of a grey blur – hovering silently over a nearby house. About a minute later it shot away, then reappeared behind me about 250 yards away on my left-hand side. The white lights were flashing while stationary, and then the red one lit up. By now they were moving away, so we carried on our journey."*

Bill Eden of the Essex UFO Group, who investigated this matter, wrote to the occupiers of the houses concerned. In return, he received a reply from a Mr Roland Lazarus, who said:

> *"I must say that I am very sceptical towards any sort of science fiction. It would, however, have been difficult for the three of us not to notice the malfunction of an electrical appliance. We were watching the TV on the 4th November, at about 7pm, when a capacitor on the TV 'blew', interrupting the picture briefly but cutting the sound off completely. This was the first time in almost 4 years that something had gone wrong with it. The cause of the malfunction remains a mystery. It was very windy that evening, and apart from the TV there is nothing else unusual I remember. Thank you for your surprising letter."*

### 7th November 1977 – Cylndrical object over Cheshire

At 4.55pm, Mr Marriot (formerly employed as a RAF radar operator) was driving through the village of Haslington, in Cheshire, when he noticed *"a flash of light"* towards the direction of Alsager, at an angle of 25 degrees. Looking upwards, he saw:

> *"...a black cylindrical disc-shaped object, displaying a blue light at each end, the size of a large helicopter."* (**Source: FUFOR, M.A. Tyrrell**)

### 8th November 1977 – Giant propeller, pear-shaped objects and UFO display

At 9.30am, Mr Paul Johnson from Doulton Road, Old Hill – a butcher by trade – happened to look up into the sky and see:

> *"...what looked like a giant propeller shooting across the sky, catching the sun; it suddenly stopped and hovered for about 30 seconds before heading away towards the south. When it stopped it started to wobble slightly. There was no noise at all. At first I thought it might have been a helicopter, but it was far too large to be that."*

*"Two distinctive pear-shaped objects"* were seen in the sky over Rowley Regis (to the north-west of Birmingham) on the late afternoon.

Housewife Ann Wood of 67, Banners Lane, Halesowen, was doing some washing when she saw:

> *"...what looked like a parachute with a mysterious metal canister hanging from it, land in Haden Hill Park."*

The police were called, who searched the area, but nothing was found.

This was followed by a report of *"a ball of orange coloured light, continually flashing"* seen at 6pm, over Oakham, in Leicestershire. (**Source: *Wolverhampton Express and Star*, 8.11.1967 – 'Police search for a UFO'**)

### UFO over Crewe

At 7.36pm, Stephen Cleaver – an investigator for the Federation of UFO Research (FUFOR) was sat in a car with Dawn Cookson, adjacent to the *Sydney Arms* public house, on the eastern outskirts of Crewe.

**Stephen:**

> *"I saw a bright light in the sky and brought it to the attention of Dawn. It was in the north-east, at an elevation of about thirty degrees off the horizon. It seemed to be moving from left to right in a semicircular motion and had a dull red light underneath it. A bleeping noise could be heard from it."*

At this point the couple were joined by four other people, who watched it performing its now classic UFO movements across the sky – from left to right, stopping, and then moving from left to right. Five minutes later, it was lost from sight. (**Sources: Personal interview/Stephen Cleaver, FUFOR**)

## Avon/Bristol UFO sighting

In the same month, a motorist (an observer with the Royal Observer Corps), was driving along the M5 Motorway, near Portishead, Avon, at 2pm, on a bright and sunny afternoon, when he saw what looked like:

> *"...an aircraft, without any wings or tail – the size of a small airliner – showing six 'portholes' along its side, heading from the direction of Bristol, towards Portishead Power Station. It stopped over the power station at a height of about 200 feet, for a few minutes, before flying away towards South Wales, over the Avonmouth; as it moved away it left behind it two exhausts or vapour trails".*

(**Source: Peter Tate, Bristol**)

## 10th November 1977 – Purple 'craft' seen over Wales

Margaret Ellen Fry – Head of the Welsh Federation of Ufologists – told us about an incident involving a couple out driving, near the village of Llandyrnog, Denbighshire, when they encountered a *"purple triangular craft"* and later complained of *"missing time"*.

According to Margaret, the couple (who expressed a wish to remain anonymous) were warned not to discuss the matter with anybody after reporting it to the RAF.

Margaret Fry

## 16th November 1977 –Mysterious globes seen over West Midlands

Three black and red 'globes of light' were seen moving across the sky over Rowley Regis, near Birmingham. (**Source: UFOSIS**)

## 18th November 1977 – Silver 'Flying Saucer' over North Humbeside

A group of seventeen children were out playing on the school field, at Wawne, North Humberside, when they saw a *"silver flying saucer"* heading across the sky – a matter they brought to the attention of their headmaster, who asked them to recreate from plasticine what they had seen. (**Source: Derick Shelton, SUFORS**)

On the same day, a brilliant white 'light' was seen in the sky, heading towards Silsden, West Yorkshire, at 7pm, by Mr Monkhouse. As it neared the horizon, it broke up into three pieces. Was this space debris, or connected with the earlier report, at Wawne? (**Source:** *Flying Saucer Review*)

## 25th November 1977 – Glowing light over Greater Manchester

A grey/green 'ball of glowing light' was seen moving backwards and forwards over Wharmton Rise, near Saddleworth Railway Station, Greater Manchester, by Mrs Brice and her friend, while returning home on the evening. (**Source: MUFORA**)

## 28th November 1977 – UFO over Southampton

A mystery 'craft' was seen over Southampton. UFO enthusiast and long-time veteran researcher with the Southampton UFO Group – Ernest Sears (now sadly passed away), was putting the cat outside, at 8.15pm, when he happened to glance up into the sky and see:

*"...a large circular object with coloured lights underneath it, with a red light at the front, a green light on one of the other edges, and a more yellow than white light underneath, which illuminated the underneath of the object. By the time I had gone in, picked up a pair of binoculars and rushed outside, it was no longer in view."* (**Source: Personal interview**)

# CHAPTER 24 – DECEMBER 1977

### 2nd December 1977 – Domed UFO over Pembroke

The *West Wales Guardian* Newspaper (2.12.1977), told of a UFO seen by Pembroke teenagers – Catherine and Brian Barnikel, who were walking home at 10pm, when they saw *"a domed object in the sky, showing three white lights on top"*, making its way slowly towards Freshwater East – which was reported to the local police, who sent two officers to interview them.

### 3rd December 1977 – UFO display over Manchester

*"Several white lights, spinning around each other in the sky together"*, were seen for approximately ten minutes, slowly moving eastwards over Oldham, Greater Manchester, at 3am, by Mrs Cheetham, driving home at the time, who *"gained an impression they may have been attached to a larger rotating object, not seen at the time"*.

At 5pm the same day, Mr Greenwood was driving along the A672, three-quarters of a mile east of Denshaw, Greater Manchester, when he noticed a flashing light, low on the horizon to the North, which was seen to hover briefly over Ogden Reservoir – the flashing being replaced by a red glow before being lost from sight

(**Sources:** *Northern UFO News*, **J. Randles/MUFORA**)

**TIMES' 2/12/77**
## In brief

## New tactics on flying saucers

New York, Dec 1.—Grenada has withdrawn a resolution to set up a special United Nations agency or department to research into unidentified flying objects and related phenomena.

Instead, it is circulating a draft resolution at the United Nations calling on Dr Wald-heim, the Secretary-General, to conduct an investigation into flying saucers, including an analysis of the benefits, prob-lems and dangers stemming from any contact with extra-terrestrial life.

At 6.28pm, three people at Castleshaw, Greater Manchester, including Mr and Mrs Bottomley, sighted a 'bright light' in the sky towards the south-east, described as:

*"...having a match sized head of pink/red colour, with a bright glow around it – bright enough to illuminate part of the sky and some of the ground below. It was then seen to move from its static position across the head of the valley, changing colour from red, orange, yellow to white, and gone in a minute."*

We were told the Bottomley's received a visit from two men, who said they were from Customs and Excise, asking for information about a nearby neighbour, the following Sunday. Whether the men were genuine or not is a matter we can only speculate on. (**Source: MUFORA**)

### 4th December 1977 – UFO sighted over Middlesex

At 5.40pm, Mr Amos and his wife of Westmoor Road, Enfield, Middlesex, along with their daughters – Jennifer (then aged 29) and Claire (then aged 4), were walking along the lane towards their house. They saw:

*"...two white 'globes of light' in the sky, quite low down, stationary over the junction with Westmoor Road. They seemed to be attached to each other. Above was a smaller red light, also apparently forming part of whatever the object was."*

An aircraft passed overhead – at which point the lights descended, making a humming noise.

The family passed underneath the three objects, which then moved away at high speed, leaving the family frightened. According to Mr Amos, even the young girl seemed agitated. (**Source: Dan Goring**)

## 7th December 1977 – UFO, Clifton Campville, Staffordshire

Pauline Broadhurst – a pleasant, friendly woman, whom we met up with, some years later – was walking home with her children, one afternoon, near the picturesque village of Clifton Campville, close to the Staffordshire border. As they passed Lullington Woods, on their left – a regular journey made most days – they saw:

> *"...an enormous orange 'globe of light' swinging backwards and forwards in the sky, as it descended towards where we were, illuminating the hedges and landscape below it. I became very frightened and bundled the children together and ran home."*

**(Source: Personal interview)**

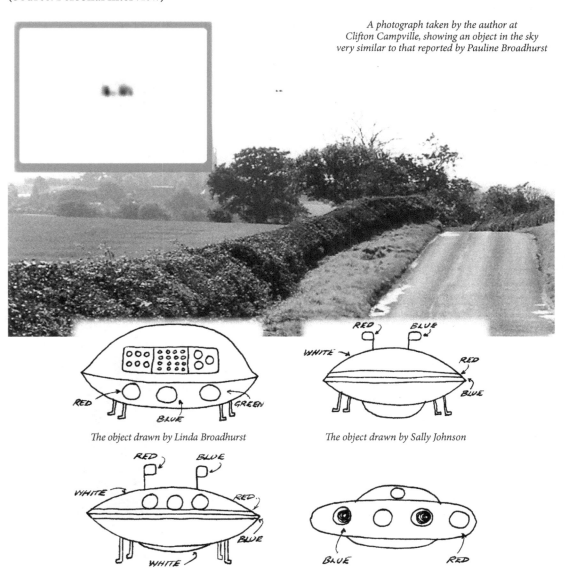

*A photograph taken by the author at Clifton Campville, showing an object in the sky very similar to that reported by Pauline Broadhurst*

*The object drawn by Linda Broadhurst*          *The object drawn by Sally Johnson*

### 8th December 1977 – UFO over Essex

Mr Michael Spicer of Wellington Drive, Dagenham, Essex, accompanied by Mr Michael McCarthy, of Birdbrook Close, and another friend, were returning from the shop at 9.30pm, close to Ballards Road.

*"We spotted six UFOs in the sky – four white in colour, the other two red. One of the red objects appeared to collide with another.*

*The next thing was that a cigar-shaped object appeared in the sky surrounded by an orange-white glow. Suddenly this disappeared from sight. We watched the others for 20 minutes, until they moved away and out of sight."* **(Source: Ron West)**

### 11th December 1977 – 'Flying Hovercraft' and three lights seen

Mr Montague Vicajee from Winton, near Bournemouth, was getting ready for work, at 7am, when he noticed a flashing light in the sky.

*"As it moved closer, I was astonished to see a 'tug'-shaped object – like a 'Flying Hovercraft' with a grey glowing centre, surrounded by a white band of light. The front of the object was slightly bulbous and showed a flashing light inset. It had no wings, or obvious means of propulsion, and was flying at a height I estimated to be 2,000 feet, moving at 100 miles per hour. Within a short time it had gone out of view."* **(Source: Leslie Harris/Mrs Vicajee)**

At 9am, Mrs B.H. Stickland of Northfleet, in Kent, wondered what had caught her newspaper boy's attention, and looked up into the sky. She saw, over Haynes Road, a long orange cigar-shaped object.

*"In the middle were three large brilliant lights and three smaller ones on each side. It hovered above the house for about five minutes, before suddenly vanishing from sight."*

**(Source: Mr M. Weaven, BUFORA)**

On the same evening, a woman motorist was driving fom Crosthwaite to Underbarrow, South Lakeland, when she noticed:

*"...three large 'lights' in the sky, over Mount Joy Hill – red, blue, and amber, in a line. The red one kept flashing on and off. I got out of the car. It was really quiet – then there was this almighty roar, like a 'souped up' car engine. The object started to move towards me, and the middle light stopped flashing. As it moved over the top of me, I saw what looked like a great big 'triangle', with three lights on its base and one on the top. It stood still in the sky for a few minutes, before slowly moving away."*

**(Source: *Westmorland Gazette*, 15.12.1978 – 'Another UFO spotted')**

### 12th December 1977 – UFO over Clifton Campville

Linda Broadhurst (daughter of Pauline, from Clifton Campville), accompanied by three friends – Sally Johnson, Georgina Ward and Lynne Watkins – were taking turns to ride a pony over heathland, known as Ward's field, close to Lullington Church, when they noticed an object in the sky approaching their position, at 4.30pm.

*"It was making this awful buzzing noise. At first, we thought it was an aircraft, in trouble, but then soon changed our mind when we saw what looked like two dull white plates, placed rim to rim, about 10 feet in diameter, with a middle section consisting of two bands – a red one above a blue one. On top were two red and white flashing lights, apparently attached to silver cylinders on its surface. The UFO was about eight feet in diameter and we could*

*The four children involved in the main encounter, from left to right: Linda Broadhurst, Sally Johnson, Gina Ward and Lynne Watkins*

*see a row of three portholes, set into its upper side. Every fifteen seconds or so it rotated anticlockwise, showing a slightly curved white protrusion on its underside, surrounded by a rectangle, containing four dark 'L' shaped objects that looked like landing legs. Panic set in. The horse tried to bolt, unseating one of the girls. We all ran away, feeling very frightened."* **(Source: Personal interview)**

## 25th December 1977 – Close encounter, Surrey … burn marks found

On Christmas Day, 1977, Keith Lane from Kenley, Surrey, (close to Kenley Aerodrome), went out to feed his pet rabbits and guinea pig. As he was doing this, he became aware of a 'man' who appeared to be between 6-7 feet tall, standing at the bottom of the garden.

*"He was wearing a one-piece silvery suit – like an Astronaut. He had a white belt and the shoes were joined to the trousers. The 'man' had a long forehead, with eyes showing red pupils, surrounded by blue – glowing, like cat's eyes in the dark. He had long sandy hair. I was frightened and ran into the house, where I remained for the rest of the day."*

The next morning, Keith ventured out when he was shocked to find the guinea pig dead in its hutch. The rabbits were unharmed.

At 6.30pm on Boxing Day, Keith was startled by the appearance of *"two small people"* – one about five feet tall, the other four feet – who were identical in appearance to the person he had seen the day before, standing about seven feet away from the kitchen door. He shouted out in alarm, and the 'figures' vanished instantly before his parents arrived.

UFO Investigator – Roy Fisher – attended and, after interviewing Keith, drove onto the Aerodrome (then used for HGV testing) and discovered a forty feet circular mark, burnt into the tar and grass, which had not been seen by the workmen there before.

**(Sources: Dan Goring, 'Earth-link', October 1972/Derek Mansell/Roy Fisher, 'Contact UK')**

## 30th December 1977 – UFO sighted over Crymych, Dyfed, in Wales

Mrs M.B. Rees wrote to Peter Paget, following his appeal in a local newspaper with regard to sightings of UFOs.

At about 4.30pm, Linda Rees, her daughter (then aged 10), and her friend – Heather Morgan (then aged 11), were on their way to visit a local pet donkey at a nearby farm, when they sighted a UFO rushing across the sky making a whistling noise.

# BACK TO THE BEGINNING

## UPDATES

WE now journey back to the beginning of the book with regard to the UFO sighting made by three Bessingby factory cleaners while on their way to work on January the 21st 1977 one of whom was Lesley Buttle. She was interviewed in 2014 by Paul Sinclair UFO author of *Truth Proof* and is the last living witness to the sighting.

**Paul:**

*"When I interviewed Lesley I never thought another witness would contact me to say that they had seen something very similar, close to the location the Britax cleaners encountered the incredible UFO. But that is exactly what happened in early December 2017. What's more Estella Moyce-Timson lives less than 100 yards from Lesley Buttle, yet neither knew of each other's sighting or have ever spoken in all of that time.*

### Estella Moyce-Timson

A surprising new development took place recently (2017) when an Estella Moyce-Timson (now 55 in 2018) contacted Paul after reading *Truth Proof* and told him she thinks she saw the same object when 15 years old at the time and that she remembers it as clearly today as when she saw it all those years ago with her mother.

**Estella:**

*"We lived on the council estate at West Hill – the allotments sat between our home and the Bessingby industrial estate. My mum actually kept one of the allotments and we spent most of our free time there digging and planting.*

*Access to and from the allotments was obtained by walking along the industrial estate. We always left the allotments just before it got dark and part of our walk home took us past Britax PLG. [The same factory where Lesley Buttle worked as a cleaner.]*

*We noticed an unusually bright gold light in the sky; interesting enough to make us stop and observe it. It then slowed, got lower and lower, until it appeared to be just above the factory roof. Me and my mum were amazed by this thing, it just descended and hung over the factory roof for a while. It was a golden orange colour and was spinning around really fast. We could not hear any sound and it's hard to say how big it was. But it looked quite large, as big as a car from where we stood.*

*What it did next however was really strange; it rose up into the air in a sort of hooping movement* then came back down again. It continued to do this all the way along the factory roof. We watched it in amazement. When it reached the end of the buildings it began performing the same peculiar movements all the way back to where it started. Another thing was that I cannot remember seeing any lights on in the factory, which was odd because we always walked home just before dark and the lights were usually on."

### Paul Sinclair

"Another interesting point, if we assume that the sightings were on the same day, was that Estelle and her mom would be leaving the allotments around the same time that Lesley and her co workers were arriving to do there cleaning at the factory. Of course it is impossible to say that the Lesley Buttle sighting and Estella's occurred on the same day. But I think there is a strong possibility that they did. The area around the allotments was where the UFO was seen.

Both sets of witnesses were close to Britax PLG and Lesley Buttle and her work colleagues say the factory had come to a standstill when they arrived to clock in. That could account for the factory being in darkness when Estella and her mom passed.Of course, we will never know for sure, but what is certain is that in January 1977 something outside of human understanding was seen and experienced at Bessingby."

Size of object in comparison to the factory's

### 17th February 1977 – UFO sighting at La Aurora *Special Feature*

Whilst the following incident did not take place in either the UK or the USA it is worth including if only to illustrate the danger that surrounds the presence of a UFO taking into consideration that we have been unable to trace the witnesses, although we have no reason to believe it is genuine in nature.

#### Previous sightings reported

It took place at a ranch run by eleven farmhands and 730 herd of cattle nine miles south of Salta, Uruguay on 3000 acres of land owned by a Mr Angel Maria Tonna (then aged 52) and his two sons, 19 and 22 years of age. It appears that between the period of February and March a dozen UFO sightings took place around the locality – witnessed by members of the Tonna family and farm hands.

#### Bright light seen over farm

At about 4am Mr Tonna and his foreman Juan Manuel Fernandez were driving 80 cows into the barn for milking when the lights (powered by a generator) went out. This was followed by the appearance of a bright light seen at the east end of the barn. Mr Tonna at first thought there had been a power outage and that hay kept in the barn had caught fire. He ran towards the source of the light accompanied by his dog Topo (Dunce in Spanish).

> *"I heard a noise and saw a fiery disc, like two plates placed face to face hovering a short distance above the ground behind the barn."*

He stood and watched the object until his foreman told him the cows were running away, accompanied by a frenzied barking from other dogs nearby.

At this stage the '*disc*' began to move in a southerly direction breaking off the branches of a tree near the barn as it did so in a peculiar rocking motion before coming to a halt and hovering over some trees about 100 yards south, at a height of 60 feet in the air.

### Approaching the UFO

Then it moved eastwards moments later but halted over a concrete bath that the cows used to disinfect themselves. By this time Tonna and his dog, a 60lb black and brown police dog, had made their way to the west side of the yard which was illuminated by light coming of the '*disc*' and climbed the fence.

The dog and its master moved towards the UFO which turned in mid air and began to move towards them, coming to a halt about 60 feet away. Topo ran toward the UFO on the attack but stopped and sat down a on a small mound some 15 feet away looked up and howled.

### Tonna:

> "*When the object began moving towards me I noticed six beams of light, like small wings, three on each side. Suddenly I felt electric shocks in my body and an intense heat hit me. I had to throw my arms over my face. After this the object moved away changing in colour from bright orange to red, increasing its speed as it did so. Several minutes later it was last seen close to the first, about half a mile away to the south when it was then lost from view.*"

After it had gone the generator began to run again but didn't produce any electricity because the wires were burned out. The whole incident had lasted some ten minutes Tonna's 19-year-old son Tulio, a second veterinary student at the University at Salto, was also witness to the event.

### 'Topo' affected – later found dead

After the incident the dog refused to eat or drink, moved around normally but declined to leave the house, which was, of course, all out of character. Sadly and bizarrely, 'Topo' was found dead on the same mound where he sat and howled at the UFO.

### Post-mortem conducted

A post-mortem was conducted on the animal by a vet from North University in Salto, accompanied by Tulio Tonna and three other second year students. According to a copy of the autopsy report, it was ascertained:

1. The hair along the animal's spine was sticky but completely hard.

2. The fat under the skin was found on the outside – which meant it had to have been melted and then come through the pores solidifying when on the outside.

3. The dog had been exposed to a very high temperature that can't be achieved naturally by the animal.

4. All the blood vessels had been bleeding very much and all the capillaries were broken. The rupture of the blood vessels was caused by an increase in temperature that couldn't be normal.

5. The liver, normally dark and red, was completely yellow, caused by a high fever. All the blood vessels were yellow too.

6. With all the blood vessels broken, the animal started bleeding inside and lost so much blood that 48 hours later the amount of blood he had circulating was insufficient and he died of a heart attack.

7. When the skin was removed from the dog, no bruises were seen or marks; none of the hair was burned.

8. Conclusion: Something very hot had caused this.

Mr Tonna's right arm, which he had put up to shield his eyes, began hurting. Several days later, Dr. Bruning Herrera, a friend of the Tonnas, examined Mr Tonna and found the underside of his arm very red and, after being told of the circumstances, decided the irritation was caused by some kind of radiation. Eventually the condition cleared up with no lingering after-effects.

We came across a very interesting article, written by Mr Pablo Villarrubia Mausó, who told of his own investigation into the incident some 20 years later. We emailed Pablo, hoping to obtain further information in mid-January 2018, and will update the reader as time goes on.

### What happened at La Aurora? *by Pablo Villarrubia Mausó*

*"I left Montevideo behind and was heading toward the city of Salto on the Argentinean border, riding a dilapidated bus in order to rescue from oblivion the events which occurred one distant February 17th, 1977. The central protagonist of the story was the owner of the La Aurora ranch, a man named Angel María Tronna. The victims included one dog, several sheep, a bull and one horse – gravely affected by an object come from afar.*

*The first thing I did upon arriving was making a straight line toward the office of the El Pueblo newspaper to consult old newspapers, which would put me on the track of the "Tonna Case". The Saturday the 19th edition was already legendary, since it presented the first news item on the macabre event.*

*On Sunday, February 13th, 1977, at 5.30am, Julio Cesar Rattín, (18), the youngest son of Angel Tonna, witnessed a UFO at a distance of some 150 metres, suspended over a copse of eucalyptus trees. It was a light-emitting disk that illuminated a broad swath of countryside. On the following day, Monday at midnight, Tonna's wife, Elena Margarita Rattín, was watching TV before going to bed, when a blackout suddenly occurred. Upon going outside to insure the operation of their generator, she noticed an intense glow over La Aurora. Frightened, she ran back into the house.*

### Newspaper reports on incidents

*It was the February 20th, 1977 edition that announced half a page saying "UFO in a ranch near the Daymán: Seen on three occasions". The anonymous journalist said that at 04:00 on February 17th, Tonna, his children and some farmhands, witnessed a strong light coming from behind a shed in which they stored feed. It was then that they saw a 'flying saucer', measuring some 3 metres in diameter at an altitude of 15 metres.*

*'The cows were frightened and stampeded, trampling one of the workers; the dogs howled in terror and we couldn't contain our astonishment. I was able to notice that the lights of the farm and the vicinity were totally out and that the generator 'coughed', threatening to seize up. The disk moved slowly, almost in a zigzag motion, and after passing over the pasture pond it headed toward the eucalyptus copse – the same one as on Sunday – and, after a while, we didn't see it again', Tonna told the journalist."*

### Marks found in the crop

The journalist interviewed the children and farmhands of the property. All versions agreed. *Tonna spoke of the strange prints that had emerged three months ago on the pasture, shaped like a horseshoe, 40 to 50cm. wide and with some parts more deeply sunk into the ground than others. It had a diameter of three metres and a variety of mushrooms began to grow inside it. At first the grass was burned but another type of grass soon sprang up to replace it.*

In spite of the assortment of data offered by the journalistic account, there were even more important elements missing – some which Angel Maria Tonna and his people decided not to tell the reporter from El Pueblo.

### Mummified dogs

*"It wasn't easy for me to find out more about La Aurora. I asked a few people on the street about the subject; even though 20 years had gone by, the memory of the event was still fresh in the minds of many citizens. Some said it had all been a hoax, a lie, and others believed that it was real and were even aware of the appearance of 'unidentified objects' in the region for a few years now."*

### 'Flying Saucer' sighted another witness

Even luckier ones had also witnessed the transit of 'Flying Saucers' over the county, such as twenty-year old Andrea Carpanesi.

*"What I am going to tell you took place in early 1997, at around 23:30 hours, in front of the house in which I live. I was with my friend Cecilia, and looking northward an intense light appeared. The entire neighbourhood was looking at it. It was almost orange in colour, making a pendulum movement. It lasted five minutes. Seeing such things is commonplace around here", Andrea said.*

### Pablo:

*"Could you find out if it was a satellite or an aircraft?"*

### Andrea:

*"I called the weather bureau and was told that no satellites were flying overhead, nor weather balloons or aircraft.*

*They couldn't tell me what it was either, but I can tell you something else that's very interesting…*

*Around 1993 I studied at the Universidad de Salto. The word spread that the School of Veterinary Medicine had two very strange dogs. With one of my friends, we sneaked into one of the labs, since it was forbidden to see these animals. I remember it all perfectly because it scared me. We saw a dead dog that had been propped up 'alive'. It was intact and even looked alive. It was black in colour and medium-sized. Some students said that for unknown reasons, both this and another dog which I couldn't see did not decompose or didn't do so with the normal speed associated with death. Furthermore, they added that they had been found at the La Aurora ranch. Nothing further was ever said about the subject."*

That very same day Pablo headed to the School of Veterinary Medicine. Everything he heard upon asking about dead dogs at La Aurora was a *"we don't know"* and an almost unbearable silence accompanied by not very friendly glances.

### Journalist – Carlos Ardaix

The next step in assembling this puzzle was to find journalist Carlos Ardaix, one of the first to appear after the incidents of February 1977, who welcomed Pablo into his home and told him about his contact with Angel Tonna.

### Carlos:

*"At that time I hosted a radio show with a considerable following. It was when Angel Maria Tonna phoned me and said: 'If you want to know the truth about La Aurora and why the city's lights went out, come over'. I went with two or three people from the radio station. When we arrived Tonna was still rather upset. He told me that at 04:00 hours they had seen*

*a light behind the shed and thought that it was on fire. The horses, the dogs . . . all of the animals were frightened. Tonna walked to some 50 metres of where the apparatus was. It approached slowly and Angel fell to the ground, covering his face with his arm to avoid the powerful light. 'Later the object vanished at high speed', the newspaperman explained. There was talk of burned or severed wires.*

*When I reached the ranch, the steel wires were still cut and the cables of the electrical facility. The engine's piston broke down, and a very expensive breeding bull died slowly. I understand that an autopsy was performed on it at the School of Medicine and no cause of death was established. The same happened to several sheep, whose wool was singed black and left like rough wafer. A very fierce dog that Tonna kept died little by little. Tonna had a skin eruption on the arm that he used to shield his face from the light."*

**Pablo – Had he any reason to doubt Tonna's information?**

**Carlos:**

*"No, he seemed very sincere. In any event, as a journalist, I tried to find other witnesses. One of the farmhands had already seen something similar near the site. I visited other farms near La Aurora, since I thought a local may have seen the UFO. I asked a foreman and he told me hadn't seen anything at night. As we walked out, a farmhand chopping wood told me: 'We all saw what happened at night, but we were forbidden to speak of it'. After that we transmitted Tonna's recording over the air. There was a chain reaction. Many people started visiting the site, like those Americans who wanted to take him back to the U.S. for testing.*

**Pablo – Do you recall who these men were?**

*"No. It was said at the time that they were from NASA, but I'm not sure. I think there was an American journalist [among them]. At the time the Salto Grande dam was being built and there were Japanese engineers staying at the farm. One physician -Dr. Menoni –discovered, through some photographs, that there was considerable radiation in the trees at La Aurora. The Japanese confirmed it on their measurement devices.*

**Pablo – What about the burns on Tonna's arm?**

*"It was a burn that would reoccur sporadically. The electrocardiogram machine wouldn't work when the electrodes were placed on him. That's what two doctors I know told me. After two years the burns began to fade. It was something truly strange that could've had something to do with radiation."*

**Pablo – What about power blackouts?**

*"No one has been able to explain why there were so many blackouts in 1977. On the night on which the events played out in La Aurora, there was a half-hour long blackout. In following days there were others, always whenever UFOs appeared."*

**Pablo – Could there have been something more behind the events – human manipulation perhaps?**

*"Never! I can tell you that the breeding bull he had died, and it was worth a fortune. That wasn't a joke. The pedigree horse didn't die ... he was a stud and was rendered sterile."*

**Pablo –** *Is it true that the ranch became a place of pilgrimage?*

*"Yes, but Angel Tonna, in recent years, is sick of receiving callers and has chosen not to let anyone in and to refuse interviews.*

*I understand because he wants to work normally, look after his animals and his property. So many people came from all over the world, like American ufologists James Hurtak, Bob Pratt, and Pedro Romaniuk from Argentina. Tonna showed me a letter in which Antonio Ribera claimed to be interested in visiting La Aurora, but he couldn't come. The most controversial was a visit by Neil Armstrong – the first man on the Moon. No one knows why he visited."*

**Pablo – Do these pilgrimages still go on?**

*"Sometimes entire buses of people come seeking cures. Yes, they think the place was blessed by a supernatural force. It was decided to build a crypt to Padre Pío there and don't ask me why. The people who find the warning sign advising them to stay away from La Aurora cross the road where they find the chapel of ten priests that makes miracles, healings."*

### Radioactivity on the farm

**Pablo:**

*"On the following day I tried contacting Tonna and his relatives, using the phone numbers featured in the local directory. After some frustrated events, I managed to speak to one of his sons, the veterinarian, and he told me that his father no longer spoke of Angel Tonna. The matter was closed for him.*

*My only alternative was to open other fronts. One of these was to locate Doctor Juan María Menoni, the same one who took photographs in the area which showed traces of radiation. 'I'm not an ufologist', he said, 'but I became interested in the case at the time. When I visited the site, I found that part of the fence had been melted. The generator and the motor had burned out. I took a sample of tree bark that had been burned by the UFO. A photographer friend suggested that I place the piece of bark over a strip of 35mm film. When we developed the film some strange spots appeared on the film.'*

*Without a word, Menoni went to his office and returned with some photo enlargements, which showed the result of the vegetable matter's exposure. It's curious. It seemed to be charged with radiation, but where was the radiation coming from? It must've been from the mysterious 'Flying Saucer'.*

*A few days later, in Buenos Aires, I had an interview with famous parapsychologist and ufologist Antonio Las Heras, who had visited La Aurora in 1978 to look into the case.*

*'What happened there drew my attention. I saw the trees, the toppled eucalyptuses, almost uprooted, as though a giant hand had played with them. I saw the branches ripped off by a UFO's effects. In fact, they looked like someone had smashed them, making them tumble over and over. I found calcined rock with vitreous formation on the sandstone. For vitrification to occur, the temperatures must be in excess of a thousand degrees [Centigrade]. I saw a giant mushroom, measuring a metre and a half in diameter, standing inside the strange marks left by the UFOs. Only radiation could have mutated those living organisms.'*

*"Las Heras told me that Tonna had been accompanied by a police dog that fateful night.*

*'The animal died three days later. They said that it had no blood, as though it had been absorbed through its flesh, which had developed an inconsistent appearance, like flesh that has been boiled. The dog's skin was burned in several patches and its tail hairs were bristled like wire. No one was able to offer a diagnosis for what occurred', he said, shaking his head."*

### Pablo – What happened to the bull?

*"It was a show animal of great value and it died with the very same symptoms as the dog, but after a week. The horse – a stallion – was left sterile. The sheep deaths were also mysterious; they had a sort of band around their bodies which passed through their withers. It was really a burned patch, as though a branding iron had been applied."* – according to Tonna.

### Pablo:

*"That made me react associating the facts with the enigmatic manifestations of the infamous Chupacabras, but much later in the mid-Nineties. A large amount of farm animals turned up dead in several Latin American countries, generally bled dry, attacked by an unknown creature or force. Uruguayan ufologist – Jorge Monsalve, whom I couldn't locate, also interviewed Tonna around the time. In his book –* Encuentros Cercanos con OVNIS *(Montevideo, 1995) – Monsalve explains how he arrived in time to see the Normandy bull, imported from France, still alive. Tonna asked the man to touch the animal's horns: That being said, I extended my hand and [the horn] practically crumbled in my finger, a sad and disagreeable experience."*

(Source: The *Appro Bulletin*, August 1977/What happened at La Aurora? *by Pablo Villarubia Mausó*)

### David Cayton, a specialist in the field of animal mutilations and personal friend, had this to say:

*"I did not start investigating UFOs until October 1993, after I had taken an early retirement from British Aerospace in January of that year. I then later started looking at the animal mutilation cases in 1997, then teamed up with Phil Hoyle in 2001.*

*I was not aware, until your email, outlining this very interesting and compelling 1977 animal, UFO event, along with the farmer and son's witnessing of all the odd features, which these days I guess, are now more fully realised by myself and others.*

*All the elements are there ... good witness visual, first-hand accounts of the craft's odd zigzag movements and light beams, etc., the localised heat effects, the responses of the frightened animals, including the poor dogs, the post-mortem findings of the very unusual state of organs, skin, hair and the blood, along with the strange discoloration of organs such as the liver, also the electrical effects to machinery and power cables, etc.*

*The harmful (presume ionization) radiation damage to skin and underlying tissues and what is most significant to me, is the sterilization of the male horse! Pity we do not know more about the prize bull and the sheep body state.*

*The residual radiation contamination is not, these days, that unusual ... similar effects, for example, on the tree trunks in Rendlesham Forest!!! The curved horseshoe ground markings are not that unusual either. Phil found these on a farm we visited on more than one occasion, in Shropshire, where sheep mutes had happened in that same field! In those areas the ground was 'baked dry and hard' but the grass was dying out. Phil can concur about this."*

## 1976/77 – British Serviceman sights cigar-shaped UFO over Catterick Army Camp

David Pritchard contacted us in 2017, after learning that we were in the throes of completing the revised *Haunted Skies* Volume 4 book covering the period of 1976-1977.

*"In 1976, during the long hot summer of that year, I was in the army based at Catterick Camp, Cambrai Barracks, 5th Royal Inniskilling Dragoon Guards, at the time Royal Armoured Corps training regiment.*

*On the afternoon of the sighting, I was in the barrack block, which was right on the perimeter of the camp looking over the moors. Suddenly I had the urge to look out*

Catterick Camp "arrowhead" (1972)

*Catterick Camp*

*of the window, not just out but to twist and look upwards to the roof. As I did this, a huge silver self-illuminated object appeared. It was a huge cigar-shaped object, 30 to 40,000 feet high up in the sky, about 30 degrees above the horizon and leaving a vapour trail. Suddenly the vapour trail shot back inside the 'cigar', which then disappeared in a blinding flash. I felt elated that I'd seen a UFO and thought to myself I'm going out on to the moors to see if I could see anything else, but then realised it wasn't worth bothering as they had by now gone. I was working at that time in the Officers' Mess. One of the jobs was to put out the daily newspapers first thing. All the local papers were full of sighting reports from all over the region. This confirmed that my sighting had been a genuine one of a UFO."*

This wasn't the only time UFOs had been sighted from this location. In 1972, this object was reported over Catterick Army Camp.

**In May/June 1973** Lance Corporal Mike Perrin, and his colleague – Trooper Carvell, from Catterick Army Camp, were taking part in a regular exercise on Bellerby Moor, at 11pm – a lonely and desolate spot on the edge of the Yorkshire Moors – when the radio fitted to their Landrover failed, followed by the headlights fading and then extinguishing completely.

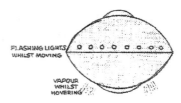

After attempting to remedy the problem they decided to wait, hoping the fault would correct itself, when Mike noticed something approaching in the sky, silently, about half a mile away. In an interview conducted with Barry King, he told him:

*"It stopped at a distance of, maybe, 100 metres, hovering some ten feet above the ground. It was shaped like a rugby ball with a row of small, circular, windows around its middle section. Through*

*these windows shone white lights, which seemed to flash. There was also some form of vapour issuing from the lowest part of the object, together with a slight buzzing sound emanating from it.*

*After it left, the radio and lights came back on."*

After arriving back at their base, they reported the matter to their Superior Officer, and were promptly arrested and charged with being drunk and leaving war department property unattended!

On the following afternoon, the two men decided to revisit the scene of the encounter and discovered a burnt circle of grass, with a diameter of 30 feet, on the other side of some woods. Mr Perrin notified his Commanding Officer of the situation and suggested the MOD be informed. He was told it was of no interest to them, although he believes the incident was later secretly investigated. When he asked if he could check with nearby radar and military installations for any information on the UFO he and his partner had seen, they were refused permission to do so.

## 21st October 1977

A silver domed object was seen in the sky over Batley, West Yorkshire, at 10.30am on 21st October 1997.

At 9.45pm on the same day, 30-40 small lights were seen moving erratically in the sky over the Catterick Garrison area of North Yorkshire, at an estimated height of about 3,000 feet, until 11pm.

## UFO landing at Warminster

In 2012, we went to see Lance Coldwell, from Chitterne – a small community on the edge of Salisbury Plain, Wiltshire.

He told us about a mysterious UFO incident which had happened at the family home, at 24 Whitbourne Springs, Corsley, Cley Hill Farm, during the summer of either 1977 or 1978, when aged seven years of age.

The first Lance learnt of what had taken place had been over the breakfast table, during conversation with his mother – Valerie Ann Coldwell – and her friend, 'Aunt' Janet, who spoke of having seen a UFO outside the house, during the night.

**Lance told us:**

*"Although I didn't see anything, I did notice my Aunt's (she was not really my aunt but a lifelong friend of my mother and a regular visitor to the house) face, which was very red – as if she had been sun burnt. The next*

**A circle of burnt grass**

TROOPERS Mike Perrin and Titch Carvell saw a UFO while on an Army exercise on the Yorkshire moors.

Mike, 27, says: "It was silvery, the size of about five Land-Rovers, and dome-shaped.

"It had portholes, and inside lights were flashing red and white.

"I tried frantically to start our Land-Rover, but the engine was totally dead.

"The object was hovering about 50 yards from us. It made a curious, buzzing noise.

"After five minutes it shot off, and all the power returned to our Land-Rover."

Mike, who was in the Royal Armoured Corps, has now left the Army.

"It's Army policy to dismiss UFO reports," he says.

"But next morning we went back with a sergeant. We found a large circle of burnt grass where the object had hovered."

*thing that happened was that I looked outside and saw about eight men in the garden of the house, examining the front lawn, which had a burnt ring cut into it, about six feet in diameter. Some of them had what looked like metal boxes and were taking measurements. Two of them were wearing white suits and poking around the brickwork.*

*My father, Dennis, went out to see them and was told by them that this was not a matter he or the family should discuss with anyone, which he took as an implied threat rather than open to discussion."*

After the men had gone, Lance went outside and examined the burnt ring left in the lawn and saw that the brickwork, some two feet off the ground, forming the outside wall of his grandmother's bungalow, was badly burnt and that some of the facings on the bricks had expanded outwards – as if subjected to considerable heat.

*"I know that my Nan – Mrs Jessie Joynes – was awoken during the night by something she heard, but went back to sleep. I decided to keep quiet and wait until my Mum had passed away. Now that my Dad died a few weeks ago, I felt that this matter should be brought to the attention of the public, as up to now nobody knows about it. I am trying to find out where Janet is currently living, as we have lost touch with her. She was, at the time, married to an American USAF serviceman, Randolph, who was then a British Taekwondo champion and running a guest house with him at Bridgwater. All I can tell you about him is that she divorced him years ago and that he has a son called Terry Randolph (using the fist name as surname?)"*

Lance was to discover that Janet was later regressed, although he has no idea as to who performed the regression, or where, but he understands she did report some missing time. From further conversation with Lance we learnt that, originally, Janet and his mother had been very interested in the UFO subject and that this interest went back to the 1950s.

**Lance:**

*"I also know that my Mum and Janet used to visit Longleat Estate, many years previously, when both very young, and had an experience there which also involved missing time, but they refused to tell me exactly what had occurred.*

*They went sky watching locally, but as the years fell away, although Janet's interest never waivered, my Mum seemed to lose some interest – too busy running the household, I suppose."*

Unfortunately, with matters such as these, nobody thought to take photos of the damage, and the whereabouts of Janet, who is the main witness to what happened, is currently unknown.

We have no reason to suppose that the version of events given by Lance is not genuine and would like to say that we offer our condolences to him for the recent death of his ten year-old son, who died from a terminal illness. Lance tells us, with pride, that his son was very much a *Dr. Who* buff, who asked for only two wishes before his death; one was to appear on the set of *Dr. Who* at Cardiff, the other was to own a Pug dog. The first was granted.

## UFO over Norwich

In October 2010, we spoke to Swindon-based Corrine Thorby – then a representative for OARS Management, Consultancy and Promotions, a qualified Para-psychologist, Psychic Practitioner, and remote viewer, having trained with The College of Management and Science, in London, with regard to giving a talk on the Warminster community radio station, Swindon, hosted by DJ Clint Denyon. Corrine – a charming woman, with

considerable experience in the field of psychic research – told what she saw, one summer evening, in July 1977/1978:

> *"After playing tennis with my sister, she decided to walk home to our mobile home park in Stratton Strawless, a few miles out from Norwich, leaving me to stay on in the tennis court. I decided to lie back on a grassy knoll and look up into the sky, when I saw a massive object moving very slowly through the air, going towards the direction of the manor house in the park. It was so big that it covered most of my view and was triangular, or arrowhead in shape, silvery-white and shiny but not overly smooth. There were lots and lots of lights on it, too – like windows of a skyscraper lit up, but in triangular form. I was so shocked and in awe that I went home and told my Dad but, unfortunately, he dismissed this. I went to bed in absolute remembrance of this event. It is still clear today as it was then. At eight years-old, I will never forget the awesomeness and size."*

**We would like to thank Vicky Jane Hyde for her assistance and encouragement with these books.**

## REST IN PEACE

Peter Hall, the father of Joanne Elizabeth Hanson, my daughter in law, passed away in February 2018. We honour his memory.

# DISCLAIMER

Should we have inadvertently missed anybody, we unreservedly apologise and will credit the copyright in *Haunted Skies,* Volume 12.

Thanks go to many people who assisted us with putting this book together. They include Nick Pope for the foreword, David Sankey, Steven Franklin, David Bryant and Wayne Mason for their illustrations. Bob Tibbitts for the design and typesetting of this volume. Phil Mantle for his assistance. Not forgetting those whose sightings and reports are contained within the pages of this book, some of whom have sadly left us.

All statements made by the people in the book involved are opinions expressed by them and should be treated as such.

These books have cost us a great deal of money to produce, but we strongly believe that this information forms part of our social history and rightful heritage. It should therefore be preserved, despite the ridicule still aimed at the subject by the media.

If anyone is willing to assist us with the preparation of any illustrations, it would be much appreciated. We can be contacted by letter at **10 Oaklands Grove Bromsgrove, Worcestershire B61 OAF**, by telephone **01527 279199**, mobile **07983 766958** or email: **johndawn1@sky.com** Website: **www.hauntedskies.co.uk**

## Volumes 1 to 6 *not* currently available – Being Revised and Updated

**Volume 1 of *Haunted Skies* 1940-1959** *(Foreword by Timothy Good)*

We present sightings from the Second Word War. They include many reports from allied pilots, who describe seeing unidentified flying objects, while on bombing missions over Germany. Some pilots we interviewed told of being ordered to intercept a UFO; one pilot was even ordered to open fire! In addition to these are reports of early close encounters, involving allegations of abduction experiences.

Another report tells of strange 'beings' seen outside an RAF Base. We also outline a spectacular sighting, in 1957, that took place in Bedfordshire, which appears identical to that seen over Oregon by employees of the Ames Research Laboratory, San Francisco. There are also numerous reports of 'saucer', 'diamond' and 'cigar-shaped' objects seen during these years.

**Volume 2 of *Haunted Skies* 1960-1965** *(Foreword by Jenny Randles)*

We re-investigated what may well be one of the earliest events, involving mysterious crop circles discovered in June 1960, at Poplar Farm, Evenlode. A 'V'-shaped UFO over Gloucestershire, and an example of a early 'Flying Triangle' over Tyneside in early September 1960. This type of object attracted much media interest in the early 1980s, following attempts by the Belgium Air Force to intercept what became labelled as 'Triangular' UFOs. This book contains many reports of saucer-shaped objects, and their occasional effect on motor vehicles. We also, wherever possible, include numerous personal letters and interviews with some of the researchers. We should not forget the early magazines, such as UFOLOG, produced by members of the (now defunct) Isle of Wight UFO Society.

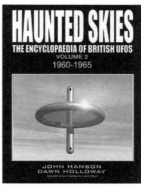

**Volume 3 of *Haunted Skies* 1966-1967** *(Foreword by Nick Redfern)*

This was two years before manned landings took place on the Moon. In October 1967, there was a veritable 'wave' of UFO sightings which took place in the UK, involving cross-shaped objects, reported from Northumberland to the South Coast, with additional reports from Ireland and the Channel islands. (The police in the USA also reported sightings of 'Flying Crosses'). The sightings took place at various times, mostly during the evening or early morning hours, and involved an object which was manoeuvrable, silent – and at times – apparently flying at a low altitude. Attempts were made by the police and various authorities to explain away the sightings as Venus, based on the fact that the planet was bright in the sky during this period, which is clearly, in the majority of sightings, not the answer.

**Volume 4 of *Haunted Skies* 1968-1971** *(Foreword by Philip Mantle)*

This book begins with a personal reference to Budd Hopkins, by USA researcher – Peter Robbins.

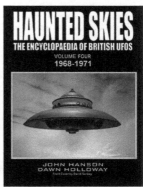

We outline a close encounter from Crediton, in Devon, which was brought to the attention of the police. Further police sightings of UFOs have been tracked down from Derbyshire, and a police chase through Kent. Multiple UFO sightings occur over the Staffordshire area, which are brought to the attention of the MOD. UFO researchers – Tony Pace and Roger Stanway – travel to London to discuss the incidents with the MOD. Close encounters at Warminster are also covered. A domed object at Bristol and further UFO landings are covered. They include a chilling account from a schoolteacher, living near Stratford-upon-Avon, and a 'flying triangle' seen over Birmingham.

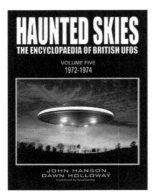

**Volume 5 of *Haunted Skies* 1972-1975** *(Foreword by Matt Lyons, Chairman of BUFORA)*

Further examples of UFO activity at Warminster, involving classic 'sky watches' from such locations as Cradle Hill, was the focus of worldwide attention during this period. In addition to this are reports of mysterious footsteps heard. A visit from the 'Men in Black', and other amazing stories, form just a tiny part of some amazing material collected by us, over the years, during personal interviews with the people concerned. UFO fleets are seen over Reading, and a landed saucer-shaped object is seen at Lancashire.

A UFO, containing aliens, is seen at close range over Worcestershire. A local councillor also described seeing what he believes was an alien spaceship, with occupants. There is also an investigation into the famous Berwyn Mountain incident, when it was alleged, by some, that a 'craft' had landed.

**Volume 6 of *Haunted Skies* 1976-1977 Jubilee edition** *(Foreword by Kevin Goodman)*

Strange globes of light, seen moving in formations of three (often referred to as triangular in overall shape). Warminster, Wiltshire – reports of mysterious black shadows, flying globes of light and a triangular-shaped UFO seen over Cleeve Hill, near Cheltenham by police officers. There is also an investigation into a number of reported landings of alien craft around the Dyfed area, in February 1977. We present some original illustrations, drawn by children at the local school (which will be reproduced in colour, in a later edition of Haunted Skies). A triangular UFO is seen over Stoke-on-Trent. Comprehensive details were also obtained, regarding Winchester woman, Joyce Bowles – who was to report many encounters with UFOs and their alien occupants.

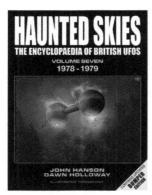

**Volume 7 of *Haunted Skies* 1978-1979** *(Foreword by David Bryant)*

The famous debate into UFOs, held at the United Nations, is covered. A UFO landing at Rowley Regis, West Midlands – involving housewife Jean Hingley – labelled by the Press as the 'Mince Pie Martian' case. Many original sketches and additional information supporting her claims are offered. Another classic UFO sighting is re-investigated, following interviews held with Elsie Oakensen – a housewife from the Daventry area – who sighted a dumb-bell shaped UFO while on the way home from work. Thanks to Dan Goring, editor of EarthLink we were able to include a large number of previously unpublished sighting reports from Essex and London. We also include a close encounter from Didsbury, Manchester involving Lynda Jones, who is known personally to us.

**Volume 8 of *Haunted Skies* 1980** *(Foreword by Philip Mantle)*

This book covers the period of just one year and is now, for the first time in the *Haunted Skies* series of books, published in colour. Unfortunately, due to the increase in pagination and the use of colour, the price has been raised, but still represents extremely good value. The first part of the book covers the period from January to November 1980. This includes numerous reports of UFO sightings and encounters. In addition to this, we outline our investigation into the Zigmund Adamski death, and the UFO sighting involving Todmorden Police Constable Alan Godfrey. In the second part, which covers December 1980, we present a comprehensive overview of the events that took place in Rendlesham Forest, thanks to the assistance of retired Colonel Charles Halt and long-standing UFO researcher, Brenda Butler.

**Volume 9 of** *Haunted Skies* **1981-1986** *(Foreword by Nick Redfern)*
Over 450 pages, many in colour

The authors point out that the majority of the information contained within the *Haunted Skies* series of books will not be found in declassified UFO files, catalogued in the Public Records Office, Kew, London.

*This book contains:*

UFO sightings over RAF Woodbridge, Suffolk – the scene of much interest during the previous month; a landed UFO at South Yorkshire; UFOs seen over Kent – harrowing close encounters between UFOs and motorists are outlined. These include a report from three women, driving home along the A5 in rural Shropshire (UK), which can be contrasted with a similar allegation made by three women from Kentucky, USA. A close encounter over the M50 Motorway, Gloucestershire; a couple from Hampshire tell of their roadside encounter – which left the husband with some strange marks on his body; a man out fishing, in Aldershot – who was approached by aliens; mysterious apports of stones that occurred, over a number of years, at Birmingham, West Midlands, involving the police – who staked out the locality in a bid to catch the offender. In addition to this, falls of coins and stones in other parts of the world are also outlined.

Although primarily covering British UFO sightings – wherever space permits (always in short supply) – we now include other forgotten worldwide cases of interest, brought to the attention of the reader. One such incident tells of a triangular UFO, seen over Arizona; another of a UFO sighted by a Russian astronaut.

A bizarre story involving David Daniels, who approached a number of prominent worldwide UFO researchers during the early 1980s – he alleged he was from the Pleiades and claimed to be able to metamorphosise from a human body to a reptilian. While it is difficult to believe rationally that this could be true, the authors tell of visits made to influential people, such as the head of the MOD, and The Lord Hill-Norton. Fact is stranger than fiction!

**Volume 10 of** *Haunted Skies* **1987-1988** *(Foreword by Nick Pope)*
632 pages, many in colour

Includes a focus on UFO cases reported from USA, Australia and New Zealand, 1940-1962.

Volume 10 of *Haunted Skies* catalogues the results of over 20 years research into reported UFO activity by the authors. The majority of those sightings and personal experiences will not be found in any declassified MOD files. Despite promises by their department to release specific individual files from 1971 (which we brought to their notice), the situation remains unchanged.

This volume covers the period of 1987-1988; which documents not only British UFO activity but also UFO activity from New Zealand, Australia and the United States, and forms an ongoing process by the authors to document such matters. In addition, a number of historical UFO cases between the periods 1940 and 1962 is also presented.

The book contains over 600 pages – many in colour – including numerous original illustrations relating to increased UFO activity over the Essex area. In addition to this, the authors outline a mysterious incident in 1987, involving claims of a UFO crash-landing in Nottinghamshire, and a spectacular sighting of goblin-like creatures that invaded a farm in Kentucky. A number of thought-provoking images, captured on camera, are shown from locations such as Cumbria, Rendlesham Forest and the Sedona area of the United States.

**Volume 11 of *Haunted Skies* 1989-1990** *(Foreword by Charles I. Halt, USAF Col. Ret.)*
756 pages, many in colour

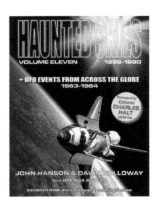

Includes a focus on UFO cases reported from UK, USA, Australia and New Zealand, 1963-1964.

Volume 11 contains over 750 pages with a foreword written by retired USAF Colonel Charles Halt – then the Deputy Base Commander of RAF Woodbridge – during the now famous UFO incident that has attracted worldwide attention, which took place in late December 1980. In this Volume the the authors continue their examination of further chronological reports of UFO activity over Great Britain, USA, Australia, New Zealand and Tasmania, for the period 1989-1990.

They also include previously unpublished material from the late Essex UFO researcher Ron West, which shows that the Essex area, like its Belgium and European counterparts, was the source of much UFO activity involving sightings of the Flying Triangle .

There is also an examination of historical UFO reports covering the period of 1963-1964, which includes sightings from the archives of Project Blue Book for the first time. In addition, the Volume outlines the valuable commitment made by the researchers themselves and their efforts to preserve what forms part of our important social history, rather than relying on other dubious sources of information.

The authors point out that very few of the UFO sighting reports published in the *Haunted Skies* books will be found in any declassified MOD files.

**Volume 1 Revised – *Haunted Skies* 1939-1959** *(Foreword by Timothy Good)*
628 pages, many in colour

The original Volume 1 of *Haunted Skies* (320 pages) covered the period 1940-1959, with a foreword submitted by Timothy Good, and was published in 2010.

Due to the early books being removed from sale in late October 2015 by our ex-publisher, we were obliged to republish the book ourselves, which then gave us full control – now the volume has twice as many pages as the early one.

This is not a reproduction of the original black and white book. It includes many additional UFO reports from RAF servicemen, accompanied by photos and images, wherever possible, in colour.

We have now gone even further into the past and presented sightings of strange objects from the turn of the Century.

In this unique book you will read of numerous inexplicable close encounters, some involving humanoid figures, red glowing objects, ghostly figures, a number of reports of landed 'craft', allegations of abduction, dogfights with UFOs, gremlins – and our review is only up to the first 100 pages!

People asked us to publish in colour; we have done that. People asked us to document as much as we could; we have also done this to the best of our ability.

No one else (as far as we know) has ever compiled such an incredible amount of UFO social history – which should be preserved for posterity. Make of it what you will.

**Haunted Skies Wiltshire** *(Foreword by Nick Pope)*
Over 700 pages, many in colour

*Haunted Skies Wiltshire* is another in a series of unique books on the UFO subject, co-written by retired Police Officer John Hanson and his partner – Dawn Holloway. The couple have made many personal visits, over a period of 20 years, to interview members of the public living in the Wiltshire area, in order to preserve the history of reported UFO activity.

This volume contains approximately 1,000 images in over 700 pages – in colour and black and white. They include photographs, sketches, private letters and illustrations, many of which have not been previously published.

Whether it's 'sky watching' from the now famous Cradle Hill, outside the lovely town of Warminster – host to some incredible UFO sightings back in the halcyon days of the 1960s/1970s, recorded by local journalist Arthur Shuttlewood – or perhaps a visit to the famous *Barge Inn* at Honey Street, Alton Barnes, overlooking the famous 'White Horse', or the magic of nearby ancient sites, such as Silbury Hill, Avebury Stone Circle, Adam's Grave, West Kennet Long Barrow, or Stonehenge, the authors have been there and enjoyed every fascinating moment.

Whatever the reason, no one can deny the breathtaking beauty of what this wonderful magical county has to offer in exceptional landscapes, and the possibility that strange objects may be captured on film or photograph.

The locality is rich with not only legends and myths but reports of UFO sightings – along with their occasional occupants – and a huge number of mysterious crop circles which abound each year, attracting tourists from all over the world, eager to see for themselves the intricate, dazzling formations which have been the subject of so much media interest over the years.

We hope you enjoy this book, as much as we have putting it together.

*John & Dawn*
**www.hauntedskies.co.uk**

**The Halt Perspective** *(Foreword by Nick Pope)*
Over 780 pages, many in colour

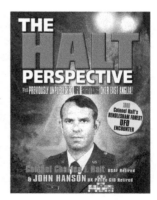

Over three nights running, in December 1980, a series of UFO encounters occurred at RAF Bentwaters and United States Air Force Woodbridge – twin bases, in Suffolk.

*"As the Deputy Base Commander in a senior management position, I knew most of the main witnesses to the reported sightings, and was involved in investigating these incidents. Additionally, as many of the readers will know, I was a witness myself to UFO activity taking place in the nearby forest. I wasn't sure what to make of what I and the other airmen saw. Other than briefly reading a book as a teenager, I never gave any thought to UFOs, although I had read one or two out of interest.*

*I asked UK retired Police Officer, John Hanson, to assist me with the publication of this book in order to set the record straight, instead of relying on the continuing rumours* about what did or didn't take place. Ironically, when initially confronted with the unexplained, I did everything in my power to keep the events quiet. Over the years there has been so much rubbish and sensational accounts given in the media surrounding the allegations made, who talk of missing time, alien beings meeting with the base commander, and so forth – more in keeping with science fiction than reality! I decided it was time to let people know exactly what took place and then make up their own minds, rather than trusting assessments made by people who weren't there and continuing publication of so much misinformation over the last 36 years. My own personal perspective on what took place needs to be told for posterity's sake."* **Colonel Charles I. Halt USAF Retired**

**Volume 2 Revised – *Haunted Skies* 1960-1969** *(Foreword by Nick Pope)*
622 pages, many in colour

*Haunted Skies* Volume 2 Revised – The history of the UFO presence on Earth – the files that Governments don't want you to see! Foreword by Nick Pope, endorsement by Irena Scott, Ph.D. John and Dawn along with V.J Hyde proudly present their latest unique book, which covers the now forgotten period of UFO history spanning 1960-1969. Many people have given us support over the years; some of them include, Betty and Freda Turpin of Coronation Street fame (aka Betty Driver), Bill Chalker, Colin Andrews, Colonel Charles Halt, Colonel Wendelle C. Stevens, Edgar Mitchell, Ex-Canadian Defence Minister – Paul Helyer, Gordon Creighton, Graham Shuttlewood, Kevin Goodman, Steve Wills, Bob Tibbitts, Malcolm Robinson, Moira McGhee, Nick Pope, Philip Mantle, Robert Hastings, Roy Lake, 'Busty' Taylor, Maria Wheatley, Polly Carson, Pat Delgado, Mathew Williams, Robert Salas, Jenny Randles, Tim Good, Trevor James Constable and many more. This revised *Haunted Skies* book represents another colossal undertaking of work, involving the spectacular presentation of hundreds of forgotten UFO sightings from police officers, RAF pilots, and members of the public, following over 20 years research by the authors – and, of course, the valuable contributions made by the researchers themselves. This book is not about us but about them and our joint efforts to ensure that this information is preserved for future generations. Our journey of discovery covers various peaks of UFO activity, including the short-lived phenomena that became labeled as the 'Flying Cross', which was to plague the later part of the UK in 1967. This book, like the others, is published in colour and includes reports from the United States. It contains approximately 600 photos, sketches, illustrations, images and supporting witness testimonials.

**Volume 3 Revised – *Haunted Skies* 1970-1975** *(Foreword by Howard Hughes)*
438 pages, many in colour

This book, with a foreword by BBC Radio presenter Howard Hughes, contains another huge slice of recorded UFO activity for the period between 1970 and 1975. There are many notable UFOsightings – one even by John Lennon over New York, following which he handed over a mysterious egg-shaped object to Uri Geller.

A visit to the Nazca Lines by the late, well-respected UFO researcher, Mr Omar Fowler . . .

A secret meeting in England with Dr J. Allen Hynek – an outstanding sighting, of what appeared to be alien craft, by a Tewkesbury man and a Sussex Councillor with what looked like 'beings' seen inside the craft.

These are only a tiny few of a massive amount of sightings painstakingly collected by the authors, covering day-by-day, another period of history which is now nearly 50 years old!